Iraq in Wartime

When U.S.-led forces invaded Iraq in 2003, they occupied a country that had been at war for twenty-three years. Yet in their attempts to understand Iraqi society and history, few policy makers, analysts, and journalists took into account the profound impact Iraq's long engagement with war had on the Iraqis' everyday engagement with politics, with the business of managing their daily lives, and on their cultural imagination. Starting with the Iran-Iraq war, through the First Gulf War and sanctions, Dina Rizk Khoury traces the political, social, and cultural processes of the normalization of war in Iraq during the last twenty-three years of Ba'thist rule. Drawing on government documents and interviews, Khoury argues that war was a form of everyday bureaucratic governance and examines the Iraqi government's policies of creating consent, managing resistance and religious diversity, and shaping public culture. Khoury focuses on the men and families of those who fought and died during the Iran-Iraq and First Gulf wars. Coming on the tenth anniversary of the U.S.-led invasion of Iraq, this book tells a multilayered story of a society in which war has become the norm.

Dina Rizk Khoury is Associate Professor of History and International Affairs at The George Washington University. Since 2005, she has been writing on the contemporary history of Iraq, particularly on violence, sectarian politics, and war and memory. She is the author of *State and Provincial Society in the Ottoman Empire* (Cambridge 1997).

Iraq in Wartime

Soldiering, Martyrdom, and Remembrance

DINA RIZK KHOURY

The George Washington University, Washington, DC

CAMBRIDGE
UNIVERSITY PRESS

CAMBRIDGE UNIVERSITY PRESS
Cambridge, New York, Melbourne, Madrid, Cape Town,
Singapore, São Paulo, Delhi, Mexico City

Cambridge University Press
32 Avenue of the Americas, New York, NY 10013-2473, USA

www.cambridge.org
Information on this title: www.cambridge.org/9780521711531

First published 2013

Printed in the United States of America

A catalog record for this publication is available from the British Library.

Library of Congress Cataloging in Publication data
Khoury, Dina Rizk.
Iraq in wartime : soldiering, martyrdom, and remembrance / Dina Rizk Khoury.
pages   cm
Includes bibliographical references and index.
ISBN 978-0-521-88461-7 (hardback) – ISBN 978-0-521-71153-1 (paperback)
1. Politics and war – Iraq – History – 20th century.   2. War and society – Iraq –
History – 20th century.   3. Iraq – Politics and government – 1979–1991.
4. Iran-Iraq War, 1980–1988 – Political aspects – Iraq.   5. Iran-Iraq War, 1980–1988 –
Social aspects – Iraq.   6. Persian Gulf War, 1991 – Political aspects – Iraq.   7. Persian
Gulf War, 1991 – Social aspects – Iraq.   I. Title.
DS79.7.K46   2013
956.7044–dc23   2012040130

ISBN 978-0-521-88461-7 Hardback
ISBN 978-0-521-71153-1 Paperback

In Memory

of

Adel Rizk, whose remembrance of Nabatiyye nourished him
through years in the desert, war, and debilitating illness
And for Iraqis
May memories of a place sustain them wherever they may be

The neutron bomb is highly intelligent.
It distinguishes between
An "I" and an "Identity."

And now
I remember trees:
The date palm of our mosque in Basra, at the end of Basra
a bird's beak,
a child's secret,
a summer feast.
I remember the date palm.
I touch it. I become it when it falls black
without fronds,
when a dam fell, hewn by lightning.
And I remember the mighty mulberry
when it rumbled, butchered with an ax ...
to fill the stream with leaves
and birds
and angels
and green blood.
I remember when pomegranate blossoms covered the sidewalks.
The students were leading the workers parade ...

The trees die
pummeled.
Dizzied,
not standing, the trees die.

from "America, America" by Saadi Youssef

Contents

Illustrations, Maps, and Table

Illustrations

Maps

Table

Acknowledgments

This book was born, more than six years ago, out of a lunch conversation in Foggy Bottom with my Cambridge University Press editor, Marigold Acland. I did not know at that time that I would, as I was writing the histories of Iraqis at war, embark on a journey that evoked my personal history. I am thankful for Marigold's patience as I am to Sarika Narula for seeing the book to production.

I would not have been able to write this book without the stories of Iraqi men who fought in the Iran-Iraq and First Gulf wars. I am grateful for their willingness to be interviewed and for their generosity in sharing their experiences. I have changed their names to protect their privacy. Many will only read this book when it is translated into Arabic. Although I have not reproduced the words of each one of them, their collective experience has shaped the book's narrative of war. I only hope that if, as Joan Didion says, all writers sell someone out, I have not done so in a manner that makes their stories unrecognizable to them.

A significant part of my research entailed stays in Amman and Damascus, where a large number of displaced Iraqis have settled. I was able to conduct research, make contacts, and altogether organize my life with the help of a number of individuals. Hala Fattah, a historian, friend, and facilitator for all researchers of things Iraqi who flocked to Amman after the U.S. invasion, provided me with entry into the community of Iraqi exiles and intellectuals. Geraldine Chatelard, then head of the French Institute of the Near East in Amman, answered my many questions about the displaced Iraqi community. Lucine Taminian, senior researcher at The American Academic Research Institute in Iraq's Jordan office, helped with contacts and with information based on her rich experience in conducting research in the oral history of Iraq. Sundus Shakir and her family made concrete to me the meaning of survival and resilience in the face of sanctions, war, and dispersal. Sundus provided me with contacts, fed me, and insisted, despite all evidence to the contrary, that she and her family could lead "normal" lives in Jordan. Awad Ali spent hours telling me his story, transcribing interviews, and educating me on the state of the first Iraqi refugees in Jordan. Ali Bader shared his experience and his insights into the generational politics of Iraq and introduced me to a vibrant community of artists and intellectuals of the nineties. Conversations with Awwad and Ali, together with Haider Saeed and Dhiaa Najm al-Asadi, all men who came of age in the late seventies and eighties, proved crucial for my understanding of the cultural politics of Iraq. Last but not least, my stay in Amman would not have been half as pleasurable without the hospitality and conversations provided by Aysar Akrawi and the late Adnan Habboo; Jenny and Mustafa Hamarneh, who sheltered me in their lovely Madaba home and whose friendship has been one of the constants in my life; and Nasri and Zeena Khoury, who found a space for me in their Amman home and who shielded me from family obligations.

In Damascus, Ziad Turkey al-Jazzaa and Roula Atallah found Iraqis willing to talk to me and introduced me to the alternative cultural life of Damascus. Ziad, a cinematographer and photographer, told me his story and answered my question on the implosion of media and visual culture during the Iran-Iraq war. Peter Harling, whose work on Iraq in the nineties remains among the best available to researchers, alerted me to the complicated politics of Iraqi Ba'thist refugees in Syria. I am grateful for Gabe Huck and Theresa Kubasak for including me in their work with Iraqi students through the Iraqi Student Project as well as their visits to Damascus churches and Syrian monasteries. Samar Hamarneh was a great companion as well as educator in the cultural and social life of Damascus. She, Hala, and George Farah guided me through the elusive specialness of Damascus, particularly its older neighborhoods.

Despite the centrality of oral interviews to the story this book seeks to tell, it would not have been possible to write without the access to the unique archive of the Ba'thist state available at the Iraq Memory Foundation, now housed in the Hoover Institution. I owe a debt to Peter Sluglett, who vouched for me when I first started my research in early 2007, when the archive was just becoming available to scholars outside the intelligence and human rights communities. I deeply appreciate his friendship and unfailing support over the years. I am grateful

to Kanan Makiya for his support and to Hasan Mneimneh for his help
in tackling the enormous archive of the Iraq Memory Foundation. At
the Hoover Institution, where the archive was moved in 2009, I am
indebted to archivists Ahmad Dhia and Haidar Hadi, who are working
at developing a reasonable cataloguing system, and to the librarians in
the reading room who continue to accommodate researchers working on
the archive. Thanks to invitations by Paul Gregory, two summer work-
shops on comparative analysis of authoritarianism organized by him and
Mark Harrison allowed me to conduct research and to engage scholars
working on the Soviet Union. I am also grateful to a number of research
assistants who have helped me over the past five years. Chief among
them is Mustafa Hadji, who toiled for hundreds of hours to tabulate the
school registers. Maria Kornalian and Christine Murphy, both students
of George Washington University, also provided materials for different
parts of the book. My thanks go as well to sociologist Faleh Abdul Jabar
and cultural critic Fatima Mohsen for their insights into the politics and
culture of Ba'thist Iraq. Muhsin al-Musawi was kind enough to answer
questions about cultural policy during the Iran-Iraq war. Ziad Turkey
al-Jazzaa and Anas Yousef helped transform the scanned images of Iraqi
newspapers and publications into better resolution printable images.

The breadth of scholarship and intellectual exchanges among my colleagues at the history department at The George Washington University
where I have taught for the past twenty years created an environment
that allowed me to move between early modern history where my earlier
expertise lay, to the history of the recent past, the period covered in this
book. I am particularly grateful to Bill Becker, who as chair was supportive of my work and of my requests for leave from teaching to complete it. Discussions with my comrades in reading, Mona Atia, Johanna
Bockman, Elliott Colla, Ilana Feldman, Melani McAlister, and Andrew
Zimmerman, have enriched the analyses in this book in innumerable
ways. Long conversations with Joseph Sassoon about the content of the
archive, the organization of the Ba'th, and the frustrations of research
have often helped make the project less overwhelming. Najwa al-Qattan
and Larry Trittle have listened and offered insight at various stages of
the research and writing of this book. Virginia Aksan has read most of
the chapters of the manuscript and has offered valuable suggestions. My
deepest thanks go to Kate Rouhana, my copy editor, who tamed my prose
and insured that I did not go on unnecessarily.

A number of organizations were generous enough to fund this project.
A John Simon Guggenheim fellowship for the year 2007–8 allowed me

to begin research in the Iraq Memory Foundation archive. Two travel grants from The American Academic Research Institute in Iraq, in 2007 and 2009, funded my research in Amman and Damascus. The Institute of Middle East Studies at The George Washington University underwrote a trip to the Hoover Institution and the cost of illustrations for the book.

Alfred, Zayd, and Waleed have each in his own way contributed to this book. They have listened to me when I could think and speak of nothing else and have endured the narrowing of my world and their exclusion from it. They are, as imm Adel used to say, "*hasheeshet 'umri.*"

Note on Translations and Transliteration

This book is meant as much for a general reader as it is for a specialist. I have avoided the use of Arabic terms as much as possible and included a translation in the text whenever an Arabic term is mentioned.

I have generally followed the transliteration guidelines of the *International Journal of Middle East Studies* but have not used diacritical and long vowels marks. I have also avoided adding the symbols of "alif" and "ayn" when these appear at the beginning of personal and place names unless it is necessary. This will mean that readers of the English text who know Arabic might find it difficult to translate the English back to Arabic. I apologize for the inconvenience, but my choice will make it easier for non-Arabic speakers to follow the text.

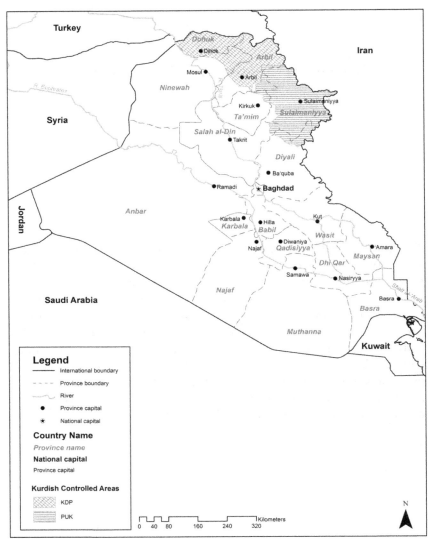

MAP I. Iraq: Provinces and principal cities. Designed by Ryan Sloan.

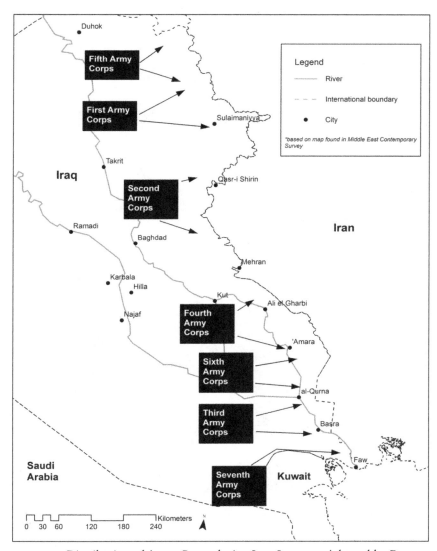

MAP 2. Distribution of Army Corps during Iran-Iraq war. Adapted by Ryan Sloan from Middle East Contemporary Survey.

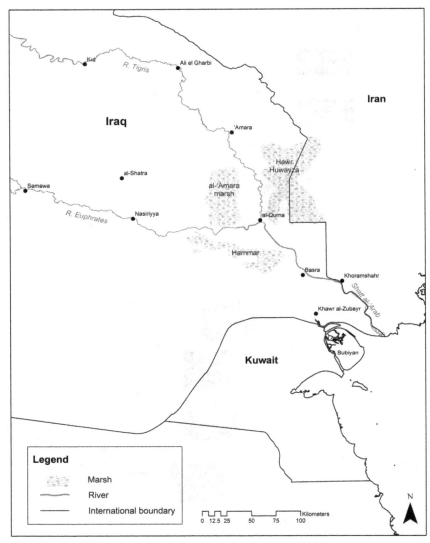

Kut

R. Tigris

Ali el Gharbi

Iraq

Iran

'Amara

al-Shatra

Hawr.
Huwayza

Samawa

al-'Amara
marsh

R. Euphrates

Nasiriyya

al-Qurna

Hammar

Basra

Khoramshahr

Shatt al-Arab

Khawr al-Zubayr

Kuwait

Bubiyan

Legend

Marsh

River

International boundary

Kilometers
0 12.5 25   50   75   100

N

MAP 3. Iraq: Principal southern towns and marshes. Designed by Ryan Sloan.

I

Introduction

When U.S.-led forces invaded Iraq in 2003, they occupied a country that had been at war for twenty-three years. September 22, 1980 marked the beginning of an eight-year war with Iran that cost both countries more than a million lives and transformed their social and political landscapes. War's end brought no relief to Iraqis. On August 2, 1990, Saddam Hussain made the disastrous decision to invade Kuwait. In January 1991, a coalition of twenty-eight countries, led by the United States and Britain, initiated a devastating bombing campaign that lasted for forty-two days, destroyed a large part of the Iraqi infrastructure, and caused tens of thousands of deaths. In the immediate aftermath of the First Gulf War, a massive uprising nearly toppled the regime, which in turn unleashed its violence against its own population. Despite the end of hostilities, the imposition by the UN of the most comprehensive embargo ever enforced on a nation, accompanied by periodic bombing by the United States and Britain, was effectively a continuation of war. By the end of the Ba'thist regime in 2003, war had become the norm rather than the exception. The result of this normalization of war has been the militarization of Iraqi politics and society, the brutalization of public culture, and the creation of irreconcilable divisions within Iraq.[1] Yet in the domestic buildup to the U.S.-led invasion, less than a handful of American policy makers, academics, or commentators devoted much analysis to the centrality of the imperatives of war making in shaping the nature of Iraqi state power,

---

[1] Isam al-Khafaji, "War as a vehicle for the rise and demise of a state-controlled society: the case of Ba'thist Iraq," in Steven Heydemann (ed.), *War, Institutions and Social Change in the Middle East* (Berkeley: University of California Press, 2000), pp. 258–91.

the manner by which the Iraqi regime governed its population, or war's impact on Iraqis' understanding of citizenship and belonging.[2] This book is an attempt to bring war front and center to the study of Iraq. It focuses on the political, social, and cultural processes and consequences of the normalization of war over more than a generation.

Because the thrust of the analysis presented in this book examines the processes of normalization, I am less interested in war making as a state-strengthening/weakening enterprise than in war as a way of governing that structures everyday lives.[3] At the same time, war was central in shaping and transforming the state's institutional and cultural practices.[4] In addition, the engagement with war and sanctions radically altered Iraqi citizens' social and legal rights and created a culture of commemoration that produced new ways of perceiving and describing community and self. The book tells the story of the normalization of war under the Ba'th by focusing on key categories of people – soldiers, deserters, prisoners of war, and martyrs' families – all of whose mobilization, control, and acquiescence were central to the state's ongoing ability to wage war and who were therefore the target of myriad state policies.

---

[2] A fascination with Saddam Hussain and his politics among policy analysts and commentators helped paint an overly simplistic picture of Iraqi politics that paralleled in many ways Hussain's fascination with himself and his need to project his power. See, for example, Ofra Bengio, *Saddam's Words, Political Discourse in Iraq* (New York: Oxford University Press, 1998).

[3] There is a rich literature on the role of war making in the formation of early modern European states and societies. The most succinct remains Charles Tilly, *Coercion, Capital and European States, AD 900–1990* (Cambridge: Basil Blackwell, 1990) and Charles Tilly (ed.), *The Formation of National States in Western Europe* (Princeton: Princeton University Press, 1975). As will become clear throughout this book, I am deeply indebted to Foucault's notions of power as practice and rule as a set of techniques of governing. I am also indebted to the notion of "state effect" elaborated by Timothy Mitchell. Michel Foucault, "Governmentality," in Graham Burchell, Colin Gordon, and Peter Miller (eds.), *The Foucault Effect: Studies in Governmentality* (Chicago: University of Chicago Press, 1991), pp. 87–104 and Michel Foucault, *Security, Territory and Population*, Michel Senellart (ed.), (New York: Palgrave Macmillan, 2009). Michel Foucault, *The Birth of Biopolitics*, Michel Senellart (ed.), (New York: Palgrave Macmillan, 2008). Timothy Mitchell, "Society, Economy and the State Effect," in George Steinmetz (ed.), *State/Culture: State Formation After the Cultural Turn* (Ithaca: Cornell University Press, 1999), pp. 76–97.

[4] Heydemann (ed.), *War, Institutions, and Social Change in the Middle East*, pp. 1–30. Among the first serious attempts to tackle the role of war in state formation in the Middle East, Heydemann's introduction draws attention to the normalization of war and militarism as a constituent of state–society relations in the region. The focus of most of the articles, however, is on the role of war making in building the state's capacity.

The first part of the book provides a brief historical context and then analyzes the organizational and bureaucratic practices of the state and the Ba'th Party in mobilizing and waging the Iran-Iraq and the First Gulf wars as well as surviving the uprising and the embargo. It addresses the evolution of categories of inclusion and exclusion in citizens' rights based on military service and martyrdom and delineates the everyday practices of Iraqis as they attempted to navigate these ever-changing rights. The second part concentrates on the cultural policies of the Ba'th, in particular its sponsorship of a visual culture, literary forms, and rituals that glorified the "war experience" and sanctified death. It contrasts the "war experience" propagated by the state with the memories of that experience relayed to me by Iraqi veterans. The concluding chapter explores the ways questions of citizenship, martyrdom, and memory are contested and reshaped by the post-Ba'th government and Iraqi citizens. I argue that current politics and rhetoric of members of Iraq's political elite and their detractors are to a significant degree the extension of the politics of the Iran-Iraq war and the Iraqi uprising. Amid the clamor for de-Ba'thification and the sectarian and ethnic politics of Iraq, few among the leadership are willing to accept their responsibility in creating and perpetuating the politics and culture of militarism and victimization that began with the Iran-Iraq war.

War as Governance

The normalization of war is neither a symptom of Iraqi exceptionalism nor simply a product of the militarism of the Ba'thist regime. Rather it is a condition Iraq shares with a number of other countries, democratic and authoritarian, in the post–Cold War period. In parts of Africa, the gradual erosion of the political authority and economic resources of post-colonial states has reconfigured African nations into enclaves controlled by warlords.[5] The fall of the Soviet Union and its satellite states was followed by the proliferation of conflicts that have elicited much commentary on the increasingly ubiquitous links between violence by states and non-state actors and the deployment of economic and political power. In Israel and Palestine, where a state of perpetual war has become the norm, scholars have studied the constitutive role that militarism, occupation,

[5] Jean François Bayart, Stephen Ellis, and Béatrice Hilou, *The Criminalization of the State in Africa*, trans. Stephen Ellis (Bloomington: Indiana University Press, 1999) and Achille Mbembe, *On the Post-Colony* (Berkeley: University of California Press, 2001).

and resistance play in Israeli state power and the socialization of Israelis and Palestinians.[6] In Iran, the continued influence of the Iran-Iraq war – termed the "Sacred Defense" by the Iranian government – on politics and society has been examined.[7] Closer to home, the drastic transformation in the political and legal culture of the United States after September 11, 2001 provides ample evidence of the ways in which war and issues of national security have become integral to the politics of everyday life.[8]

Nonetheless, Iraq's engagement with war during the last twenty-three years of Ba'thist rule is unique in many respects. Within that period, the country experienced four different kinds of war: the Iran-Iraq war was a conventional war fought between two nation-states deploying large infantry divisions along national borders; throughout much of the 1980s and 1990s, the Iraqi state waged a war of counterinsurgency against sections of its population; the First Gulf War pitted a Third World army with a limited and debilitated military war machine against the military technological prowess of the only surviving superpower in the post–Cold War era; and finally, the UN-sanctioned embargo, which Joy Gordon characterized as an "invisible war," entailed severe limitation of Iraq's territorial and economic sovereignty and the deployment of a belligerent

---

[6] For a survey of this trend in scholarship on Israel, see Zeev Rosenhek, Daniel Maman, and Eyal Ben-Ari, "The study of war and the military in Israel: an empirical investigation and reflective critique," *International Journal of Middle East Studies*, 35 (2003), 461–84. See also Baruch Kimmerling, *The Invention and Decline of Israeliness: State, Society and the Military* (Berkeley: University of California Press, 2005), pp. 208–29, and Neve Gordon, *Israel's Occupation* (Berkeley: University of California Press, 2009). For Palestine, see Yezid Sayigh, "War as leveler, war as midwife: Palestinian political institutions, nationalism, and society since 1948," in Heydemann (ed.), *War, Institutions and Social Change in the Middle East*, pp. 200–39, Laleh Khalili, *Heroes and Martyrs of Palestine: The Politics of National Commemoration* (Cambridge: Cambridge University Press, 2009), and Nasser Abufarha, *The Making of the Human Bomb: The Ethnography of Palestinian Resistance* (Durham: Duke University Press, 2009).

[7] Haggay Ram, *Myth and Mobilization in Revolutionary Iran: The Use of the Friday Congregational Sermon* (Lanham: American University Press, 1994), Peter Chelkowski and Hamid Dabashi, *Staging the Revolution: The Art of Persuasion in the Islamic Republic of Iran* (London: Booth-Clibborn editions, 2000), Christopher de Bellaigne, *In the Rose Garden of the Martyrs: A Memoir of Iran* (New York: HarperCollins, 2005), Farideh Farhi, "The antinomies of Iran's war generation," in Lawrence Potter and Gary Sick (eds.), *Iran, Iraq and the Legacies of the War* (New York: Palgrave Macmillan, 2004), pp. 101–20, and Roxane Varzi, *Warring Souls: Youth, Media and Martyrdom in Post-Revolutionary Iran* (Durham: Duke University Press, 2006).

[8] Judith Butler, *Precarious Life: The Powers of Mourning and Violence* (New York: Verso, 2006), Carlo Galli, *Political Spaces and Global Wars*, Elisabeth Fay, trans. (Minneapolis: University of Minnesota Press, 2010); Slavoj Zizek, *Violence* (New York: Picador, 2008), and Wendy Brown, *Regulating Aversion, Tolerance in the Age of Identity and Empire* (Princeton: Princeton University Press, 2006).

humanitarianism that threatened the biological security of entire civilian populations.[9]

Clearly, the process of rendering these seismic ruptures in Iraqis' lives into part of the business of living was no small undertaking. How did the imperatives of war making, counterinsurgency, and embargo survival affect the deployment of the state's power and resources? What kind of social, security, and cultural practices did its various bureaucracies develop in the face of these different forms of war? How did war change the politics of everyday life and redefine the parameters of acquiesce and resistance among Iraqis?

Until the outbreak of the Iran-Iraq war, Ba'thist state policies had been ordered by the twin political and social policies of development and corporatism. Ba'thist society was organized vertically by political party, professional, and labor organizations that mobilized the population over political and social agendas and linked the population directly to the state. The Iraqi state, with the help of the Ba'th Party, managed labor and professional organizations, disbursed resources, and oversaw what it perceived as the modernization and welfare of its citizens.[10] As a state focused on development, the primary target of its policies were social categories of people like women, children, workers, peasants, illiterate citizens, intellectuals, and youth. As a one-party state, it framed rights of access to citizens' social and economic rights in both negative and positive terms. Citizens enjoyed these rights only if they did not belong to categories of people deemed threatening to the security of the party and the state. These included members of outlawed political parties and their families and those who belonged to certain ethnic groups. On the positive side, citizens' rights granted to those who served the state in desired ways, notably by belonging to the Ba'th party hierarchy, had privileges denied to others.

To undertake development and to ensure that access to resources was apportioned according to political and security concerns, the Ba'thist state, flush with the rents accruing to it from the nationalization of the oil industry in 1972, expanded its bureaucracies that dealt with the population's welfare and with state security. As Partha Chatterjee has succinctly

---

[9] Joy Gordon, *Invisible War, The United States and The Iraq Sanctions* (Cambridge: Harvard University Press, 2010).

[10] Peter and Marion-Farouk Sluglett, *Iraq Since 1958: From Revolution to Dictatorship*, revised edition (London: I.B. Tauris, 2001) and Eric Davis, *Memories of State, Politics, History, and Collective Memory in Modern Iraq* (Berkeley: University of California Press, 2005), pp. 148–75.

put it, the object of the developmental and welfare state was not the individual citizen with universal political equal rights but rather a multiplicity "of population groups that are objects of governmentality – multiple targets with multiple characteristics, requiring multiple techniques of administration."[11] It is at the level of "multiple techniques of administration," as targets of both the state's development and security policies, that Iraqis encountered the state in their everyday lives and experienced the full impact of the different wars over the last twenty-three years of Ba'thist rule.

The onset of the war with Iran transformed the nature of the Iraqi state. No longer able to allocate resources to development, it poured its resources into financing the war. In an incisive but schematic article on the relationship of war making to state power in Iraq, Isam al-Khafaji has argued that the war with Iran transformed the Iraqi state from one dependent on oil rents to one dependent on "strategic rents," based on its ability to pose as the defender of the "eastern flank of the Arab nation" and to extract funds from oil-rich Gulf states fearful of the spread of Iran's brand of revolutionary Islam. As a result, its developmental and corporatist policies were jettisoned in favor of policies geared toward the militarization of its population and a personalized and paternalistic form of power dominated by Saddam Hussain. al-Khafaji, among others, points to the weakening of state capacity as a result of the Iran-Iraq war, a weakening that escalated into failure after the First Gulf War.[12]

More significant, and less well studied, are the implications of war making on the nature of the Iraqi state's bureaucratic practices. The administrative bureaucracies of the state, the party, and the military now focused on managing the state's national security and on counterinsurgency concerns. However, because war making is as much about managing population and territory as it is about the allocation and disbursement of resources, a primary concern was the recruitment and retention of men and the control of the insurgent territories in the northern and southeastern part of the country. Thus, to understand how this transformation from a developmental and corporatist to a national security and counterinsurgency state affected ordinary Iraqi lives, we need to look at how the "techniques of administration" of the state and party bureaucracies

[11] Partha Chatterjee, *The Politics of the Governed, Reflections on Popular Politics in Most of the World* (New York: Columbia University Press, 2004), pp. 35–6.
[12] al-Khafaji, "War as a vehicle for the rise and demise of a state-controlled society" and Charles Tripp, *A History of Iraq*, 2nd edition (Cambridge: Cambridge University Press, 2002), pp. 193–292.

evolved during wartime. Central to this change was the expansion, bureaucratization, and securitization of the Ba'th Party, the only legal political party in Iraq. Equally important was the shift in the categories of people targeted by the social and security policies of the state. Soldiers, deserters, insurgents, and martyrs' families became the primary objects of state policies.

The Iraqi state was able to wage the longest war fought in the twentieth century, and to do so with a relatively small population and little previous experience in prolonged warfare. That it was able to do so is largely attributable to the state and the Ba'th Party's ability to develop institutional and organizational practices that transformed war into the politics and practice of everyday life. The Ba'th Party became the means of organizing society to fight both internal and external enemies. Thus, the most noticeable change in the politics of the regime during the Iran-Iraq war was the transformation of the Ba'th Party from a corporatist party with an agenda focused on economic and social development to a national security and counterinsurgency party. It became involved in monitoring dissent, organizing popular committees in support of the war, monitoring correct political behavior at the front, and punishing deserters and absentees. In both the Kurdish north and in the southern areas of Iraq, the party became the clearinghouse for counterinsurgency operations against rebellious populations.

Throughout the 1980s, the Ba'th remained central to governance. Despite the diminishing strength of its ideological appeal, Ba'thist cadres developed techniques to survey citizens, particularly those directly affected by the war, and manage their social lives. They mediated between the population and various state institutions and ensured that claims and complaints by soldiers' families, prisoners of war, and martyrs were heard. The extent to which Iraqi citizens framed their daily struggles in terms of complicity or resistance to the regime was quite limited. For most of Iraq's population during wartime, the Ba'th Party, to use Derek Sayer's phrase, defined the "boundaries of the possible."[13] Within these boundaries, most of the politics of everyday life during wartime was shaped by the negotiation over specific claims to entitlements rather than politics writ large. This was politics conducted in increments, but politics nonetheless.

---

[13] Derek Sayer, "Everyday forms of state formation: Dissident remarks on hegemony," in Gilbert Joseph and Daniel Nugent (eds.), *Everyday Forms of State Formation: Revolution and the Negotiation of Rule in Modern Mexico* (Durham: Duke University Press, 1994), p. 375.

This is not to say that outright resistance to the Ba'thist regime did not exist. But that resistance did not take the form of organized party opposition, except in the insurgent Kurdish north and on the southeastern borders with Iran. It manifested itself most clearly with significant resistance to the war and took the form of desertion, dereliction of duty, or surrender to the enemy. Other, more subtle forms of resistance took place as well, most notably through the organization and attendance of Shi'i rituals of mourning. Thus, despite the extension of party and state control over the population, the hegemony of both was at all times tenuous. The need on the part of both party and various security apparatuses of the state to resort to violence to control men and territory points to the limits of state power rather than its hegemony.

The brittleness of the regime and the limits of obedience of the Iraqi population were on exhibit during and after the invasion of Kuwait in 1990. The First Gulf War, the March 1991 uprising, and the ensuing sanctions imposed on the regime led to drastic reworking of the institutional and organizational practices of Ba'thist rule. Commentators who have attempted to make sense of Iraqi politics in the last thirteen years of Ba'thist rule have focused on the "re-tribalization" of Iraqi politics and the rise of sectarianism.[14] However, the most persuasive presentation of Iraqi form of rule in the 1990s is that it was despotic and marked by extreme improvisation. It drew on tribalism, sectarianism, Ba'thism, and a host of new categories to reward and punish its citizens.[15] The result was a method of rule that oscillated between charity and mercy. The regime created a market of entitlements in titles, positions, and access to precious resources that transformed the relationship of the state to the party as well as to citizens. It made access to these entitlements dependent on the charity of the ruler and on his ability to reward and punish. The corruption and the privatization of entitlements that ensued, together with the enactment of multiple laws and regulations governing reward and punishment, created what can aptly be described, following Slavoj Zizek, as a "regime of mercy." Writing about the greatly weakened regimes of the Eastern Bloc in the 1980s, Zizek draws our attention to the techniques of

---

[14] Amatzai Baram, "Neo-tribalism in Iraq: Saddam Hussein's tribal policies 1991–1996," *International Journal of Middle East Studies*, 29 (1997), 1–31 and Tripp, *A History of Iraq*, pp. 253–71.

[15] David Baran, *Vivre la Tyrannie et lui Survivre, L'Irak en Transition* (*Living Tyranny and Surviving It: Iraq in Transition*) (Paris: Mille et Une Nuits, 2004), pp. 27–149. For the improvisational nature of postcolonial regimes, see Achille Mbembe, "The banality of power and the aesthetics of vulgarity in the post-colony," *Public Culture*, 4 (Spring 1992), 1–30.

these regimes in devising laws that criminalized so many aspects of public life that they assigned potential guilt to almost every citizen. These laws were not meant to be implemented in any consistent fashion but rather were designed as a projection of the rulers' power through their ability to forgive infractions and be merciful.[16] In Iraq, together with the creation of expensive spectacles in support of the regime's pronouncements, these methods of rule projected state power even as they highlighted its episodic presence in Iraqis' lives.[17]

By the time of the Ba'thist regime's fall in 2003, the Iraqi state and the Ba'th Party had devised a variety of practices to rule Iraq's population. The first part of the book analyzes these practices and argues that they helped normalize war and left a profound imprint on the manner in which the Iraqis targeted by state policies resisted these policies and made claims on the state's resources.

The War Experience and Memory

Soon after the outbreak of hostilities of the Iran-Iraq war, Iraqi state media began propagating a view of the war experience (*tajrubat al-harb*) as formative of the Iraqi citizen and subject. The war experience and its meaning became the cornerstone of the Iraqi state's attempts to transform the Iraqi self, particularly the male self. Attempts at shaping the public culture of heroism and manliness and of death and mourning were regulated by incorporating war celebrations with commemoration rituals under the purview of neighborhood party officials. Educational, cultural, and media institutions and organizations contributed to the creation of what can best be described as a memory discourse that set the parameters within which Iraqi soldiers and intellectuals narrated their war experience. These parameters were challenged after the First Gulf War, which brought massive violence and displacement of large sections of the Iraqi population.

Until the Iran-Iraq war, Iraqis had no experience with total war. In contrast to Western Europe, where death for the nation was sanctified in the nineteenth century by national governments and various civic organizations, the creation and dissemination of the war experience as constituting an essential part of the Iraqi self was a strictly state-controlled enterprise. Unlike the European case where volunteers and their communities

---

[16] Zizek, *On Violence*, pp. 158–9.
[17] This aspect of spectacle in weak states is nicely formulated by Lisa Wedeen as "acting like a state" in her article, "Seeing like a citizen, acting like a state: exemplary events in unified Yemen," *Comparative Studies in Society and History*, 45 (2003), 680–713.

played an important part in the cultural and commemorative practices that characterized what George Mosse has called the "myth of the war experience," the Iraqi state monopolized literary output as well as commemoration of fallen soldiers.[18] As Iraq had no prolonged experience of war on which its leadership could build, it had to invent what constituted the war experience. It drew on the militant liberationist ideology of the Ba'thist version of Third Worldism, with its anti-imperialist rhetoric and emphasis on the need to create "new men and women," and molded this message to convince Iraqis that war with Iran was an extension of the Ba'thist revolution. It also drew on the visual and literary cultural output that had developed around the world wars in Western Europe and the Soviet Union.

The promotion of a heroic narrative of the war experience was a conscious policy articulated by the Ba'th leadership and by Saddam Hussain in an effort to link the war with what it called the "generation of the revolution," whose war experience was to mark a new phase in the heroic advancement of the Ba'thist nation. In doing so, the government sought to address the urgent questions raised by the war regarding its legitimacy as a liberationist Third World state committed to modernization and social distribution of wealth. The erosion of its support, particularly among intellectuals, was born out of its suppression of leftist opposition within the Ba'thist Party itself and from its liquidation of the Communist and Shi'i Islamist parties in the late 1970s. It was compounded by its policy of controlled privatization that challenged the "socialist" program espoused by a significant portion of its membership in the early 1970s and supported by the Communist Party. In addition, the war with Iran further strained Iraq's credentials as a revolutionary anti-imperialist beacon of Arab nationalism confronting Zionism. Instead, the Ba'thist regime now faced fighting a popular revolutionary state more anti-imperialist and anti-Zionist than itself.

To propagate the official version of the war experience, state cultural institutions and party organizations disseminated a memory discourse that sought to construct and regulate the Iraqi experience of military and other war-inflicted violence. Unlike the project to manipulate the historical memory of Iraqis for the purposes of shaping public culture analyzed by Eric Davis, the memory discourse initiative marked an ambitious attempt by the state to regulate the inner emotional self of the Iraqi

---

[18] George L. Mosse, *Fallen Soldiers, Reshaping the Memory of the World Wars* (New York: Oxford University Press, 1990).

individual as he or she experienced war. Its power lay in its ability to personalize as it homogenized, not only through coercion but also through the "taken for granted" shared memory of war. Unlike the Lebanese case, where there existed no single dominant memory discourse on the Lebanese civil war, the memory discourse disseminated by the Iraqi government during the Iran-Iraq war was dominant.[19] More important, its deployment by institutions of public culture marked the emergence of memory and martyrdom as categories of experience through which individuals or communities could make claims for social and political rights through the construction of difference based on degrees of participation in suffering incurred as a result of war.[20]

Memory discourse as propagated by state institutions was a discourse of power. But the war experience was not a fabrication. It was grounded in the reality of living in a society at war. Some writers challenged the official version of the war experience during the Iran-Iraq war, but their questioning remained muted compared to the bombastic narrative disseminated by mass media outlets. I have, therefore, attempted to compare some of the elements of the sanctioned version of the war experience with the remembrances of soldiers who fought in the Iran-Iraq and First Gulf wars. As will become clear, while these remembrances often challenged the official version of the war experience, they attested to the power of the vocabularies and images the state deployed to define it. The war experience, for most of these soldiers, was as generational as it was brutalizing. It shaped them as men as it transformed their experience of their nation.

The centrality of the heroic and loyal Iraqi soldier to the war experience was severely tested in the First Gulf War and its aftermath, because large segments of the Iraqi military took part in the ensuing uprising.

---

[19] Sune Haugbolle, *War and Memory in Lebanon* (Cambridge: Cambridge University Press, 2010), and Lucia Volk, *Memorials and Martyrs in Modern Lebanon* (Bloomington: Indiana University Press, 2010).

[20] In my analysis of memory discourse, I have drawn on Wendy Brown, *Regulating Aversion*. Brown's concern is with the ubiquitous presence in U.S. public culture of the "tolerance discourse" and its impact on issues of social and economic justice as well as identity politics. She attempts to trace the governmental and regulatory functions this discourse performs and links it with the crisis in the legitimacy of the late capitalist state. While the Iraqi deployment of the memory discourse is different in many respects, Brown's analysis of that discourse as regulatory and patently nonpolitical is quite useful in understanding the functions of that memory discourse in Iraq. The literature on memory, war, and nationalism has proliferated since the 1990s, but has now peaked. The journal *History and Memory* has been central in defining its contours. For a critical assessment, see Kerwin Lee Klein, "On the Emergence of Memory in Historical Discourse," *Representations*, 69 (2000), 127–50.

Instead of the heroic soldier, the Iraqi that epitomized the new war experience was the hapless civilian victim of the violence of war, the gritty survivor of the sanctions regime. She or he could only survive this new form of total war, euphemistically referred to as "the difficult days," by belonging to the nation of "the patient ones" who persevered in the face of adversity. Nowhere was this shift more noticeable than in the commemoration of the dead. The prototypical martyr was no longer the heroic fallen soldier, but rather the civilian victim of U.S. bombardment and the UN-imposed embargo. The state, however, had lost its tenuous monopoly over the national memory discourse. It did not have the wherewithal to systematically enforce it because its ability to finance the institutions that produced it was severely curtailed by the sanctions. Nor could it stem the tide of writings that challenged this discourse, which flooded in from the Iraqi diaspora that escaped Iraq in the 1990s. Another equally important influence in shifting the language of remembrance and claims to that of victimization was the pervasiveness of the humanitarian discourse of the UN and other nongovernmental organizations that were monitoring the effects of the sanctions – a trend that continues, albeit in a different form, in post-invasion Iraq.

Sources and Methodology

Government Documents

The bulk of the book is based on research in Iraqi government archives, press and literary sources, and interviews with Iraqi soldiers and intellectuals who fought in the wars or witnessed the 1991 uprising. The archival sources I drew on were digitized copies made available by the Iraq Memory Foundation in Washington, DC, when I began my research in 2007, sources now in the Hoover Institution at Stanford University.[21] I used two collections: the North Iraq Data Set (NIDS) and the Ba'th Regional Command Collection (BRCC). The NIDS consists of digitized documents (more than 2.5 million) originally given to the U.S. government by the Patriotic Union of Kurdistan (1992) and the Kurdish Democratic Party (1993), both parties in control of the Kurdish region that had maintained autonomous rule and U.S. support after the First Gulf War. The documents were airlifted to Washington, DC, and eventually digitized by

---

[21] The Iraq Memory Foundation was established in 2003 by Kanan Makiya as an outgrowth of the Iraq Research and Documentation Project at the Center of Middle East Studies at Harvard University. The Foundation and Harvard have since parted ways.

the Defense Intelligence Agency. Copies were then passed on to the Iraq Documentation and Research Center, the precursor of the Iraq Memory Foundation.[22] The BRCC was taken over, with the U.S. Army's help, by Kanan Makiya, head of the Iraq Memory Foundation, in 2003 and eventually transported to the United States. The BRCC comprises an estimated 3 million pages of documents from the Ba'th Party Regional Command headquarters in what is now the Green Zone. All of these have been digitized, but they are only now being indexed by archivists at the Hoover Institution.[23]

The Iraq Memory Foundation has generated a great deal of contentious debate among students and observers of Iraq who question the manner of the archive's acquisition, its ownership, and access to the documents.[24] Kanan Makiya, the Foundation's founder, was a vocal supporter of the U.S.-led invasion and occupation of Iraq as the only means to dislodge Saddam Hussain's dictatorship. The Foundation was created in 2003 to document human rights abuses committed by the Ba'th regime, whether by recording testimonies or archiving state papers, to ensure that history will not repeat itself. This sentiment is echoed by organizations that have sprung up to document the horrors of World War II, Stalinism, and the Khmer Rouge, among others, and to deal with the human costs of authoritarian regimes. From the beginning, however, the Foundation's mission was enmeshed with the politics of the U.S. invasion of Iraq. Critics point to the fact that the Ba'th Party documents seized in 2003 were a result of Makiya's close connections to Bush administration officials. They insist that these documents fall under the purview of international legal norms that make it imperative that all cultural property, including archives, be protected by the occupying power as such property belongs to the nation under occupation. Their seizure by a private entity such as the Iraq Memory Foundation and their transfer to the United States constituted an act of cultural pillage and a violation of the laws of war. Makiya argues that he was instrumental in rescuing these records because they were threatened by destruction or looting at the time of their seizure.

Matters came to a head in 2008, when the Iraq Memory Foundation turned custody of these records over to the Hoover Institution, long

---

[22] file://IRDPSelect/Select/info/hm.htm accessed March 10, 2007. The holdings also include some seven hundred fifty thousand documents captured in Kuwait in 1991.

[23] http://iraqmemory.org/en/Projects_Documentation.asp. These holding comprise 6,420 boxfiles containing 2,764,631 pages.

[24] Michelle Caswell, "'Thank you very much, now Give them back': cultural property and the fight over the Iraqi Baath records," *American Archivist*, 74 (2011), 211–40.

known for its collection of documents on dictatorial regimes. Saad
Eskandar, the director of the Iraq National Library and Archive, and his
supporters in the international community of professional archivists and
librarians have stated that these archives have been acquired in clear contravention of international law and are the property of the Iraqi nation
and its national institutions. The Iraq Memory Foundation maintains
that it never claimed ownership of the material and was merely holding it
in trust until the Iraqi government could reclaim and maintain it.[25] At the
moment, the documents are at the Hoover Institution. Negotiations are
under way to return the original documents, if not the digitized copies, to
the Iraqi government. Despite such promise, the manner of transfer and
ambiguity over the timing of the repatriation of the documents continue
to plague the negotiations.[26]

   The question of access to these archives, digitized copies of the original
documents, has generated some debate and misinformation. Researchers
who make the trip to Stanford have access to the archives, although these
remain difficult to navigate despite an ongoing process of cataloguing
and indexing. There are, however, a number of restrictions on the use
of names, quotation, and reproduction. In addition, the nature of the
archive as a document of a dictatorial and often violent regime, many
of whose informants and perpetrators, not to mention its victims, are
still alive, raises a host of ethical and moral issues for researchers. While
archivists are undertaking a process of redacting some names, there is
as of yet no consistent policy for handling the challenges of privacy and
safety these archives raise.

   There is no doubt that these issues will eventually be resolved as the
politics of the U.S. invasion and occupation recedes. As of this writing,
however, the use of these archives by scholars raises a difficult ethical
conundrum. Does the researcher who uses these archives grant legitimacy

----

[25] Hugh Eakin, "Iraqi Files in US: Plunder or Rescue," *New York Times*, July 1, 2008. http://
www.nytimes.com/2008/07-01/books/01hoov.html.

[26] Mr. Eskandar, however, has a bigger fight on his hands: the retrieval of some 100 million
Iraqi government documents in possession of the Department of Defense. The Minerva
controversy, saad eskander, http://www.ssrc.org/essays/minerva/2008/10/29/eskander
accessed June 8, 2009. In a report issued by Saad Eskandar after a May 2010 meeting with the Hoover Institution, Eskandar stated that the Iraq Memory Foundation
archives will return to Iraq and that the Hoover Institution and the Iraq National Library
and Archive will work together to preserve the archive. However, it appears no agreement was reached on the immediate return of the archives to Iraq. Bruce Montgomery,
"Immortality in the secret police files: The Iraq Memory Foundation and the Baath Party
archive," *International Journal of Cultural Property*, 18 (2011), 309–36.

to their manner of acquisition and their current contested status? Or is the use of the archive for the purpose of producing historical knowledge about Ba'thist Iraq a separate issue altogether, one divorced from the politics of their acquisition?

The ethical ambiguities surrounding the current status of the Ba'th Party archives does not mean, at least in the case of this researcher, that the use of the archive lends legitimacy to the manner of their acquisition or to the continued presence of the originals at the Hoover Institution or at other locations in the United States. The use of the Iraqi government archives by independent researchers allows for a less ideologically charged study of Ba'thist Iraq, one that critically engages the politics of empire, nationalism, humanitarian intervention, and memory. The Ba'th archive at the Hoover Institution remains unique in that it offers researchers a window into the workings of a postcolonial authoritarian state in the Middle East. More problematic in the long run is the privileged access that the presence of these archives, at the Hoover Institution and elsewhere in the United States, has allowed Western scholars with funding and means to study Ba'thist Iraq at the same time that this access is unavailable to Iraqi citizens who need to study their history.

Despite all these caveats about issues of seizure, provenance, and access, I am grateful to Hasan Mneimneh, the head of the documentation project at the Iraq Memory Foundation, who gave me unfettered and unconditional access to the digitized copies of the documents in Washington, DC. His help in the early stages of my research as well as his direction in sifting through the mass of documents were crucial for my research. Nonetheless, the sheer volume of the sources and the lack of consistent indexing and annotation for the majority of the documents were overwhelming. In the end, I chose to work on the NIDS material that was digitized and, for the most part, annotated for my analysis of the 1980s, particularly on issues that pertain to recruitment, desertion, punishment of dissent of soldiers, and control of the war narrative. The bulk of the documents are drawn from the security offices of the government in Sulaimaniyya, Dohuk, and Arbil in the Kurdish north. Northern Iraq was the base for Kurdish as well as other opposition parties and was the favored escape route for men trying to flee the army during the war. Thus, while the documents focused on regional issues, their content was of national significance.

The majority of my research is based on the Ba'th Regional Command Collection. Although some documents exist for the 1970s, the bulk was produced after 1980, with the most abundant and detailed material produced in the 1990s. While digitized, these documents are much more difficult to use. The greatest challenge was trying to disentangle the complex web of structures within the Ba'th under which these documents were produced, their significance, and the way they affected policy. The Ba'th Party was run like a state with military, police, intelligence, professional, educational, labor, and peasant organizations. How these different components of the party worked with one another and how the relationship with the state institutions changed over time is one of the most difficult problems for the independent researcher to solve. I attempted to get around this problem in four ways: first, by using material produced consistently over time and that involved the same party organization, such as the school registers. These surveys of the political affiliation of matriculating middle and secondary school students were conducted by party cadres between 1983 and 2002. I based my conclusions on the surveys of students matriculating in the sixth secondary. Second, I used material that involved reports on an event such as the 1991 uprising and analyzed these reports. Third, I chose categories that appeared consistently over time in the documents and traced them. For my study, the categories of "escape and desertion" and "prisoners of war" seemed to have dominated the attention of the Ba'th in the 1990s, because these two categories of people carried with them the most potential for political dissent. Finally, insofar as it was possible given the rudimentary indexing of the material, I chose documents filed under the various regional bureaucracies of the Ba'th, such as the regional bureaus as well as documents listed under the various popular organizations, such as the General Federation of Iraqi Women. The archives of the Ministry of Defense and the Ministry of Interior are now in the possession of the U. S. government. I could not consult them despite the fact that this book is on war and its conduct.

A word needs to be said about the reliability of these documents as sources of information on Iraqi society and the workings of the Iraqi state. Like all documents of this sort, the fact that they exist as records, regardless of the information they yield, is in itself a subject of study. Who wrote these documents? Who constructed their categories? How did these authors present the information? How did the documents change over time, and why are they reproduced at several levels in the chain of command? These questions cannot be addressed in a book such as this one, but I have tried to address some of them in my analysis of the impact of war on the relationship between the state, the Ba'th Party, and citizenship in the first part of this book. As for the kind of information these records yield, one needs to cautiously weigh the evidence against the ideology that underpins the creation of information in one-party state systems: for example, the need to create statistics that paint a certain picture of the country or the need to find foes to maintain a power structure dependent on informants who subsist simply by fingering enemies. What emerges from these documents is a picture of a state and a party awesome in their ability to monitor and control dissent and skillful in manipulating their resources to reward loyal citizens with a largesse that belied the country's poverty. But that is more a picture that the state and the party wanted to believe than it is reality. In other words, these documents represent the party's creation of its own world. This is particularly evident in the kind of information kept out of the reports of local party cadres as these went up the chain to the General Secretariat of the party and then onto the Office of the Presidency. Having said that, however, these documents do provide valuable information on Iraqi society, not only on the world of the Ba'th. One often has to read them against the grain, very much like we have learned to read the documents of the various colonial officers of former imperial powers to mine them for information about the peoples they ruled.

Interviews

War lends itself to story telling, as it represents one of the most dramatic encounters between the private individual and public events. In Iraq, as elsewhere in societies at war, the war story has been very important to control, particularly as it pertains to the experience of soldiers who fight and die for the cause. European and American wars have produced a rich literature by soldiers who have written of their experience and helped shape the debate about war and its impact on their lives and on society at large. The literature has done much to debunk the mythology built around the war. In the Middle East, in Lebanon, Palestine, Israel, and Iran, challenges to the official or homogenous versions of the war narrative continue to appear in literature, film, and other art forms.

Until recently, little had been heard from the soldiers who fought in Iraqi wars. There are myriad reasons for this silence. Perhaps the most obvious is the fact that there has been no period of peace in Iraq to allow soldiers to write and think with some distance about their experiences. More significant, however, is the view of Iraqi intellectuals and the current political elite that soldiers who fought in Iraq's wars were not fighting national wars but Ba'thist ones. Their lives and deaths carried no independent meaning outside the official version of their war experience presented by the Ba'thist state. Therefore, it was important for me to interview soldiers and to contrast the official version of the war story with their remembrances. I conducted my interviews over the summer of 2007 and the spring of 2009 in Amman and Damascus, with nineteen soldiers, of whom only four were men who had enlisted in the armed forces. I also interviewed eight other men who had been witnesses to both wars and to the 1991 uprising, although they had no combat experience. My aim was not to record the history of confrontations or to verify certain facts; rather it was to get a narrative of the soldiers' experience of violence and death. Their stories are incorporated into nearly every chapter, but they are also analyzed as narratives in the second part of the book.

Except for two soldiers, all the interviewees had become displaced after 2003. They came from different sectors of Iraqi society as well as different regions of the country. They are far from representative, how-ever. Although Kurds fought in the regular Iraqi army, most who were organized into military units were members of the National Defense Battalions posted in the northern region to fight the Kurdish insurgency. I was unable to go to Iraqi Kurdistan to interview any of these soldiers. As a result, the story I tell in this book is poorer. At the same time, my intent was not to create a sample that would help social scientists generalize about soldiers' experience, but rather to present the multitude of narra-tives that lays bare the claim that there is a unified war story of heroism and sacrifice.

Oral history is a process that involves two people from radically dif-ferent backgrounds trying to construct a narrative of a life experience. Three factors seem to have shaped these interviews: first, my gender and national origin. My gender set limits on how much men were willing to tell me about their experience, particularly as it pertained to personal feelings on issues of masculinity, death, and killing or their daily banter in the trench. On the other hand, my unfamiliarity with life in the mili-tary allowed them to recreate their experiences in vivid terms that they might not have been compelled to use with a military historian or a man with a deeper familiarity with a soldier's life. My national origin as a Lebanese displaced by war played a positive role, as I was an outsider to Iraqi politics and shared with my informants a prolonged experience with violence. The second factor had much to do with the location of these men in time. They were refugees whose lives in their host countries were precarious. Their own country was wracked by violence and occu-pied by foreign forces. They tended to place their recollection of the wars within the context of the current violence and with their state as displaced persons. A number of them commented on the relatively orderly way that the Iran-Iraq war occurred as opposed to the current one, where there were no rules and there was no place to hide. Many stressed the fact that there were Iraqis of all sects in their units, highlighting the belief that sectarianism was new to Iraq. So, despite the sheer misery of their experience on the front, their remembrance was sometimes infused with nostalgia. The third factor that played an important part in the way the narrative of the wars was constructed was the fact that few of these men had told their experience as a story and incorporated it into their own life histories. Of the nineteen men I interviewed, only three, all intellectuals who had dabbled in journalism, told their story in a linear manner and attempted to make sense of the politics and meaning of the wars. Significantly, they spoke in literary Arabic (*fusha*) and had a remarkable memory of dates and battles, in clear contrast to others whose narratives had no such clarity. The majority had previously shared fragments of their war experience, but they had never attempted to tell the story as a whole. In part, this is due to their dispersal and the lack of independent forums, such as veteran and other organizations that could have helped give meaning to their experience as soldiers. An equally important factor, however, is the lack, at the time of my interviews, of a unifying national narrative on which there is an Iraqi consensus. Such narratives would have provided the context within which to frame their personal stories. By contrast, the European, American, and Israeli soldiers who fought the various wars have adeptly challenged the official narratives of these wars precisely because there was a modicum of a national consensus, albeit manufactured, about the war story.

2

Iraq's Wars under the Ba'th

The history of the Iran-Iraq (1980–8) and First Gulf (1991) wars, as well as the twelve-year, UN-imposed sanctions regime (1991–2003), is best understood within three contexts: the ideology and the internal politics of the Ba'thist state; the threat the Iranian Revolution posed to regional political order and Iraq's place in it; and the emergence of a new global order led by the United States and increasingly administered by various international organizations such as the UN working closely with the United States to manage conflict and punish "criminal" regimes.

Iraq's invasion of Iran in September 1980 was motivated by ideological factors as much as by political calculation. The Islamic revolution in Iran challenged the Ba'thist secular ideology of revolutionary Arab nationalism and threatened Iraq's ambitions for a regional leadership role. The anti-imperialist rhetoric of the Islamic revolution and the Iranian people's ability to dislodge the Shah of Iran, a powerful U.S. ally, through peaceful means generated considerable excitement in the Arab world, the population of which had grown disillusioned with Arab nationalism. Unlike the Islamic Republic of Iran, the Ba'thist regime had come to power through a military coup, not a popular mandate. In July 1968, Ahmad Hasan al-Bakr, a Ba'thist army general, became president, and, less than a year later, appointed his kinsman Saddam Hussein vice chairman of the ruling Revolutionary Command Council, the highest legislative and executive body in Iraq.

Despite its initially narrow base, an estimated five thousand party members, the Ba'th Party insisted on defining itself as a revolutionary party and on defining its regime as a vanguard of Arab revolutions and part of Third World revolutionary anticolonial regimes. The Ba'th borrowed heavily from the rhetoric of liberationist movements and from Arab nationalist ideology. Iraq, according to the leaders of the Iraqi Ba'th, was a nation at arms organized to fight a war against poverty, underdevelopment, and what the ideologues termed "backwardness" in the name of creating modern Iraqi citizens and a strong Ba'thist party committed to the "revolution" of Arab "socialist Iraq." The economic and social programs envisioned by the political report of the 1974 Eighth Party Congress aimed at creating a "socialist and revolutionary" Iraqi citizen, a Ba'thist who would become the model for other Arabs.[1]

Much of the regime's legitimacy among its population came less from commitment to this vision than from its nationalization of Iraq's oil industry in 1972. Not only did nationalization reinforce the regime's anti-imperialist credentials, the revenue from oil also allowed it to embark on an ambitious development program. Under the rubric of "socialism," the state invested in agriculture, industry, health, and education, becoming the country's largest employer.[2] The 1970s saw an expansion in the Iraqi middle class, working primarily in the public sector. It constituted the social base of the regime.[3]

Despite making great strides in social services and infrastructure development, the Ba'th regime had to navigate the landscape of Iraqi politics with a mixture of accommodation and repression. Alongside challenges from the military, the Ba'thists had to contend with the Iraqi Communist Party (ICP), the Kurdish Democratic Party (KDP), and the Shi'i Islamist parties, particularly the Da'wa Party. The ICP had had a long history of organizing among professional syndicates and labor organizations. Despite suffering repression and internal divisions in the 1960s, it remained the most effectively organized party in the early 1970s. The ICP drew its followers from the southern cities of Iraq and had a substantial constituency in the Kurdish cities of the north.

Conscious of the precariousness of its popular support, the regime forged an alliance with the Communists, known as the National Patriotic Front, in 1972. Despite the legalization of the Communist Party and the

---

[1] Ba'th Arab Socialist Party, *Revolutionary Iraq, 1968–1973, The Political Report Adopted by the Eighth Regional Congress of the Ba'th Arab Socialist Party-Iraq* (np: 1974).

[2] Ibrahim Maroun, *L'économie Pétrolière pour L'économie de Guerre Permanente, Étude Socio-économique des problèmes du Dévelopment en Irak* (Beirut: Lebanon University Press, 1986).

[3] Farouk-Sluglett and Sluglett, *Iraq Since 1958*, pp. 230–66, and Isam al-Khafaji, "The parasitic base of the Ba'thist regime," in Committee Against Repression and for Democratic Rights in Iraq (CADRI,) *Saddam's Iraq, Revolution or Reaction* (London: Zed Press, 1986) pp. 73–88.

appointment of Communist ministers, however, the regime continued its policy of arrests and repression. The National Patriotic Front was formally dissolved in 1978, long after it had become an empty shell and most Communists had been imprisoned or killed or had fled Iraq. At the same time, bolstered by the passage of a law that same year that outlawed all other parties, the Ba'th successfully supplanted the Communists in all professional and popular organizations.[4]

The more serious challenge to the regime came from the KDP and its leader, Mustafa Barzani. The Kurds, an ethnic minority with a distinct language, had intermittently waged a nationalist insurgency since Iraq's founding in 1921. By the 1960s, the KDP had become the main representative of Kurdish nationalist aspirations. When the Ba'th Party came to power in 1968, its leaders worked at forging a solution to Kurdish demands for autonomy and national rights. In 1970, the KDP secured an agreement with the Ba'thist regime, known as the March 11 Manifesto, which allowed Kurds use of their language in schools and government institutions, limited autonomy, some form of representation in national politics, and the appointment of Kurdish administrators in Kurdish regions. In areas where Kurdish majorities were in question, particularly in the oil-rich area of Kirkuk, a census was ordered to determine whether these regions fell under Kurdish autonomous rule.

However, despite its agreement on paper, the Iraqi government did not undertake the census, fearing it would reveal that Kirkuk was indeed predominantly Kurdish. Soon after the Manifesto was signed, the regime embarked on a policy that displaced Kurdish peasants from the Kirkuk region and the Kurdish areas of Diyali province and resettled them in central and southern Iraq. Arabs from other parts of Iraq received incentives to resettle in the contested areas in order to change the demographic balance in a more favorable direction. Barzani complained about these policies and suspected that the long-promised census was going to be postponed until the ethnic composition of the area was changed.[5]

By the spring of 1974, a full-fledged insurgency was under way in the Kurdish areas, with the KDP drawing support from Iran, the United States, and Israel. That same year, on the anniversary of the March 11 Manifesto, the government unilaterally placed the Kurdish areas designated in the agreement as Region of Autonomous Rule under a special

[4] Johan Franzén, *Red Star over Iraq: Iraqi Communism before Saddam* (London: Hurst and Company, 2011) pp. 185–248.
[5] The Fayli Kurds were Shi'a who inhabited an area on the Iraqi border with Iran stretching from Khaniqin to Amara. Farouk-Sluglett and Sluglett, *Iraq Since 1958*, p. 158.

ministry administered from Baghdad and controlled by the government. The regime began a dual policy of economic development accompanied by a redrawing of districts and settlement of Arabs in the predominantly Kurdish areas. The disputed Kirkuk region was excluded from the Region of Autonomous Rule and made into a province.[6] Much of the insurgency's logistical support depended on open borders as well as funding and arms from Iran. In 1975, the Shah of Iran and the Iraqi government resolved a number of outstanding border issues and the Algiers Agreement was signed. The Shah withdrew his support of the Kurds in exchange for concessions on the Shatt al-Arab waterway and other border areas in central Iraq. The Kurdish insurgency collapsed and its leader fled the country.

The regime continued its policy of Arabizing certain areas of Iraqi Kurdistan while the Kurdish nationalist movement sought to regroup in exile. By 1977, the movement, now split between the KDP under the leadership of the Barzanis and the Popular Union of Kurdistan (PUK) under the leadership of Jalal Talabani, began to wage a low-intensity guerilla war in the Kurdish areas. At the outbreak of the Iran-Iraq war, they were poised to offer their help to the Islamic revolutionary government of Iran.

Equally problematic for the Ba'thist regime was the restiveness of sectors of the Shi'i majority population who were drawn to Islamist politics. Although the overwhelming majority of Iraqi Shi'a is Arab, a minority is descended from Iranian families who settled in Iraq during the Ottoman period. The holy cities of Najaf and Karbala are central to the formation of Shi'i communal identity. The first houses the mausoleum of Ali, the first *imam*, and it has historically been the premier, if not sole, center of Shi'i learning. Successive Iraqi governments had to devise various methods to erode the independence of the clerical establishment and keep it from entering politics. During the first decade of Ba'thist rule, these methods included tighter control of Shi'i seminaries, the appointment of government-approved clerics to preach in mosques, and the sponsorship of Shi'i clerical leaders who willingly disavowed politics.

If Najaf is the intellectual center of Shi'i life, Karbala is its emotional core. Tens, if not hundreds, of thousands of Iraqi Shi'a converged annually in the month of Muharram to commemorate the death of Hussain the son of Ali and the third *imam* of Shi'i Islam, at the hand of Yazid, the

---

[6] Ibid., p. 17. The boundaries of the Region of Autonomous Rule excluded about half of the Kurdish areas, including Kirkuk, Jabal Sinjar, Kifri, and areas around the border with Iran. The new provinces of Ta'mim (with Kirkuk as its center) and Salah al-Din (with Takrit as its center) ensured Arab predominance.

son of the Ummayyad Caliph in 680 CE. The battle in which Hussain
was killed is reenacted over several days, and the reenactment culminates
in the ritual beating of breasts and flagellation on *'Ashura*, the tenth day
of Muharram, the month of Hussain's death. The potential for using this
passion play, which chronicles the death of the grandson of the Prophet
who had set out to reclaim his rights from an unjust ruler, to channel
political dissent was great. The Ba'thists, therefore, maintained tight control of *'Ashura* processions and of the traditional day of mourning forty
days after that (*al-arba'in*).

While the Shi'a in Iraq had a sense of communal identity, they belonged
to the same parties as their Sunni and Christian compatriots and did
not organize around sectarian agendas. The Iraqi Communist Party had
adherents among the urban middle and lower middle class as well as the
working class, particularly in southern cities such as Basra and Nasiriyya.
The Ba'th Party's brand of Arab nationalism also attracted a large number of middle-class Shi'a in the sixties. When, in the late seventies, the
Ba'th became the only legal party in Iraq, Shi'a, like others, joined the
ranks at every level in its hierarchy. However, during this same period,
underground Shi'i Islamist parties experienced a surge of followers due
to several factors. First, these parties formed part of a region-wide trend.
Islamist parties challenged secular nationalist movements on the grounds
that these movements and the governments they supported had not delivered on their promises of social development and political liberation.
Second, within Iraq, the gradual elimination of the ICP diminished the
opportunities for Shi'i political involvement in secular parties. In addition,
the upper echelon of the Ba'th Party was gradually taken over by men
perceived as more loyal to Ahmad Hasan al-Bakr and Saddam Hussein
drawn from Takrit, their hometown, and the areas of north central Iraq.

Most important for the development of Shi'i political activism, however, was the rise of a number of intellectually innovative Shi'i clerics
angered by the secular and socialist policies of the Ba'th, particularly
regarding issues of land reform and women's rights. They called for an
activist brand of Shi'i Islam. Consequently, political parties with exclusively Shi'i agendas and constituencies gained in strength and number.
While many Shi'a continued to look to the chief religious scholar,
Ayatollah Abu Qasim al-Kho'i, for guidance in their lives, other scholars
challenged Kho'i's quietism and accommodation of the Ba'thist regime.
Among the most visible of this group was Ayatollah Muhsin al-Hakim,
whose children helped found an opposition movement in Iran during
the Iran-Iraq war. Ayatollah Muhammad Baqir al-Sadr provided inspiration for the Da'wa Party. Finally, Ayatollah Khomeini, exiled to Najaf

by the Shah's government in 1965, contributed to the political and intellectual ferment.

Shi'i grievances coalesced around a number of issues. Some, such as the lack of adequate representation in various government institutions and the allocation of government funds to the predominantly Shi'i southern regions, were negotiable. The regime addressed them by investing more heavily in the south and ensuring that more Shi'a were accepted into institutions of higher learning and employed in public sector jobs. Political demands, however, were harder for the regime to accommodate. The regime dealt harshly with the clergy who were hostile to the secular ideology of the Ba'th and reacted violently to the Da'wa Party, which called for the establishment of an Islamic government.[7] The advent of the Ba'th to power ushered in a period of harassment of non-pliable Shi'i clerics accused of disloyalty to Iraq because of their connections to Iran.

In April 1969, while Iraq was engaged in a dispute with Iran over control of the Shatt al-Arab waterway, al-Bakr asked Ayatollah Muhsin al-Hakim to condemn the Iranian government's refusal to succumb to Iraqi demands. When al-Hakim refused, the government used his refusal as an excuse to expel twenty thousand Iraqis of "Iranian affiliation" and to close Kufa University and confiscate its endowment.[8] Together with the removal of the Shi'i Fayli Kurds in 1971, this latest expulsion highlighted a practice that the Ba'thist government would engage in periodically as its relations with Iran deteriorated. Iraqi Shi'a branded of "Iranian affiliation," whose families had lived in Iraq for generations, found themselves designated as a fifth column, their rights circumscribed, and their fate subject to Iraq's relations with Iran.

Shi'i activism was propelled to the center of Iraqi politics in February 1977. Part of the Muharram commemoration of the death of Hussain entailed a massive cleric-led pilgrimage from Najaf to Karbala. On February 5 and 6, the underground Da'wa Party turned the march of some thirty thousand people into a protest against the government. In the ensuing riots, several people were killed and two thousand were arrested, including a number of clerics. A special court convened to investigate the events and sentenced eight clerics to death and others to prison.[9] These events highlighted the organizational strength of the Da'wa Party and alerted the government to the growing power of activist clerics to mobilize their followers around public religious commemorations and

[7] Tripp, *A History of Iraq*, pp. 193–223 and Faleh A. Jabar, *The Shi'ite Movement in Iraq* (London: Saqi Press, 2003).
[8] Tripp, *A History of Iraq*, p. 201.
[9] Ibid., p. 216 and Farouk-Sluglett and Sluglett, *Iraq Since 1958*, p. 198.

in spaces associated with Shiʻi forms of worship, venues more difficult to monitor and control.

Shiʻi political activism took on regional dimensions in the wake of the Iranian Revolution of 1979 that threatened to upend the relationship between Iraq and Iran. The Iraqi government had keenly watched the erosion of the Shah of Iran's power over the course of 1977–8. Relations with the Shah of Iran had been turbulent. Disputes over borders, particularly over the division of the Shatt al-Arab waterway, were compounded by competition over the projection of political influence in the Gulf. The conflict over borders and regional influence carried international repercussions since the two nations were allied to the opposing poles in the Cold War. The Shah had turned Iran into the premier power in the Gulf with U.S. military support and encouragement. The leaders of Baʻthist Iraq had ambitions to challenge this hegemony and turned to the Soviet Union for the training and supply of its armed forces. Relations became particularly tense in 1971 when Iran occupied three small islands in the Gulf after the British withdrew from the Trucial States and the United Arab Emirates came into existence. It was a clear bid on the part of Iran and its ally, the United States, to supplant the British and exert hegemony in the Persian Gulf. Relations deteriorated further when Iran funneled arms and funds to the Kurdish insurgency in 1974 in an attempt to destabilize Iraq, now bound to the Soviet Union by the 1972 Treaty of Friendship and Cooperation. The war with the Kurds proved costly for the Iraqi government in both arms and men. Although interested in weakening the Iraqi regime, the Shah had no intention of supporting the Kurdish bid for autonomy since he had a sizable and restive Kurdish minority within Iran itself. By the winter of 1975, both governments were ready to take up the offers of mediation proposed by Jordan and Egypt. The Algiers Agreement was signed in March 1975. The Shatt al-Arab boundary was set at the Thalweg Line (the median line of the deepest channel of the waterway), and Iran agreed to abandon its claim to territories on the frontier with central Iraq. At the same time, the agreement and the treaty that accompanied it implied that any Iraqi claims, resurrected in 1980, to Khuzistan, where Arabs constituted a significant portion of the population, were laid to rest because the area fell within the accepted line of demarcation of the Shatt al-Arab waterway. The Iranian government agreed to close the borders with Iraqi Kurdistan and to end its aid to the Kurdish insurgents.[10]

---

[10] Dilip Hiro, *The Longest War, The Iran-Iraq Military Conflict* (U.S.A: Routledge, 1991), pp. 7–39.

The 1975 Algiers Agreement settled, at least for a short time, the border dispute between Iraq and Iran and effectively ended the 1974 Kurdish insurgency. Equally important, the agreement signaled a shift in Iraq's position in the region and its alliance with the Soviet Union. It was welcomed by the conservative governments of the Gulf as well as Saudi Arabia, until then wary of Iraq's alliance with the USSR and its militant nationalist rhetoric. While the Iraqi regime continued to use militant rhetoric and maintained its relations with the Soviet Union, it gradually moved to mend relations with the United States and its more conservative allies in the Gulf. Behind this shift in foreign policy lay the ambition to carve for Iraq a leadership role in the region – an ambition rendered realizable by President Sadat's visit to Jerusalem in 1977, effectively removing Egypt from its role as a leader in the Arab world. The Baghdad Summit, convened in November 1978, was an attempt to position Iraq as the leader of Arab governments seeking a unified reaction to Egypt's decision to sign a peace treaty with Israel in March 1979.

The fall of the Shah's regime and the founding of the Iranian Islamic Republic in February 1979 had more far-reaching regional ramifications than even the Israeli-Egyptian peace treaty. Although the Iraqi government recognized the Islamic Republic, it was acutely aware of the potential threat the Iranian revolutionary example posed to its hold on its own Shi'i population and to its revolutionary credentials. The regime's fears were not unfounded. Shi'i Islamist organizations soon began organizing. Matters were compounded by the appeal across the Middle East of the Islamic Revolution as a peaceful mass uprising against an oppressive and seemingly impregnable U.S.-supported regime.

In July 1979, Saddam Hussain pushed aside President Ahmad Hasan al-Bakr and installed himself as president of the republic, head of the Revolutionary Command Council, secretary general of the Ba'th Party Regional Command (the only sanctioned party in the country), and head of the armed forces. Along with this concentration of power, Saddam Hussain began cultivating a personality cult that linked him to the nation, the people, and the Ba'th "successes." He had begun his career in the shadows of the Ba'th hierarchy, creating and running the party's security services. After the Ba'th seized power, he was instrumental in eliminating its enemies and consolidating its power. Drawing on the support of his and al-Bakr's clan networks in Takrit, he created a core of high-ranking party cadres loyal to him and ruthless in their pursuit of opponents.

Hussain had gradually become the linchpin of Iraqi foreign policy in the 1970s; he was now its main architect. He had become convinced that the chaos engendered by the Iranian Revolution provided a perfect opportunity for Iraq to assert its power in the region, reclaim the concession it made to Iran in the Algiers Agreement, and contain the appeal of revolutionary Shi'ism. For its part, the Iranian government believed that its revolution was exportable. It therefore extended support to Shi'i Islamist parties in Iraq, whose confrontation with security forces continued throughout 1979.[11]

The Iran-Iraq War

A series of events in the spring of 1980 provided the background to the beginning of the war with Iran. In March, the Iraqi government took severe measures against the Islamists, arresting and executing a number of Da'wa and other militants and making membership in the Da'wa Party a crime punishable by death retroactively.[12] As a result, Ayatollah Muhammad Baqir al-Sadr, who had earlier sent a congratulatory note to Khomeini, issued a verdict declaring the Ba'th un-Islamic. In April, a member of a small Islamist group tried to assassinate Deputy Prime Minister Tariq Aziz at Mustansiriyya University in Baghdad. The government immediately arrested and executed al-Sadr and his sister, Bint al-Huda, and placed Grand Ayatollah al-Kho'i under house arrest in Najaf. In addition, Iraq bombed the Iranian town of Qasr-i Shirin and expelled tens of thousands of Iraqis of "Iranian affiliation."[13] By early September, a series of border skirmishes culminated in the Iranian shelling of the Iraqi border towns of Khanaqin and Mandali, resulting in a number of casualties. On September 17, with great fanfare, Saddam Hussain tore up the Algiers Agreement in the National Assembly and declared Iraqi sovereignty over the entire Shatt al-Arab waterway. On September 22, Iraqi troops entered Iran.

The Iraqi government had thought of its entry into Iran strategically and had not prepared for either a long-term occupation of Iranian territory or for a long war.[14] The war was conceived as a war of "demonstration," in the words of political scientist Charles Tripp.[15] The goals were: to force

---

[11] Tripp, *A History of Iraq*, pp. 223–53 and Hiro, *The Longest War*, pp. 7–39.
[12] Hiro, *The Longest War*, p. 35.
[13] Estimates put the number of expelled at forty thousand. Tripp, *A History of Iraq*, p. 230.
[14] Lieutenant General Ra'id Majid Hamadani, *Qabla 'an Yughadiruna al-Tarikh* (*Before History Leaves Us Behind*) (Beirut: Arab Scientific Publishers, 2007), pp. 55–7.
[15] Shahram Chubin and Charles Tripp, *Iran and Iraq at War* (Boulder: Westview Press, 1988), pp. 53–67.

the Iranian government to make concessions on borders; to dissuade it by force from supporting Shi'i Islamist groups; and to establish Iraq as the premier power in the Gulf. These expectations were dashed when Iran refused the first offer of a ceasefire agreement on September 28, 1980. By the spring of 1982, Iranian forces had regained most of their conquered territory and Iraq unilaterally withdrew its forces to the internationally recognized borders in June. The war then turned into a war of "survival" waged to maintain the regime in power against the stated aim of Khomeini, who made peace conditional on the fall of Saddam Hussain and his party. Several coup attempts, purges in the Ba'th Party and the armed forces, executions of military leaders, and a counterinsurgency against the Kurds that turned genocidal in 1988 bespoke the increasingly draconian measures the regime had to undertake to wage this longest of late-twentieth-century wars.[16]

The war was fought on difficult terrain along the 800-mile border. In the south, marshes and intricate waterways separated the two countries and made the movement of military equipment difficult. In the north, high mountain ranges, snow covered in the winter, presented insurmountable terrain for tank movement and provided an effective shield for insurgents. Iraq was at a dual disadvantage: its main cities were closer to the Iranian border (Baghdad was 40 miles away, Basra 12 miles, whereas Tehran was 530 miles away); and its population (14 million) was much smaller than Iran's (42 million). Much of the confrontation took place in trenches and was characterized by periods of intense fighting followed by a stalemate. A series of offensives and counteroffensives marked by the occupation of narrow strips of land made it difficult for either country to claim victory. Nevertheless, the war can be divided into three distinct periods.

The first months of the war saw Iraqi victories with the occupation of Khorramshahr (Muhammarah) and the advance of Iraqi troops into Iranian territories. By November 1980, Iraq had occupied about ten thousand square miles of Iranian territory and declared it had reached its objectives.[17] Iraqi forces crossed the Karun River, lay siege to the strategic city of Dezful, and attempted to take the island of Abadan in order to ensure a gateway to the Gulf. The tide began to turn against Iraq in September 1981, when Iraqi forces were dislodged from around Abadan. By December 1981, Iranian forces had regained some 70 percent of their

---

[16] Ibid., pp. 57–61.
[17] Hiro, *The Longest War*, p. 43.

FIGURE 2.1. A group of Iraqi soldiers tears an Iranian flag after overrunning the city governor's office in Khorramshahr, Iran, November 1, 1980 (AP photo/ Zuhair Saade).

conquered territories.[18] By May 1982, Iranian forces had recaptured Khorramshahr and taken tens of thousands of Iraqi soldiers, a great portion of them from the Popular Army, as prisoners of war. Iraq announced a unilateral ceasefire in June 1982 and withdrew to the internationally recognized borders (Figure 2.1).

The withdrawal of Iraqi forces and the loss of Khorramshahr – the conquest of which the regime had touted as a restoration of its Arab population to the Iraqi fold – created a severe crisis for the Iraqi leadership. The losses were compounded by shortages and the curtailment of the ambitious development projects that had provided legitimacy for the regime. Austerity measures were imposed and the "guns and butter" policy promised at the beginning of the war was jettisoned in the face of dwindling national reserves.[19]

To deal with the political fallout, Saddam Hussain moved to consolidate his power within the Baʿth, to centralize decision-making processes in the Office of the Presidency, and to redefine the war as one of survival, a war "imposed" on Iraq by Iran's refusal to agree to peace despite

[18] Ofra Bengio, "Iraq," *Middle East Contemporary Survey*, 6 (1981–2), 582.
[19] Ibid, p. 583.

repeated offers by Iraq. Soon after the withdrawal in June 1982, Saddam Hussain convened the Ninth Regional Party Congress of the Ba'th Party. The party leadership anointed Saddam Hussain the chief ideologue and his words became the guiding principle of Ba'thist education and political mobilization. In addition, the congress de-emphasized the "socialist" aspects of its economic programs, paving the way to a policy of liberalizing the economy, allowing private entrepreneurs to become subcontractors of the state by providing them with low-interest loans and tax concessions.[20] To further consolidate his power, Saddam Hussain turned the Office of the Presidency into a primary center of decision making by staffing it with six ministerial special advisers. Thus, the crisis of 1982 helped in consolidating the power of Saddam Hussain.[21] To appease the army generals who had chafed under his interference in military decisions, Hussain relaxed his policy of promoting and rewarding officers based on their Ba'thist affiliation.[22]

The second phase began a war of attrition and culminated with the devastating loss of the Faw Peninsula to Iran in February 1986. It was the deadliest period of the war and the most destructive, as each country bombed its adversary's cities and oil infrastructure. Iraq survived this period thanks in no small part to the decision of the U.S. government to provide economic subsidies for grain purchase. Beginning in 1983, Iran launched a series of attacks on Iraqi defensive lines in the south, middle, and north of the country. In the south, Iranians organized troops in human waves to capture the Basra-Baghdad highway and hoped to capture Basra and incite its Shi'i population to rebel against the regime. The Iraqi Fourth Army Corps put up fierce resistance. The Iranians captured Mehran, in the middle section of the country, from the Second Army Corps and pushed their troops thirty miles into Iraq. In the north, where the Iranian-supported Kurdish insurgency had gained ground, the Iranians succeeded in pushing back the First Army Corps from Iranian border towns and made inroads in areas east of Panjawin. By 1984, much of the fighting was concentrated in the south, where Iranian troops attacked the Third and Fourth Army Corps and captured the oil-producing island of Majnoon in Hawr al-Huwayza, signaling a major Iraqi loss. As the fighting concentrated in the south, a new army command, the East Tigris Command, was established to run the defensive operations around the

---

[20] al-Khafaji, "The parasitic base," pp. 77–88 and Farouk-Sluglett and Sluglett, *Iraq Since 1958*, pp. 230–66.

[21] Chubin and Tripp, *Iran and Iraq at War*, pp. 84–122.

[22] Hiro, *The Longest War*, pp. 58–95 and Bengio, "Iraq," 592–3.

southern marshes. In the north of the country, the KDP, the PUK, and the ICP mounted attacks on the Iraqi army in the rural areas outside the cities of Dohuk, Sulaimaniyya, and Arbil. The ranks of Kurdish guerilla forces, the *peshmerga*, swelled with deserters from the government-sponsored Kurdish military forces, the National Defense Battalions.[23] Meanwhile, the Shi'i Islamist opposition parties had united under the umbrella of the Supreme Assembly of the Islamic Revolution in Iraq (SAIRI). Sponsored and funded by Iran, its military wing, the Badr Brigade, fought alongside the Iranian army.

The beginning of 1986 saw a concerted effort by Iran to conquer Basra and to break the Iraqi defensive line around the southern marshes. Unable to do so, Iran directed its attention to the Faw Peninsula. On February 6, it mounted a successful attack on the Faw Peninsula, conquering it in a massive, well-planned military operation that caught the Iraqi army unprepared. Shaken to the core, the Iraqi regime sent in the Republican Guard to support the Seventh Army Corps in an unsuccessful counteroffensive that decimated whole regiments within the Guard.[24] To counter the loss of Faw, Saddam Hussain pushed his military to conquer Mehran, but lost it again to an Iranian offensive.

The loss of Faw and the unsuccessful attempt to take Mehran created a serious crisis for the regime. Saddam Hussain called an extraordinary meeting of the Revolutionary Command Council at which he installed his cousin Ali Hasan al-Majid as director of security and delegated the reorganization of the Military Office of the Party to him. Some reshuffling of the Revolutionary Command Council leadership also took place, and the military received greater freedom in setting strategy. The regime allowed for the voicing of complaints by its citizens against the corruption of state organs and party officials, thereby deflecting criticism from Saddam Hussain to state institutions and party organizations.[25] Citizens had much to complain about. The war had created economic hardship, led to the deaths of hundreds of thousands of Iraqi men, and created labor shortages. So critical was the shortage of men that the government conscripted some one hundred twenty-five thousand male university teachers and students, a practice it had avoided in fear of alienating a critical element of society.[26]

---

[23] Hiro, *The Longest War*, p. 150.
[24] Ofra Bengio, " Iraq," *Middle East Contemporary Survey*, 10 (1986), 364. al-Hamadani, *Qabla 'an Yughadurana*, pp. 116–26.
[25] Bengio, "Iraq," p. 369.
[26] Hiro, *The Longest War*, p. 175.

The last two years of the war saw intense involvement by the international community to resolve the conflict as its costs escalated.[27] Iraq had initiated a tanker war in 1984, hitting Iranian oil carriers in the Gulf as part of a campaign to disable the oil-producing capacities of Iran. Soon after, both countries were engaged in a tanker war that threatened oil shipping in the area and led Kuwait, the closest country to the conflict, to ask for Soviet protection of its oil tankers. The Soviets agreed and the United States soon followed. The reflagging of oil tankers meant that Iran's attacks threatened to involve its government in conflict with the United States and the Soviet Union, a situation it wanted to avoid at all costs. At the same time, the war on the ground began to turn in Iraq's favor. Better military intelligence, provided with U.S. help, together with the decision to use the elite Republican Guard more heavily in the war, allowed Iraq to regain most of its lost territory and to repulse Iranian attacks. In the spring of 1987, the regime decided to direct its energies to suppressing the Kurdish insurgency. By the winter of 1988, the Iraqi government had begun a well-organized military campaign to remove the Kurdish population from its villages through a scorched earth policy. The Anfal (Arabic for spoils of war) campaign, as it was called, together with the bombing of Halabja, a Kurdish border town that had fallen to the Iranian forces, marked the beginning of the end for the Kurdish insurgency. While Kurdish insurgents and their Iranian allies continued to control parts of northern Iraq, Iran was unprepared for the Iraqi offensive to capture Faw on April 16, 1988. On July 18, 1988, Iran unconditionally accepted UN Resolution 598. Fighting continued until August 20, when a ceasefire agreement came into effect.[28]

The Iraqi regime painted the end of the war as a great victory. This triumphalism, however, was deployed to mask the problems that plagued Iraq. The war had been costly at many levels. Politically, Saddam Hussein had succeeded in tightening his hold over the Ba'th Party and the security services, but his supremacy remained tenuous. Threats came from within his extended kin, whom he had used to maintain his control over the state machinery, and from the military he himself had elevated to a position of prominence. Two assassination plots were uncovered in 1988 and early

---

[27] The intelligence was provided by Saudi-owned AWACS, piloted by Americans, and approved by Washington.

[28] Hiro, *The Longest War*, pp. 129–52 and Human Rights Watch, *Genocide: The Anfal Campaign against the Kurds*, 1993, http://www.hrw.org/reports/1993/iraqanfal/ANFAL1.htm accessed October 27, 2010.

1989 and Hussain used them to purge the military and his own inner circle of those suspected of disloyalty.[29]

In 1989, inspired in part by glasnost in the Soviet Union, and fueled by the regime's need to reshape postwar popular politics, the climate was ripe for increased political openness. The government called for parliamentary elections and loosened press censorship. It soon became apparent, however, that the elections and press freedoms were designed by the government to reflect its own narrow vision of postwar Iraq. Participation in the war effort was made the crucial determinant of eligibility of candidates running for office. As for freedom of the press, the regime encouraged complaints against state institutions and party officials, but disallowed criticism of the political system as a whole.[30]

The regime's attempts to make participation in the Iran-Iraq war central to the postwar political arrangement had much to do with the war's vast social costs. In 1987, one year before the war ended, out of a total population of 2.6 million Iraqi men aged eighteen to forty-five, 1.7 million were in arms.[31] The deployment and death of large portions of the productive male population led to labor shortages. One and a half million Egyptians and other Arab laborers were imported to run the agricultural, industrial, and service sectors of the economy, and at times to help transport goods to the front. Women were called upon to fill public sector positions, and by 1988 accounted for 31 percent of the labor force in that sector, and one-forth of the total labor force.[32]

The economic costs of the war were also staggering. Iraq emerged burdened with a foreign debt of $50 to $82 billion U.S. dollars, the bulk of it owed to Kuwait and Saudi Arabia. Unemployment, caused in part by the demobilization of soldiers and the dismantling of the war economy, as well as an increase in the demands for social services, severely stressed the state's ability to create jobs and meet the population's social needs. In response, the government accelerated the rate of privatization that had begun during the war and introduced fees on some public sector services. Consequently, inflation rose 35 to 40 percent, and complaints about government and party officials enriching themselves at the expense of Iraqis who had sacrificed for the nation permeated the press.[33] In 1988, declining oil prices worsened Iraq's economic woes, as did the curtailment of

---

[29] Tripp, *A History of Iraq*, pp. 248–53.
[30] Ofra Bengio, "Iraq," *Middle East Contemporary Survey*, 13 (1987), 376–80.
[31] Hiro, *The Longest War*, p. 195.
[32] Ibid., pp. 110 and 133.
[33] Bengio, "Iraq," *Middle East Contemporary Survey*, 13 (1987), 390–5.

its oil production due to the destruction of some of its oil production facilities. To deal with this crisis, the Iraqi government attempted to persuade the Organization for Petroleum Exporting Countries to restrict production quotas and raise oil prices. Saddam Hussain tried to persuade Kuwait and Saudi Arabia to initiate the rise in oil prices and expected them to consider the $40 billion dollars they had extended Iraq in loans as a gift. While Saudi Arabia was willing to forgive the loans, Kuwait did not succumb to pressure and the Iraqi regime's language became increasingly belligerent throughout 1990.

The regime's bellicose language was a result of the mindset of its leaders after the Iran-Iraq war. During and in the immediate aftermath of the war, a military-industrial complex fueled by the building of a military infrastructure, the manufacture of light arms, and the development of chemical weapons increasingly swallowed up state resources.[34] The war cemented Iraq's position as the primary policeman of the Gulf and a bulwark against the Iranian Islamic Republic. After the war, some three hundred thousand Iraqi soldiers remained deployed on the Iraq-Iran border, and Iraqi troops occupied 920 square miles of Iranian territories. Iraq continued to demand, as a "victor," that the eastern shore of the Shatt-al-Arab waterway remain under its control. Relations with Washington had improved during the war, culminating with the exchange of ambassadors. All these factors contributed to the view among Iraq's leaders that military solutions to diplomatic problems were desirable.

The First Gulf War and the UN-imposed Embargo

When attempts by the Arab League to mediate the conflict with Kuwait failed, Iraq felt confident enough to invade Kuwait on August 2, 1990. It did so at what it perceived was a particularly opportune moment. The opposition in Kuwait had boycotted elections to the Kuwaiti National Council in June, creating the illusion that the al-Sabah family's domestic support was eroding. Furthermore, Saddam Hussain seemed to believe that the international community, headed by the United States, would regard the invasion as an attempt to hasten a negotiated settlement by military means. The illusion of quick resolution was reinforced by the ease of the conquest itself. It took Iraq twenty-four hours to occupy Kuwait. Kuwait's ruler, Shaykh Jaber al-Sabah, fled, as did some three

---

[34] Phebe Marr, *The Modern History of Iraq* (Boulder: Westview Press, 2003), pp. 221–3.

hundred thousand Kuwaitis and hundreds of thousands of expatriate workers and their families.

The extent of Saddam Hussain's miscalculations soon became apparent. The international community and the Arab League condemned the invasion. The UN Security Council passed a series of resolutions, most notably Resolution 660 calling for Iraq's unconditional withdrawal from Kuwait and Resolution 661 imposing an embargo on Iraq. Days after the occupation, the Bush administration began to seriously consider a military option. The first contingent of U.S. troops was deployed to Saudi Arabia on August 7. The Bush administration justified what it dubbed "Operation Desert Shield" as strictly defensive, seeking to protect Saudi Arabia and American oil interests in the region. The United States, however, began a concerted diplomatic effort to gather an international coalition of forces, including some from Egypt, Syria, and Morocco, in preparation for a military confrontation with Iraq. By early fall, it had succeeded in bringing on board twenty-eight countries. On October 31, the Bush administration decided to deploy more troops to Saudi Arabia, and by November 8, Bush announced that the United States had decided to double its troop numbers to four hundred thirty thousand, the largest deployment since the Vietnam War. From that point on, a military confrontation was clearly inevitable.

Neither the U.S. Congress nor a majority of the American population was convinced of the military solution. The Bush administration had to convince these constituencies that the United States' decision to move from its initial goal of protecting its oil interests in Saudi Arabia to liberating Kuwait from the clutches of another "Hitler" was supported by an international community and would be sanctioned by the UN. Despite repeated efforts by Jordan, the PLO, France, and the Soviet Union to mediate and signs of willingness to make concessions on the part of Saddam Hussain, a deadline for unconditional withdrawal was set for January 15, 1991 and approved by UN Resolution 678, which authorized war against Iraq. The U.S. Congress followed suit on January 12, only three days before the deadline mandated by the UN resolution.[35]

The invasion of Kuwait, and Iraq's official annexation of Kuwait as its nineteenth province on August 8, created a crisis for the Iraqi leadership. Perhaps most important was the justification for the occupation of an

---

[35] The literature on the First Gulf War is voluminous. I have relied in my summary on Dilip Hiro's excellent *Desert Storm to Desert Shield: The Second Gulf War* (New York: Routledge, 1992), pp. 190–316.

Arab country that had been viewed as a close ally only two years earlier. Exhausted by eight years of war and suffering from economic austerity, Iraqis were not ready for the hardships brought on by the UN-imposed embargo and the human costs that a military confrontation with a coalition of twenty-eight countries could bring. By October, rationing and shortages of fuel were widespread.[36] The regime had dubbed its military operation "The Call," alleging that the invasion came in response to a call by Kuwaiti leaders for an uprising to overthrow the al-Sabah family. Few believed this justification, particularly given that few Kuwaitis collaborated with the occupation. Two other justifications for the occupation carried more credibility with the Iraqi and Arab public: Iraq had a historical claim to Kuwait since the British had drawn borders between the two countries after World War I: the invasion was merely an attempt to rectify an historic injustice. What made matters worse, according to this logic, was that rich Kuwait had refused to allow Iraq access to the sea by leasing it the islands of Warba and Bubayan and was pumping oil from the contested oil field of Rumayla, even after Iraqis had lost their lives trying to defend it from Iran. The regime's initial appeal to pan-Arabism and to historic grievance gradually gave way to anti-imperialist and anti-Zionist rhetoric used by the regime to bolster its regional as well as its international standing quite cynically and to great effect. Preparation for the war had taken place during the first Palestinian intifada and the large-scale immigration of Soviet Jewry into Israel in the wake of glasnost. The American rhetoric about the "New World Order" created by the end of the Cold War and the United States' role as the great enforcer of law and order against the "evil" of Saddam Hussain allowed the Iraqi regime to present the war as a fight against imperialism. Throughout the months leading up to the war, the regime bolstered this argument by linking its withdrawal from Kuwait to Israeli withdrawal from the occupied territories, Lebanon, and Syria. Why, the Iraqi government asked, were the international community and the UN so bent on Iraqi withdrawal from Kuwait when UN resolutions had also called for the withdrawal of Israel from the lands it occupied? This argument initially provided a cover of legitimacy and popular support for Iraq in the Arab countries.

Once it became clear that war was inevitable, the immediate challenge for Saddam Hussain and a small coterie of advisers and generals

---

[36] Ofra Bengio, "Iraq," *Middle East Contemporary Survey*, 14 (1990), 405. Najib al-Salhi, *al-Zilzal (The Earthquake)*, 1998 http://www.Iraq4all.dk/Zlzal/Zm.htm accessed April 28, 2008.

he consulted before his decision to invade was how to maintain control of Kuwait and Iraq and ensure his regime's survival. Ali Hasan al-Majid, head of the Northern Bureau of the Ba'th Party and architect of the Anfal campaign, was appointed governor of Kuwait. In Baghdad, Saddam Hussain surrounded himself with a small group of loyal kinsmen, including his two sons, Uday and Qusay, who did little to apprise him of the real repercussions of the war. Despite the escalation in the language by different military leaders of the Bush administration that war would devastate the Iraqi infrastructure and would debilitate Iraqi military capabilities, Saddam Hussain continued to worry about his survival.

The Iraqi military had seen the gains made during the Iran-Iraq war dissipate. On August 14, Saddam Hussain sent a letter to the Iranian president offering to withdraw Iraqi troops occupying Iranian territory, to exchange prisoners of war, and to return to the border agreement over the Shatt al-Arab waterway as spelled out in the Algiers Agreement. While freeing some three hundred thousand men for the Kuwaiti theater of operations and ensuring Iran's neutrality in the looming conflict, the offer alienated the leadership of the Iraqi armed forces. To counter the threat from the upper echelon of the officer corps, Hussain made some personnel changes before deploying some one hundred thousand soldiers, led by six divisions of the elite Republican Guard, to invade Kuwait.[37]

By the beginning of hostilities on January 16–17, Iraq had called up its reserve and mobilized, according to U.S. and Israeli intelligence, 9 percent of its citizens, some 1.5 million men, to fight. The numbers might have been exaggerated by the U.S. military to justify its use of disproportionate force in the war. Memoirs by Iraqi generals as well as Ba'th Party documents point to the great difficulties the state encountered in getting men to show up at military recruitment offices.[38] Nevertheless, Popular Army as well as infantry divisions from the regular armed forces were stationed in cities in Kuwait, while the Republican Guard remained in strategic locations outside main population centers.[39] Despite the massive mobilization of troops, the Iraqi military leadership had no illusions about the war's outcome. Its main concern was not regime survival but

---

[37] Ibid, p. 102.
[38] Hiro, *Desert Shield to Desert Storm*, p. 397 estimates that the Iraqi forces engaged in war numbered about three hundred sixty thousand, eighty thousand of which surrendered and became prisoners of war in the last days of the ground war, another one hundred eighty thousand of which were bombarded by allies, and some one hundred thousand of which had withdrawn from Kuwait before the ground war started to protect the regime.
[39] Hiro, *Desert Shield to Desert Storm*, p. 253.

the preservation of the bulk of Iraq's military capabilities and ensuring that the conflict did not result in an occupation of Iraqi territory. The Iraqi regime was disappointed on both counts.[40]

The war, upgraded from "Desert Shield" to "Desert Storm" by the U.S.-led coalition, lasted for forty-two days. From January 16–17 until February 24, the coalition forces led an air campaign to soften Iraqi military targets in Kuwait and to disable Iraqi command and control structures. From the beginning, however, the air war targeted the civilian infrastructure and inadvertently led to the loss of civilian life, referred to in the parlance of the U.S. military as "collateral damage." The much-touted precision-guided missiles were used to great effect, but the bulk of the ordnance that fell on Iraqi cities, particularly Baghdad and Basra, was not as precise. Power plants, bridges, and communication networks were hit, as were shops and, in one case, a shelter housing more than 400 Iraqis, most of them women and children.

The Iraqi armed forces took a beating and Iraqi cities experienced the full impact of a bombing campaign that dwarfed anything their populations had experienced during the Iran-Iraq war. The United States and its allies designated February 24 as the date for the beginning of the ground offensive, unless Iraq withdrew all its forces unconditionally from Kuwait and accepted all UN Security Council resolutions including those asking for war reparations and weapons inspections. During the days leading up to the ground war, the Soviet Union offered two peace plans, which were accepted by the Iraqi government but rejected by the United States. Iraq agreed to abide by Security Resolution 660, begin withdrawing from Kuwait, nullify its annexation of Kuwait, and sign a ceasefire agreement. It refused to accept all other UN Security Council resolutions, however, thus allowing the U.S. government and its allies to dismiss the peace plans as insufficient. On February 24, the U.S.-led coalition began its ground offensive to liberate Kuwait. A day later, the Iraqi Revolutionary Command Council ordered troop withdrawal from Kuwait and Iraqi troops began their pullback. Contesting Iraq's claim of unilateral troop withdrawal from Kuwait, the U.S. military blocked all routes for Iraqi troops back into Iraq and, on February 26, bombarded retreating Iraqi soldiers on the Jahra-Basra highway, the Jahra-Umm Qasr road, and the Umm Qasr-Baghdad-Nasiriyya road. The bombardment continued until President Bush declared victory on February 28 and called for a ceasefire, which Iraq accepted two hours later.[41]

[40] al-Hamadani, *Qabla 'an Yughadiruna*, pp. 221–48.
[41] Hiro, *Desert Shield to Desert Storm*, pp. 514–20.

In April, UN Resolution 687 set the provisions for the implementation
of the ceasefire, ushering in twelve years of international control of the
Iraqi economy and military. Among its many provisions, the ones that
would have the most effect were those that made Iraq's economic recov-
ery dependent on the control of its military capabilities. A UN peace-
keeping force would remain at its border. Iraq needed to pay reparations
to Kuwait for the damage it had visited on the country. Furthermore,
the resolution established the mechanisms of monitoring Iraqi compliance to provisions concerning the dismantling of its weapons systems,
including the destruction of its nuclear, biological, and chemical weapons
capabilities. Under the provisions of Resolution 661, failure to conform
to any of the conditions of the resolution extended the comprehensive
embargo imposed on Iraq.[42]

The Gulf crisis and the war that ensued set the parameters of U.S.
policy in Iraq for the next twelve years and gave birth to the means
of implementing it. Sanctions, weapons inspections, and selective use
of force were deployed to ensure a policy of containment of Saddam
Hussain's regime. Furthermore, the crisis and the war transformed the
UN as an international organization and linked its Security Council, if
not its other humanitarian organizations, to U.S. interests. For the next
twelve years, the UN oversaw and gave legal sanction to the harshest
and longest embargo ever imposed on a nation, reshaping the meaning of humanitarianism and linking it with the political agenda of its
most powerful states.[43] More troubling was the transformation in the
conduct of war and the disproportionate use of the technologies of violence against populations of states singled out as "criminal" states. In
the 1990s, the United States, Britain, and France used so-called surgical strikes against Iraq for its non-adherence to UN Security Council
resolutions with no UN oversight and little accountability as to the laws
governing more traditional wars. The transformation of the UN's role
and the uncontested ascendency of the United States helped undermine
Iraqi sovereignty, created a humanitarian crisis for Iraq's population,
and paradoxically helped the Ba'thist regime, now greatly weakened, to
survive until 2003.

The Iraqi armed forces' fear that the war would end up compromis-
ing Iraqi sovereignty and destroying its military capability proved well

---

[42] UN Security Resolution 687 is reproduced in Hiro, *Desert Shield to Desert Storm*,
   pp. 540–8. At thirty-four articles, it was one of the longest UN resolutions ever passed.
[43] Joy Gordon, *Invisible War*.

founded. Sensing the scale of the impending catastrophe and the threat to his regime, Saddam Hussain had ordered the early withdrawal from Kuwait of tens of thousands of his elite forces before the ground war started. Some eighty thousand Iraqi troops had surrendered to the allied forces, effectively becoming prisoners of war, and close to one hundred eighty thousand had been pounded by the allied forces. Destruction of the army's military hardware was extensive as well.[44]

The Bush administration had hoped that the war would bring about the fall of Saddam Hussain, but thought his removal would be at the hands of the military to ensure a stable transition. Instead, his regime faced a chaotic uprising that started in the predominantly Shi'i south and spread to the Kurdish north. Although the Damascus-based Iraqi opposition insisted that the uprising was a national rather than a sectarian one, Iran's support of the uprising sealed its fate in the south. Saddam Hussain could claim that the uprising was the work of Iranian "saboteurs" and did not reflect the popular anger. Furthermore, the Bush administration and its Saudi ally had no desire to see an Iranian-style regime in Iraq. They therefore allowed the Iraqi regime to use helicopter gunships to subdue the rebels and stood by watching as units of the Republican Guard pounded the cities of the south. The suppression of the uprising in the south was bloody, and, by May 1, some sixty-eight thousand Iraqi refugees had fled to camps in Rafha in Saudi Arabia or crossed the border into Iran.[45] In the north, Kurdish rebels, now under the umbrella of the Kurdish Front, succeeded in taking over the major cities in Iraqi Kurdistan and held onto the crucial town of Kirkuk. The prospect of an independent Iraqi Kurdistan did not appeal to Turkey, another important ally in the coalition, and the Bush administration chose not to interfere. By March 28, the regime had reestablished its hold over the rebellious areas.

The rebels in the south were unsuccessful in mustering international or U.S. support. The Kurdish uprising in the north, however, led to the establishment of an autonomous regional government in Iraqi Kurdistan, in large part because the Kurds successfully internationalized their predicament. The suppression of the uprising in the north led to the exodus of some 2 million Kurds across the Iranian and Turkish border. Fearful that the Iraqi regime would use chemical weapons and follow the same policy it had used in its Anfal campaign, Kurds fled across harsh terrain and in difficult weather conditions.

---

[44] Hiro, *Desert Shield to Desert Storm*, p. 397.
[45] Marr, *Modern History of Iraq*, p. 251.

The humanitarian crisis that ensued, together with Turkey's concern over the large number of Kurdish refugees within its borders, induced the Bush administration to launch Operation Provide Comfort. Initially conceived to provide humanitarian aid to the Kurds and to ensure their safe return to their homes, Operation Provide Comfort spawned a series of measures that further eroded Iraqi sovereignty. To protect fearful Kurds, the United States imposed a no fly zone north of the thirty-sixth parallel, effectively prohibiting any military activity, including the flying of aircraft as far north as Mosul. Next, UN-administered safe havens were established in Kurdish areas. The presence of the UN and the establishment of the no fly zone gave the Kurdish Front some leeway to negotiate an agreement with the central government. Over the next months, the Iraqi government ceded control of the Kurdish north to the Kurds, but maintained its hold over Kirkuk. By 1992, the Kurds had succeeded in forming a Kurdish regional government that remained outside the effective control of Baghdad.

The Iraqi regime had survived the war and the rebellion, but at great cost to itself and the nation. The uprising and its suppression created deep fissures within Iraqi society, led to the rise of sectarianism, and removed predominantly Kurdish areas from the control of the central government. Equally problematic were the curtailment of Iraqi sovereignty and the disintegration of Iraq's economy and its human capital resulting from the UN embargo. The war and the uprising provided a forum for the Iraqi opposition in exile, grown exponentially in factions and numbers, to begin preparing for the regime's eventual demise. From 1991 until the regime fell in April 2003, events in Iraq were shaped by two factors: first, the insistence of the United States and its allies on Iraqi compliance to UN resolutions, particularly Resolution 687 calling for disarmament; and second, the Iraqi regime's reaction to measures instituted by the UN and the United States and its allies to curb Iraq's sovereignty and dislodge Saddam Hussain from power.

Much of the policy governing the sanctions regime and the program of weapons inspection imposed on Iraq was made by the UN Security Council and shaped by the will of the United States and its allies who were permanent members of the Council.[46] Ostensibly, the United States and its allies' main interest lay in destroying Iraq's military capabilities so

---

[46] France's policy toward sanctions and toward the weapons inspection program was more ambiguous than that of Britain. It did take part in airstrikes on Iraq in 1994 and 1996, but objected to the joint U.S. and British military operation, Operation Desert Fox, in 1998.

that it could not pose another threat to the region. There were two areas of contention between the UN Security Council and the Iraqi government: the first was the weapons inspection program, namely the conduct and the prerogatives of the weapons agencies; the second was the management of the sanctions regime and its impact on the Iraqi population.

The weapons inspection program posed existential problems for the Iraqi regime. Resolution 687 decreed that the economic embargo on Iraq would not be removed until weapons inspectors were persuaded that all of Iraq's weapons of mass destruction had been accounted for and destroyed. Inspectors were to be allowed unlimited access to facilities for housing these weapons, including those of the crucial security apparatus and the presidential palaces. Inspectors would penetrate the deepest recesses of the regime's power and threaten its survival. Thus, not only was Iraqi territorial sovereignty destroyed, so was the regime's ability to shield its opaque power structure. By 1996, inspectors were satisfied that most of Iraq's nuclear and chemical weapons and long-range missiles had been accounted for and destroyed. However, other weapons systems, particularly biological weapons, were not accounted for, in large part because documentation of these indicated they might be hidden in Saddam Hussain's palaces. The UN Security Council decided that sanctions were to remain in place. In December 1998, the United States and Britain initiated Operation Desert Fox against security facilities and a number of Saddam Hussain's palaces. It effectively ended inspection until 2001, enabled Saddam Hussain to claim that the weapons inspection program was a tool of American interests, and further weakened international support for the embargo.[47]

The weapons inspection program was aimed at the heart of the regime and effectively destroyed Iraq's military capabilities. The economic embargo's purpose was to create such internal pressure on the regime as to force the Iraqi population to rebel against it. The UN Security Council, dominated by the United States, insisted on maintaining and managing the embargo despite reports of UN and humanitarian organizations on the deleterious impact of the sanctions on the Iraqi population.[48] The economic embargo's impact had far-reaching consequences – in both economic costs and humanitarian terms. The economic costs are easily

---

[47] Marr, *Modern History of Iraq*, pp. 266–90 and Gordon, *Invisible War*, pp. 20–38.

[48] Gordon, *Invisible War*, analyzes the conflict between the political and humanitarian goals of the organization through a study of the workings of the sanctions committee founded to administer the embargo. Sarah Graham-Brown, *Sanctioning Saddam: The Politics of Intervention in Iraq* (London: I.B.Tauris, 1999).

quantified. Resolution 661 prohibited all UN member states from import-
ing or exporting goods from Iraq. Iraq's economy was highly dependent
on revenue generated by the sale of its oil. Fully two-thirds of its food
consumption came from imports. Economists estimate that Iraq's GDP
fell by one-half to two-thirds of its prewar level by 1997.[49] Hyperinflation
meant that the vast majority of Iraqis employed in the public sector saw
their buying power evaporate. Per capita income declined from its prewar
level of $3,500 to $450 in 1996.[50]

Equally devastating were the humanitarian consequences of the economic embargo. Malnutrition became a severe problem, affecting 22
percent of children under five. The sanctions took their toll on the ability of the state to invest in the crucial areas of health and education.
Health problems associated with lack of water treatment and medicines
increased. The impact of the sanctions on the educational sector was
drastic. In 1977, Iraq's literacy rate stood at 78 percent; by 2000, 23
percent of Iraq's children did not attend elementary school, in large part
because the government could not build enough schools to accommodate
them.[51]

The history of the implementation of the sanctions regime was a
struggle within the international community regarding the politics of
humanitarian intervention and its costs. For Iraq, the conflict over the
terms of the sanctions and their implementation had more to do with
questions of national sovereignty and the limited benefits it could get
by ceding more control of its economy to the UN. The struggle to maintain sovereignty was most clearly evident in the government's rejec-
tion and then acceptance of what became known as the Oil for Food
Program.

In February 1996, Iraq accepted UN Resolution 986, which allowed
its government to sell a portion of its oil to finance the purchase of food,
medicines, and other goods deemed necessary to maintain its population.
It was a bitter pill for the regime to swallow.[52] Under the terms of the resolution, Iraq could sell one billion barrels of its oil every ninety days. The
proceeds from the sale were placed in an escrow account controlled by a

---

[49] Gordon, *Invisible War*, p. 21.
[50] UNICEF, "Iraq watching brief: Child protection," prepared by Josi Salem-Pickartz, July
2003, p. 2.
[51] UNICEF, "Iraq watching brief: Overview report, July 2003", prepared by Biswajit Sen,
p. v–vi.
[52] Iraq had refused an earlier resolution, Resolution 706, passed in August 1991, on the
grounds that it severely curtailed its sovereignty, gave control of the economy to the UN,
and promised to make a very small difference in alleviating the situation of Iraqis.

committee in the UN. The committee then divvied up the income between a fund to compensate Kuwait, paying the costs incurred by the weapons inspection program, and recouping the costs incurred by administering the Oil for Food Program. The Iraqi government's share of the proceeds came to a little over 50 percent.[53] The program was clearly designed to help sustain the populations' basic humanitarian needs without allowing Iraq any funds to rebuild its economy and human capital. The serious erosion of the Iraqi government's control over its economy was compounded by the limited impact of the Oil For Food program in providing long-term sustenance for Iraq's population.[54]

Conclusion

Over the course of twenty-three years, the Iraqi population experienced three kinds of war: the conventional Iran-Iraq war, fought by large infantry divisions between nation-states with comparable resources; the First Gulf War, marked by the disproportionate use of force and by the deployment of sophisticated technologies of violence; and what Joy Gordon has called an "invisible war" that combined the use of economic sanctions with surgical air strikes. The outline of the political history of these wars and their impact on Iraq's elite political power structures provides only a glimpse of their inestimable human costs.

First is the matter of the number of dead combatants.[55] At the moment, the only available source for researchers is the surveys conducted by the Ba'th Party of matriculating male students in fifteen of the eighteen provinces of Iraq for the year 1998–9.[56] These list the number of the fallen in each student's family during the Iran-Iraq war and the First Gulf War. They provide a rough estimate of the percentage of the dead within each province, but they need to be used with caution. The Ba'thists did not survey each school, nor did they include the number of missing or injured soldiers. The surveys represent the list of those considered

---

[53] Gordon, *Invisible War*, p. 25.

[54] Ibid., p. 26.

[55] The politics of counting the dead in the Iran-Iraq and First Gulf wars are controversial. Not only are the actual numbers still unavailable, the question of who among the two main sects in Iraq suffered the heaviest casualties has become fodder for the sectarian reading of Iraqi history. Furthermore, the body count of the First Gulf War has generated some controversy between the U.S. military and humanitarian and other international organizations.

[56] The three provinces of Iraqi Kurdistan were not surveyed as they were outside the control of the central government in 1998.

martyrs by the regime.[57] Nevertheless, they provide a useful barometer. The losses are unevenly distributed across Iraq, with some southern provinces such as Dhi Qar and Muthanna and central provinces such as Diyali and Ta'mim accounting for larger losses than other provinces. The percentage of loss among Baghdad's population is the lowest in the country, standing at 4.6 percent, while that of the southern province of Muthanna is the highest at 10.5 percent.[58] Generally, rural areas and poorer urban neighborhoods account for higher percentages than average. Nationally, for every 100 male students listed in the registers, there was an average of 6.3 dead combatants. The population of the fifteen provinces listed in the registers was, in 1997, a little more than 20 million. Assuming that half that number is male, then, one can estimate that the death toll among combatants for both wars was six hundred thirty thousand.[59] That amounts to 3.2 percent of the population, among the highest percentage of fallen soldiers per national population in the major wars of the twentieth century.

Civilian casualties of these wars were also substantial. Bombing by Iran and by the coalition forces resulted in civilian deaths and injuries, but their numbers were not as high as the casualties caused by the regime. The genocidal policies of the Ba'thist regime toward its Kurdish population resulted in the death of tens of thousands.[60] In addition, estimates of those killed in the suppression of 1991 numbered at least several thousand.[61] The wars displaced hundreds of thousands of Iraqis. By some estimates, some two hundred thousand Iraqis were expelled from Iraq because they were of "Iranian affiliation." Hundreds of thousands more were displaced during and immediately after the First Gulf War. By the late 1990s, more than 3 million Iraqis had left Iraq.

Iraq's history under the Ba'th was marked by a series of ruptures caused by different kinds of war. The political history of these wars and their human costs provides only a glimpse into the profound manner in which these wars structured the everyday lives of Iraqis and transformed

---

[57] These registers list matriculating students in the third and sixth secondary classes. The numbers and percentages listed here are of students matriculating in their sixth year of secondary education.

[58] See Appendix I for distribution.

[59] Population numbers are for the year 1997 and are drawn from http://citypopulation. mobi/Iraq.html accessed February 7, 2011.

[60] Joost Hiltermann, *A Poisonous Affair: America, Iraq, and the Gassing of Halabja* (Cambridge: Cambridge University Press, 2007).

[61] Human Rights Watch, "Endless Torment: The 1991 Uprising in Iraq and its Aftermath." (1994) www.hrw.org/file://G:\Iraq926.htm accessed June 12, 2008.

the manner by which state and party bureaucracies mobilized and governed the population. The rest of this book attempts to tell the story of this transformation in the lives of Iraqi citizens as they came to grips with the everyday forms of control instituted by the state and by the Ba'th Party that sought to integrate wartime conditions into the routine of living.

3

The Internal Front

Making War Routine

I thought when the [Iran-Iraq] war started that it will end in a month, then two
months, then three. Then I was convinced that it would end before I am graduated from college. But when I became a soldier [1984], I thought the war will
never end.[1]

Tareq Ali, a Baghdadi from a middle-class family, describes how he
learned to live his life with war. His statement underscores the success of the government and the ruling Ba'th Party in normalizing the
Iran-Iraq war and making it part of the everyday life of citizens. How
was the government able to turn what should have been a short exceptional interlude into an enduring reality? What were the mechanisms
of ensuring the public's obedience and support? How were the war's
social costs managed at home? What sort of disciplinary and bureaucratic practices developed to ensure the continuous circulation of men to
the front?

   Partial answers to these questions lay in the regime's ability to transform
war into a way of governing – a set of techniques to educate, reward, discipline, count, and survey its population on what it dubbed the "internal"
front. The Ba'th Party was central to this project. It is important not to
view the process of turning war into part of everyday life as simply a
product of directives of an authoritarian regime foisted on a passive population. What emerges from examining the workings of the Ba'th Party is
a process more complex and dynamic. On one hand, the Ba'th Party was

---

[1] Interview with Tareq Ali, Amman, Jordan, July 14, 2007.

instrumental in securing citizens' obedience through monitoring dissent and ensuring the dissemination of the sanctioned version of the war story. On the other hand, the Ba'th Party acted as a social organization, ensuring that the impact of the war was borne by the population and effecting the social policy that governed the day-to-day lives of Iraqis.

Managing the War

The regime used the Ba'th Party, the only legal political and popular organization in Iraq, to manage a great deal of the social and security consequences of the war. By 1977, the Ba'th Party had become part of the state, its leadership incorporated into the Revolutionary Command Council.[2] Its 1974 political program had included a social agenda of reform along "socialist lines" and drew heavily from the program of the Iraqi Communist Party as well the Soviet Communist Party, which had trained its cadres.[3] By 1982, its program had jettisoned its socialist and reformist rhetoric for the program and words of what it called the "the leader-necessity."[4] Saddam Hussain and his decisions were to be the arbiters of all social development programs and all political rulings. In effect, many commentators concluded, the Ba'th Party had become the instrument of the leader's decisions, as had the Revolutionary Command Council.

The concentration of power in the person of Saddam Hussain and a close circle of loyal advisers, mostly civilians, increased during the war. By the early 1980s, a series of Revolutionary Command Council resolutions assigned to the Office of the Presidency the power to intervene in resource allocation, in entitlement disbursements, and in the punishment and pardon of those who committed infractions against the state. A cult of personality, reminiscent of that of Stalin during World War II,

---

[2] Tripp, *A History of Iraq*, p. 216.

[3] Ba'th Arab Socialist Party, *Revolutionary Iraq, 1968–1973, The Political Report Adopted by the Eighth Regional Congress of the Ba'th Arab Socialist Party-Iraq* (np: 1974). The 1972 Friendship Treaty with the Soviet Union provided for establishing relations between the Ba'th Party and the Communist Party of the Soviet Union so that the former could learn from the latter's organizational experience. Oles M. Smolansky with Bettie Smolansky, *The USSR and Iraq, the Soviet Quest for Influence* (Durham: Duke University Press, 1991), p. 18.

[4] Ba'th Arab Socialist Party, *The Central Report of the Ninth Regional Congress of the Ba'th Party* (np: June 1982), p. 8 http://www.almoharer.net/iraqi_files/ninth_regional_congress82.htm accessed February 16, 2010.

developed around Saddam Hussain.[5] On January 7, 1980, five months
after the war began, he told his people:

> Iraq is victorious in the face of the great conspiracy. Iraq is a fortress of action
> and hope to achieve the rebirth of the Arab nation and return its rights: You have
> started a new era of uplift of your nation, the party, the people, the army and
> Saddam Hussein are now in a condition of unity. The spirit of victory is present in
> the heart of every martyr's mother who walks her son to this wedding. We salute
> those who want peace with Iraq and the Arab nation within Iran.[6]

The party was central to the war effort, particularly in maintaining the
support and obedience of the "people" in the face of the losses on the
front and the army's insatiable demands for manpower. This was
possible because the party that Saddam Hussain viewed as one with the
people had become a bureaucracy that managed not only the political,
but also the social aspects of Iraqis' lives.

The bureaucratization of the Ba'th Party began in the 1970s, but escalated and changed during the Iran-Iraq war. At the outbreak of the war,
the party had succeeded in consolidating its hold over Iraqi political life. It
eliminated those within its own party ranks who opposed Hussain's policies. It successfully displaced the communists within the women's, labor,
and professional unions, and secured its position within the armed forces.
While its power as the only legal party in Iraq was paramount in 1980, its
authority over the everyday lives of Iraqis developed during wartime and
was intimately bound with a process of expansion in its territorial reach
and the systematic collection of information about the people who came
under the jurisdiction of its various branches and divisions. During the
1980s, the party's administrative apparatus expanded to include different
planning and implementation committees. In addition, other committees
were created to ensure that decisions were implemented and information
was recorded and archived.[7] The party's different departments ran parallel to the state's military, security, social, and educational institutions. Its

---

[5] John Barber and Mark Harrison, *The Soviet Home Front* (London: Longman, 1991).
Without using the Russian archive it is difficult to tell the extent to which Iraq's conduct
during the war mimicked that of the Soviet Union during the Second World War. The
similarities in the role of the Ba'th to that of the Communist Party of the Soviet Union are
remarkable, as are the similarities in the conduct of the Soviet security forces, NKVT, and
that of the Iraqi government's and party's security forces, particularly in Kurdish areas.

[6] *al-Jumhuriyya*, January 7, 1980, 1.

[7] BRCC 01–2140–0003–0003 to 0010. This is a progress report submitted by Sa'd Mahdi
Saleh, the head of the Baghdad Bureau. In his introduction, he indicates that the period
between 1985 and 1989 was marked by the systemic development and professionaliza-
tion of the administration in marked contrast to the earlier period.

secretariat presided over departments and directorates that specialized in collecting information, processing information provided by different institutions and ministries about the population, dispensing of members' requests, organizing political indoctrination, and a wide array of functions that pervaded Iraqis' everyday lives.[8]

The party was organized territorially around five bureaus: Northern, Middle, Southern, Euphrates, and Baghdad.[9] These regional bureaus oversaw the branches, divisions, and subdivisions within the party organized along provinces, counties, and districts that often corresponded to administrative units. Between 1985 and 1989, the number of Ba'th Party offices grew until almost every corner of Iraqi urban centers, if not all Iraq's rural areas, had a Ba'th Party office and/or popular organization attached to the party office, particularly in politically restive areas. The leadership of the Southern Bureau created four branches and thirteen new divisions,[10] and that of the Northern Bureau expanded to include twelve new branches, forty new divisions, and ten new subdivisions.[11] At every level of the party hierarchy, different offices had representatives from the General Federation of Iraqi Women, the Federation of Iraqi Students and Youth, and other popular organizations. Local Ba'th Party offices had a security branch that provided a link to the local internal security apparatus.

Two sources provide an idea of the organization and membership of the party: the reports of regional bureaus and the collection of school registers created by the party of matriculating male students. Although not comprehensive, they reflect larger membership trends. Two appear to have predominated. The first trend was a push to recruit members and create new divisions in areas where government control was most tenuous, using the Ba'th to maintain authority over society during wartime.

[8] BRCC 01–3763–0001–0012. The document is a diagram of the sections and directorates of the Ba'th Party Regional Command Secretariat. It is not dated, but appears to have been drawn from a box of documents that date from the 1987–8 period.

[9] The Bureaus' territorial reach was often reworked according to security concerns. In the second half of the 1980s, the Northern Bureau included the provinces of the Region of Autonomous Rule, Arbil, Sulaimaniyya, Dohuk, Ninewah, and Ta'mim. That of the Euphrates included the provinces of Najaf, Karbala, Qadisiyya, Muthanna, and Babil. The Southern Bureau included Basra, Maysan, Wasit, and Dhi Qar, while the Middle Bureau covered Salah al-Din, Diyala, and Anbar.

[10] BRCC 01–3212–0001–0549.

[11] BRCC 01–2140–0003–0079 and 0054. The reports of the Northern Bureau cover August 1985 to March 1987 and March 1987 to August 1989. Under the direction of Sa'd Mahdi Saleh, the Baghdad Bureau grew by two branches and ten divisions between 1985 and 1989.

Thus the Northern and Southern Bureaus oversaw the greatest expansion in membership and in Ba'th Party working cadres, while the Baghdad Bureau suffered a net membership loss between 1985 and 1989, despite growth in its organizational structure.[12] The second trend was the expansion in recruitment among a younger generation of Iraqis from within the school system.

Party cadres in leadership positions numbered several thousand. Those who led bureaus, particularly the crucial Baghdad, Northern, Euphrates, and Southern bureaus, were old-time Ba'thists who had firm ties to Saddam Hussein from his early party days.[13] The upper echelon was drawn from longtime party stalwarts with decades of experience in the Ba'th. Except in insurgent Kurdish zones in the north, where appointments were viewed as a hardship, almost all members of the party leadership were drawn from the local population. In 1988, the Baghdad Bureau membership numbered 19,274, some 5 percent of the total population under its authority. Less than 1 percent of the membership had leadership positions administering branches, divisions, and subdivisions within the party apparatus.[14] The percentage of leadership positions within the party to overall membership figures was similar in the Northern and Southern Bureaus.[15] The disparity in numbers between the leadership cadres and the party base created a strain on the party's ability to carry out its ambitious plans for expansion. To offset the leadership shortfall

[12] BRCC 01–2140–0003–0012 and 0013. The Baghdad Bureau reports that in 1989 its membership had dropped to 192,740, down from its peak in 1985 of 272,192 members, out of a total population of 3,841,268. Thus its membership dropped from 7 percent of the population to 5 percent in 1989. Part of the loss could be explained by the redistricting of certain areas in Baghdad taken out of the Baghdad Bureau and placed in the Middle Bureau. However, even Sa'd Mahdi Saleh had to admit that declining membership was due to the war. See also Joseph Sassoon, *Saddam Hussein's Ba'th Party: Inside an Authoritarian Regime* (Cambridge: Cambridge University Press, 2012), p. 52.

[13] The Southern and Euphrates Bureaus alternated between Mizban Khidr Hadi and Abd al-Ghani Abd al-Ghafour in the 1980s, the Northern Bureau was run by Muhammad Hamza al-Zubaydi and Ali Hasan al-Majid, while the Baghdad Bureau was run by Sa'd Mahdi Saleh.

[14] BRCC 01–2140–0003–0016. The population covered by the Baghdad Bureau came to over 3.8 million. The members in leadership positions were divided among the branches (13), membership in branches (38), membership in divisions (230), and membership in subdivisions (1,221). There were also 6,352 full working members, 2505 trainees, 1,406 candidates; the rest were divided between advocate (70,459) and supporter (110,516).

[15] BRCC 01–2140–0003–0071 to 0072. In March 1987, overall membership in the area covered by the Northern Bureau stood at 205,991, about 5.4 percent of a population of 3,760,244. They were divided between the Northern Bureau executive (6), branches (46), divisions (199), and subdivisions (1,116). The rest were divided between full members (4,606), candidates (2,194), advocates (51,718), and supporters (146,106).

and its inability to recruit adults, the Ba'th turned its recruiting efforts to school-aged young adults. Of the 95,477 male secondary school students matriculating in ten of Iraq's eighteen provinces in 1987–8 for which school registers are available, 60.8 percent belonged to the rank of supporter, 20.5 percent to the rank of advocate, and 4 percent to the rank of advanced advocate.[16] In contrast to membership percentages in the overall population, those of the school-aged population were remarkably high. Despite that, these numbers do not always indicate a straightforward trajectory of growth and promotion within the party. Rather they bespeak the party's efforts to bring under the umbrella of its various organizations an increasing number of Iraqis. All members met at regular intervals for organized activities, from sports and arts events to education and indoctrination sessions. The depth and territorial reach of the Ba'th Party positioned party cadres at each branch to play a crucial role in managing the war on the home front and to do so in a manner particularly suited for the local realities of their area.

The war turned the Ba'th Party into an organization focused on security in the widest definition of the term. Not only did it monitor dissent and discipline the population, it also was involved in ensuring that goods and services were available to citizens. By the end of the war, local Ba'th offices nationwide were dealing with the daily lives of those affected by the war. The Ba'th ensured that Iraqis had access to services provided by various government ministries of state. It facilitated privileged access to employment government enterprises, educational institutions, and other state organizations, not only for party members, but also for conscripted soldiers, their families, and the families of martyrs. To do so, local party bureaucrats, as well as party officials at the front, surveyed citizens considered key to the functioning of the state at war. Students, soldiers, martyrs and their families, deserters, those who failed to report for military duty, and those who were absent without leave (heretofore absentee soldiers), were now part of a kind of knowledge that had as its main objective control of a population at war, the disbursement of rewards and punishments, and the management of war's repercussions.

The Ba'th had become less a political party with an ideological core than a means of managing state security and Iraqis' social lives. The logic governing this transformation was spelled out in the Central Report of the Ninth Regional Congress in 1982. Iraq, according to this report,

---

[16] Registers analyzed are those of Anbar, Babil, Baghdad, Basra, Diyali, Karbala, Najaf, Ninewah, Ta'mim, and Wasit. For a breakdown, see Appendix II.

had moved from the politics of the National Front of the 1970s into a "popular democracy" in which popular and professional organizations presented their constituencies' needs directly to the leadership. Saddam Hussein ensured the workings of this "popular democracy" by:

> initiating genuine profound, living relations with the people. Comrade Saddam Hussein allows every citizen to contact him by telephone, receives scores of citizens every week ... and visits every corner in Iraq, acquaints himself with citizens' living conditions, asks them about their problems.... Comrade Saddam Hussein's own method in his relation with the people ... adds a profound and human dimension to the democratic practice in the society built up by the Party in Iraq.[17]

Party cadres institutionalized this "human dimension" of "democratic practice" through what Ba'th Party documents described as "cohabiting" (*mu'ayasha*) and the "perpetuation of ties" (*idamat sila*).[18] The exponential expansion of party membership had more to do with citizens' ability to access social privileges and to navigate the state and party bureaucracies. To reword Hannah Arendt's characterization of bureaucracies, everybody was a Ba'thist but nobody was a Ba'thist.[19]

This is the broad outline of how the exigencies of war reshaped the Ba'th Party. The picture that emerges is of a pervasive organization that infiltrated all aspects of social and political life in Iraq. To a certain extent, this assessment is borne out by the Ba'th Party sources. But these sources also reveal that the bureaucratization of the party, the multiplication of its functions at home and on the front, meant that the directives coming from its secretariat were often shaped by the practices of its cadres working on the ground. The leadership cadres of the party were quite small, and their abilities were circumscribed by members drawn from the lower ranks of the party who lacked the commitment to party ideology and authority that its leadership envisioned. The party gradually turned from a relatively efficient organization of social and political control in 1980 to a collection of regional and local bureaucracies whose governance encompassed a large number of social as well as political issues. Thus, rather than regarding the party as a highly centralized, all-powerful behemoth, it is more instructive to see it as a sum total of local practices that were as much a function of the conditions at home as they were

---

[17] *The Central Report of the Ninth Regional Congress of the Ba'th Party*, (np: June 1982), pp. 22–3.
[18] The terms will be discussed further later in the chapter.
[19] Hannah Arendt, *On Violence* (U.S.A: Harvest Book, 1970).p. 38. Arendt speaks to the greater bureaucratization of life as a "rule of Nobody ... Where all are equally powerless. We have tyranny without a tyrant."

of directives coming from its General Secretariat and the Revolutionary Command Council.

The Internal Front

The Iran-Iraq war caught Iraqis at the end of the summer vacation. It had been a busy summer for many Baʿthist popular organizations, including the General Federation of Iraqi Women, as they fanned out across the country to participate in a national literacy campaign. Iraqi youth had come home from camps run by the Federation of Iraqi Youth, after weeks of activities that covered sports and visual and performance arts, as well as a dose of Baʿthist indoctrination.[20] The Federation of Iraqi Students had finished its summer work camp, entitled the Heroes of Qadisiyya, where fifty thousand students of both sexes, dressed in khaki military-style outfits, built 240 houses for peasants.[21] The Popular Army, the Baʿthist Party militia, which at that point was primarily a militia that undertook civil defense as well as internal security, had run summer camps where young men and women were trained in the use of arms. The pages of the daily *al-Jumhuriyya*, the most widely read newspaper in Iraq, were replete with reports of a society organized as a kind of utopia along Soviet lines, one in which all parts worked in tandem to create a militant modern society. Particularly during the first two years of the war, when the government had not yet exhausted its reserves, it was intent on maintaining what it called "mobilization for development" alongside the mobilization for war. Mass media messaging emphasized the link between the two kinds of mobilization.[22] The former aimed at the creation of a modern Iraqi society, while the latter aimed at defending the achievements of the Baʿthist revolution against the attack of an Islamic revolution bent on destroying such achievements.

The Baʿthist regime harnessed the militant organization of society for the mobilization of its population during wartime. The effort of the local Baʿth Party branches was multidimensional. However, three components proved essential: disseminating the official war story at the local level, managing the social repercussions of the war, and managing dissent and desertion. In all three efforts, party cadres on the ground were aware of

---

[20] *al-Jumhuriyya*, August 12, 1980. Hazim Najm, a Basrene who was a member of the Baʿthist youth organization, Talaʾiʿ, spent summers in these camps. Interview with Hazim Najm, Amman, Jordan, July 27, 2007.
[21] *al-Jumhuriyya*, August 28, 1980, 1.
[22] *al-Jumhuriyya*, December 8, 1980, 4.

the differences in the social, political, and communal composition of the populations that came under their branches' jurisdiction. They understood that what the state dubbed the "internal" front was a highly differentiated place consisting of populations divided by political histories, ethnicity, sect, locality, and class. In particular, the war was experienced differently in the southern areas of Iraq, which in effect became part of the battlefront, and the relatively safe central areas, particularly Baghdad. The northern Kurdish regions as well as the southern regions were targeted for intense monitoring and surveillance, as they became a haven for a large number of deserters who had fled the front to hide or join the insurgency.

The party's function was thus twofold: to ensure that the war's costs were borne by the population and to help security services track down dissenters and deserters. Local party branches were organized around several departments. These were then divided into committees.[23] The local branches of various popular party organizations such as the General Federation of Iraqi Women, the Federation of Labor, and the Federation of Iraqi Students and Youth worked closely with the local Ba'th branches. The lines and functions between these committees were quite fluid as was the division of labor between the popular organizations and the party. For example, cultural committees of local party branches, in cooperation with popular organizations, focused on disseminating the official war story and organizing support for the war. As the war progressed, the party branch offices and popular organizations took on the role of counting, monitoring, rewarding, and punishing families that had members affected by the war. The General Federation of Iraqi Women played a crucial role as a mediator between the cultural, social, and security components of the work of the party at the local level. The transformation of the Federation's role from serving a developmental and social agenda to one intimately bound to the managing of the war's social and political repercussions provides insight into the ways in which the war was managed at the internal front.

Managing the War Story
The cultural committees within the party disseminated the official version of the war and shaped the message to fit the political, sectarian,

---

[23] For a general description of these committees' roles, see Sassoon, *Saddam Hussein's Ba'th Party*, pp. 34–70. The most important for our purposes were the cultural, social, security, and military committees; the last was responsible for recruiting volunteers for the party militia. Taha Yasin Ramadan, *Qadisiyyat Saddam wa al-Jaysh al-Sha'bi* (*Qadisiyyat Saddam and the Popular Army*) (Baghdad: The General Leadership of the Popular Army, 1988).

or ethnic composition of their local constituencies. They invested time and resources in institutions and organizations of public culture, particularly those of television, print media, visual arts, and performing arts. The party's Directorate of Political Guidance oversaw the production of television programs and documentaries and employed an army of artists and intellectuals to bring the war story to the home front. The content and impact of this organization on Iraqi public culture will be addressed in later chapters. What is of interest here is how the official version of war was disseminated among party cadres and the general public.

The Iraqi media's official narrative of the origins of the Iran-Iraq war was that it started with a series of confrontations that escalated into a full-fledged conflagration. These began with the attempt on Deputy Prime Minister Tariq Aziz's life at Mustansiriyya University by "agents of the Persian regime" in April, which culminated in the bombing by Iran of the border towns of Khanaqin, Mandali, and Maydan on September 4. Thus, the beginning of the war was not the internationally accepted date of September 22, when Iraqi troops crossed the international border with Iran, but the date the Iraqi government was provoked to respond to Iranian aggression. The war was therefore a defensive one, imposed on a nation threatened by an Islamist revolutionary regime that wanted to destroy its achievements.[24] This war narrative gained added credence among Iraqis once Iran refused several Iraqi offers of ceasefire agreements, particularly after Iraq unilaterally declared withdrawal from Iranian territories it had conquered in June 1982. By February 1983, when the Iranian offensive to capture the Basra-Baghdad road was under way, the majority of Iraqis was convinced that theirs was a defensive war fought to maintain their national territories, even if not all were convinced that the war was unavoidable or that the regime had not initiated it. Propaganda aimed primarily at linking the nation's defense to that of the Ba'thist leadership and to Saddam Hussein.

The war with Iran was named Qadisiyat Saddam or the Second Qadisiyya, the first being the battle fought in 636 CE under the leadership of Arab Muslim leader Sa'd bin Waqqas against the Persian Sassanian Empire.[25] Saddam Hussein's likeness graced all posters, murals, and

[24] See, for example, the narrative of the origins of the war on the cusp of its first anniversary published in *al-Jumhuriyya*, August 23, 1981, 3.
[25] Much has been written on the personalization of the war and the personality cult it engendered. See for example, Amatzia Baram, *Culture, History and Ideology in the Formation of Ba'thist Iraq, 1968–89* (New York: St. Martin's Press, 1991), and Ofra Bengio, *Saddam's Words, Political Discourse in Iraq* (New York: Oxford University Press, 1998).

photographs depicting aspects of the war, a fact that has elicited commentary and substantial scholarship.[26] Although few Iraqis accepted the link between the first and second battles, in practical terms, the naming meant that the battle was intertwined with the personality cult of Saddam Hussain. The personalization of the war was bolstered by the Khomeini's declared war aim – the fall of Saddam Hussain and the Ba'th regime.[27] Khomeini was nicknamed Ayatollah "May God protect me" (*'a'uthu billah*), a play on his name, "the sign of God" (Ayatullah), and was vilified in the media as a corrupt, greedy, evil, feminized, and deluded man of religion.[28] The personalization of the war meant that the security apparatus and the party interpreted any criticism of the war's conduct as criticism of Saddam Hussain himself. By March 1986, the Revolutionary Command Council issued an amendment to article 225 of the penal code number 111 that made it a crime to insult the president of the Republic.[29] Insulting the president included such vaguely defined actions as casting doubt on the veracity of the communiqués issued by the armed forces recording the heroic victories of the Iraqi army, changing the television channel when the president was giving a war speech, and any attack on party or military personnel involved in the war effort. Reporting on such infractions was particularly important in the Kurdish areas as well as in the southern cities that had a Da'wa and/or Communist presence.[30]

A large component of the propaganda campaign launched by the Ba'th in cooperation with various state ministries and professional organizations focused on reporting, analyzing, and disseminating the leader's different war pronouncements. The fifth and sixth sections of the Central Report of the Ninth Regional Congress in 1982 provided a blueprint for local party cadres.[31] They dealt with two pressing issues: justifying the war in the wake of the retreat of Iraqi troops from Iranian territories, and facing the appeal of the religious activism of the Iranian revolutionaries, euphemistically called the "religious question," to Shi'i as well as Sunni

---

[26] Davis, *Memories of State*, pp. 176–99.

[27] Hiro, *The Longest War*, pp. 34–58. By March 1981, Khomeini's declared goals were regaining the lost territories and bringing down the regime of Saddam Hussain.

[28] The demonization of Khomeini began early in the war. *al-Jumhuriyya* weekly, September 14, 1980, ran a cartoon entitled Ayatollah "May God protect me."

[29] Joost Hiltermann, *Bureaucracy of Repression, The Iraqi Government in its Own Words* (New York: Human Rights Watch, 1994), p. 141.

[30] NIDS/serial 321621 and NIDS/serial 717060.

[31] The Ba'th Arab Socialist Party-Iraq, *al-taqrir al-markazi li al-mu'tamar al-qutri al-tasi'*, June 1982 (*The Central Report of the Ninth Regional Congress*, June 1982) (Baghdad: np, 1983), 182–304.

Iraqis. The General Secretariat instructed local party cadres to draw on these two sections to persuade their cohorts that the war was justified and its conduct proper. Qadisiyat Saddam was an "imposed" war because Khomeini and Iran – historic haters of the Arabs – refused offers of a settlement that restored Iraq's territorial rights. Khomeini's "gang" was supported by an imperialist and Zionist conspiracy to divide Iraq and other Arab countries into powerless statelets organized along narrow sectarian and ethnic interests. Party cadres need look no further than the divisions within the Arab ranks: Syria and Libya allied themselves with Iran against Iraq. Despite its Ba'thist credentials, the Syrian regime had actively suppressed the Palestinian resistance in Lebanon in 1976. It stood helpless as the Israelis invaded and occupied Lebanon in 1982, wreaking havoc on an Arab country as they eliminated the presence of the Palestine Liberation Organization. The war on Iraq was only one symptom of a region-wide retreat by Arabs in the face of Zionism and imperialism. The heroism of the Iraqi people and their leader lay in their ability to stand firm against this onslaught.[32] Appeals both to the uniqueness of Iraq's history and to its leadership of the Arab world, as well as accusations of conspiracies aligned against it despite its willingness to sue for peace, reinforced Iraqi nationalism and highlighted the importance of defending the country's integrity and sovereignty. Bolstered by a persuasive reading of regional and international politics, this rationale allowed the regime to convince a public wary of the leadership of the Ba'th and Saddam Hussein.

The religious question presented the regime and the party with two challenges: how to attack the Islamic revolutionary and anti-imperialist Iranian regime without appearing to criticize religion, and how to deal with the appeal of a revolutionary brand of political Islam that presented a more authentic alternative to the secular Third World rhetoric of the Ba'th. The Ninth Party Congress report had to account for what it officially described as the "religious phenomenon," that is to say, the increasing appeal to Iraqis, even those within the Ba'th Party membership, of religion.[33] According to the official Ba'thist line, the failure of Arab regimes

---

[32] Ibid., 226–62.

[33] Ibid., 300–1. In a remarkable admission of the growing appeal of religion to Ba'th Party cadres, the report addressed the increased attendance by lower-ranking Ba'th Party members (supporters and advocates) of mosque prayers. This is supported by the report issued by the head of the Northern Bureau in June 1980 to the General Secretariat detailing the manner in which party cadres should combat the spread of political Islam in the wake of the Islamic Revolution. The report frankly addresses that appeal among

in their fight against Zionism, together with the party cadres' lack of gen-
uine commitment, explained why Iraqis were increasingly turning to religion. Party cadres were reminded that Ba'thist ideology was not against
Islam. Rather, Islam and Ba'thist ideology formed the core of a belief system that had at its center the liberation of Arab lands and the modernization of the Arab nation. Islam was, first and foremost, a liberationist and
revolutionary ideology that brought the tribes of Arabia to the center of
old civilizations and allowed them to forge a new civilization marked by
its brilliance and its Arabness. By contrast, the Islamist movements of the
late twentieth century were reactionary, sectarian, and bent on destroying
all the accoutrements of modernity. To counter Islamist claims that the
nationalism was borrowed from the West and not authentic, party cadres
should insist that the idea of the Arab nation had existed since antiquity,
predating even the rise of Islam. Furthermore, Islamists were reminded
that the most dangerous and oppressive example of the twinning of religion and state was Zionism. Along with the Iranian regime, Zionism
served as a powerful example of the dangers of politicized religion.[34]

These arguments formed the broad outlines of the party's stance on
the war and on the Islamic revolution. Ultimately, the war was understood and perceived by Iraqis as a national war and as a war between
two distinct versions of organizing society, one along Islamic and the
other along secular lines.[35] However, despite the opposition of the secular
to the religious, the Ba'th Party and the regime deployed the use of religious scholars in Sunni areas and attempted to control Shi'i scholars and
monitor rituals in predominantly Shi'i areas. Much of the propaganda
unleashed by the different institutions of public culture in Iraq explained
the conflict around three binaries: Persian against Arab; modern against
medieval; and Arab Islam against Persian Islam. Local party branches
highlighted one or another aspect of these binaries depending on the
population under its jurisdiction.

In the Kurdish region, where the Kurdish Democratic Party and the
Patriotic Union of Kurdistan were leading an insurgency against the
regime, drawing on the support of Iran, local Ba'th Party chapters geared

the youth, university students, and party cadres. BRCC 003–1–1–0371 to 0374. At the
same time, the party tasked members of its popular organization, the Office of Peasants'
Cooperatives, particularly in the southern countryside, with working among the religious
establishment and infiltrating *husayniyya* meetings in Basra, Dhi Qar, and the Ahwar.
BRCC 003–1–1–0375 to 0385.
34 The Ba'th Arab Socialist Party-Iraq, *al-taqrir al-markazi*, 264–304.
35 Soldiers I interviewed focused on Iran's intention to take over Iraq and expressed hostility to the theocratic form of government of Iran.

their message to appeal to Kurds. These local chapters reported directly to a special section in the General Secretariat of the Ba'th that was to administer the political, security, and military affairs of the north. Among its many functions was the recruitment and monitoring of the paramilitary forces of the National Defense Battalions from Kurdish tribes loyal to the regime. The propaganda efforts of the party drew parallels between what it dubbed "Persianism" with Zionism and ensured that the populations in the north did not join either Kurdish nationalist or communist opposition parties. The regime was also concerned that the Islamic revolution would appeal to the more religious elements of the population in the north. Thus, when Muhammad Hamza al-Zubaydi, then head of the Northern Bureau of the Ba'th Party, visited Dohuk in September 1986, he spoke to party members and leaders of the local popular and professional organizations at party headquarters. He reassured them that although there had been some attacks by Kurdish insurgents in the area, the "saboteurs" had been destroyed. These as well as the opposition groups who worked with them, he said, constituted a fifth column effectively destroyed by the "heroes of the north." Cognizant of the appeal of the Iranian brand of revolutionary Islam, he asked his audience not to believe rumors spread in Friday sermons that Khomeini represented true Islam. Labor organizations as well as other popular organizations should work closely at supporting the war effort.[36] In the mixed Kurdish and Assyrian region of Zawita in Salah al-Din, activities of the local Ba'th division included visiting the church as well as establishing contact with student organizations in schools and with public sector employees to prepare for their recruitment into the Popular Army.[37]

Members of the General Federation of Iraqi Women organized women's meetings to talk about the treachery of Jalal Talabani, the head of the PUK, the importance of being watchful of any hostile coverage or rumors about the war effort, and Saddam Hussain's latest interview with soldiers.[38] The educational sessions of party members were more specific. The regime's attempt to appeal to the ethnic nationalism of its Arab population by defining the war as an eternal struggle between the Persian and Arab civilizations did not carry much weight in the Kurdish regions of the north. Rather the appeal had to focus on the links between imperialism, its local agent, the state of Israel, and the regime of Iran. The clear

[36] NIDS/serial 55557 to 555564.
[37] NIDS/serial 273584 to 273591. Report by the local Ba'th branch dated November 1985. The Zawita division of the Salah al-Din branch included forty-nine villages.
[38] NIDS/serial 555567 to 555569.

message to the Kurdish population in Dohuk fused the interests of Iran, Israel, the United States, and Kurdish nationalists.

Despite the regime's avowed secularism, it was acutely conscious of the appeal of the Iranian brand of revolutionary anti-imperialist Islam, even among Sunnis. The Ministry of Endowments and Religious Affairs was charged with training and funding religious scholars and speakers to disseminate the "correct" version of Islam and to inform their followers that the war with Khomeini was imposed by a regime that had as its aim world hegemony in the name of a "false Islam." In Kurdish areas, the policy of the state appears to have taken place at the expense of established religious scholars instead making use of ambitious and more pliable but less well-trained laymen. In one telling report written by the *imam* (prayer leader) of al-Abyad mosque in March 1982, the author reassured the party that the *ulama* (religious scholars) of Arbil had remained loyal to the regime because of the latter's investment in the economy, culture, and infrastructure of the Kurdish area around the city. He then went on to report:

For the past two years of the war that was imposed by Khomeini – the Iraqi people are fighting for survival – the *ulama* were active in unveiling the enemy to the Iraqi people and took to their mosques and pulpits to defend the revolution. They visited the front, I was among the group that visited twice to give a lecture to soldiers and to embolden them – The *ulama* also used the radio and television to tell people to support the revolution and to encourage deserters and those who have not joined or were late in joining the army to stand against Khomeini – despite the criticism of some who have sold their conscience to foreigners and spread propaganda for the enemy. A Committee of Enlightenment and Education was created to organize meetings with the masses in villages and in the city to expose the enemies. The Ministry of Endowments gave each member 30% of his salary and no less than 20 dinars monthly. Members were to meet twice a month. But the Arbil committee has done nothing thus far – its members have taken extra money and the people who joined it were not educated or drawn from good social elements.[39]

The *imam* requested that the committee be dissolved and replaced with one that had more established scholars at its helm. Clearly, in addition to focusing on the more secular aspects of the war, the regime attempted to create a cadre of Sunni preachers that would help disseminate the official narrative of the war. By 1985, party cadres worked with these local prayer leaders to deflect popular skepticism of the regime's claims of victories.[40]

[39] NIDS/serial 833734, 833735, 833736.
[40] NIDS/serial 555602. In September 1986, when the Iranians had made inroads in the midsection of the country in areas under the control of the Third and Seventh Army Corps

The southern areas of Iraq, concentrated around Basra, Dhi Qar, and Maysan provinces, were militarily crucial for several reasons. The agricultural hinterlands of the cities of Basra and Amara were destroyed to make way for the movement of heavy war machinery and troops. The marshes in Maysan province were a haven for deserters and the Iraqi government was at all times suspicious that deserters might receive local support. Dhi Qar province was the home of a major military base as well as a training center for conscripts and reservists. The cities of Amara and Basra were hubs for troop deployment, and they became the areas for the services associated with a war economy. Bus depots and train stations overflowed with troops going to and from the front and military hospitals, hotels, and other facilities were filled with soldiers, journalists, and myriad others associated with managing and reporting on the war. In addition, the populations of these provinces had historically opposed the regime. In particular, the cities of Basra and Nasiriyya had until recently been Communist Party strongholds, and the Da'wa Party had supporters in Maysan and Dhi Qar provinces. A great number of the Iraqi conscripted infantry was drawn from the Shi'i population of the southern and Euphrates regions. It was vital to both the regime and the party that this population did not succumb to the revolutionary Shi'ism of Iran and that of exiled Iraqis who had relocated to Iran.

The regime invested heavily in the Holy Cities of Najaf and Karbala, and attempted to co-opt Shi'i scholars and institutions of learning. Local party branches tailored the war narrative in ways that would counter the potential appeal of Iran. A pliable Shi'i religious establishment in Najaf and Karbala had already issued opinions that refuted Khomeini's interpretation of Islamic jurisprudence.[41] At the same time, Hujjat al-Islam Kashif al-Ghita' expressed his support by stating that Iran was the aggressor in the war.[42] More problematic for the regime was the control of Shi'i rituals. Of particular concern to the government were specific rituals associated with Imam Hussain's death on the tenth day of the month of Muharram ('*Ashura*) and the ritualistic march to Karbala forty days later known as the Visit of the Fortieth (*ziyarat al-'arba'in*). In 1983, one hundred twenty thousand Iraqis converged on Karbala for the '*Ashura* commemorations and four hundred fifty thousand made the visit to the

---

in the southern sector of operations, the Dohuk subcommittee on religious affairs within the party called on prayer leaders to use loudspeakers in their call to prayer and to pray for victory for Iraq and its leader as well as for the souls of martyrs.

[41] *al-Jumhuriyya*, April 2, 1980, 1. BRCC 003-1-1-410 to 414.
[42] *al-Jumhuriyya*, February 23, 1981, 4.

city on *ziyarat al-arbaʿin*. Furthermore, a great number of Baʿthist Party members, particularly at the entry level of supporter, participated in these rituals as did soldiers and deserters. Women constituted some 70 percent of the participants and they set up their own gatherings to mourn the death of Imam Hussain (*taʿziya*).[43]

The regime's official stance on Shiʿi rituals was spelled out in a report issued in March 1984.[44] Shiʿi rituals presented twin threats to the nation: they were associated with an Iranian brand of religious practice that was "foreign" to Iraqi Shiʿism, and they represented vestiges of a premodern social order that stood in contradiction to the modern Baʿthist nation. While monitoring played a great part in keeping the rituals under control, the party cadres assigned equal importance to persuading their constituencies through educating them on the achievements of the "revolution," the correct stance of the Baʿth toward religion, and the Arab origins of Shiʿi Islam. Different popular organizations, as well as public media and the Ministry of Endowments and Religious Affairs, were assigned specific tasks to tailor these points to youth, women, and party cadres. The regime regarded processions and gatherings organized by citizens set up to commemorate the death of Hussain as potential venues for criticism of the government. Officials characterized these commemorative rituals as "incorrect practices" of religion contrary to the Baʿthist view of modern new men and women. The central aim for popular organizations and party cadres was to engage in an educational project that had at its heart the "modernization of thought." The report directed Baʿth Party cadres to focus in a "persistent and consistent manner on the achievements of the revolution that are national and socialist and that mesh with the instructions of religion particularly the laws that govern social welfare and the care of the handicapped and elderly."[45]

---

[43] BRCC 023-4-4-0518, 0519 and 0522. The Revolutionary Command Council and National Security Council held an extraordinary session on December 1, 1979 to address the appeal of the Islamic Revolution and to spell out a policy to combat it, including infiltrating mosques, establishing good relations with religious scholars, and using women to infiltrate popular Shiʿi rituals. BRCC 003-1-1-410 to 414.

[44] BRCC 023-4-7-0000. The report was issued by the Organizational Committee (*al-lajna al-tanzimiyya*) of the Baʿth Party. It was based on the collation of information from different regional party organizations, the directorate of general security, and the directorate of the police covering the events of Muharram and the *al-arbaʿin* for the year 1983. The committee consisted of Ali Hasan al-Majid, then director of the party secretariat, Fadhil al-Barrak, the director of general security, the head of the police, and leadership of the Baghdad, Euphrates, Middle, and Southern bureaus (0470).

[45] BRCC 023-4-7-0525.

The report emphasized the high level of women's participation in these rituals as well as their leadership role in the sponsorship of processions and gatherings. The report's authors asked local members of the General Federation of Iraqi Women to remind women that these practices were potentially harmful to their and their children's health. Women should be discouraged from wearing the traditional black robe (*'abaya*) as this was a sign of "backwardness." Female Ba'thist cadres were asked to attend women's gatherings (*ta'ziya*) and to ensure that readings included material that elucidated the achievements of the party and the revolution. Foremost among these achievements was the support of women's rights.[46] Equally important was the eradication of "incorrect practices" among the many youth who attended. Their presence betrayed a lack of proper inculcation in the values of Ba'thist youth and left their "immature minds" open to Da'wa Party interpretations of Islam. The General Federation of Iraqi Students and Youth focused its efforts on inculcating Ba'thist values. To counter the attraction of Shi'i rituals to the youth, the Federation organized trips of youth to the rear lines of the war front to have them cohabit with soldiers fighting the Persian enemy.[47]

Modern versus traditional and incorrect versus correct practices were the two binaries that governed the Ba'thist message around the rituals of *'Ashura* and the *ziyarat al-arba'in*. They were meant to discourage Iraqis from participating by appealing to them as modern citizens of an Iraqi nation. More important, the Ba'thist cadres pitted the principles of "true" Islam against Khomeini's "distorted" version of Islam. The human dimensions of Islam were transformed by the Iranian regime into political sectarianism. The origins of this distortion were supposedly located in the historic hostility that Persians have had to the Arabness of Islam as exemplified by Iranian attempts to marginalize the Arab origins of imams Ali and Hussain. Even the "incorrect practices" of Shi'i rituals were marginalized as foreign, particularly Persian, infiltration into the heart of the Arab Shi'i community in Iraq.[48]

The ethnicization of Shi'ism, that is to say the distinction between Arab (true and spiritual) Shi'ism and Persian (political and sectarian) Shi'ism became the cornerstone of the education program set up in southern areas. Party cadres, however, were careful not to frame their educational endeavors in communal terms. Instead, they personalized the attack on

---

[46] BRCC 023-4-7-0529 and 0530.
[47] BRCC 023-4-7-0531 and 0532.
[48] BRCC 023-4-7-0523 to 0525.

the Iranian brand of Shi'i activism by targeting Khomeini. In Amara, for example, a party leader suggested that Khomeini's appeal was to be combated by claiming that he was hostile to "Arab Islam" because he denigrated the Arab origins of Islam.[49] In the Euphrates region, in Najaf and Karbala, the party's emphasis on the historical hatred between Persians and Arabs was reinforced and linked to the heroic person of Saddam Hussain, who protected Arab honor in the second battle of Qadisiyya.[50]

In the Kurdish and Shi'i regions, the party's faithful framing of the war was bolstered as well by the strategic use of rumors. Both the Iraqi and the Iranian regimes maintained tight control on the news, and rumors became a crucial technique for creating discontent or reassuring the public. Party cadres were trained to disseminate certain rumors and combat others. In the particularly problematic areas of the south and the north, this mission was always perilous. On one hand, rumors were often based on an element of truth, and addressing them meant an admission by the regime that a problem existed. For example, in the wake of the Iranian attack on the southern marshes in 1983, the Ministry of Interior sent a circular to all Ba'th Party branches asking that its members combat Iranian rumors that the regime had executed a number of marsh residents. The Iraqi government was well aware that such rumors were meant to stir sectarian allegiances among the marsh population. Party cadres broadcast programs that highlighted the heroism and support of the marsh inhabitants. At the same time, they were instructed to conduct such interviews with utmost secrecy to deflect any perception that some of the marsh residents were in fact hostile to the Ba'thist regime and had been cooperating with the Iranians.[51] In addition, the Iranian regime used Da'wa Party members exiled in Iran to spread rumors. Its declared aim was the conquest of Basra, where the Shi'i population would rise against the regime in support of its co-religionists in Iran. The Da'wa and other opposition parties appealed to sectors of the Shi'i population who had had relatives imprisoned or executed by the regime. They were asked to spread rumors of the imminent conquest of Basra and defeat of the Ba'th.[52]

---

[49] BRCC 01-3212-0001-0006 to 0012 Kanan Makiya, *The Republic of Fear, The Politics of Modern Iraq* (Berkeley: University of California Press, 1998), pp. 73–109; Davis, *Memories of State*, pp. 148–99.

[50] BRCC 01-2162-0001-0368.

[51] NIDS/serial 745815. These rumors were not groundless. They came in the aftermath of a public execution of deserters in the sports arena in Maysan province. See Chapter 4.

[52] NIDS/serial 833806.

The use of rumors became especially important to bolster the propaganda of the regime, which insisted on claiming victory despite all evidence to the contrary. By 1985, Iran had begun to make headway in both the southern and northern fronts, and the bodies of the dead provided incontrovertible truth of the cost of the conflict, as did the reports of soldiers coming home on their monthly furloughs. It was important for the regime to reassure its citizens that the current stalemate on the battlefront was about to end. The internal security branch offices were charged with manufacturing rumors to be circulated to different areas of Iraq. In May 1985, in the wake of the visit of the minister of state for military affairs to the Soviet Union, party cadres were directed to circulate several rumors: Iraq had obtained new weapons that could reach and destroy cities deep within Iran; antiwar demonstrations were erupting in Iranian cities; a great number of Iranians had fled to Turkey and neighboring countries as a result of aerial bombardment.[53] In the Kurdish areas, where Kurdish insurgents were joined by deserters as well as fighters from opposition parties, the rumors emphasized the weakness of the Iranian regime and its callous attitude toward its ethnic groups. The security offices of Arbil district spread rumors that, at the last meeting between Khomeini and the religious establishment, a decision was made to liquidate all ethnic groups in Iran except the Persians, and that divisions existed within the Da'wa Party along Persian-Arab lines.[54]

The shaping and control of the official version of the war was one of the most important functions of the local branches of the Ba'th Party. Not only did they ensure the propagation of the regime's message, they also became the main organizers of the numerous public ceremonies related to the war. Whether celebrating soldiers on Army Day or commemorating those fallen in the war on Martyr's Day, the Ba'th Party cadres played a central role in shaping the public perception of the war. However, the Iran-Iraq war expanded the role of the party from managing the war story to managing the social consequence of war.

Managing the Social Repercussions of the War: Cohabiting and Perpetuating Ties

For most Iraqis, the first realization of the human costs of the war came with the procession accompanying the coffin of a fallen soldier or with the cries of women in the neighborhood who had been informed of a

[53] NIDS/serial 745884.
[54] NIDS/serial 745815.

beloved soldier's death. Mazin al-Hadithi, an eighteen-year-old student from Haditha who had his sights on attending the prestigious Academy of Fine Arts, had thought of the war as a distant event and did not pay much attention when the official celebrations of the fall of Khorramshahr (Muhammarah) blanketed the news media. He recalls the moment when he saw the body of the first martyr from Haditha brought in a coffin draped with the Iraqi flag:

> The first event of the war that shook Haditha was the advent of a martyr after seven days of the war ... his name was Jinan, he was a Christian, a handsome young man. They brought him with a celebration and fired rounds in the air. It was a big event. We could not imagine that half the Iraqi people were going to be dragged into war and be draped with a flag. We found this first one very difficult.[55]

The Ba'th Party played a pivotal role in managing the social repercussions of war at the local level. Whether dealing with the families of the fallen soldiers or those of prisoners of war and the missing, the party became a social organization with great leverage. At the heart of its endeavor was the systematic effort to keep records of those affected by the conflict. The information was, according to the three-year report of the head of the Ba'th organization of the south, pooled in "chambers of information":

> to understand the party and society. They [the chambers] were organized in all the party sub-divisions [ninety-eight of them in the south], and information was ordered along certain categories for every group and condition. This is to be in the service of the party and society and to facilitate control and absorb what society will create whether that be negative or positive.[56]

To facilitate and routinize the Ba'th's management of the social consequences of the war at the local level, party cadres counted the number of war dead, prisoners of war, and missing within their jurisdiction. They worked in conjunction with the military committee to keep a census of the families of martyrs who belonged to the party and the Popular Army as well as those martyrs with no political affiliation.[57] The Military Office of the party kept a file on each martyr that recorded his name, military rank and unit, residence, and manner and place of death. Political commissars

[55] Interview with Mazin Hadithi, Damascus, Syria, March 1, 2009.
[56] BRCC 01–3212–0001–0549. This is the report issued by the office of the Southern Bureau covering the years 1985–8. Information between brackets is my own.
[57] NIDS/serial 690925 to 690936. This is a report of the Maysan branch of the party for the months of August and September 1988.

on the front who were attached to every battalion provided the information on martyrs.[58] In the insurgent Kurdish north, records were almost
exclusively focused on the dead among party members and did not
include those among the National Defense Battalions, the Kurdish military force that fought the insurgents alongside the government.[59] Keeping
such records had a dual function: assess the level of social work that
the different popular organizations and the party had to do to maintain
peace at the home front; and enable the party to monitor those families
most inclined to political discontent.

While "absorbing" the "negative and positive" impact of the war was
fueled by the party's concern with obedience and security, the party cadres' work also had an important social dimension. To map the social
lives of Iraqis affected by the war, cadres used the terms "cohabiting"
and "perpetuating of ties." The terms denoted two very specific practices
spelled out clearly in party documents and systematized through division
reports. Cohabiting consisted of living with the affected sectors of society
to study the repercussions of the war, report on them to the local and
regional offices, and identify ways to ensure that complaints were heard
and needs met. Visiting families of those affected by the war was the cornerstone of the policy of "cohabiting" and the "perpetuating of ties." By
the end of the war, it became incumbent on cadres to visit the families of
martyrs a certain numbers of times each month and submit reports about
them to the branch. Visits, according to one report, "should be organized and meaningful so that the sacrifices of the martyrs are acknowledged and remembered." In addition, cadres should take care to foster
pride in the children of martyrs, prisoners of war, and those missing in
action. The families' needs should be serviced to establish relationships
and strengthen them, and to link them to the party's daily struggle. Most
important, records should be kept of the times the families were visited
and the services performed to aid these families.[60]

[58] BRCC 01–2459–0002–0003 to 0185. For example, in September 1986, the military office
of the Yarmouk branch of the party sent a memo to the General Secretariat seeking the
promotion and induction of 170 soldiers, most of whom had died in the fierce battles of
Hawr al-Huwayza, East Tigris, and East Basra between late 1985 and September 1986.
Eighty of the fallen soldiers had no political affiliation (Independents), while fifty-five
were at the entry level of supporter. The dead were drawn from all over Iraq. Thus, it is
not clear whether the list is confined to those within the jurisdiction of the branch.

[59] NIDS/serial 1289398 to 1289399. The division of Gorbag had five cells that had lost 114
martyrs, had 21 missing in action, and 26 prisoners of war for the years 1982–8.

[60] BRCC 01–2162–0001–0376 to 0377. The instructions covered the families of the party
militia but echoed those issued to cover the families of other martyrs.

The Committees to Oversee the Affairs of Martyrs and the Missing were set up to help these families navigate the bureaucratic and institutional hurdles they faced as they attempted to deal with a bewildering number of decrees and laws governing compensation for the relatives of war victims. The committees defined their mission as one of "perpetuating ties" and acted as a conduit for the families' requests and complaints as reported by party cadres and members of popular organizations such as the General Federation of Iraqi Women and the Federation of Labor. The committees distributed forms for families to complete to process their complaints and, in the process, created an information pool about soldiers and their families. Requests and complaints could then be forwarded up the party hierarchy as well as to the Ministry of Defense, the Ministry of Justice, and other relevant state institutions. Thus, because of their close proximity to the populations with which they cohabited, these committees mediated between the different institutions of state and the requests of local constituencies.[61]

Party cadres grappled with a host of issues in their dealings with families affected by war. First, they needed to define the scope of their purview. Were they to cater only to party members' families or to the population at large? The dilemma was particularly acute when dealing with martyrs' families. The Ba'th Party policy toward martyrs evolved over time and in fits and starts. At the beginning of the war, martyrs within the party were elevated posthumously within the party hierarchy. More significant, those who had died with no party affiliation were inducted into the party after death.[62] The Ba'th practice of inducting and promoting the dead was partly informed by the ideology of a regime that insisted on the unity between nation, party, and state. It was a fiction that the regime needed to maintain during the long war and a policy in which the recipient of the party's largesse did not have much say. Questions governing the exact definition of who was considered a martyr were not academic. The state's wartime rewards system

---

[61] BRCC 01–3496–0003–0000. Information is based on a report issued by the Southern Bureau for the year 1984. The report also included accounts from Ba'th branches nationwide.

[62] This practice seems to have started as early as 1981, but it is not clear whether it became standard practice. *al-Jumhuriyya*, June 30, 1981. Local branches continued to report on the induction into the party of martyrs who had been independent. In a memo dated June 29, 1986, the Yarmouk branch of the party informed the General Secretariat that it had decided to accord the membership to those martyred within its district. BRCC–01–2459–0002–0001.

depended largely on a hierarchy of rights-based, precise definitions of martyrdom.[63] For the Ba'thists working on the ground, it was important to become educated in these rights as they visited the families of martyrs in their areas. Directives emanating from the General Secretariat called on local branches to work with popular organizations and unions to facilitate the cumbersome paperwork.[64]

Party cadres were able to shape policy on certain social issues and to influence decisions on the management of citizens' social lives. Their intervention was based on their assessment of the social needs of individuals and families affected by the war. Two examples serve to illustrate how the process worked on the ground. The first concerns the issue of inheritance, one of the most vexing problems faced by martyrs' families. Widows would clash with their in-laws and children over the martyr's salary and other generous compensations. The Ministry of Justice was supposed to settle such disputes, but the next line of appeal was the visiting party cadre. Thus in 1983–4, the Baghdad, Dhi Qar, Wasit, and Maysan Committees to Oversee the Affairs of Martyrs and the Missing asked that the Ministry of Justice facilitate the paperwork of the martyrs' families on inheritance matters and redefine the rights of minors to the inheritance of their dead fathers' property.[65] These and other recommendations were often taken up to the Office of the Presidency and resulted in laws issued by the Revolutionary Command Council that covered matters of inheritance and compensation.[66]

The second problem that seems to have elicited a great deal of complaints from citizens had to do with the collection of salaries of the war dead, missing in action, and prisoners of war. Widows and wives of those missing or imprisoned complained of their inability to live on the salaries of their husbands who had been gainfully employed or who had been farming their land before conscription. In addition, they found it difficult to process the paperwork necessary to receive their husbands' salaries from the Ministry of Defense's Directorate of Salaries located in Baghdad. Party cadres in most of the provinces of Iraq requested that the

---

[63] These rights will be the topic of Chapter 6.
[64] NIDS/serial 329089.
[65] BRCC 01–3496–0003–0062, 0137, 0143, and 0145 to 0147.
[66] These laws will be discussed in Chapter 6. The Office of the Presidency had a special section that dealt with party affairs directly. On matters covering soldiers, martyrs, prisoners of war, and the disabled, the Office gradually played a more important role than the Ministry of Defense.

local Directorate of Military Recruitment process the soldiers' salaries. Their request was granted by presidential order in 1984.[67] In addition to helping facilitate the everyday lives of citizens affected by the war, party cadres conducted regular education sessions on new laws governing disbursement of entitlements and a host of other issues that touched on the maintenance of life during wartime. While these meetings often started with a formulaic praise for the leader and the revolution, they seem to have mostly focused on more prosaic life issues.[68]

Party cadres played a central role in coordinating civil defense in cities shelled by Iran. Between November 1986 and January 1987, for example, Iran launched a major offensive in southern Iraq that sought to capture Basra. Heavy shelling of the city and its hinterland resulted in wide-scale destruction and civilian deaths. Party cadres reported on these losses and mediated the requests of citizens before the Ministries of Health, Industry, Education, and other institutions that catered to the various social needs of those affected by the war. When Basra and its environs were emptied of their residents to avoid casualties, party cadres helped manage the process. They conducted regular meetings with various heads of clans to explain the situation, solicit their cooperation, and ensure that popular anger against the shelling remained under control.[69]

By the end of the war, the Ba'th Party had come to play a crucial role in managing the social cost of the war for all citizens affected by it. Its concern was no longer with its members alone. In its role as a social organization, the party was often responsive to the demands of the people in the areas under its purview and contributed, in part, to shaping policy based on these demands. As a result, the party helped normalize the war in ways that would have been difficult to imagine had Iraq not been a one-party state. However, the social dimensions of the party's dealing with the families of martyrs, the missing in action, and prisoners of war should be understood as integral to its concern with security. These were families prone to opposing to the regime, and maintaining close watch over them through "perpetuation of ties" was deemed vital.

The limits of the regime and the party's ability to make war a part of everyday life and their increasing reliance on violence became evident in their handling of dissent and desertion.

[67] BRCC 01-3496-0003-0064.
[68] BRCC 01-3496-0003-0356.
[69] BRCC 01-2062-0001-0355 and 0374 to 0490.

Managing Dissent and Desertion

The majority of men who fought the war with Iran were conscripts rather than volunteers. As the war grew longer and costlier, it became more difficult to persuade them to continue fighting, even if they believed that the war was necessary to defend the nation. Particularly after the battles of 1984 and 1985, desertion among the rank and file increased exponentially. The Iraqi government viewed desertion as a traitorous act. As a result, the war blurred the distinction between political dissent and desertion. Not only were the regime, the party, and the security apparatus engaged in monitoring and suppressing dissent and public criticism of the war, but increasingly, desertion was treated by the legal and security apparatus as the gravest of political and social threats. Whereas in the 1970s much of the party's work with the security apparatuses of the state had focused on battling political enemies, in the 1980s, their purview was extended to pursuing, apprehending, and executing deserters. From party documents and the multiple laws and Revolutionary Command Council directives that governed desertion and absenteeism, it is clear that the state and the party were greatly concerned with the problem. The draconian measures imposed on deserters and their families, coupled with repeated Revolutionary Command Council declarations of amnesty for absentee soldiers and deserters, speaks to the regime's attempts to balance its need for manpower with the political implications of desertion.[70] While it is difficult to parse out from the sources the ratio of desertion among conscripted and enlisted men, it is safe to assume that desertion and absenteeism were rampant among conscripts. Not only did desertion present an explicit challenge to the regime's narrative of the war as a heroic national struggle, deserters often joined the opposition in Iran or the Kurdish areas of the north. If they did not, they lived in hiding in Iraq, relying on family and friends for support. Such support was seen as politically dangerous, and the regime and party developed mechanisms to monitor and punish all those who sheltered deserters and absentee soldiers, as they had done and continued to do to those who had any connections with political enemies.

---

[70] BRCC 01-2162-0001 is a booklet issued by two military lawyers in 1989 detailing the development of laws and regulations governing desertion and absenteeism during the Iran-Iraq war. Absenteeism was defined as failure to report to military or reserve duty for five days after an assigned date. Desertion was defined as failure to report to duty after thirty days. After the Revolutionary Command Council issued amnesty decrees, deserters and absentee soldiers were allowed anywhere from a week to thirty days to report to their units or to Ba'th Party offices (pp. 0016 and 0017). These laws applied to conscripted and enlisted soldiers. They did not apply to members of the Popular Army.

Desertion was also perceived as a social threat, as deserters often engaged in illicit trade, found work in the private sector, or became part of an informal service economy.[71] The Kurdish regions under insurgents' control, as well as the southern marshes, became a haven for deserters from all over Iraq as they could hide and join the burgeoning underground economy based on servicing deserters trying to flee the country or to live invisibly. Some joined the insurgents, in most cases voluntarily, in others after being coerced into joining by rebels anxious to increase their numbers. Others navigated the thin line between criminality, political dissent, and rebellion. Well aware of the political and social threats of desertion, the regime and the party gradually developed practices that addressed both facets of the problem, initially adapting techniques used to monitor and punish political dissidents, but eventually surpassing them as the problem worsened.

The Ba'th Party became one of several security organizations on the home front charged with pursuing deserters. In addition to the general security apparatus, it worked with its military branches on the front, as well as with military intelligence.[72] Special squads were formed within the party's security committee and attached to its "sub-committee for the pursuit of deserters."[73] These were granted wide latitude in their work, eventually becoming exempt from any legal proceedings against them by citizens who were harmed or who lost property as a result of the squads' actions.[74] By the mid-1980s, the pursuit, interrogation, and punishment of deserters had developed into a series of routine practices that conflated political dissent with desertion. In particular, party organizations were tasked with mounting regular campaigns to pursue deserters and report on their operations. In one such report presented by the head of

---

[71] The social fallout of desertion was of great concern to the government and the party. They attributed to it the increase in crime, particularly smuggling, in the northern areas. Deserters often rented rooms in hotels or with families, became unlicensed taxi drivers, or smuggled goods from Iran. See for example NIDS/serial 815719 on the increase of lawlessness and NIDS/serial 815847 on how families helped soldiers rent rooms in hotels under false names.

[72] The directorate of military intelligence within a military sector often sent inquiries and information to general security service and asked for help in apprehending deserters and absentee soldiers. The security service then enlisted the help of the local party security committee to locate deserters. See for example, NIDS/serial 815719, dated December 20, 1986.

[73] It is not clear from the records when these squads were formed within the party security apparatus. They appear in the record in the second half of the 1980s, when desertion had become a large problem for the regime.

[74] BRCC 01–2162–0001–0015. In addition, the injury of a potential culprit by a squad pursuing him was no longer subject to criminal investigation.

the Southern Bureau to the General Secretariat on the accomplishment of the party, the apprehension and execution of deserters is presented as a major organizational achievement.

The period from 1986 to August 1988 saw major operations on the southern front with a great number of casualties. "The battles," according to the Southern Bureau's director:

resulted in a large number of deserters from the army and they increased the crime in the city [Basra] by stealing. We worked actively at limiting the crimes of the people. Our party organizations were given the authority to execute [deserters] and we were very successful in apprehending a great number of deserters. We also worked at persuading their families to surrender deserters.[75]

Some 67,522 deserters were caught. Of these, 7,832 were apprehended, 58,943 surrendered (presumably after a Revolutionary Command Council's decree of amnesty), 432 died during pursuit, 193 were executed, and 122 were injured.[76] Only twelve of these deserters belonged to the outlawed Da'wa Party. The Northern Bureau processed some 82,957 deserters and absentees between August 1985 and March 1987; the Euphrates Bureau processed 8,348; and the Baghdad Bureau processed 11,806 in the last years of the war.[77] While quite large, these numbers do not reflect the overall number of deserters, as many surrendered directly to their military units after the Revolutionary Command Council issued a general amnesty.

The political and social ramifications of deserting were clearly spelled out by a report of the Euphrates Bureau less than a year after the war ended. The report assessed the dangers posed to national security and social cohesion by demobilized soldiers. In particular, it offered a trenchant analysis of the ennui and cynicism of a generation of young men who had spent their youth at the front. A special section was devoted to an analysis of deserters and absentee soldiers. They were, according to the report, excluded from their rights as citizens of the nation. The work of the party was to educate the public that desertion was treason. Desertion created an atmosphere of crime and lawlessness and undermined public safety. The example of family members bringing in deserters or reporting them was cited as the highest act of loyalty to the nation; nonreporting

[75] BRCC 01–3212–0001–0546 to 0550.
[76] It is not clear if these numbers cover the years of 1985–8 or if they are confined to the last two years of the war.
[77] BRCC 01–2140–0003. For the Northern Bureau numbers, see pages 0082 and 0083. These were mostly deserters from the National Defense Battalions. For the Euphrates Bureau, see page 0125, and for the Baghdad Bureau, see page 0035.

families were to be punished. In one telling report, the security committee of the Baghdad Bureau sent letters to such families encouraging them to inform the committee of their relatives' whereabouts and brought families to a special field set up to execute deserters so families would have no illusions about the gravity of their relatives' crime of desertion.[78]

The social threat of desertion to public safety and family well-being was but one aspect of the party's function. More important was counting deserters at the end of the war. Local party offices, positioned in neighborhoods and schools, were tasked with creating a special register for every deserter that was to include information about him and his family. Through these registers, it would become possible to monitor the deserter's movement.[79]

Less knowable to the party and more difficult to control than desertion and open political dissent were the more diffuse acts of resistance the Iraqis used to avoid military service and to voice political discontent. For example, male students made use of a law that allowed them to continue matriculating even if they failed a year of study. They deliberately failed, thereby postponing their graduation and thus their conscription in the hope that the war would end before they finished school and were forced to join the army. Teachers were well aware of this tactic and some became complicit.[80] By 1984, the problem had become widespread enough that the Council of Ministers viewed it as a national phenomenon that had to be addressed. The Baghdad Bureau of the party, the Federation of Students and Youth, and the Ba'thist Union of Teachers then convened meetings in secondary schools and colleges with failing students and their parents as well as with college and secondary schoolteachers. The heads of universities were reminded that "they have to live up to their party's loyalty by ensuring that there is no failure of students in their university."[81] The degree to which such warnings worked is difficult to gauge. However, oral interviews with soldiers confirm that the practice remained quite common throughout the war.

The transformation of local Ba'th party branches and divisions into bureaucracies that managed the social and security consequences of the war was greatly facilitated, indeed maintained, by the cooperation of the local branches of the General Federation of Iraqi Women (GFIW).

---

[78] BRCC 01–2140–0003–0037.
[79] BRCC 01–2161–0378 to 0379.
[80] A number of conscripts I interviewed mentioned their failing the matriculation class of secondary schools and colleges to avoid joining the military.
[81] BRCC 01–2185–0002–0117.

More than any other popular organization, the GFIW changed from an organization primarily focused on the management of social issues of development to one concentrated on monitoring, counting, and surveying soldiers' families and managing the regime's message.

The General Federation of Iraqi Women

From the beginning of the war, the party and the regime positioned women as a primary force in the mobilization of the population. The rhetoric of the party and the various institutions of public culture linked the role of women to the defense of two central components of Ba'thist ideology: the first was the defense of the nation, and the second was the preservation of women's achievements under the Ba'thist "revolution." The Ba'th Party had made the issue of women's rights and women's integration into the workforce a cornerstone of its modernization project.[82] By the mid-seventies, the General Federation of Iraqi Women was active on several fronts: it called, with limited success, for reforming the Personal Status Law that defined rights of inheritance, marriage, and divorce; it was instrumental in mobilizing for social programs of development; and it worked steadily on expanding its organizational reach to encompass other popular organizations and its geographic reach to include urban centers and provincial towns.[83] All these activities were central to the creation of a militant, activist, and liberated woman committed to the nation and the program of social and national development of the Ba'thist state. Women's activism was understood as part of the war on underdevelopment and traditionalism. The war against the Islamic Republic became part and parcel of a war to defend the progress of women under the Ba'th.

The war created a slew of challenges for the leadership of the Federation. Among the most pressing was setting priorities. Should the national war against Iran and the defense of the Ba'thist "revolution" take precedence over equality? Until the mid-1980s, most of the Federation's leadership's public rhetoric saw in the war an opportunity to press forward on issues of equality and integration into the workforce precisely because of the

---

[82] The Eighth and Ninth Party Congresses devoted a special section to the "achievements of the revolution" on women's rights.

[83] Achim Rohde, *Facing Dictatorship: State-Society Relations in Ba'thist Iraq* (London: Routledge, 2010), pp. 80–5. See also, Nadje al-Ali, *Iraqi Women: Untold Stories from 1948 to the Present* (London: Zed Press, 2007). For the importance of expanding the Federation's reach, see report NIDS/serial 527871 to 527957, the years 1977–9. The Dohuk branch of the Federation reports on its close cooperation with student, worker, and peasant organizations. The report also proposes expanding its work through cooperation with Ba'th Party branches in areas where it had no offices.

manpower shortage and the need to mobilize all sectors of the population. Thus, in a special issue of the *al-Jumhuriyya* newspaper devoted to the role of women in war, Amal al-Sharqi, a Federation leader, argued that men and women had equally important roles to play in the war. She stressed the public role of women working in factories, fighting in the civil defense and the Popular Army, and serving in the rear lines as nurses and doctors.[84] Sajida al-Musawi insisted on the active role of women as bearers of arms. Women could no longer be relegated to the home front but were now part of the war front as well. Women's expanded role in the public arena was made possible, argued Dr. Fawzia Attiya, because of the induction of women into the Popular Army in 1976 and the opening up of the armed forces to women at the ranks of officer and deputy officer.[85]

The regime rewarded the Federation's activism by issuing amendments to the Personal Status Law in 1983 and 1985 to accord more rights within the family to individual women.[86] Buoyed by such concessions, the executive committee of the GFIW felt strong enough to submit a working program to the Twelfth Congress of the Federation that focused on legal reform in labor laws to protect women in the workplace.[87] The opportunities afforded by the war to women's rights would not last through the 1980s.

The war produced new realities for women as it did for men. In particular, the increase in the number of households headed by widows, wives of missing, and wives of prisoners of war created what has been called in the context of wars elsewhere a "crisis of patriarchy."[88] Women who headed households faced a series of confrontations with kin over entitlements and pensions. At the same time, the regime was acutely aware of the scale of the loss of life caused by the war. By the second half of the 1980s, defeats at the front, deaths, and desertion led to a policy reversal. Women were encouraged to return home, produce more children, and strengthen the family. These policies were followed by a series of Revolutionary Command Council decrees governing reproduction, marriage, and women's inheritance that reversed the advances made at an earlier stage of the war.[89]

---

[84] Hiro, *The Longest War*, p. 133.

[85] *al-Jumhuriyya* weekly, October 5, 1980, 8–9. According to Rohde, *Facing Dictatorship*, p. 89, the Popular Army had enlisted about forty thousand women by 1981.

[86] More will be said on these rewards and the Revolutionary Command Council decrees governing them in Chapter 6.

[87] Rohde, *Facing Dictatorship*, p. 91.

[88] Elizabeth Thompson, *Colonial Citizens* (New York: Columbia University Press, 2000).

[89] Noga Efrati, "Productive or reproductive? The role of women during the Iran-Iraq war," *Middle Eastern Studies*, 35 (1999), 27–44, and Rohde, *Facing Dictatorship*, pp. 95–7.

The reversal on issues of rights was partially offset by the great expansion in the GFIW's organizational reach. By 1987, more than eight hundred fifty thousand women were members of the General Federation of Iraqi Women. Its branches reached 62 percent of Iraqi neighborhoods in rural and urban areas, and 30 percent of urban women had become members.[90] Thus, the Federation acquired more depth as offices were set up at district levels. The Federation's reach and activities touched every aspect of the war effort. It cooperated with other popular organizations such as the Federation of Iraqi Labor to found women's offices to conduct censuses of working women and educate them. It coordinated training sessions for nurses needed at the front with the Ministry of Health and Social Services. It played a leading role in training for civil defense. It set up tents for returning furloughed soldiers to welcome them home, and visited their families in their absence. It spearheaded campaigns to collect from women gold "donations" for the war effort. It was at the forefront of disseminating the war story. Finally, it was crucial in dealing with families affected by the war. Like all Ba'th Party offices, the Federation kept careful record of the number of activities it undertook. Thus in 1987, for example, it carried out 104 types of activities, many focused on propaganda in support of the war effort. For example, the Federation prepared 709 victory tents to welcome furloughed soldiers; organized 3,005 campaigns to see them off to the front; undertook 6,890 visits to wounded soldiers in hospitals; and organized thousands of events in support of the war and the "beloved leader."[91]

Managing the war's social costs, however, increasingly involved the Federation in surveillance of families and reporting on dissent. This aspect of the Federation's work remained unacknowledged in its official pronouncements. Thus in the 1986 report of the executive committee to the GFIW, Congress's proposed social and political aims included improving schools and nurseries, offering counseling services for pregnant women, and other social projects, but widows and the rights of females heading households were not mentioned. Nor were these families' social needs addressed.[92] While absent from the official pronouncements, reports written by local Ba'th Party offices and sent to the General Secretariat, and, presumably, reports sent to the main Federation office in Baghdad, point

---

[90] Manal Yunus Abd al-Raziq al-Alusi, *al-Mar'a wa al-Tatawur al-Siyasi fi al-Watan al-'Arabi* (*Women and Political Development in the Arab Nation*) (Baghdad: Ministry of Culture and Information, 1989), appendix IV, p. 320.

[91] Ibid., appendix V, pp. 321–5.

[92] Rohde, *Facing Dictatorship*, p. 91.

to the centrality of the problem of death and desertion to the Federation's work on the ground.

The importance of women to the business of reporting and monitoring dissent was clearly articulated in 1981. At a Revolutionary Command Council meeting in December focused on reorganizing the party's security services, the GFIW was called upon to visit the families in more "conservative" areas where male party cadres were not welcome.[93] This policy was reiterated in 1984, when women were asked to attend the private readings organized by Shi'i women during Muharram.[94] Thus, as a matter of policy, the Federation was enlisted as an arm of the party and the state to penetrate the family domain. The mechanisms employed by the local branches of the Federation in addition to female party members included regular visits to families of soldiers, dissidents, deserters, and prisoners of war. Federation members recorded the number of these visits and submitted reports to local party branches. In addition, women visited families of martyrs and prisoners of war and reported any criticism of the regime or the war effort and any expressions of support for outlawed political parties.

By the end of the war, the Federation played a crucial role in tracking families affected by the war, setting up systems of social support such as daycare and education, facilitating access to state resources, and maintaining a vigilant watch for any signs of political or social discontent. This twinning of its social and security roles broadened the organization's social and political reach, but severely compromised its claim to represent women's rights. In a remarkable admission, Manal Younus, head of the Federation, wrote in the party newspaper, *al-Thawra*, in March 1987: "during Iraq's defensive battle, Iraqi women became a security service defending the revolution, defending it by serving as perfect informants for the responsible security service ... the woman showed no sign of fatigue, she always pursued victory and progress."[95]

Conclusion

Within a few weeks of the conclusion of hostilities with Iran, party cadres expressed deep concern about the war's political, security, and social consequences. The political agenda for the party was to build on the "victory"

[93] NIDS/serial 695799.
[94] BRCC 023–4–7–0531 and 0532.
[95] Quoted in Rohde, *Facing Dictatorship*, p. 98.

by integrating the meaning of Qadisiyat Saddam into the educational programs of Ba'thist cadres and the general population. It was also important for the party to remain vigilant in its pursuit of deserters and to watch for hostile activity. However, the war's social impact was deeply troubling. Demobilizing hundreds of thousands of troops at once threatened to disrupt the social and political peace the party had tried to maintain at home. Thus, local branches of popular organizations met with party cadres to discuss ways to manage the behavior of the returning militarized male population.[96] No less important was the impact of the war on family structures. When, in 1988, the Ministry of Interior issued a report on the spike in the number of murders, particularly honor killings, leaders of local party branches were quick to point out that the absence of males from families during the war with Iran was behind the increase.[97]

By the end of the Iran-Iraq war, the local branches of the Ba'th had developed into small bureaucracies crucial for the management of the war's social and political consequences. Intimidation, surveillance, and violence were part of the party's repertoire, choices its leadership had embraced to expand its functions and authority during wartime. In particular, its role in the southern and northern areas of Iraq served to highlight regional and ethnic distinctions and created irreparable fissures within Iraqi society. Yet it is important not to view this process of bureaucratization and securitization of the party as simply one in which the population was victim to a monolithic state and party structure intent on subjugating every aspect of citizens' lives. While that was certainly the aim and ideological core of the Ba'thist state, the men and women who managed the lives and deaths of the population within their jurisdiction were proficient in the language of the party, but adept at framing it in local terms and within local constraints. Furthermore, they were drawn from the populations that came under their purview, whether these were Kurdish or Shi'i. The affected population played a part in making claims to their entitlements and calling for the government and the party to respond to their daily needs. Perhaps most important was the transformation of what the state considered political. During the Iran-Iraq war, the regime no longer exclusively framed one's politics as a choice between being a Ba'thist or a "saboteur," but increasingly as one of being a soldier or a deserter.

---

[96] BRCC 01–2126–0001–0360 to 0377.
[97] BRCC 01–2126–0001–0394 to 0456. This is a report issued by the Ministry of Interior and sent to all Ba'th bureaus for comments.

4

Battlefronts

War and Insurgency

The propaganda machine of the Iraqi government painted the war as an extension of a Ba'thist revolution that fused the leader, nation-state, and party in a violent but necessary defense of the nation. Fighting at the front forged a sense of national unity that could override social and communal divisions. The Ba'thist state had fashioned what its ideologues defined as an "ideological army," one penetrated by Ba'thist army officers and overseen by Ba'thist commissars committed to the state and the party's vision of the nation.[1] In reality, the military leadership and the Ba'th Party premised the conduct of war on policies that had less to do with forging national unity and more to do with security. The regime's security and the maintenance of the state's territorial sovereignty became the driving force of the war after 1982, when Iranian troops began making headway into Iraqi territory, drawing on the support of Kurdish and other opposition parties in the north and in the southern marshes. Thus, the regime was waging two kinds of war at the same time: a war of national security and a war of counterinsurgency.

The line between the two kinds of war was quite fluid, as evidenced by the regime's handling of two of the war's most important components – the management of men on the front and the management of territory. The first concerned the mobilization, training, loyalty, and retention of men as fatalities and desertion increased and as the insurgent north and the southern marshes became a magnet for those fleeing the front. To

---

[1] Ahmad Hashim, "Saddam Husayn and civil-military relations in Iraq: The quest for legitimacy and power," *Middle East Journal*, 57 (2003), 9–41 and Andrew Parasaliti and Sinan Antoon, "Friends in need, foes to heed: The Iraqi military in politics," *Middle East Policy*, 7 (2000), 130–41.

manage these two issues, the regime followed a two-pronged strategy. First, it invested resources and expanded the reach of the Ba'th Party propaganda on the front. Second, it developed a system of distinctions to reward and punish performance on the front, monitor dissent, and ensure outward ideological conformity. The system entailed classifying the battlefront into territorial sectors, particularly in the south and north, where massive state interventions and shelling by Iran created enclaves marked for population movement, property destruction, and, in the case of the Kurds, the physical elimination of populations.[2]

The effect of these strategies was far-reaching. On one hand, the experience of conscription, training, and battle brought a generation of men from different social and communal backgrounds together on an unprecedented scale and forged a sense of Iraqi patriotism and generational solidarity. On the other, the war's length and brutality, coupled with Ba'th Party practices and the conscripts' perceptions of social inequalities at the front, created deep resentment against the regime and the party. In the end, the war exacerbated regional and ethnic divisions within Iraq and failed to forge an "ideological army" committed to the Ba'thist notion of nationalism. More important for subsequent developments in Iraq were the official practices of creating legal, spatial, and cultural distinctions that gave sanction to state violence and served to frame the massive rebellion against its institutions in the aftermath of the First Gulf War.

Conscripts in an "Ideological Army"

Iraqi men drafted into the Iraqi armed forces had to contend with two bureaucracies. The Ministry of Defense was responsible for enlisted men (who voluntarily joined the armed forces) and officers graduated from military colleges and for the recruitment, training, and management of conscripts on the front. Equally important was the Ba'th Party bureaucracy that existed at every level of the armed forces. The Ba'th Party had come to power bent on eliminating any threat of a military coup emanating from the armed forces. The leadership purged the armed forces of

---

[2] My analysis of spatial hierarchies created by state violence has benefited from readings of Franz Fanon, *The Wretched of the Earth*, trans. C. Farrington (New York: Grove Weidenfeld, 1991) pp. 35–41; Achille Mbembe, "Necropolitics," trans. Libby Meintjes, *Public Culture*, 15 (2003), 11–40; and Eyal Weizman, *Hollow Land: Israel's Architecture of Occupation* (New York: Verso Press, 2007). Fanon focuses on colonial state policies; Mbembe extends the argument to new forms of violence in the postcolonial world; and Weizman is particularly insightful on the link between militarization of space and spatial knowledge created by modern technologies.

troublesome army officers and developed the concept, no doubt based on the Soviet model, of creating an "ideological army."[3] By 1979, when Saddam Hussain acquired formal control of the party as well as leadership of the armed forces, the upper echelon of the military was dominated by officers drawn from the areas around Takrit, al-Dur, and Mosul.

The Ba'thification of the army was a routine and often opaque enterprise. The Ba'th Party instituted a bureaucracy to oversee the admission of potential recruits into military academies, the professional and technical schools that provided staff to the armed forces.[4] By the mid-1980s, party cadres in local divisions nationwide surveyed male students in matriculating classes in part to determine their eligibility for military colleges and schools.[5] In addition, the Ba'th placed commissars at various levels of military divisions, down to the level of platoon, to ensure loyalty within the forces, oversee applications for promotion, and gather intelligence on political activity within the armed forces. The locus of Ba'thist control was the Military Office of the Ba'th Party, attached to the Office of the Presidency and operating independently of the General Secretariat of the Ba'th Party. It ran separate party offices in all military training camps as well as the seven army corps that provided the bulk of the ground forces during the Iran-Iraq war.[6] The party also dominated the Directorate of Military Discipline, the equivalent of the Military Police. Finally, the Directorate of Political Guidance, established as early as 1973, ensured that the armed forces inculcated the ideology of the Ba'th.[7]

---

[3] For a useful comparison between the relation of party and military in communist countries and Iraq, see Ahmad Hashim, "Civil-military relations," pp. 21–3.

[4] The process of culling applicants to academies did not only place through one department or section of the Ba'th. The Section on Military Technical Schools examined applicants who were to be trained in military support technologies such as the planting of mines or radio communications. The Directorate of the Affairs Sessions oversaw several divisions that collected information on applicants to academies for training members of the security apparatus and on recruits in military camps and academies, and cleared applicants to professional schools, such as medical and engineering schools, whose education was to be funded by the Ministry of Defense. Every student who wanted to enter the armed forces applied to the recruitment office of the Ministry of Defense, which then sent his application to the party's Directorate of Military Training Sessions to clear the applicant. BRCC 01–2496–0106–147.

[5] Sassoon, *Saddam Hussein's Ba'th Party*, pp. 129–45.

[6] BRCC–1–2479–0004–0000. The Military Office (*al-maktab al-'askari*) was formed in 1962. In 1986, the head of the Military Office was Ali Hasan al-Majid. Military branches were organized on the front line but maintained close contact with military committees in the civilian branches of the Ba'th Party. The branches were Dhi Qar, Yarmouk, Basra, Baghdad, al-Walid, al-Rashid (First Army Corps), al-Qadisiyya (Third Army Corps), and sections in the Fifth and Sixth Army Corps. By 1989, these branches had expanded to ten. BRCC 01–2124–0000–0011.

[7] Hashim, "Civil-military relations," p. 23.

The war with Iran created new challenges for the regime. The need for manpower on the front strained its ability to pursue the Ba'thification of the armed forces, particularly among conscripts. The armed forces expanded during the war from twelve to sixty divisions, the overwhelming number of them infantry. The rank and file and lower-ranking officers within these divisions were mostly drawn from conscripts whose training was rudimentary and whose military cohesiveness was weak. For military leaders, this problem – together with the politicization of military decisions – lay at the heart of the poor performance of the rank and file within the armed forces.[8]

The war, however, provided opportunities for non-Ba'thists. The need for technical expertise opened up training academies to recent graduates who were not active party members.[9] Recruitment into the military academies was no longer premised solely on ideological conformity to Ba'thist principles, but rather on the absence of any hostile political activity on the part of the applicant or his family. The loss of a large number of mid-ranking Ba'th officers opened the ranks to new and more diverse officer corps drawn from different areas, including the Shi'i south.[10] This was particularly the case in the regular armed forces, unlike the elite Republican Guard. While there are no data to confirm the largely impressionistic assessment of these trends, some data are available from the records of the Military Office of the Ba'th Party that list the number of fallen and missing in action in different campaigns. A record of soldiers fallen between January and July 1986 in the middle sector (Jwarta and Panjawin and Mandali) is instructive. Of the eighty-six soldiers listed, many of them belonging to an elite and mobile unit of commando forces (*maghawir*), six were officers who had attained a relatively high Ba'thist rank of advanced advocate, eleven others belonged to the rank of advocate, and the majority belonged to the entry-level rank of supporter.[11] Even within the elite

[8] Lieutenant General Ra'id Majid Hamadani, *Qabla an Yughadiruna al-Tarikh*, pp. 60–114. Lieutenant General Hamadani was in the armed forces during the war and offers a strong indictment of the politicization of decision making and lack of preparedness of the rank and file.

[9] Staff Colonel Ahmad al-Zaydi, *al-Bina' al-Ma'nawi li al-Quwat al-Musalaha al-'Iraqiyya (The Structure of Morale of the Iraqi Armed Forces)* (Beirut: Dar al-Rawda, 1990), pp. 80–8. The colonel defected to Kurdistan early after the invasion of Kuwait. His is a decidedly sectarian reading of army politics, but he draws on his experience serving on the front during the Iran-Iraq war.

[10] Ofra Bengio, "Iraq," *Middle East Contemporary Survey*, eds. Haim Shaked and Daniel Dishon, 8 (1983–4), 470–6.

[11] BRCC 01–2459–0002–0193 to 0198. The numbers of the dead are divided evenly among Baghdad, Basra, Diyali, and Ninewah provinces, with smaller numbers drawn from other provinces.

corps of the infantry divisions of the Republican Guard, viewed as the bulwark against threats to the regime, party affiliation had ceased to be most determinant factor of induction into the Guard, although party rank was factored for promotion.[12]

Ba'th Party commissars saw the expansion of the armed forces as both threat and opportunity. Growth in numbers threatened the party's hold on the armed forces and presented an opportunity to position the party as the regime's primary instrument to ensure obedience, manage rewards and punishment, and intervene during periods of military crisis. Commissars were officers with military ranks, although not all had gone to military academies. The leadership of sections dealing with intelligence, promotion, and political indoctrination had to consist of high-ranking Ba'thists, while the commissars in security, defense, and administration were military recruits. These did not have to belong to the higher echelons of the party bureaucracy, and often came from its lower ranks. Commissars coordinated with their military counterparts on training, replenishing troops, administrative affairs, furloughs, the reward and punishment of soldiers, the removal of the dead and injured from the front lines, and the maintenance of morale. The Directorate of Political Guidance played a pivotal role at every level of the armed forces, and the vast number of artists, journalists, and media personalities it employed became the lynchpin of a sophisticated campaign to link the internal front with the war front and maintain control of what it dubbed "the morale" of soldiers on the front (Figure 4.1).

The Directorate of Political Guidance

Like all governments at war, the Iraqi regime was singularly aware of the importance of controlling the war's narrative and maintaining the troops' morale. It used the Ba'thist Directorate of Political Guidance within the Ministry of Defense to manage coverage of the battles at the front, disseminate information about different battles, and ensure that its troops received a heavy dose of propaganda and were entertained.

---

[12] BRCC 01-2459-0002-0299 to 0482. The ledger contains a request from the Military Office of the party to the General Secretariat requesting the posthumous induction and/or promotion of those killed in two Republican Guard units into party hierarchy. The men of the First and Second infantry units had been killed between February 15 and February 25, 1986 in the battle of Faw. Of the 175 dead, 79 were at the level of advocate and 96 at the level of supporter. Another significant number is that of the units of Republican Guard killed in Mehran between July 3 and July 6, 1986. Of the fifty-two killed in one unit, forty-four were listed as having no party affiliation. See pages 0584 to 0694 of the same ledger.

FIGURE 4.1. Iraqi soldiers on the southern front in Iraq, along the border with Iran, June 18, 1984 (AP photo/Don Mell).

The Iran-Iraq war was fought on television screens in Iraqi homes, as well as on the radio. It was the first war in which extensive coverage, albeit of a propagandistic type, was made available to the Iraqi public, linking Iraqis of all stripes to the developments on the front. As the options for most Iraqis were quite limited – one official television station and two official radio stations – the Directorate of Political Guidance had a captive audience. Press coverage, visits to the front by journalists, filming of battle scenes, and the education of schoolchildren and other members of the Iraqi public brought to the front to cohabit with fighters were managed by the Directorate. One of its central functions was to create a sense of shared experience between Iraqis on the home front and soldiers in the trenches. At the battlefront, its primary concern was to persuade soldiers to continue fighting and to boost their morale by offering entertainment as a reprieve from war. At the same time, the Directorate's leadership played an important role in disciplining soldiers, particularly those exhibiting "negative phenomena," a euphemism used to describe a host of problems, including dereliction of duty, desertion, and lack of enthusiasm.

The commissars of the Directorate were present at every level of the military hierarchy ranging from battalion to division. They were usually headquartered in the rear lines of these units. For many conscripted soldiers, working with the Directorate offered an attractive, if often temporary, way out of serving on the front lines. High-ranking commissars were drawn from the party's upper echelon, but most of the rank and file were conscripted soldiers drafted from educational and fine arts academic institutions that were closed to non-Ba'thists. Thus, soldiers conscripted into the Directorate had to have attained a certain level in the Ba'th hierarchy without having to be full members.[13] The Directorate drew on a young and talented group of Iraqi men aspiring to make their mark in the arts. In television, radio, and theater, as well as the visual arts, these men helped frame and disseminate the regime's war narrative.

The Directorate had to gear its message to Iraqi conscripts who came from different backgrounds and educational levels. The vast majority of them were not Ba'thists. Many joined the party at its lowest level. In part to appeal to the more educated among them, the Directorate began issuing a daily newspaper, *al-Qadisiyya*. It was widely circulated on the front.[14] In addition to battle coverage, its pages offered commentary on social and cultural issues that went well beyond the interests of the Directorate's traditional officer corps. The paper reflected the interests of the expanding number of educated Iraqi conscripts swelling military ranks. While its political pages, particularly its front and editorial pages, might not have had much credibility among educated soldiers, the cultural and social pages provided respite from the unrelenting barrage of propaganda. At times, this outlet even allowed for veiled challenges to the official war narrative.[15]

It was, however, to the soldiers at large that the Directorate's main efforts were aimed. While indoctrination remained part and parcel of the meetings of party commissars on the front, the message of the Directorate's

[13] Interview with Waddah Hasan, Amman, Jordan, June 21, 2007. These included the College of Education, the College of Letters, and the Institute (later College) of Fine Arts whose graduates usually staffed the educational and cultural institutions of Iraq.

[14] The daily was geared to a wider readership than the more specialized monthly publication, *The Guardians of the Nation* (*Huras al-Watan*).

[15] I have not had access to the *al-Qadisiyya* newspaper of the 1980s, although I examined issues from 1990 onward. My conclusions are based on interviews I conducted with Waddah Hasan, who worked in the Directorate between 1981 and 1984, and with Haytham Ali, who worked as a war journalist during this period.

various programs for most of the rank and file was different. The programs eschewed political indoctrination in Ba'thist ideology in favor of a propaganda effort geared toward demonizing and belittling the enemy and exulting in the martial values of Iraqi soldiers. The Directorate's mission was twofold. First, it aimed to inculcate a "fighting" spirit among soldiers and to convince them of the "justness" of the Iraqi cause. Second, the Directorate saw its effort as a way of mitigating the soldiers' "psychological problems during war" such as depression, paranoia, and suicide and general psychological breakdown.[16] To that end, commissars stationed in the rear lines of units were tasked with maintaining contact with their superiors and providing regular reports on morale, especially any "negative phenomena."

A few months after the war began, the Directorate issued instructions to all its branches in different army corps detailing the content of a daily radio and a weekly television program devoted to the armed forces and broadcast in different army units as well as to the public at large. The programs were meant to bring the war front into Iraqis' homes and to provide a simple patriotic message about their armed forces in a fast-paced manner. The radio programs began with what Iraqis called the "*dibaja,*" a formulaic preamble on the latest pronouncement of the leader on the glory and performance of the armed forces. Commentators then gave the official version of Iranian politics and military preparedness, taking care to counter rumors heard among soldiers about Iranian victories.[17] They reported on battles, interviewed soldiers at the front, and hosted poets and singers. These reports were tightly controlled. Commissars chose the soldiers interviewed to highlight the heroism of the armed forces. During attacks on enemy lines, radio programs brought in popular poets to sing the praises of the army and the leader and broadcasted patriotic songs.

The language used to describe the enemy drew on a repertoire of racial, political, and gendered terms from an Iraqi Ba'thist rereading of Islamic history and from the Iranian regime's own description of its war aims. Perhaps the most distinct was the continuous use of the term "Persian Magians" to allude to the Iranian enemy. The term drew on the reworking of the word *shu'ubiya,* a cultural trend led by literati of Persian origin during the high Islamic Middle Ages, specifically during the Abbasid period, when Baghdad was the cultural capital of the Islamic world. In

---

[16] NIDS/serial 4581 to 4591. The phrase was used by a study issued by the office of the Ministry of Defense and sent by the Directorate of Political Guidance to all army corps.

[17] Ibid. The report from the Directorate in the Ministry of Defense to its counterpart in the First Army Corps stationed in Arbil is dated December 1980.

its original usage, the term denoted merely a literary trend that assigned more weight to the cultural contributions of Persians over Arabs. In Iraqi Ba'thist ideology before the war, it represented all that fell outside the political and cultural order that the Iraqi Ba'th defined as Arab and Iraqi. Thus, the Iraqi Communist Party was described as *"shu'ubi,"* as were all intellectual trends that did not conform to the Ba'thist Party line.[18] During the war, the term acquired a racial meaning linking it to the pre-Islamic term *Magians* (*majus*), which early chroniclers of Islam had used to describe the religion of the ancient Persians. To counter Iran's claims that it was an Islamic political and moral order, the Iraqi regime associated the modern Iranians with their Persian, un-Islamic ancestors. The Directorate of Political Guidance insisted all radio announcers and political commissars use the term when speaking about the Iranians.[19] Supporting the racism of the propaganda was a language of hate, including a slew of epithets used to dehumanize the enemy. For example, the enemy was often described as a rat or a cockroach.

Troops at the front made reference to a set of distinguishing characteristics, often caricatures, designed to belittle the Iranian soldier and contrast his performance with the heroism and manliness of the Iraqi fighter. These stereotypes served as visual and linguistic shorthand for portraying the enemy. The Iraqi soldier "danced at the shoulders of death." If his conviction in the "justice" of the Iraqi cause was not strong, then he should be reminded "of the value of his manhood."[20] In the press circulated on the front, photographs of soldiers depicted them posing with victory signs on tanks or armored vehicles, clean-shaven except for the requisite mustache that the idealized manly soldier was to sport in imitation of Saddam Hussain. Iranian soldiers were photographed either as captives or as corpses, with unshaven faces and bodies in positions of subjugation.[21] The Iraqi soldier was nicknamed *Abu Tahrir*, the father of liberation (presumably of Muhammarah), and contrasted with the Iranian soldier who was young, inexperienced, and driven by irrational, unquestioning belief in the creed of obscurantist Iranian *mullas*.[22] The image of fanatical and ignorant Iranian soldiers was reinforced by Iran's

---

[18] Makiya, *Republic of Fear*, pp. 216–28; Davis, *Memories of State*, pp. 122–33.

[19] NIDS/serial 4581 to 4591. The entire study is included in sheet number 31177.

[20] Ibid.

[21] See Chapter 7.

[22] Interview with Waddah Hasan, Amman, Jordan, June 21, 2007. Hasan wrote for the radio station at the front and told me of a popular comedian, Imad Badan, who contrasted *Abu Tahrir* with the Iranian soldiers.

FIGURE 4.2. Cartoon by Khdeir, "Abu Tahrir," *Alif Ba'*, March 5, 1986. Iranian soldiers looking onto the boot of Iraqi soldier Abu Tahrir: "Strange! Where are our people.... I don't see except darkness."

strategy of sending young recruits in human waves across the terrain of southern Iraq with wooden keys to heaven tied around their necks and green bandanas on their heads. Iraqi soldiers were convinced that their Iranian counterparts were brainwashed into believing that they were to liberate Karbala from the godless Iraqi regime, rewarded by entry into paradise. Thus, while the Iraqi soldier fought in a regular army organized around units, the Iranian soldier was effectively part of an unorganized mob, indistinct and incapable of rational action. The regime that sent its youth on these suicidal missions was bent, according to the Directorate, on conquering Baghdad and creating the same kind of political and cultural order that produced these men. The contrast between the manly and courageous Iraqi soldier and the youthful and irrational Iranian soldier echoed the Ba'thist attempts back home to paint the Iranian regime as obscurantist and bent on destroying the Iraqi achievements of modernization (Figures 4.2–4.5).

The extent to which Iraqi soldiers were swayed by these distinctions is difficult to gauge. Certainly, the prospect of living in an Iraq ruled by an Islamic government did not appeal to many soldiers, who simply stated that they did not want *hukm al-malali* (the rule of *mullas*) and who spoke with great sarcasm about the rulers of Iran.[23] Ultimately, however, the Directorate sought to convince soldiers that Iraq was fighting a national and defensive war. The shelling of Iraqi cities, particularly of Basra, together with the well-publicized aim of the Iranian leadership of

---

[23] My interviews of Iraqi soldiers were not representative or statistically significant. I should also say that these interviews were conducted in 2007 and 2009, at a time of great Iranian influence in Iraq. These conclusions cannot be quantified.

FIGURE 4.3. Cartoon by al-Karkhi, "Keys to Heaven," *Alif Ba'*, November 5, 1980. Iranian clerics looking at a soldier: "He has taken a dozen keys [to heaven] and he is still crying."

conquering parts of the south in the hope of a Shi'i insurrection, provided incontrovertible proof that Iraqi soldiers were fighting a war to preserve national sovereignty against sectarian politics. In the first few years of the war, the support for these claims among the armed forces, particularly among enlisted men, appears to have been strong. As the war progressed, however, and the long stalemate of the middle years led to an increasing number of casualties, the support for the war, particularly among conscripts, eroded. Desertion and dereliction of duty mounted, as did the efforts of the party and the military to convince its armed forces that the war was an imposed one created by Iran's refusal to accept a ceasefire agreement. The centrality and limit of propaganda as a tool of a national defensive war is evidenced by the Ba'th Party's Military Office's report on the "negative phenomena" within the armed forces, particularly among the rank and file. Issued in October 1986, the report was an attempt by

كاريكاتير

وجبة (الــــلا)

FIGURE 4.4. Cartoon "The *Mulla's* Meal," *Alif Ba'*, October 29, 1980.

the Military Office to reckon with the devastating loss of Faw to the Iranians in February of that year and to explain to officers as well as to the rank and file the decision to take the Iranian city of Mehran in retaliation, only to lose it soon afterward. Much of the blame for these losses was laid at the feet of the ordinary soldier, lower-ranking officers, and Ba'th Party commissars who had not been diligent in their reporting on problems of morale and corruption within the armed forces.[24]

Most troubling for the commissars who wrote the report was the lack of commitment of the rank and file. They were not the heroes of the modern Iraqi nation portrayed in the propaganda. They deserted, sometimes infiltrated enemy territory as a unit in the Kurdish north, surrendered to the enemy preferring captivity to fighting, or committed acts of sabotage

[24] BRCC 01–2479–0004–0341 and 0342.

FIGURE 4.5. Cartoon "The Khomeini Mentality," *al-Jumhuriyya*, October 26, 1980. A group of Iranian clerics, led by President Bani Sadr, carrying a man representing the Iranian people and pushing him into a pot entitled the "Khomeini mentality." The man holding the pot is Khomeini.

by destroying military hardware and giving information to the enemy. The lack of commitment was attributed by the head of the cultural committee within the Military Office to several factors. Among the most important was the lack of consciousness on the part of the ordinary Iraqi soldier, who was viewed as having firmer ties to his kin, tribe, ethnicity, and class than to the nation. These "traditional" and "backward" ties persisted because soldiers had not been sufficiently inculcated with the modern values and achievements of the Ba'thist revolution.[25] Thus, even after a decade of education in Ba'thist ideology and more than six years of intense propaganda at the front, the Iraqi conscript remained reluctant to die in defense of the "achievements of the revolution." Part of the solution to the problem, at least for the Directorate of Political Guidance and the cultural committees attached to various army corps, was more education.[26]

"I Have Become a Hero Despite Myself": Reward, Survival, and Punishment

A macabre joke circulated among some conscripts in the late 1980s. A soldier who had lost both of his arms during a battle was hospitalized and then sent back to the front. When his commanding officer was asked why,

[25] Ibid., pp. 0257 to 0273.
[26] BRCC 01–2479–0004–0155 to 0162. By 1986, the Military Office of the Ba'th Party coordinated sections devoted to information, intelligence, security, defense, provisions, political guidance, and administration of promotions and rewards.

he replied that the army could use the handicapped man to deliver letters wedged between his teeth. When this same man lost a leg at the front, he was asked again to join his unit. His commanding officer explained that he could be used as a wiping cloth.[27] The joke highlights the dispensability of a soldier's life to the regime as it underscores the state's increasingly desperate measures to find what conscripts described as "kindle for the furnace" of war. Although every able-bodied Iraqi man aged eighteen to forty-five was at some time conscripted into either the armed forces or the party militia during the war, the need for manpower was particularly important because Iran's population was nearly triple that of Iraq. So acute was the shortage of men at the front, the Iraqi regime had to resort to recruiting non-Iraqi Arabs, particularly Egyptians and Sudanese, to fight by offering them financial incentives. For Iraqi soldiers, the length of the war was made all the more unbearable by the lack of reprieve from serving. All who were eligible served multiple times on different fronts and moved between units to replenish reorganized divisions decimated by the war. Young men, freshly graduated from high schools and academies of higher education, provided a constant pool of draftees as the death toll among soldiers mounted and desertion became a problem. Almost every Iraqi family had one, often two or three, men serving on the front. It would seem that war, like death, was the great equalizer. Yet the war made some men more equal than others.

The men who fought on the front fell into several categories: the professional army of volunteers trained in military academies, subject to military rules of promotion and retirement, and housed in or around various military bases; reservists who had completed their two, later three years, of compulsory military training and had returned to civilian life before being called to the front. In addition, soldiers who belonged to the party militia, the Popular Army, were given cursory training and thrown into battle, often to disastrous effect. In the Kurdish north, the National Defense Battalions, a paramilitary force of Kurdish conscripts, fought with the government against the Kurdish insurgents. Finally, conscripts drafted during the war had no familiarity with military life until their shortened training sessions before their posting directly to the front. For most, this marked the first time they had lived in close quarters with other Iraqi men drawn from different social and regional backgrounds.[28] The experience

---

[27] Interview with Tareq Ali, Amman, Jordan, July 14, 2007.
[28] These comments are based on nineteen interviews I conducted with soldiers in the summer of 2007 and spring of 2009. All belonged to infantry divisions: four were enlisted men and the rest were conscripts.

forged a common vocabulary among them. Their familiarity with the officers and Ba'thist commissars, their survival after certain battles, their involuntary and intimate knowledge of the breadth of Iraq's geography, and the rhythm of a life centered around intense and chaotic fighting followed by a lull all served to create a sense of shared experience.

Several distinctions dominated the way conscripts remembered their shared experience. These were often described in the language of military difference between the officer corps and the rank and file, between conscripts and enlisted men, between soldiers and the Popular Army and Ba'thist commissars ensconced in the rear lines and infantry men at the front. Underlying those differences was another set of social and cultural distinctions. Conscripts spoke of distinctions between those connected to certain officers through ties of patronage and those who were not, between Kurd and Arab, and between Kurds who served in paramilitary forces and Kurds who joined the guerillas. No less important for soldiers were differences between urbanite and country peasant, college graduate and barely literate, and those from certain parts of Iraq and others drawn from Mosul and Takrit, who dominated the upper echelons of the officer corps. Rewards, survival, and punishment on the front had as much to do with these distinctions as they had to do with military performance.

Over the course of the war, the Revolutionary Command Council issued numerous decrees granting members of the armed forces, conscripted and enlisted, entitlements to property as well as privileged access to state services. The lion's share of these entitlements went to the officer corps, although benefits accruing to martyrs' families covered all ranks and categories of men in the army. The regime sought to provide incentives for soldiers by promising to compensate their families should they die. In addition, Saddam Hussain expanded the military rules governing the assignment of medals and rewards to allow him to dispense medals of courage and transform the entitlements that accompanied such medals. He framed the rewards as grants in return for the performance of a noble deed (*makruma*), given by the munificent holder of the highest military office in the country, Saddam Hussain, to honor the loyalty and sacrifice of his soldiers. In addition, soldiers granted medals received financial benefits and consumer goods that surpassed compensations historically associated with promotion and reward within the rules spelled out by the Ministry of Defense.[29] The new policies were paternalistic, designed

---

[29] For Revolutionary Command Council decrees issued in the first year of the war, see, for example, *al-Jumhuriyya*, May 11, 1981, 1; May 17, 1; May 27, 1. For grants of

to highlight the role of Saddam Hussain as the father of the nation at war, a patriarch who dispensed monetary and other gifts. By incentivizing military performance with money and goods, the leadership of the regime attempted to turn soldiering into mercenary enterprise. Under the new rules, the Ministry of Defense rewarded soldiers and officers with money and cars commensurate with their rank. In a successful military operation, for example, an officer was awarded six thousand dinars, an assistant officer three thousand, and a corporal one thousand.[30] As the war grew longer and more costly, Saddam Hussain issued a series of directives that associated the performance of certain military tasks with specific monetary awards. Thus, in 1983, prizes were given to soldiers who removed Iraqi martyrs from no-man's-land (fifteen hundred dinars), captured Iranian soldiers (five thousand dinars), and brought the body or tags of a dead Iranian combatant to his unit's headquarters (one thousand dinars).[31]

The regime's policy undermined the autonomy of the military establishment and its professionalism. Its immediate impact, however, was to open up the military hierarchy to a crop of new officers and soldiers by offering venues of social mobility. It is difficult, however, to determine the extent to which the regime bestowed these honors and entitlements based on merit. Although military officers within units in cooperation with military intelligence chose the soldiers to put forward after successful military operations, their names had to be cleared with Ba'thist commissars at the front before they were sent further up the military hierarchy. Certainly, there was room for corruption and political patronage. More problematic was the expansion of an officer corps that had undergone shortened training before being promoted. Some were appointed to their posts through connections to party or other officials. Together with the Ba'th Party commissars, they became the bane of the rank-and-file soldier's life at the front. Their very corruption, however, provided soldiers with the opportunity, however narrow, to negotiate their survival. In particular, conscripts who could establish relations of patronage with officers and political commissars managed much better than those who did not have similar relations. It helped them avoid the front lines as long as possible, although the majority ended up with battle experience.

land, medals, and consumer goods by Hussain, see *al-Jumhuriyya*, September 2, 1981, 1; September 10, 1.

[30] NIDS/serial 39 to 60. The document comes from military intelligence from the northeastern sector after a battle in the Shaykhan region in 1987.

[31] NIDS/serial 865574 to 0865576.

One of the most pervasive corrupt practices among the officer corps was the manipulation of furlough. Together with the persistent use by the officer corps of conscripts to run personal errands, the problem was the most worrisome for the commissars reporting on the morale of the rank and file. Every Iraqi soldier had a monthly furlough of a week in periods of calm, or a few days during periods of intense engagement. Many had to travel several days, taking public transportation. Particularly for young conscripts, the furlough provided critical respite from the front. Officers were well aware of this and soon used their ability to issue papers to reward and punish to their advantage. Mazin Hadithi, for example, was a budding artist when he was drafted in 1983. He fought in some of the fiercest battles in Faw and Basra. He spent the first few months of his service in the rear lines working in the office of the Directorate of Political Guidance in the Third Army Corps, drawing maps of the terrain for operations in the Basra region. Soon, however, he found himself in the trenches of the front lines. His comrades tried to ease his terror and dissuade him from deserting by taking him to his commanding officer. Like Mazin, the officer came from Anbar province. The officer sent the young artist to the brigade headquarters to paint a large mural of Saddam Hussain. Mazin's painting allowed him to avoid the front lines for another six months, but he soon found himself back in the trenches. Over the following four years, he bribed his officers to obtain unauthorized furloughs and to extend authorized ones.[32] Mazin was one among many soldiers who made use of a network of officers adept at selling fake papers, whether identity cards to facilitate the movement of absentee soldiers or deserters, or papers allowing unauthorized furloughs. Not all soldiers were as shrewd as Mazin or had access to funds or talents to bribe their commanding officers. Officers as well as party commissars often used furlough to punish conscripts. By 1986, the manipulation of furlough by the officer corps had become such a widespread phenomenon that the Military Office of the party tasked military intelligence and the Directorate of Political Guidance with monitoring and disciplining officers and commissars who engaged in the practice.[33]

The corruption of party commissars and some of the officer corps undermined the professionalism of the armed forces but provided conscripts with an avenue for negotiating their survival. The majority of conscripts, however, were not able to use any ties of patronage. Among conscripted soldiers, a wealth of information spread on techniques to

[32] Interview with Mazin Hadithi, Damascus, Syria, March 1, 2009.
[33] BRCC 01–2479–0004–0278.

injure oneself without eliciting the suspicion of the officers or commissars.[34] Desertion was rampant. Many soldiers deserted more than once, returning to their military units after the Revolutionary Command Council issued many of its amnesty decrees. No overall statistics are available for the rate of desertion, but the example of an infantry division of three thousand in the Second Army Corps provides a clue. Nearly a quarter of that division deserted, many of them repeatedly.[35] Soldiers did so with great difficulty, because they were fully aware that they and their families were subject to surveillance and punishment. Those who fled to the southern marshes were periodically raided by the military and the Popular Army or forced to join the opposition forces of the Islamist parties. Kurdish deserters from the regular armed forces had more choice. They could join the Kurdish paramilitary organizations and serve in the counterinsurgency campaign against Kurdish guerillas or be inducted into the *peshmergas* of the Kurdish nationalist parties.

The Ba'th Party oversaw the recruitment, training, and indoctrination of two major militias: the Popular Army and the Kurdish paramilitary forces. Regional bureaus were responsible for recruiting and training the Popular Army. As the party militia, the Popular Army served two functions: first, it allowed the party to claim that it was contributing militarily to the war effort; and, second, it helped create a mass militarized society in which every citizen contributed to national defense. The leaders of the various party bureaus were continually anxious to report on the numbers of men and women trained for the party militia. Ostensibly, men who joined the party militia did so voluntarily. In reality, while many initially volunteered, the majority were conscripted by cadres who carried out periodic campaigns to recruit school-aged and older men into the militia. Party cadres were expected to provide a certain number of able-bodied men from their assigned neighborhoods. The "volunteers" were then sent to training camps and organized into units. From 1985 to 1988, for example, the Southern, Northern, and Baghdad bureaus recruited and trained more than one hundred ninety-five thousand Iraqis, the overwhelming majority of whom were males.[36]

---

[34] al-Zaydi, *al-Bin'a al-Ma'nawi*, pp. 274–9. Interview with Waddah Hasan, Amman, Jordan, June 21, 2007.

[35] BRCC 01-3370-0000-0670 to 0700. The number of deserters was 756. Of these, approximately 160 had deserted more than once. The ledger of the Second Army Corps is dated 1987 to 1988.

[36] For the Southern Bureau, see BRCC 01-3212-0001-0550. For the Baghdad Bureau, see BRCC 01-2140-0003-0020 to 0026, and for the Northern Bureau see 0086 to 0088 in the same box file.

In the early years of the war, the party militia was tasked with overseeing occupied Iranian territories. At the front, their performance was disastrous: against insurgents and deserters, however, they were invaluable. A significant percentage of the men participated in deserter pursuit operations and were also crucial in the counterinsurgency campaign against the Kurds. They manned observation posts and supported the armed forces.

The major paramilitary organization in the Kurdish areas was the National Defense Battalions.[37] It had its origins in the 1960s during the government's counterinsurgency campaign against the Kurdish guerillas. Exploiting tribal divisions among the Kurds, the Ba'thist government in the 1970s recruited tribal leaders and allowed them to draw on their followers to form militias. Soldiers serving in these battalions carried light weapons and policed Kurdish areas, often providing intelligence to the army. During the war with Iran, their leaders came under the operational command of military intelligence and the leadership of the army corps stationed in the northern sector. However, the Northern Bureau of the party was responsible for setting and implementing policy for the Battalions, reporting on its leaders' political activities, and maintaining control over the Kurdish conscripts within its ranks.[38]

The Northern Bureau's official policy in its recruitment of the Battalions painted the endeavor as part of its effort to civilize and modernize its Kurdish population, an attempt to transform them from tribesmen into citizens of the Iraqi nation.[39] To that end, a presidential decree required that military-aged men residing in the Region of Autonomous Rule join the Battalions. The rhetoric of the party and the regime, however, belied actual practice. From the beginning, the Battalions was organized along tribal lines. Kurdish tribal leaders were tasked with recruiting men for their units and accorded authority over the soldiers in their Battalions, even if the traditional basis of that authority had long dissipated.[40] Many

---

[37] The *Afwaj al-Khafifa* (Light Cavalry). The Military Office of the Ba'th party oversaw the Afwaj, the Kurdish equivalent to the Popular Army. Created in 1984 to counterbalance the tribal paramilitary contingents of the National Defense Battalions and to inculcate Ba'thist ideology in Kurdish soldiers, the Afwaj soon became a haven for deserters and volunteers looking to make a living and obtain arms. NIDS/serial 745803 to 745805.

[38] Ibid.

[39] BRCC 01–2140–0003–0112 and 0113. The report of the Northern Bureau was presented by its head, Muhammad Hamza al-Zubaydi, and covered the period of August 1985 to March 1987.

[40] The official title of the tribal leader of Battalions was "consultant" or *mustashar*, an innocuous title that hid the extent to which the Battalions was crucial to the military operations of the government in the Kurdish north, as it also hid the extent to which these "consultants" were subject to its power.

had become instruments of government policy. Those deemed ineffective or whose loyalty was in doubt were replaced by others within their clan or were ordered to disband their units. Others chose to rebel or switch sides and were summarily executed.[41] Battalion leaders came under the jurisdiction of party branches in predominantly Kurdish areas. Training camps, education sessions, and the pursuit and apprehension of deserters and absentees accompanied by close surveillance of both leaders and the soldiers became central to the security operations of the Northern Bureau.[42] In 1987, the Bureau oversaw 147 Battalions with close to two hundred five thousand men, comprising almost 10 percent of the total Kurdish population under its purview.[43]

In addition to its use as an arm of counterinsurgency operations, the Iraqi government viewed the Battalions as a means of absorbing young Kurdish conscripts, providing them with employment, and dissuading them from joining the rebels. The success of the government and the Ba'th was limited, as the large number of deserters among the Kurdish Battalions attests. Desertion was rampant, and the Kurdish north became a military zone of operations where men switched sides continuously and where the choice for Kurdish fighters was quite narrow. They could either join the insurgents or fight in the Battalions. If they chose the first, they and their families lived precariously and were subject to harsh measures of deportation and imprisonment. If they chose the latter, they became part of an apparatus of repression and pariahs among their Kurdish compatriots who referred to them sarcastically as *jahsh* (donkey fowl).

[41] BRCC 01–2140–0003–0113 to 0117. One leader had his Battalion cancelled, and he was arrested because he claimed that he had 500 soldiers in his unit, although he had only 90. Another was disbanded because of "negative aspects," a euphemism used to describe lack of effectiveness and loyalty. Two others were executed and their units disbanded because one had failed to fight alongside the armed forces in a battle against Iranian units, and another had attempted to assassinate the head of the Fifth Army Corps. The leader of the 24th Battalion, for example, rebelled in Mankish within Dohuk province and was executed.

[42] BRCC 01–2140–0003–0071 and 0072 and 0107 to 0117. The Ninewah, Ta'mim, Arbil, Sulaimaniyya, and Dohuk branches of the party all had Battalions attached to their offices.

[43] BRCC 01–2140–0003–0071 and 0072. In 1987, the population under the purview of the Northern Bureau was 3,760,244. Of these, 2,064,712 were Kurds. The numbers of Battalions are on page (0117). Five of these Battalions were disbanded in 1987. By the time Ali Hasan al-Majid declared the end of the Anfal campaign in August 1989, the Battalions had grown to 321 units and included some 412,636 soldiers. This increase can only be explained by the forcible induction of Kurds into the Battalions after the end of the Anfal campaign, page (0057).

Two stories of deserters drawn from the records of the security apparatus of the north illustrate their bind. By the time the security men had
captured Ahmad in Arbil in 1986, he had fled his unit in the National
Defense Battalions several times. Military intelligence accused him of
collaborating with the enemy because he carried with him a letter from
the opposition Kurdish parties allowing free movement between the
areas under their control and Iran. When conscripted, he joined a unit
of the National Defense Battalions in Kirkuk, was sent to the southern front to Khorramshahr, and deserted soon afterward. He rejoined
the Battalions after a general amnesty, but subsequently continued
to desert. In 1983, he fled to the regions controlled by the Kurdish
insurgents.[44]

Mas'ud's story appears in a directive issued by the Special Court in
Kirkuk to different agencies on a ruling concerning his crime. Security
men had arrested him because he carried arms, a crime punishable by
life imprisonment, in the Region of Autonomous Rule. To compound his
problems, he was a deserter and was punished by the confiscation of
his property. He had served in the communication section of the First
Army Corps in Dezful and had fled his unit in 1982. He met with a
Kurdish insurgent and asked to join the *peshmergas*. However, he was
refused, because he could not find someone acceptable to the insurgents
who could vouch that he was trustworthy. Rejected by the *peshmergas*,
he went back to his village outside Sulaimaniyya and worked as a day
laborer and lived with his aunt until he was arrested.[45]

For most conscripts, desertion was an extremely dangerous undertaking, as was any attempt to survive by retreating in the face of enemy
fire. Execution squads were ubiquitous on the front lines. Led by Ba'thist
commissars and clad in olive-colored uniforms with a red band on their
sleeves, the squads' members were usually stationed at the rear of the
battle lines.[46] Squad members were drawn from different parts of Iraq
and assigned to military divisions across different sectors of the front. In
the heat of battle, when heavy losses of junior officer corps left many conscripts leaderless, the execution squads played a crucial role in ensuring
that conscripts did not flee. As one officer told Haytham Ali, an *al-Thawra*
reporter, the war made heroes of men despite themselves. Unable to flee
the front (because they faced execution) or desert (because they would

---

[44] NIDS/serial 740811 to 740814. I have changed the name of the arrested deserter.
[45] NIDS/serial 716597 to 716599.
[46] Interview with Ammar Hasan, Damascus, Syria, August 16, 2007. Ammar was posted to
one such squad.

be relentlessly pursued and their families ostracized), they stood their ground because they had few other options.[47]

Hamza Jubayli was only fifteen when he was "volunteered" into the Popular Army in 1980. By 1987, he had become a seasoned soldier whose unit was attached to the East Tigris Command. Of all the battles he survived, the 1987 battle known as *al-Hisad al-Kabir* (The Great Harvest) in East Basra was among the deadliest. His description of the front lines provides the best window into the mayhem and death of the battle:

There is a leader of several officers who directs the units that are coming for the battle in the area of Dayr, near Basra. They tell these units, "*Yalla*, go, enter from this road, find the unit that is going to the front." It does not matter whether this unit is carrying provisions and military hardware or not, nor does it matter if it has fuel or not. "*Yalla*, enter." You enter from Dayr and continue to the outskirts of Basra, an area called Tannouma. All its houses are boarded up. It has no people, like a city of ghosts. Then, from Tannouma you go towards Iran. You come across the position of the execution squad. It was responsible for the execution of those who retreat. They were not military men but party people. I had heard of them but had not seen them until now. In Nahr Jasim, I saw them. They had a red band. We went into an area of thick groves through a rough road and we found a huge number of missiles. It is something a civilian cannot imagine. When I passed the execution squad, I saw a group of Sudanese men, maybe six or seven and about four or five Egyptians. I don't know what brought them to this place. They were using them to carry materials and goods. They were in front of me when I saw a missile or two hit them. They were torn to pieces (Figure 4.6).[48]

Prisoners of War: Ideology, Conversion, and Betrayal

In its first release on the violation of humanitarian law on the part of Iran and Iraq, the International Committee of the Red Cross singled out the situation of prisoners of war. Both governments subjected captured combatants to summary execution and hampered the repatriation of the wounded and sick. They used "prohibited force" against captives, forced them to endure ideological indoctrination, and pressured them to inform on their fellow prisoners.[49] The conclusions and recommendations of the report were based on the limited access its staff was granted to the prison camps in Iran and Iraq. The report reflected the committee's increased concern over the treatment of captives, particularly in Iranian prisons.

[47] Interview with Haytham Ali, Amman, Jordan, August 8, 2007.
[48] Interview with Hamza Jubayli, Damascus, Syria, April 28, 2009.
[49] Elvire Corboz, "Uneasy humanitarianism, the ICRC and the prisoners-of-war during the Iran-Iraq conflict," unpublished MA thesis, Faculty of Oriental Studies, Oxford University (2005), 19. Ian Brown, *Khomeini's Forgotten Sons, The Story of Iran's Boy Soldiers* (London: Gray Seal, 1990), pp. 97–117.

FIGURE 4.6. Iran-Iraq war: Situation between Amara and Basra (Jacques Pavlovsky/Sygma/Corbis).

Neither country adhered to the Geneva Convention's laws governing the treatment of prisoners of war, despite both being signatories. Instead, each country used the other's mistreatment of captives to make its case against their enemy in the international arena, particularly at the UN. The Iraqi government pointed to the execution of prisoners of war by the Iranians after the battle of Bostan on December 1, 1981 as proof of Iran's disregard for humanitarian law. It highlighted revolts by Iraqi prisoners against their Iranian captors, the most famous of which was the revolt at Gorang prison in October 1984.[50] The execution by the Iraqi military of Iranian prisoners of war is not well documented, but reports by

[50] Federation of Arab Journalists, *No to War, Yes to Peace: Stop the Gulf War, Save Iraqi POWs* (Baghdad, np, 1986).

journalists as well as Iraqi opposition parties suggest that it was regular. Soldiers fighting on the front lines confirm these reports as well.

The execution of prisoners of war was in clear contravention of international humanitarian law. However, for most surviving prisoners, the prison camps and the insidious disciplinary policies of both regimes in these camps left a longer lasting political and social impact. Iranian and Iraqi regimes subjected prisoners to all manner of identity erasure, both as legal persons and as human beings.[51] For Iraqi prisoners, the process took place over more than twenty years. Prisoners captured between 1980 and 1983 were repatriated in 1990. More than forty thousand prisoners returned that year. However, between twenty thousand and thirty thousand prisoners remained in Iran throughout the 1990s, with a group repatriated at the cusp of the fall of the Ba'th regime.[52] The International Committee of the Red Cross had not been granted permission by Iran to register many of the prisoners.[53] As captive combatants in enemy camps, they had no protection under international law. Nor was it clear to the Iraqi government if the men unaccounted for at the front were taken prisoner or simply missing in action until the International Committee of the Red Cross confirmed their imprisonment. Thus, their government could not even attempt to protect their rights until their names were registered with the Red Cross.

Prisoners of war, whether Iranian or Iraqi, became pawns in the war of ideologies between the two regimes. Iraqi authorities subjected Iranian prisoners to reeducation meetings and used their Iranian allies, the

[51] Corboz, "Uneasy humanitarianism," pp. 47–93. The first exchange of prisoners of war after the conclusion of hostilities took place in the summer and fall of 1990. According to a report issued by the International Progress Organization in May 1989, of the 70,000 Iraqi prisoners of war, only 46,098 prisoners were registered with the ICRC in Iran's sixteen prison camps. The remaining twenty-four thousand were unregistered. The number of Iranian prisoners of war released by the Iraqi government was 37,861.

[52] al-Qadisiyya, March 24, 1997, 2. There were several unilateral exchanges of prisoners during the 1990s, some facilitated by the International Committee of the Red Cross. As of 1997, however, more than twenty thousand prisoners had not been repatriated. The International Committee of the Red Cross, working with the Iranian government in 2003, gives the figures of these prisoners of war released over the course of twenty-three years. By 2003, 56,712 Iraqi prisoners had been repatriated: more than 4,600 declined to be repatriated. http://www.icrc.org/eng/resources/documents/misc/5x5drb.htm accessed March 4, 2011.

[53] The Iraqi government was more forthcoming in allowing Iranian prisoners access to the International Committee of Red Cross. However, in 1986, it refused to allow the Committee access to unregistered Iranian prisoners in retaliation for Iran's recalcitrant policy on Iraqi prisoners. It also stage managed visits by journalists to schools set up for prisoners of war. See Brown, Khomeini's Forgotten Sons, pp. 50–6 and 67–70.

opposition group Mujahid-i al-Khalq, to create divisions among Iranian prisoners. The Directorate of Political Guidance of the Ba'th Party used Iranian prisoners of war in "education" sessions to convince Iraqi deserters of the weakness of the Iranian regime and its evil intentions toward Iraq.[54] Additionally, the Iraqi government kept prisoners who belonged to the armed forces, doctors, and other technical personnel in secret prisons and interrogated them, hoping to collect information about Iranian military capabilities.[55] However, the Iranian regime's attempt to indoctrinate Iraqi prisoners was at a different level than that of the Iraqi regime. While the Iraqi regime's main aim appears to have been the extraction, frequently through torture, of information from its Iranian captives, the Iranians were more interested in transforming their captives. Iraqi prisoners suffered, often at the hands of their own compatriots, a systematic and relentless policy of "conversion" aimed at destroying their former identities and creating new ones. The practice sowed divisions among prisoners' ranks and forged hierarchies of power within the prison system based on degrees of collaboration with the Iranian authorities and their Iraqi allies. The repercussions of these practices were profound – not only on the prison population – but also on the manner in which their families were treated at home as well as the prisoners' reintegration into Iraqi society once they returned to Iraq.

Reports on the treatment of Iraqi prisoners in Iranian jails began filtering into Iraq after the repatriation of injured and sick prisoners through the mediation of the International Committee of the Red Cross and Turkey soon after the beginning of hostilities. It became clear that the Iranian government was using the Iraqi opposition in Iran, particularly members of the Da'wa Party and followers of Muhammad Baqir al-Hakim, to persuade Iraqi captives to recant their allegiance to the Ba'th Party and to its leader and join the opposition in Iran. Once back in Iraq, the released prisoners were visited by party cadres and asked to provide the names of Iraqi prisoners collaborating with the enemy in Iran (Figure 4.7).[56]

Given that Iran repatriated only 2,762 prisoners between 1980 and 1989, the party did not methodically collect information on the working of the prison camps. When more than forty thousand prisoners returned in the fall of 1990, the Iraqi regime, together with the Ba'th Party, began

54 BRCC 01–2479–0004–0290.
55 Corboz, "Uneasy humanitarianism," 37, and Brown, *Khomeini's Forgotten Sons*, p. 99.
56 BRCC 01–3496–0003–0046 to 0048.

FIGURE 4.7. Iran-Iraq war: Iraqi prisoners of war (Jean Guichard/Sygma/Corbis). Prisoners are holding pictures of Khomeini and Iraqi cleric Muhammad Baqir al-Sadr executed by the Ba'thist regime.

to systematically process the prisoners and debrief them. The Party created forms, questionnaires, and a system of reward and punishment for returning prisoners based on the information they provided about themselves and others who collaborated with the Iranian regime. The information from these records provides the basis of the following analysis of life in the prison camps in Iran. Although returning prisoners often provided formulaic praise for the leader, a large number of the debriefed prisoners had, at some point, collaborated with the Iranians or fought with the Badr brigade, the paramilitary arm of the Iraqi Shi'ite opposition parties in Iran. Others were Ba'thist commissars who had, by their own reckoning, heroically resisted the attempts of their collaborating compatriots to break them. All, however, offer quite consistent descriptions of life at the camps.

The Iranian regime viewed the prison camps as ideological schools and recruitment centers. Drawing on the treatment of their own domestic political prisoners, prison authorities pressured and often tortured their Iraqi captives. Their purpose was not to obtain information about enemy capabilities, as their captives remained in prison for a long period after their initial interrogation. Rather they sought to transform the prisoners into "believers" (*mu'minun*).[57] Once they "converted," prison authorities designated them as repentant (*tawabun*). It is not clear from the reports what exactly such a conversion entailed.[58] The process began when prisoners were asked to give allegiance to Khomeini using the Islamic term *bay'a*. Prison authorities forced Iraqis to partake in political education meetings in which pro-Khomeini and anti-Ba'thist slogans were chanted. In addition, the leaders of Friday prayers within the camps were Iraqi "converts" who gave sermons on the utopian Islamic form of government under Khomeini. Interrogators as well as converts demanded that Ba'thist prisoners, particularly those who belonged to the higher echelons of the party, recant their Ba'thism, associated with the figure of Saddam Hussein and with the secularism of the un-Islamic order.[59] Non-Muslims, such as Mandaens and Christians, were pressured to convert to Islam and endured education sessions set up as debates with religious scholars to persuade them to leave their faith. When minority prisoners refused to convert, they were isolated in separate cells or taken to prison camps known for harsh living conditions.[60]

The impact of these policies on the prison population was devastating. To survive, a large number of prisoners "converted," although the majority did not partake in the disciplining or torture of other Iraqis. In effect, they became complicit in a policy in which access to the necessities for survival was predicated on their suspending their former identities, informing on other prisoners, or participating in their discipline. Rebellion within the prison camps was rampant. The Gorang prison rebellion of 1984 was the most publicized because it took place while the International Committee of the Red Cross was visiting the prison. Hunger strikes and confrontations with Iraqi prisoners and their Islamist parties' allies in the prisons were frequent. Attempts by Iraqi prisoners, sometimes led by military officers or Ba'th Party commissars, to organize cells within prison camps led to punishment of the organizers and participants. Ultimately, however, the mode of operation for most prisoners was survival.[61] While the leadership of the prison camps, that is to say, the guards, the proselytizers, and the torturers came from the Shi'i south,

[57] Ervand Abrahamian, *Tortured Confessions, Prison and Public Recantation in Modern Iran* (Berkeley: University of California Press, 1999) offers an insightful analysis of the aim of torture and recantation in a highly ideological regime such as Iran's in the 1980s. Torture methods include waterboarding, solitary confinement, and whipping.

[58] BRCC 01–3665–0001–0106.

[59] BRCC 01–3665–0001–0006 to 0053.

[60] Interview with Abu Mukhlis, Amman, Jordan, August 7, 2007.

[61] BRCC 01–3665–0001–0053 to 0054.

"believers" were from across the Iraqi ethnic, sectarian, political, and socioeconomic spectrum.

A remarkable report by a high-ranking Ba'th Party commissar from Najaf who was taken prisoner in 1982 and released in 1990 addressed the widespread phenomenon of Iraqi collaboration in prison camps. Part of the problem was the concerted propaganda efforts of the "turbaned" ones and their allies among the Communist Party, the Da'wa Party, the Kurdish nationalist parties, and those Iraqis of "Iranian affiliation" who had been expelled from the country. The Iranians allowed these groups to form military units within the camps, and they led the interrogation and education committees and they were the torturers. The Iranians and their allies, according to this report, were able to recruit about seven thousand prisoners to join the Badr brigade. The core of the penal and the propaganda apparatus of the camps was made up of recruits from the Islamist and other opposition parties and those prisoners known as the "repentant" who managed the camps' cultural and social life. The rest of the prisoners, however, became "believers" because they had despaired that the war was going to end and found the camp life too difficult. They were from all classes and included doctors, military officers, and Ba'thists, as well as members of the poorer classes from all areas of Iraq.[62]

Ba'th Party commissars and their counterparts at home kept close record of the prisoners of war and their families. At home, Ba'th Party cadres distributed the letters from prisoners sent to their families through the International Committee of the Red Cross after having read them to make sure that they were politically innocuous. Visits to families of prisoners of war by party cadres were not only meant to "perpetuate ties," but also to ensure that these families remained under surveillance.[63] Party commissars who had been prisoners themselves devised a system of classification that assigned guilt to collaborating prisoners of war according to a hierarchy used by the regime in the 1990s to reward and punish returning prisoners. Soon after the largest repatriation of prisoners took place in the summer and fall of 1990, the regime designated the prisoners who had "converted" as "apostates," using a religious language that echoed that of the Iranian regime. The use of the term "apostate" by the regime emphasized that these prisoners had betrayed their sacred duty to their nation and hence deserved their exclusion from rights as citizens. It was up to the Ba'th Party and the regime to determine the extent of their

---

[62] BRCC 01–3665–0001–0098 to 0102.
[63] BRCC 01–3212–0001–0696 to 0703.

inclusion, backed by information gathered by commissars on the individuals' level of collaboration within the prison camps.[64] Many of these
prisoners declared "apostates" in 1990 played an important role in the
uprising that shook the foundation of the Iraqi regime in March 1991.

Managing Territories of War and Insurgency

The leadership of the armed forces divided the war front into the northern, middle, and southern sectors. For much of the war, the southern
and northern sectors saw the largest deployment of men and military
ordnance and experienced the heaviest fighting. Of the seven army corps
divided among these sectors, the First and Fifth were deployed in the
north, while the Third, Fourth, Sixth, and Seventh Army Corps were
stationed in the south. Mobile units of Special Forces as well as divisions of the Republican Guard supported the army corps divisions, the
vast majority of them infantry. After 1982, when Iraq had to preserve its
defensive positions in the face of the Iranian push into Iraqi territory, the
regime developed a series of techniques to alter the physical and human
landscape of Iraqi Kurdistan and southeastern Iraq. Its aim was to push
back as well as to defend these territories threatened by Iran, to eliminate
any topographic and human barriers that allowed for the control of territory by Iranian-supported insurgent Kurds and Shi'i Islamist parties,
and to deal in an effective way with the problem of deserters by depriving
them of a refuge.

To a large degree, the logic informing the policies used by the military
and the Ba'th Party drew on the counterinsurgency techniques used in the
1970s against the Kurdish guerillas. The Kurds were familiar with these
techniques: the designation of areas of guerilla activities as spaces to be
"cleansed," the destruction of villages, the forcible movements of populations and their resettlement.[65] The 1980s marked a qualitative and quan-
titative shift in the techniques used by the regime. For the first time, the
southeastern territories of Iraq were militarized and remapped according
to the security exigencies created by the war. At the same time, the Ba'th

---

[64] See Chapter 6.

[65] For a good summary on Ba'thist policies that provide a background to the Anfal Campaign,
see Joost Hiltermann, "Case Study: The 1988 *Anfal* Campaign in Iraqi Kurdistan," *Online
Encyclopedia of Mass Violence*, February 2008, http://www.massviolence.org/The-1988-
Anfal-Campaign-in-Iraqi-Kurdistan?artpage=9–11 accessed April 6, 2011. For a general
history of the Kurds, see Martin Van Bruinessen, *Agha, Shaikh and State: The Social
History and Political Structures of Kurdistan* (London: Zed Books, 1992).

Party headquarters in the northern and southern region became a clearinghouse for the actions of the military and security forces. Finally, the logic of counterinsurgency gave cover to what became a policy of ethnic cleansing of the Kurdish population that included the use of chemical weapons.[66]

On April 19, 1983, the Ba'th Party offices in the city of Amara in Maysan province hosted a special meeting to address the growing problem of deserters and absentee soldiers within the armed forces who had taken refuge in the southern frontier marshes (*al-Ahwar*) that extended from the province of Wasit to that of Basra. Ali Hasan al-Majid, then deputy of the general secretary of the Ba'th Party, the leaders of the Third and Fourth Army Corps, the director of the general security services, and the representative of the military intelligence service of the south attended the meeting.[67]

al-Majid asked the secretary of the party's Southern Bureau to coordinate plans for a military operation with the other agencies whose representatives attended the meeting. The secretary obliged and "Operation Peace" was launched. The headquarters of the military operation in Maysan included high-ranking officers from the Third and Fourth Army Corps, representatives from the Popular Army, and the police. On May 3, more than sixteen thousand soldiers drawn from the two army corps, the Popular Army, and security services undertook a military operation supported by the use of helicopter gunships. The operation lasted three days and yielded 538 arrests and 189 deaths, as well as a trove of light weapons, animals, and boats. A public execution of deserters in Maysan crowned the operation and was attended by the heads of other regional party bureaus, the leader of the Fourth Army Corps, a number of officers and soldiers from the Popular Army, and notables from the southern area. al-Majid, who had ordered the execution ceremony, provided the guidelines of the speech that the secretary of the Maysan branch delivered before the "traitors" and the attendees.[68]

The operation marked a turning point in the way the regime conducted the war on the southern front at several levels. It was the first coordinated

---

[66] Human Rights Watch conducted an investigation in 1992–3 to establish that the Anfal Campaign can be classified as genocide. Its report was issued in 1993 under the title *Genocide in Iraq: The Anfal Campaign Against the Kurds*, http://www.hrw.org/reports/1993/iraqanfal/ANFAL1.htm accessed October 27, 2010.

[67] See BRCC 01–2219–0004–0022 to 0038 for the report by the secretary of the Southern Bureau of the party. al-Zaydi, *al-Bina' al-ma'nawi*, p. 350. The operation took place after Iranian troops had crossed Hawr al-Huwayza and reached the Basra-Baghdad highway.

[68] BRCC 01–2219–0004–0031 for the public execution and 0037–0038 for the speech.

effort by the various agencies and party bureaus to deal militarily with
the problem of desertion. It followed a general amnesty for deserters that
proved effective in inducing many to surrender. Between the end of the
operation and June 27, more than fifteen thousand soldiers surrendered
or were arrested by party cadres.[69] Furthermore, the Southern Bureau of
the party, rather than the military, was designated the coordinator of a
military operation in the marsh areas. Because the regime viewed desertion as a potential act of political insurgency, it assigned the party to
manage its suppression. It would deal with the insurgent north in a similar manner.

The secretary of the Southern Bureau was quick to seize on the implications of the new realities produced by "Operation Peace." The Ba'th
Party organizations and committees and the Popular Army positioned
themselves to become a linchpin in the military operations to control the
porous borders with Iran. In his report to the Office of the Presidency
about the operation, the secretary proposed a detailed mapping of the
habitation and populations of the Ahwar region – the geographic landscape, the terrain, and waterways that offered deserters mobility – and
their congregation points. He further proposed that the administrative
boundaries of the provinces of Wasit, Dhi Qar, Maysan, and Basra be
redlined to ensure that the Ahwar areas were isolated from the towns
and larger cities of the south. A central Maysan-based committee – led
by the secretary of the Ba'th Party branch with members from the various security, military, and intelligence agencies – should spearhead the
mapping of the Ahwar region and coordinate military pursuit of deserters. Subcommittees replicating the composition and function of the
central committee were to be set up at the smallest administrative level
in the southern areas. Among the prerogatives of their local heads was
the ability to call on the military and the use of helicopter gunships to
destroy the hideouts of deserters and "saboteurs" in the Ahwar region.[70]
Over the following three years, the party's Southern Bureau coordinated
various military and security agencies' efforts to reshape the southern
marshlands of Iraq. To ensure the programmatic enforcement of the
policy, the Bureau expanded to include thirteen new divisions and four
branches.[71]

---

[69] Ibid., page 0031. The exact numbers are 12,884 surrendered and 2,843 arrested in the
southern provinces. The numbers of soldiers who surrendered to their military units is
unknown.

[70] BRCC 01–2219–0004–0039 to 0040.

[71] BRCC 01–3212–0001–0549 to 0550.

In the spring of 1985, Iraqi troops fought the bloody battle of *Taj al-Ma'arik* (The Crown of Battles) to beat Iranian soldiers who had advanced to the Basra-Baghdad highway through the Hawr al-Huwayza marsh. The regime and the military leadership in the southern sector concluded that the only way to secure the southern marshes was to create a *cordon sanitaire* empty of population and cleared of all vegetation. They had a template for such a policy at hand. In 1977–8, the regime had deported, by its own admission, twenty-eight thousand Kurdish families to create a *cordon sanitaire* along the Iranian border abutting the Sulaimaniyya province.[72] Prevented from returning to its villages, the population was resettled by the government in collective residential complexes on main highways of Kurdistan or around large cities. A similar process took shape in the south. On March 25, 1985, the Ministry of Defense sent a request to the Office of the Presidency to destroy villages and cut down reeds and palm groves in the marsh areas to secure a defensive barrier that would prevent Iranian troops from reaching the crucial Basra-Baghdad highway. By April, the committee tasked with planning the undertaking oversaw a military and civilian operation that cleared the marsh areas from the town of Uzayr in the north to the marshes of al-Qurna at the mouth of the Shatt-al-Arab waterway. More than twenty-five thousand people were uprooted and twenty-one villages destroyed. By January 1986, most of the population had been resettled in Dhi Qar province.[73] Party cadres in Basra organized trips by citizens and school-children to help clear the marshes in an effort to turn the undertaking into a popular project waged in defense of the southern front.[74] In the al-Qurna area of Shatt al-Arab, as Iranian shelling intensified, the Ba'th Party coordinated with the military to clear terrain that had been thick with palm groves.[75] Once these areas were cleared, the party set up headquarters to monitor deserters and infiltrators. These were military outposts manned by members of the party's security committees and the Popular Army. The creation of a *cordon sanitaire* in the marshlands was

---

[72] This was by no means the first deportation and resettlement of Kurds in the 1970s. In 1975, an Iraqi official admitted that fifty thousand Kurds had been deported to the southern provinces of Nasiriyya and Qadisiyya. Human Rights Watch, "Ba'athist and Kurds," *Genocide in Iraq*, p. 7. For the operation in the southern marshes, the regime drew on the expertise of the minister of the Region of Autonomous Rule. The regime made him a member of the committee that planned and oversaw the operation. BRCC 023–2–2–0030 to 0143.

[73] BRCC 023–2–2–0030 to 0143.

[74] BRCC 01–3212–0001–0546 to 0550.

[75] BRCC 01–2062–0001–0389.

not completely successful in limiting their use by deserters and Shi'i opposition party fighters allied to Iran. In January 1987, during a major military thrust by the Iranians to conquer Basra, insurgents in the marshes of
Maysan province were able to fire rockets at party headquarters.[76]

The year 1987 proved critical in escalating the scale and intensity of the
regime's counterinsurgency campaign in the southeastern marshes and the
northern areas dominated by the Kurdish insurgents. The Kurdish insurgency in the north was gaining ground and had facilitated the Iranian
military movement into Iraqi territory. In the south, Shi'i Islamist parties drew on deserters to wage a low-intensity insurgency in the Ahwar
region. Coming in the midst of a retreat of Iraqi armed forces, an attempt
on Saddam Hussein's life, and a sustained effective Iranian military campaign, the insurgencies in both areas were threatening the regime's survival. In the north, as will become clear, the legal, administrative, and
military wheels for the ethnic cleansing of the Kurdish population were
set in February 1987. In the marshes, the regime drew the outlines of a
policy that would lead to draining of the marshlands and periodic military operations in the 1990s.

In keeping with the regime's plan, the Southern Bureau coordinated
a military operation against areas in the marshlands that had a congregation of "saboteurs." The operation's tactics included using poison and
burning or blowing up houses that sheltered the targets and recruiting
deserters to undertake assassinations. The Popular Army, military, and
security agencies carried out periodic preemptive operations designed to
punish potential supporters. As in the 1983 operation, helicopter gunships were deployed to hunt down deserters and destroy the villages that
harbored them. An economic blockade was imposed on the marsh areas.
Unauthorized vehicles, including public transportation, were not allowed
into towns and villages unless they had special permission from the security apparatus. Food companies were prohibited from marketing in the
area; vendors selling food products to insurgents or deserters were subject to severe punishment. Marsh inhabitants were not allowed to sell
their fish outside the area and their boats were confiscated. At the same
time, the government began to consider the systematic implementation of
a policy it had initiated in 1985. It commissioned a study to examine the
possibility of moving the inhabitants of the marshes to inland areas that
would be easier to control. In addition, the regime considered draining
the marshlands and laying out roads to open them to easy movement.[77]

---

[76] BRCC 01–2062–0001–0345.
[77] The report is reproduced in Hiltermann, Watch, *Bureaucracy of Repression*, pp. 152–4.

The militarization and designation of the southern sector of Iraq as a territory of counterinsurgency was a direct product of the Iran-Iraq war. In the north, however, successive Iraqi governments had faced a nationalist insurgency with clear territorial claims. The framework of the Ba'thist regime's policies toward Kurdish territories developed between 1974 and 1979. These included the redrawing of administrative boundaries, the development of a bureaucratic, legal, and security apparatus that singled out these areas as potentially insurgent, and the forcible movement of rural populations into residential complexes near major Kurdish cities or in the Arab south. By the late summer of 1980, the regime could claim with some confidence that its main internal problem was not the weak Kurdish insurgency in the north and its communist allies, but the Shi'i Islamist Da'wa Party in Baghdad and southern Iraq.

The outbreak of hostilities with Iran derailed the government's attempts to settle what it termed the "Kurdish Question." The Kurdish nationalist parties and their allies mounted an effective insurgency, drawing logistical and economic support from Iran. During the first two years of the war, much of the fighting took place in the southern and middle sectors of the front and on Iranian territories. The government directed its military resources toward conquering and retaining Iranian territories and, after the beginning of 1982, to setting up defensive lines along the southern borders with Iran. In the Region of Autonomous Rule, the government retained its hold of the major cities and corridors around highways, but gradually lost control of the rural areas to the *peshmergas* of the Kurdish Democratic Party and the Patriotic Union of Kurdistan. Divisions of the First and Fifth Army Corps, headquartered in Kirkuk and Arbil, respectively, were mobilized to fight on the Iranian border. Rural military posts were abandoned or were manned by inexperienced troops from the Popular Army.

By late 1985, when the Patriotic Union of Kurdistan joined the insurgent Kurdish Democratic Party, a great deal of the rural areas bordering Iran and Turkey had become the core of the insurgent territory, while the main cities, particularly Dohuk and Sulaimaniyya, had a number of effective insurgent cells.[78] The refuge these areas provided for the increasing numbers of Iraqi army deserters, many of them non-Kurds, compounded the political and military repercussions of the loss of control of borders with Iran. Between late 1985 and 1987, the regime and the insurgents engaged in open but inconclusive warfare. The Northern Bureau and its secretary, Muhammad Hamza al-Zubaydi, played a pivotal role in

---

[78] Human Rights Watch, "Ba'athists and Kurds," *Genocide*, p. 11.

managing the diverse population under the broad outlines of a policy that would lead to the more systemic ethnic cleansing of Kurds. In March 1987, al-Zubaydi submitted a report of his tenure to the Office of the Presidency, the Ministry of the Affairs of the North, and the General Secretariat of the party. The report mapped out in detail the human, political, and topographic terrain of northern Iraq and gave an account of the counterinsurgency operations against opposition parties.[79]

During this period, the Northern Bureau's counterinsurgency campaign was overseen by the Central Coordinating Security Committee, whose meetings were attended at times by al-Majid as the representative of Saddam Hussein, the head of the Committee of Northern Affairs, as well as commanders of the First and Fifth Army Corps and military intelligence. It coordinated the various counterinsurgency operations in the area; oversaw the National Defense Battalions; reported on and punished "saboteurs"; monitored "hostile" activity within cities, schools, and university campuses; and ensured that orders issued by the Revolutionary Command Council's National Security Council were implemented.

At the heart of the counterinsurgency campaign in the north was the mapping out of territories of insurgent activity and linkage with the ethnic and religious composition of the various villages and districts.[80] Consequently, beginning in 1983, much of rural Kurdistan was designated a "prohibited area." These areas, considered "liberated" by the rebels since 1983, had been subject to an economic blockade and restrictions on entry and exit from villages. Iraqi military aircraft bombed villages intermittently, and individuals caught carrying arms were subject to life imprisonment. Government personnel, such as teachers, were withdrawn from schools.[81] Well into 1987, the Kurdish nationalist parties and their Iraqi communist allies had succeeded in creating an intricate system of hideaways and tunnels in this rural landscape, and their presence became part of the rhythm of everyday life of the villages under their control.

---

[79] BRCC 01–2140–0003–0070 to 0123.

[80] The Northern Bureau purview encompassed the Region of Autonomous Rule (Arbil, Dohuk, and Sulaimaniyya provinces) and Ninewah. However, in 1985, the province of Ninewah's party organization was split in two, one covering the province and the other the city of Mosul and its immediate environs. The Northern Bureau's area of operation extended over 85,168 square kilometers and included 3,760,244 inhabitants. Of these, 2,064,712 were Kurds, 1,696,399 were Arabs, and 99,133 were Turcoman. The designation of Arab is misleading. Assyrians, who speak a distinct language and did not self-identify as ethnically Arab, were designated as Arab by the government. BRCC 01–2140–0003–0071.

[81] Human Rights Watch, "Ba'athists and Kurds," *Genocide*, p. 6.

They had developed techniques to protect their inhabitants against periodic army incursions. Few infantry divisions were able to penetrate the "liberated" areas. Nor could the economic blockage and the restriction of movement in and out of rural Kurdistan do much to stop the inflow of goods and military hardware from Iran.[82]

Between 1985 and 1987, al-Zubaydi led a committee that included the governors of areas that came under the jurisdiction of the Northern Bureau and representatives of the First and Fifth Army Corps as well as the director of general security in the Kurdish provinces. The sphere of counterinsurgency measures and operations covered two areas: those designated as "prohibited" since 1983 (some 1,815 villages) and those villages within the Region of Autonomous Rule, as well as Ninewah and Ta'mim provinces, that had pocket of "saboteurs." The committee proposed that the economic embargo, hitherto confined to the "prohibited areas," be extended to all villages that had insurgent activities or whose inhabitants were providing foot soldiers for the "saboteurs." The committee oversaw the assessment of the property of citizens in villages that had become centers of insurgent activity outside the "prohibited area." The work of the committee was done in secret since the government anticipated the need for information in its future fight against insurgents.

Central to the mapping of villages within and outside the "prohibited areas" was the policy of destruction (*hadm*) and eradication ('*izalat*) of villages that harbored insurgents or were centers of insurgent activity. Between 1985 and March 1987, the military, at the behest of the central government, destroyed and eradicated several villages in the hope of forcing their Kurdish inhabitants to stop providing shelter and bases for insurgents. The inhabitants of destroyed villages were resettled in residential complexes, and their men were encouraged to join the National Defense Battalions.[83]

The recommendations issued by al-Zubaydi's committee called for extending the rules governing the management of the insurgency in the "prohibited areas" to all Kurdish areas that harbored insurgents. In effect, it called for a more generalized and systematic approach to the "Kurdish Question." During al-Zubaydi's tenure, however, the insurgency in the north continued unabated. In March 1987, Saddam Hussain

---

[82] Yusuf Abu al-Fawz, *Tadharis al-Ayam fi Dafatir Naseer* (*The Traces of Days in the Journals of an Advocate*) (Damascus: Dar al-Thaqafa wa al-Nashr, 2002). The author was an Iraqi communist party guerilla fighting along with the *peshmergas* during the war.
[83] BRCC 01–2140–0003–0109 to 0112.

appointed Ali Hasan al-Majid to lead the party's Northern Bureau in Kirkuk. al-Majid was mandated with coordinating the military campaign against the Kurdish insurgents meant to settle the Kurdish national question once and for all. Granted extraordinary new powers, he was to "represent the Regional Command of the Party and the Revolutionary Command Council in the execution of their policies for the whole of the Northern Region, including the Region of Autonomous Rule, for the purpose of protecting security and order, safeguarding stability, and applying autonomous rule in the region." al-Majid's "decisions shall be mandatory for all state agencies, be they military, civilian and security." In the words of the Human Rights Watch's report, al-Majid's power in the Region of Autonomous Rule was equivalent to the power of the president of Iraq.[84] Between his appointment and April 1989, he presided over and shaped a policy that transformed a war of counterinsurgency into a systematic campaign to ethnically cleanse the Kurdish areas where insurgents operated. The campaign was carried out in several stages and culminated in a series of military campaigns, eight in all, known as the *Anfal*, which included the use of a scorched earth policy, economic boycott, chemical weapons, and the forcible movement and killing of Kurdish civilians.

As head of the Northern Bureau and effective ruler of the northern sector, al-Majid coordinated a number of agencies. The military operations, the use of helicopter gunships, and the dropping of chemical ordnance were carried out by the First and Fifth Army Corps. The National Defense Battalions, the Popular Army, military intelligence of the northern sector, and security forces did much of the scouting, intelligence gathering, and policing during these operations. al-Majid issued a series of directives to instruct these various agencies on how to deal with insurgents, civilians, the wounded, and the disappeared. In the spring of 1987, al-Majid expanded the system of legal, economic, and administrative restrictions imposed on the "prohibited areas." As al-Majid put it, the decision to "destroy and collectivize" villages was meant to "draw a dividing line between us and the saboteurs."[85] The military and security agencies cooperated in redrawing a map of villages within the prohibited areas marked for destruction. Their population was given up to fifteen days to leave and resettle in complexes. Then, their houses were dynamited and

[84] Human Rights Watch, "Prelude to *Anfal*," *Genocide*, p. 3. The quote is from Revolutionary Command Council decree no. 160. See Appendix III for al-Majid's report on the number of villages destroyed. BRCC 01–2140–0003–00064.

[85] Human Rights Watch, "Prelude to *Anfal*," *Genocide*, p. 4.

bulldozed, their animals killed, and farming prohibited. To highlight the seriousness of its intent, the military used chemical weapons, a practice it had used extensively against Iranian combatants but not against its own civilian population. Between April and July 1987, 1,444 villages were eradicated, 26,399 families were forced to resettle, and 663 insurgents and more than 22,000 deserters and absentees had surrendered to the authorities.[86]

The security and party agencies relocated the uprooted population to complexes along main highways and maintained close watch over their movement. Any contact between the inhabitants of these complexes and residents of villages in the "prohibited areas" was outlawed. Alongside the military operations, a series of laws and directives deprived the civilian population of the villages of their civil rights, confiscated their property, and decreed that first-degree relatives of "saboteurs" were criminals and subject to execution. By June 1987, al-Majid decreed that all inhabitants who had chosen to remain in the "prohibited areas" were "saboteurs." Those who chose to "repent" could rejoin the "national fold" and settle in residential complexes. They needed to fill out forms and register for the upcoming census. If they did not do so, the Iraqi government would consider them a fifth column within the nation.[87] The bureaucracy and military strategy for the Anfal campaign was set. The military operation started in February 1988 and ended in August of that year. Having decreed that villagers who continued to reside in the "prohibited areas" were "saboteurs," the regime's strategy was to uproot or eliminate all the inhabitants and destroy their means of sustenance.

Three aspects of the Anfal campaign distinguish it from the earlier campaign. The first was the determination to destroy the territory's ability to sustain all forms of life. The regime made extensive and systematic use of chemical weapons not only to create fear among the population and induce villagers to flee, but also to destroy any possibility of their return to habitation and cultivation. This logic, above all, governed the use of chemical weapons in Anfal. That explains, to a large degree, why the regime did not consider the gassing on March 16 of the border town of Halabja, which had fallen briefly to Iranians with the help of the insurgents, as part of the Anfal. The regime claimed that its use of chemical weapons was justifiable in a defensive military operation against Iranians.

---

[86] BRCC 01–2140–0003–0064. The figures are from a report written by al-Majid in 1989 and submitted to the General Secretariat of the party.

[87] Human Rights Watch, "Prelude to *Anfal*," *Genocide*, pp. 18–19.

Furthermore, unlike in 1987, the military and Ba'thist leadership did not give residents of the "prohibited areas" the option of returning to the "national fold" or resettlement. Kurds who fled the military operations faced myriad dangers. A great many were killed. The army and National Defense Battalions coordinated the movement of survivors to detention camps. Others were abandoned in residential complexes where they had little shelter or sustenance. A large number were "disappeared," probably killed and buried in mass graves. For the regime, the radical suppression of Kurdish national claims made by the insurgents could only be accomplished by the physical elimination of the landscape and the population that provided them with the territory to launch their rebellion. Kurds have coined a verb to designate the victims of this kind of violence: they have been *Anfalized*. Human Rights Watch has estimated that upward of fifty thousand were killed.[88]

On September 6, the Revolutionary Command Council decreed a general amnesty for all Iraqi Kurds inside the country as well as the tens of thousands who had fled to Turkey in the last phases of the Anfal campaign. The amnestied population included deserters, Christian Assyrians who lived in predominantly Kurdish areas, as well as members of the National Defense Battalions. In effect, the regime used the amnesty to deprive Iraqi Kurds as well as the Assyrians of their civil and social rights. They could not be nominated for membership in the National Assembly, lease, buy, or sell state property, or work for private businesses contracted by the state. The decree was effective for two years. After that period, citizens who proved through "proper conduct" and "good intentions" that they had ended their "collaboration" with "saboteurs" could have their rights restored.[89] In a report on the Anfal campaign widely circulated among party organizations in 1989, al-Majid boasted that the campaign had deprived the "saboteurs" of the "human power to wage their war against the nation." It had created stability and security in the Kurdish areas and demonstrated, through the Battalions' participation in the campaign, the "deep" ties Kurds had to Iraq.[90]

Human rights organizations and the Kurdish Regional Government have viewed the Anfal campaign through the historically tortured relations of the Kurdish national movement with the central government. While the Anfal is certainly a Kurdish tragedy, it needs to be understood

---

[88] Joost Hiltermann, "Case Study: The 1988 *Anfal* Campaign in Iraqi Kurdistan."
[89] Human Rights Watch, "The Amnesty and its Exclusions," *Genocide*, pp. 1–3.
[90] BRCC 01–2140–0003–0058.

in the context of the Ba'thist regime's war against what it viewed as insurgent territories during the Iran-Iraq war. To secure its borders with Iran, the Ba'thist regime waged a counterinsurgency that sought to alter the human and physical landscape of its southern and northern borders. The regime set up the bureaucratic, military, and legal framework for the Anfal campaign in the same year it began to plan the draining and depopulation of the southern marshes. It implemented its plans for the south in the 1990s. Furthermore, the south provided the organizational blueprint for managing the campaign against the Kurds. The Southern Bureau coordinated the first sustained campaign against the population of the marshes in 1983, a model the regime followed when it assigned the task of coordinating the Anfal campaign to the Northern Bureau of the Ba'th. In its violence against insurgent territories and populations during wartime, the regime made little distinction between Arab and Kurd. It is because the Kurds were much better insurgents with a history of fighting for their national rights and expertise in organizing the territory under their control that the campaign against them was so lethal.

Conclusion

The triumphalism in the regime's postwar rhetoric concealed its disastrous political and social repercussions. It had waged a long war on two fronts, one against a national enemy and one against sectors of its own population. If the regime had managed to preserve Iraq's territorial sovereignty and national unity among its Arab population, it had destroyed any possibility of reaching a compromise with its Kurdish population. Through its practices against insurgent territories and populations in the north and south of the country, it exacerbated regional differences, reshaped the human and geographic environment, and created deep fissures among the various sectors of Iraqi society. Among its southern Arab population, particularly Iraqis who hailed from areas most affected by the war and counterinsurgency, the conflict created long-lasting grievances. The war on the marshes, a war in which both the government and the Shi'i Islamist opposition parties share blame, laid the foundation for the intense violence that accompanied the 1991 uprising and the destruction of these marshes in the 1990s. Equally troubling were the techniques developed by the regime and its various agencies, particularly the Ba'th Party, to deal with the categories of people, soldiers, deserters, prisoners of war, and "saboteurs" created by the war. Extrajudicial punishment, corruption, and paternalism, accompanied by layers of surveillance and record keeping, ensured that every Iraqi soldier on the front or his family at home were made aware of the rewards and punishments that acceptance or refusal to be part of the war effort brought. That Iraqi conscripts continued to desert in such large numbers speaks to the limits of the apparatus set up to control them.

5

Things Fall Apart

Two days before the beginning of the air war against Iraq, Waddah Hasan's editor at the *al-Qadissiyya* newspaper summoned him to a press conference. The meeting was meant to be a joint briefing by Saddam Hussain and UN Secretary General Perez de Cuellar on a last-ditch effort to avert war with the U.S.-led coalition that Waddah, like many Iraqis, viewed as suicidal for both the regime and Iraq. When Saddam Hussain entered the room without de Cuellar, Waddah and his colleagues were filled with foreboding. Hussain said that the attempts at reaching an agreement had failed, reassured those at the meeting of the strength and preparedness of the Iraqi armed forces, took questions from the journalists, and departed. The version later shown on Iraqi television omitted, according to Waddah, the moment when Hussain told journalists, "Live and die over Kuwait."[1]

Of the many hyperbolic statements Saddam Hussain made in his career, this one was closest to the truth. The war, the ensuing uprising, and the UN-imposed sanctions did not destroy the regime, but they did deplete state institutions, weaken and transform the Ba'th Party, and, perhaps most important, decimate the fabric of Iraqi society. To mobilize the population between the invasion and occupation of Kuwait on August 2 and the beginning of the air war on January 17, the regime and the party drew on the repertoire of techniques they had developed during the Iran-Iraq war. Their success was limited. The party could not justify the war as a defensive one, nor could it muster the resources to plan for what all, including the regime, saw as a struggle between the life and

[1] Interview with Waddah Hasan, Amman, Jordan, June 21, 2007.

death of the politics of Ba'thist Iraq. Internally, the regime and the party were in disarray. The Ba'th Party, so adept at managing the social costs of the earlier war, could do little in the face of the pummeling of civilian infrastructure experienced in cities like Baghdad and Basra. The ground war and the chaotic and deadly withdrawal of the Iraqi army fueled the massive uprising that followed.

The *Intifada*, as the Iraqis call the March 1991 uprising, nearly destroyed the Iraqi regime. As the most cataclysmic event in the history of Ba'thist Iraq, its meaning continues to be a flashpoint in current Iraqi politics. The regime, as well as the Shi'i Islamist opposition that dominates the politics of post-2003 Iraq, described it in sectarian terms. The latter continues to paint the Intifada as a rebellion by the Shi'i majority against the Sunni-dominated regime. The former accused the Shi'i Islamist parties of orchestrating the rebellion with Iranian support. However, the Intifada was a spontaneous, localized, and largely nonsectarian uprising. Although fueled by the breakdown of the military and the violence that accompanied the end of the First Gulf War, it was a rebellion against the routine practices of the regime and the party bureaucracy that had developed in the south during the Iran-Iraq war. In the Kurdish north, the Intifada marked the beginnings of the rudiments of a relatively autonomous regional political order controlled by the same Kurdish parties that had been victims of the regime's ethnic cleansing policies during the 1980s. In the south, the violent suppression of the Intifada marked the area and its population for an intense counterinsurgency campaign. The south became a territory of an internal war that included periodic military deployment, the transformation of the marshlands' geography, and forced population transfer. Throughout Iraq, however, the uprising and its suppression reinforced sectarian identities and regional fissures that continued to shape post-Ba'thist Iraq.

Until its fall in 2003, the regime's main goal was its own security. To that end, it engaged in two kinds of war: one against the international community, which continued to impose the UN-sanctioned embargo and attempt regime change, and one against its own population that had "betrayed" it. These wars, however, were waged under radically different international and national circumstances. Not only was it difficult for the leadership of the regime to continue drawing on Ba'thist and nationalist ideology to justify its disastrous political decisions, but it could also no longer afford to fund the state and party bureaucracies that had managed the consequences of the Iran-Iraq war. Saddam Hussain and his close advisers developed several strategies, often piecemeal and inconsistent, to survive. To combat the embargo, he and the Ba'th appealed to the language of humanitarianism to mobilize the international community against the sanctions. The social breakdown that ensued from the uprising and the embargo could no longer be addressed by appealing to the defunct Ba'th ideology. Instead, the regime began using religion as a means of social control. Weakened by the destruction visited on Iraq, the regime privatized the economy, state institutions, and security. Entrepreneurs, large and petty, drawn from all sects and ethnicities in Iraq, vied for a share of the emerging system. Ba'thist Party bureaucrats at all levels, Shi'i and Sunni clan leaders deemed loyal to the regime, martyrs' families, and thousands of state employees became adept at negotiating their own survival. The deployment of clan networks, Ba'thist connections, and communal loyalties were techniques of governing that cannot be understood simply as a manifestation of sectarianism, tribalism, or regionalism. Undergirding them was a kind of politics that can be best understood as the "politics of mercy and charity."

These techniques bespoke the regime's weakness and the state's withdrawal from Iraqi lives. Their effectiveness was episodic and irregular. They manifested the regime's obsession with projecting an illusion of power even as it lacked authority and hegemony. Iraqis, particularly in the south, were deemed traitors until proven otherwise. Their access to vital resources was made contingent on their loyalty and obedience. The increasing number of laws and decrees issued by the Revolutionary Command Council governing punishment of criminals, deserters, and "culprits" in the uprising were sporadically implemented and designed to elicit the mercy of the leader and bolster his diminishing power. With the drastic curtailment of the economic and political powers of the party and the state, the regime created a market of entitlements – in titles, positions, and access to precious resources. Access to these resources, granted as a matter of citizens' entitlement in the 1980s, was now made dependent on the leader's charity.

Despite its weakness and bankruptcy, the Ba'th Party played an important role in the management of the new order. Its cadres created information banks on the population in the aftermath of the Intifada, tracked down deserters, reported on rumors in the streets, forwarded requests for financial aid from Ba'th members to the Office of the Presidency, and organized mass public demonstrations of obedience to the regime. In many respects, its cadres continued to do what they had done during the Iran-Iraq war. However, they did so within the confines of the new politics of mercy and charity. They were far less effective than they had previously been as both a social and a security organization. If the copious Ba'th Party records of the 1990s are any indication, they point to a party, like the regime that it bolstered, more focused on form than substance.

The Mother of All Battles and the End of Days

Sabir Farah had a desk job at the headquarters of the al-Medina al-Munawarah division of the Republican Guard.[2] The al-Medina al-Munawarah was one of a number of Republican Guard units sent south to the desert outside Nasiriyya for training exercises focused on methods of intimidating Kuwaitis into conceding to the demands of the Iraqi government. On August 1, Sabir saw Lieutenant General Iyad al-Rawi, then head of the Republican Guard, poring over maps and indicating that the al-Medina al-Munawarah units should start deploying south into the desert. Most of the rank and file within the units were, according to Sabir, ordered to move, even though their weapons were not loaded and their vehicles were unequipped to avoid sinking in desert sand. Most were not told that they were expected to cross the border into Kuwait. Even Sabir, privy to the information because he was at the division headquarters, could not quite believe that the invasion had actually started. When he crossed the border and asked the Indian and Sudanese guards at the post if they were now in Kuwait, they confirmed his fears. His comrade's response to the border guards' inquiry as to why Iraqi soldiers were there was a sarcastic, "We are here to liberate Kuwait," to which the Sudanese border guards responded, "What is in Kuwait that you need to liberate? What does it mean to liberate it?"[3]

Whether Sabir's recollection of the exchange at the border crossing is accurate or not is moot. It demonstrates that the Iraqi military believed that the regime's claims were spurious and its actions arbitrary. Lack of military planning, the absence of coordination among institutions of state, party, and leadership, and the increasingly apocalyptic language employed by the regime as the looming war drew near served to highlight the sense of helplessness and impending doom that pervaded the press and personal narratives of this period. For the first time since its

---

[2] Najib al-Salhi, *al-Zizal* (*The Earthquake*), www.Iraq4all.dk/Zlzal/Zm.htm accessed April 28, 2008, p. 122. al-Salhi states that a large number of Republican Guards from the al-Medina al-Munawarah division surrendered on March 16.

[3] Interview with Sabir Farah, Amman, Jordan, July 22, 2007.

founding, the prospect of the Ba'thist state's end was conceivable, but so was the possibility of a foreign occupation of Iraq.

Meeting in Beirut in August 1990 and in Damascus in the following months, a coalition of Iraqi opposition groups began hammering out a vision of post-Ba'thist Iraq. The opposition included the Islamist Shi'i parties that had fought alongside Iran, Kurdish nationalist parties, the Iraqi Communist Party, some military leaders, and various groups who had suffered at the hands of the Ba'th, particularly during the Iran-Iraq war. The opposition issued a charter in December calling for the establishment of a democratic Iraq and urged Iraqi soldiers and civilians to rebel.[4] However, Muhammad Mahdi al-Jawihiri, the venerated leftist nationalist poet of Iraq exiled in Syria, cautioned his fellow opposition leaders that support for an uprising against the regime should be tempered by concern about foreign occupation. "All of us," he told the audience, "condemn the traitorous intervention on the part of the fascist and dictatorial Iraqi regime in the small and peaceful country of Kuwait. However, my dear brothers, there is a limit to everything, including punishment, and we will not accept crossing that limit."[5]

al-Jawihiri's warning of foreign occupation in 1991 proved premature, but it forewarned the scale of the war's destruction and the violence of the uprising that followed. The depleted Iraqi military was ill prepared for the new war technologies the coalition forces unleashed against it. Nor could it muster the same level of conscripts it had raised during the long war with Iran. Many of those called to military units simply did not show up. In areas around military bases and recruitment centers, soldiers called to the front engaged in acts of sabotage.[6] Others deserted their units in Kuwait when they were given short furloughs. The memoirs of Iraqi military leaders attest to the complete breakdown of morale and discipline among the rank and file.[7]

In Kuwait, the professional army, including the Republican Guard, became an occupying power subject to the monitoring of the Special Forces, intelligence, and various security agencies as well as Ba'th Party

---

[4] The Joint Working Committee of the Iraqi Opposition Forces, *Watha'iq al-Mu'tamar al-'Am li Qiwa al-Mu'arada al-'Iraqiyya* (*The Documents of the General Congress of Iraqi Opposition Forces*) (Beirut: np, 1991).

[5] Ibid., p. 116.

[6] NIDS/serial 2380437 to 2380459. This is a report from the Eastern Region's military intelligence headquarters from Ba'quba a month after the occupation of Kuwait. The report highlights the difficulty of getting soldiers to report for duty and their lack of discipline and drunkenness. It records some acts of sabotage and theft by soldiers in Kuwait.

[7] al-Salhi, *al-Zilzal*, pp. 1–10, and al-Hamadani, *Qabla an Yughadiruna*, pp. 237–48.

commissars. The predatory practices of the Iraqi regime's leadership in Kuwait, headed by Ali Hasan al-Majid and supported by relatives of Saddam Hussain, set the tone of the occupation and the chaotic withdrawal that followed. The Special Forces and the regime's inner circle systematically looted Kuwaiti assets. The looting by party cadres, petty officers, and soldiers paled in comparison. When the international media began reporting on the looting, the regime found scapegoats in some army officers and executed them publically in Kuwait.[8]

Communication between the leadership in Baghdad and the armed forces in Kuwait was marked by a total lack of understanding on the part of the former of the scale of the impending defeat. In a telling vignette, Saddam Hussain sent a letter to Ba'thist officers within the armed forces hunkered down in Kuwait after six weeks of air strikes. It reminded them of the greatness of the Arabs and Muslims and reassured them that the leadership of the armed forces had told him that the losses experienced by the air strikes were no more than the loss of an army corps in Qadisiyat Saddam. The officers took the missive to mean that the ground war was imminent.[9]

Within Iraq, the Ba'th Party attempted to manage the war as it had done earlier. Its cadres were hampered by several factors. Their communications with security services, crucial for collecting information on potential threats as well as deserters, was haphazard at best. The regime's leadership, which included that of the Ba'th, refused to plan for the war's aftermath and the possibility of an uprising. Thus, the party did not undertake any studies of the possible impact of the war as it had systematically during the Iran-Iraq war.[10] Coordination between the party and the various institutions and ministries of state was chaotic and intermittent. At the same time, a significant number of high-ranking cadres, and many more lower-ranking ones, fled their areas of residence in major cities like Baghdad, Basra, and Nasiriyya for safer areas.[11]

Given all these constraints in the months leading up to the war, the party played a role at several levels. It organized and armed a "volunteer" civilian paramilitary organization, *fida'iyun* (those who sacrifice themselves),

---

[8] al-Salhi, *al-Zilzal*, p. 7.
[9] Ibid.
[10] BRCC 01–3138–0000–0022 to 0027. This is a report written in August 1991 by an anonymous party member. He left it in an envelop at the General Secretariat. So critical of the military, Ba'thist, and political leadership was it that its author did not dare record his name.
[11] BRCC 01–2855–0002–0078.

to protect the regime and sent several divisions of the Popular Army to Kuwait.[12] It continued, with little success, to apprehend deserters and absentees. However, so great were their numbers and so depleted was the party of its working cadres that the endeavor seemed fruitless. Those high-ranking members sent to Kuwait abandoned their posts and returned home.[13] In the south, deserters from Kuwait flocked to the marsh area or simply returned home with little fear of being pursued.

Popular organizations such as the General Federation of Iraqi Women continued their work. Branch meetings addressed the regime's version of the invasion and ways to secure vital resources under the embargo. Together with the civil defense organizations, they provided public education on basic first aid. Teachers and students in colleges and secondary schools coordinated education sessions on civil defense.[14] The press duly reported these undertakings to reassure the public that the government and the party could deal with the impending war.

Another activity that occupied party cadres was the processing and debriefing of more than forty thousand returning prisoners of war between August and October 1990. Collecting information on those who had "converted" or had worked with the Iranian regime became particularly urgent.[15] This effort was undertaken as a coalition of opposition parties – including SAIRI, the Da'wa, and other parties funded by Iran – gathered in Damascus to discuss an alternative to the Iraqi regime. Any returning prisoners who had worked for these parties in Iranian prison camps could help foment an uprising against the regime. Thus debriefing them became essential. Cadres working in the various party divisions reported on their findings as well as on rumors circulating about the opposition. However, such reports to the General Secretariat were scarce during this period, attesting to the operational breakdown within the Ba'th bureaucracy.

The blockade on Iraq started early in August 1990, and the party, along with provincial and municipal authorities, managed the distribution of goods. Black marketeering in rations and corruption by party officials were widespread, particularly in the southern provinces. Party cadres became entrepreneurs, selling access to food and charging fees for managing the multitude of permissions and paperwork Iraqis had

[12] BRCC 024–5–2–0125 to 0127.
[13] BRCC 01–2855–0002–0185 to 0186 and 0192 to 0197.
[14] *al-Qadisiyya*, December 9, 1990, 6; December 13, 1990, 6; and December 16, 1990, 6–7.
[15] BRCC 01–3665–0001–0105 to 0108.

to obtain to live. As an example, in Basra, a high-ranking party member threatened to inform on men who had not reported to the military recruitment center unless he was paid.[16] These practices had begun during the Iran-Iraq war, but they became widespread as central control eroded during the First Gulf War. According to a report written by a Ba'th official during the March uprising, "some cadres within the party were more interested in private gain so they turned from strugglers to businessmen. This situation is known by the party organization as it is known by the citizens who can point out by name these businessmen."[17]

The disintegration of discipline and the lack of coordination among different parts of the government, party, and military were reflected in the increasingly incoherent and apocalyptic language of the leadership and the press in the months leading up to the war. The Iraqi press vacillated between analysis of the debates in the U.S. and international press on the implications of the involvement of the only superpower in a war against Iraq, the use of eschatological language to describe the division among Arabs, and the presence of American troops on Saudi soil, at the heart of the holiest sites of Islam.[18] These reports viewed the U.S. war on Iraq, like the Vietnam War, as an imperial onslaught by the sole hegemonic superpower against a Third World country. The *al-Qadisiyya* newspaper published reviews of films and books on the Vietnam War, all of them critical.[19] Many articles predicted a defeat for the U.S.-led forces, as had happened in Vietnam. That defeat was inevitable, according to one article, in no small part because God was on the side of the weak and the patient. On December 18, 1990, the Revolutionary Command Council and the Ba'th leadership published a statement in response to the escalating war rhetoric of the United States. It was addressed to the Iraqi and Arab nation:

There is a conspiracy against this nation that has been engineered by the international community and its slaves among the Arabs whose alliance serves the Americans and the Zionists.... The *umma* [Islamic nation] has been corrupted and sullied, the light of Islam has been hidden.... Iraq has risen in the name of God with its sword drawn in belief to destroy the center of spies who are agents

---

[16] Interview with Hazim Najm, Amman, Jordan, July 15, 2007.

[17] BRCC 01–3138–0000–0027.

[18] *al-Qadisiyya*, December 15, 1990, 5. The newspaper printed a translation of a *Time* magazine article on the debates in Congress about going to war in Iraq.

[19] See for example, *al-Qadisiyya*, December 20, 1990, 8 on the American media's coverage of the Vietnam War and in the same newspaper, January 7, 1991, 9, a translation of an article in *Newsweek* on a study of post-traumatic stress disorder suffered by veterans of the Vietnam War.

of the foreigner who had taken our land in Kuwait. The Gulf Arabs are not real Arabs, they are tribes [*'I'rab*] who are ignorant unbelievers.[20]

The regime had used conspiratorial and racial language against its enemies in the Iran-Iraq war. The turn to apocalyptic imagery, particularly of a religious nature, was new. It became more pronounced when the air war started and the civilian populations in the cities of Baghdad, Basra, Najaf, and Nasiriyya began experiencing the full impact of the military ordnance dropped on these cities. On January 15, 1991, Saddam Hussain decreed that the words *"Allahu Akbar"* ("God is Great") be added to the Iraqi flag. It was a cynical move, as was the use of apocalyptic imagery and language. The Iraqi press used increasingly opaque and often obscurantist language to describe the coming confrontation. According to one editorial entitled "The sacred law and the necessity of Iraqi victory":

It is the law of God, the one and only, that has become widespread and applicable in this great battle that Iraq is coming to with its leadership.... It has become the vanguard in its defense of humanity.... The sacred law will crown the victory of Iraq and defeat the dissolute unbelievers who have attacked us.[21]

Unwilling to take responsibility for its invasion of Kuwait and its subsequent refusal to withdraw, the regime resorted to framing the confrontation as one beyond history and rational action. The Mother of All Battles, the official name of the war, was one in which strategic military and political thinking was jettisoned for a logic that pitted forces beyond history in a war in which the virtuous would vanquish the evildoers. Despite the regime's cynical manipulation of religious language, its use of such language reflected the desperation and isolation of the leadership during the war.

As the air war continued to wreak havoc on Iraq's infrastructure and urban flight commenced, the regime devolved part of its decision making on questions of security to the Ba'th. On January 29, Saddam Hussain issued a letter to the General Secretariat of the Ba'th expanding its prerogatives and allowing party cadres independence in decision making during the war. The party leadership decided to oversee internal security with the help of the Popular Army. It attempted to find retired military officers and asked them to defend the regime by infiltrating the northern and southern regions dressed in civilian clothes. They were to gather information, find "unpatriotic" elements that did not support the war,

[20] *al-Qadisiyya*, December 18, 1990, 1.
[21] *al-Qadisiyya*, February 7, 1991, 3.

and execute them.[22] So concerned was the Ba'th leadership that a popular uprising against the leadership would ensue after the war, it admonished party cadres to guard the pictures of Saddam Hussain so they would not be vandalized.[23]

Apocalyptic language was not merely a cynical tool employed by the regime. It reflected the violence of the occupation of Kuwait and the ferocity of the air campaign against retreating Iraqi soldiers. It pervaded the recollections of Iraqi soldiers, U.S. soldiers, and reporters who covered the bombing campaign along the six-lane Highway 80 that started on February 26, 1991 and lasted for two days.[24] According to Tony Clifton, a reporter for *Newsweek* embedded in the Tiger Brigade that did much of the bombing:

The group of vehicles we hit included petrol tankers and tanks, so the tanks exploded in these great fountains of white flame from the ammunition.... You could see the little figures of soldiers coming out with their hands up. It really looked like a medieval hell ... because of the great flames and then those weird contorted figures.... Next morning we went up to see what we'd done ... there were bodies all over the place. And I remember at one point looking down at the track and I was up to my ankles in blood. The tracks had been filled with blood, and there were very white-faced men going round saying, "Jesus. Did we really do this?"[25]

For Sabir Farah's Republican Guard division, the retreat was chaotic and deadly. Sabir and his comrades were hungry, dirty, and buried with their equipment in trenches dug in the sand. They found out about the order to withdraw from Kuwait only when they heard the rumbling of tanks and military vehicles as they lay sleeping. Soldiers were running barefoot in front and alongside military vehicles driving toward the Iraqi border. They were running as if the "end of days" had come. They were escaping a "cyclone." Unable to save their military ordnance because they were being bombed as they retreated, they scampered like "savages" toward Zubayr, a town south of Basra. According to Sabir:

[T]he planes came to a paved highway that links Kuwait and Saudi Arabia to Iraq through the desert. They came and bombed it. The scene I saw was like a volcano ... like the volcano you see on the television or in the cinema.... I imagined

[22] BRCC 024–5–2 pages 0070–0090.
[23] NIDS/serial 2392645.
[24] Kanan Makiya, *Cruelty and Silence, War, Tyranny, Uprising and the Arab World* (New York: W.W. Norton, 1993), pp. 34–8.
[25] Quoted in Hiro, *Desert Shield to Desert Storm*, p. 388. BBC TV, *The Late Show*, June 8, 1991.

the earth turned over swallowing us and our equipment ... shrapnel was falling over our heads ... hundreds of rockets followed us all the way to Zubayr.[26]

The Intifada and its Aftermath in the South

More than one hundred thousand soldiers like Sabir returned from Kuwait over the course of a few days. According to the popular narrative, the uprising began in Sa'd square in Basra, a hub for the movement of troops during the Iran-Iraq war and the First Gulf War. It has now become part of the mythology of the Intifada that the uprising was spurred by an iconic gesture on the part of a returning soldier who shot at the picture of Saddam Hussain on February 28 or March 1.[27] True or false, the narrative of a specific act that marked the beginning of the Intifada gives coherence to what was in fact an uprising that took place simultaneously and independently in many parts of southern Iraq and spread to the Kurdish areas. However, the myth captures an essential aspect of the uprising in Basra and other parts of the south: it was fueled by returning soldiers who were hungry, defeated, bedraggled, and tired of being at war.

The uprising soon acquired a life of its own. It drew on soldiers, clan networks, returning prisoners of war, army deserters, and members of opposition parties that infiltrated into Iraq from Iran. In other words, its participants were those sectors of Iraqi society that had suffered most during the Iran-Iraq war and the First Gulf War. Between March 1 and 3, all the provinces south of Baghdad were in open rebellion. In the north, the uprising began as a series of confrontations with security forces in Kurdish towns. By mid-March, it had escalated into a military confrontation between the Kurdish Front, the coalition of Kurdish parties, and the regional security and Ba'th officials. The violence and looting that accompanied the uprising on the part of the rebels, particularly in the south, led many Iraqis who remained on the sidelines to describe the events as a *farhud*, an Iraqi colloquial term that denotes a riot accompanied by violence and dispossession of the population.[28] While the targets of the rebels' anger were often government institutions and party organizations,

---

[26] Interview with Sabir Farah, Amman, Jordan, July 22, 2007.
[27] Makiya, *Cruelty and Silence*, pp. 59–60. Makiya cites the chronology of the Intifada of the al-Kho'i Foundation in London. His 1992 book provided an important account of the uprising based on interviews with Iraqis who escaped the government crackdown and use of government documents from the Kurdish areas.
[28] BRCC 3455–0002–0053 and 0054.

FIGURE 5.1. Iraqi rebels atop a captured Iraqi armored vehicle, March 15, 1991
(Mohammad Sayyad/AP photo).

the rebels also looted museums, schools, food warehouses, and shops. In
Najaf, Karbala, Sulaimaniyya, and other cities, those associated with the
party and the security services were summarily executed, and sometimes
their bodies were mutilated.[29] By August 1991, the party requested the
government honor as martyrs 714 party members who had been victims
of the uprising.[30] The number did not include innocent civilians or members of other state institutions who did not belong to the party. In some
cities like Diwaniyya and Najaf, committees were set up to control the
violence and looting, but they were soon overwhelmed by their need to
defend their control of the cities against the military dispatched by the
regime to crush their rebellion (Figure 5.1).[31]

The regime's response was swift and deadly. Although officers as well
as a great number of conscripts had fled and joined the rebels, members of
the regular armed forces rejoined their units after the regime's first thrust
against the rebels. The Republican Guard, particularly the Hammurabi
division, played a pivotal role in the suppression of the uprising, and

[29] Human Rights Watch, *Endless Torment, The 1991 Uprising in Iraq and its Aftermath*
(New York: Human Rights Watch, 1992), p. 45. Makiya, *Cruelty and Silence*,
pp. 87–95.
[30] BRCC 01–3134–0004–0101 to 0106. Of these only eighty-nine were issued to the
Republican Guard.
[31] Makiya, *Cruelty and Silence*, pp. 63–76.

units within the army corps undertook mopping-up operations. In Babil province, the army used helicopter gunships to take over the city of Hilla just two days after it had fallen to the rebels. In Basra, which did not completely fall to rebel forces, Ali Hasan al-Majid established his head-quarters in Sa'd square and led the operation of the Republican Guard as well as the Third Army Corps assaults. By mid-March, Basra and sections of Maysan and Dhi Qar provinces had been subdued. In Najaf and Karbala, the indiscriminate shelling of Shi'i holy sites was accompanied by the killing of large numbers of rebels and their families. Altogether in much of the south, except for the city of Samawa, the rebels were only able to maintain their control of major cities for no more than nine days. In the Kurdish north, the army regained most of the area lost to the rebels, its campaign culminating in the retaking of the city of Kirkuk on March 28.

Human Rights Watch has documented the death and destruc-tion brought on by the suppression of the uprising in a special report. Summary executions and mass graves, destruction of holy sites, and the flight of more than 2 million Iraqis into refugee camps in Iran, Turkey, and Saudi Arabia was the price Iraqis had to pay for the restoration of the regime's power.[32]

Beyond counting the humanitarian costs of the uprising, however, how does one make sense of its politics? On March 15, 1991, Saddam Hussain addressed the nation and declared the end of the uprising, giving it its official name, "The Page of Betrayal and Treachery" (*safhat al-ghadr wa al-khiyana*). It was portrayed as an Iranian attempt to control Iraq. The instigators were dismissed as saboteurs who came from "behind the border." No mention was made of the catastrophic occupation of Kuwait and the Iraqi army's withdrawal. Nor was there any mention of the humiliating ceasefire agreement signed in Safwan. By April 1991, when the Kurdish uprising had also been suppressed but Iraq was los-ing sovereignty over its Kurdish areas because of the humanitarian crisis that ensued, the government press and the Ba'thist newspaper *al-Thawra* had spun the uprising as the work of "*ghawgha'iyun*," or uncontrolled mobs. "Saboteurs" disloyal to Iraq and funded by the forces of imperial-ism, Zionism, and Iran directed these mobs. In particular, the early press reports stressed the destructive nature of the uprising and the rebels' moral depravity. In an infamous series of articles, *al-Thawra* maligned the populations of the south and spoke of the Shi'a in sectarian terms.

[32] Human Rights Watch, *Endless Torment*, pp. 10–17.

Not only did the Shi'a constitute a fifth column in the heart of Iraq, they were ungrateful recipients of the benefits of modernization and development the state had brought. This reading became the official version and affected state policies in the south and mid-Euphrates regions of Iraq until the regime's demise in 2003.[33]

The opposition's version differed. A series of reports and press releases issued by an opposition group in Damascus during the uprising portrayed the government as engaged in horrific acts of violence and the rebels as forming a unified opposition seeking to establish a democratic state that was neither Islamic nor allied to Iran. From the outset, the opposition was well aware that the uprising was being interpreted in sectarian terms by the international media and by the Sunni Arab states. It was concerned that the uprising be regarded as a popular revolt supported by wide swaths of the Iraqi population. At the same time, the opposition tried to convey that the Intifada had a unified leadership and clearly defined objectives.[34] For their part, the Shi'i Islamist parties gave their own interpretation to the uprising, presenting it as a rebellion by an oppressed Shi'i population against the Ba'thist regime. Shi'i Islamist parties headquartered in Iran sent in members of the Badr brigade to help the rebels.

Party cadres reporting on the uprising offered a more complicated reading of events.[35] The Ba'thists' reports cast doubt on the government's and the oppositions' narratives. The rebels' slogans varied according to locality. Some informants stated clearly that some of the rebels had pictures of al-Hakim and Khomeini; others stressed the role of the tribes and the military in the uprising. Many simply characterized the rebels as the "*mu'arada*," the opposition, perhaps alluding to the coalition of opposition parties formed early in the war. Their reports largely attested

[33] Fanar Haddad, *Sectarianism in Iraq, Antagonistic Visions of Unity* (New York: Columbia University Press, 2011), pp. 117–32.

[34] M. al-Majid, *Intifadat al-Sha'b al-'Iraqi* (*The Uprising of the Iraqi People*) (Beirut: Dar al-Wifaq, 1991). al-Majid's book was issued in June of that year and it is clear that the information obtained by the author was received through the opposition in Iraq, international press reports, and the office of Ayatollah Muhammad Taqi al-Din al-Mudarissi of the Islamic Action Organization, who issued daily reports on the Intifada. al-Mudarissi was in the leadership of the Damascus-based opposition and participated in the conference in Beirut that the opposition organized to consider the future of Iraq. Dar al-Wifaq was funded by his organization.

[35] BRCC 01–3455–0002. Reports on the nature of the uprising, its causes, and its participants began to come into the Ba'th Party Baghdad Bureau headed by Sa'd Mahdi Salih, later speaker of the parliament, by March 10, 1991, and were issued by members of the Ba'th Party in the various southern provinces.

to the localized nature of the uprising and its leaders.[36] Reports from Najaf, Qadisiyya, Dhi Qar, and Maysan provinces, where the violence from both sides was most intense, depict the diversity of the Intifada's participants and leaders.

In Najaf, the rebellion leaders included a security officer, a food warehouse employee, a communist deserter, and the Najaf hospital director.[37] The venerable Ayatollah Kho'i, the highest spiritual authority for millions of Shi'a, did not openly support the uprising, although the reports from Najaf indicate his importance for the rebels. Concerned with the looting and the killing in Najaf, he confined himself to urging the rebels not to attack property and to bury the dead. A few days later, he was behind the formation of a central committee made up of notables and religious scholars to manage the situation in the city. The religious establishment within this committee was made up of minor clerics but had wide support from army officers who had deserted. In the rural areas around Najaf, army officers, shop owners, lower-middle-class state employees, and relatives of individuals executed by the regime seem to have played an important role in the organization of the uprising.[38] In both Najaf and Karbala, pictures of Ayatollah al-Hakim and Khomeini were openly displayed, as were slogans calling for the establishment of an Islamic republic. In the wake of the rebels' defeat in Najaf, Saddam Hussain summoned Kho'i to Baghdad and forced him to describe the rebellion as a chaotic affair.[39]

In Qadisiyya, long regarded by the regime as essential to the capital's security, the uprising was instigated, according to the earliest report filed on March 11, by returning soldiers and prisoners of war who poured into Iraq from Iranian prisons in 1990 as part of a deal struck between the Iranian and Iraqi governments after the occupation of Kuwait. The al-Yasiriyya clan played a leading role in mobilizing the rebels outside Diwaniyya.[40] Other tribes joined, including the head of the Khaza'il tribe, who was a member of the National Assembly.[41] Not all the tribes of the region supported the rebels, however. Early on, the head of a tribe in the Hamza region offered his men's services (some 170 to 200 tribesmen) to the state and provided a detailed list of those tribes leading the

---

[36] BRCC 01–3455–0002–0436 and 0437 and 0054.

[37] BRCC 01–3455–0002–0421.

[38] BRCC 01–3455–0002–0252. This is a report sent by a party member who was in the Shamiyya district when the party headquarters in Qa'Qa' was destroyed.

[39] al-Salhi, *al-Zilzal*, p. 9.

[40] BRCC 01–3455–0002–0517 and 0518.

[41] BRCC 01–3455–0002–0352 and 0353.

uprising.[42] The rebels were also supported by a substantial number of officials from the Ba'th, a number of ex-Communists, and relatives of Da'wa Party members executed by the regime.[43] The alliance of soldiers, many of them officers with tribal connections, made the uprising in Qadisiyya among the more organized in the southern and central Iraqi regions. However, the leaders of the uprising in the province clearly had little idea, beyond unseating the Ba'th, what form of government they wanted to institute.

Reports from the province of Dhi Qar are the richest in detail and the most abundant. American troops were still on the outskirts of the province and in some cases they were seen in Suq al-Shuyukh and in Nasiriyya. It was important for the government to gauge the extent of support the Americans were giving to the rebels. The most comprehensive report came from the president of the Dhi Qar branch of the General Federation of Iraqi Women and covered Suq al-Shuyukh, where the Intifada started on March 1, and Nasiriyya, where it had spread by March 2.[44] In Suq al-Shuyukh, the rebellion was dominated by clans, but included former communists and Da'wa Party members who initiated contacts with the Americans. In Nasiriyya, members of the opposition and army deserters were at the forefront. The reports stressed the role played by soldiers stranded in Nasiriyya and the potential trouble they could wreak as they abandoned their weapons and tried to find food and money to go home. Yet, compared to the rebels in Qadisiyya and Najaf, they were less organized and could not forge a disciplined leadership. Army officers do not seem to have played an important planning role. Like the rebels in other parts of Iraq, the population of Dhi Qar targeted government and party buildings, census bureaus, and military recruitment bureaus.

In Maysan province, where the marshes provided refuge for deserters and supporters of Shi'i opposition parties, the rebellion was instigated and sustained by the Islamist parties and Iraqi supporters who infiltrated into the country from Iran. Amara was flooded with soldiers trying to find transportation to take them home. Many had come from Kuwait to Amara on foot, changed into civilian clothes, and sold their arms to buy their way home. The attacks on government buildings were carried out by four categories of people: the families of those executed for belonging

---

[42] BRCC 01–3455–0002–0372.
[43] BRCC 01–3455–0002–0485 and 0486.
[44] BRCC 01–3455–0002–0337 to 0344.

to the Da'wa Party, the families who had "Iranian affiliation," deserters, and soldiers returning from Kuwait. The leaders of the uprising ran its day-to-day operations from mosques and espoused an openly sectarian Shi'i agenda.[45]

In Arab Iraq, returning soldiers and the Shi'a of the south have the singular honor of, as they put it, "breaking the barrier of fear." It is important, however, to distinguish between that fact and the conclusion that the uprising was sectarian or that its participants espoused openly Shi'i agendas. Class differences, divisions between rural and urban populations, and clan loyalties and tensions played a significant part in the level of participation among the Shi'i population in the south. Even in Najaf, Karbala, and Maysan, where rebels called for the establishment of an Islamic state and chanted Shi'i slogans, their popularity among other sectors of the population was difficult to determine. In Najaf, for example, one participant in the Intifada pointed to a clear division between a professional and mercantile middle class and the lower classes. The former expressed their grievances against the regime and joined the demonstrators on the first day of the uprising, but soon withdrew into their homes when the looting and violence began and when pictures of Khomeini and al-Hakim appeared on walls.[46] Some Shi'i clans cooperated with the regime, informed on the rebels in their neighborhoods, and were duly and publically rewarded later. Finally, while many Shi'i Ba'thist members joined the rebels, others remained on the sidelines.

The violence and patterns of participation by Iraqi rebels in the south during the Intifada can be best understood as a reaction to the practices of the state and the Ba'th during the Iran-Iraq war. While these practices were driven by national security and counterinsurgency considerations, their implementation led to the creation of specifically southern, as well as Shi'i, sectarian grievances. The use of family networks to exact punishment for individuals' infractions had a multiplier effect. This largely explains the mobilization of clan networks against or in support of the regime. The expansion of the party's organization and functions during the Iran-Iraq war played a significant part in mobilizing the rebels against it. The security services' surveillance and the Ba'th Party practices of creating information banks on families who belonged to the opposition parties in the south factored into the mobilization of clans who had family members executed or imprisoned by the regime, as did the party cadres'

---

[45] BRCC 01–3455–0277–0283.
[46] Interview with Hussain Ahmad, Amman, Jordan, June 23, 2007.

activism and centrality to the maintenance of control over deserters, prisoners of war, and their families.

In the provinces of Basra, Dhi Qar, and Maysan, a direct correlation existed between the losses in life and property incurred in the Iran-Iraq war, political persecution, and patterns of participation. In Basra province, where the border rural areas suffered most in both wars, towns like al-Qurna, Shatt al-Arab had the highest number of men executed per male student population in the province, mostly for belonging to the Communist Party. The towns also had the highest number of families affected by the war, largely because their men were martyred, had deserted or had been taken as prisoners of war.[47] In sections of Basra, certain neighborhoods suffered a disproportionate number of martyrs, and their inhabitants had more family members who had taken an active role in the uprising than elsewhere.[48] The same patterns can be detected in Dhi Qar province, with the towns of Suq al-Shuyukh and al-Shatra, and the marsh area of al-Chibayish, where inhabitants' participation in the uprising was much higher than that by residents of the city of Nasiriyya.[49] It is little wonder then, that the rebels attacked state and party institutions that had surveyed them, categorized them in family and clan networks,

[47] For al-Qurna, 2.8 percent of its 772 matriculating students had relatives executed by the regime; another 3.6 percent had family members who belonged to the opposition. For Shatt al-Arab's 158 matriculating students, 4.5 percent had relatives who had been executed, and an equal percentage belonged to the Communist Party. In al-Madina, part of Basra, nearly 10 percent of students had lost a family member in either the Iran-Iraq war or the First Gulf War (1998). While the overall average of men executed by the regime in the province of Basra in 1987–8 was 1.6 percent and men lost in the wars was close to 6 percent, these percentages of men lost to the war and to the regime's violence were higher in the rural and poorer areas of the city and province. See Appendix I for the distribution of war dead. For 1987–8, School Registers, Amn 32–01 and Amn 32–02. For 1998–9 School Registers, Hizb 61–23, 61–23, 61–25.

[48] Conclusions are based on the surveys of matriculating students conducted by the security service in 1991–2. These list the number of students who had participated or had family members who participated in the uprising. In al-Qurna, of the 1,858 students, 1.8 percent participated or had family members who had participated; in al-Madina, part of Basra, the comparable figure was 7.4 percent. School Registers, Amn 32–14 and Amn 32–15.

[49] While the total average of participants in the whole of Dhi Qar province was 1.6 percent, of al-Chibayish's 225 matriculating students, 7.6 percent had been involved in the uprising. School Registers, Dhi Qar Amn 28–14 and 29–01 and Hizb 29–02 and 29–03. In the rural area of Qada' al-Salam in Maysan province, for example, of the eleven male matriculating students, one had a brother killed in the First Gulf War, one had a brother killed in the Iran-Iraq war, one had an uncle killed in the Iran-Iraq war, one was head of the Federation of Youth in his town and his uncle was a party member, one had an uncle who was in the Communist Party, and one had a brother executed for belonging to the Da'wa Party. School Registers, Amn 25–06 and Hizb 60–37.

punished them for their families' political affiliations, drafted their men-folk, pursued deserters, and surveilled families of martyrs and prisoners of war.

Following the Intifada, the government waged a counterinsurgency campaign against the population of the south. That campaign took two forms: the systematic collection of information on individuals and families who had participated in the Intifada, and the alteration of the physical features of the southern marshes. Weeks after the Intifada was suppressed, the directorate of general security and Ba'thist cadres began systematically surveying matriculating male students in the fifteen prov-inces under the central government's control. Factored into the surveys were precise statements on the level of participation of students and their families in the Intifada. Together with the reports of Ba'thist cadres from various areas in Iraq, they constituted the basis for the government's cam-paign to punish rebels and reward collaborators.

The reports written by Ba'thist cadres on the ground during the Intifada as well as the surveys of students created a very specific kind of knowledge about the rebellious population. That knowledge provided the basis for the assignation of culpability. It shaped the way that the regime and the cadres understood the populations they surveyed and was crucial in the regime's deployment of counterinsurgency techniques. From the beginning, it was clear to those working on the ground that while the rebellion was primarily a Shi'i one, it was not by any means a rebellion by all Shi'a. It was, therefore, essential to weed out those who were amenable to rehabilitations – those who proved loyal – from those who constituted a threat to the regime's security. These surveys of matriculating male students were particularly important in the southern and mid-Euphrates regions. Until the Intifada, these surveys had served as the basis for excluding from select higher education institutions those students who had family members who belonged to opposition parties, were deserters, or were of "Iranian affiliation." After the Intifada, the parameter of exclusions was widened to include those whose families had been rebellious. These surveys established a systematic hierarchy in which levels of participation were used to "rehabilitate" those who had shown loyalty and contrition after the Intifada and to punish those who remained intransigent. In this way, the surveys helped shape what became the politics of mercy exercised by the regime in the 1990s. One was culpable as was one's family, but mercy and access were granted depending on the level of participation in the resistance. For the first five years following the Intifada, these surveys screened out those who had participated from access to institutions of higher learning, police, and security academies. They also helped determine the level of rehabilitation allowed "culprits" who sought their entitlements, ration cards, and other social services.

While these information-gathering activities in the south resembled an invisible counterinsurgency campaign more so than they had done in the 1980s, the transformation of the geographic and human terrain of some southern areas was a continuation of the counterinsurgency practices initiated during the Iran-Iraq war. The circumstances under which the regime conducted this campaign, however, were radically different. Much weakened militarily and domestically, plagued by porous borders, and subject to increased monitoring by international humanitarian agencies, the regime was less able to inflict the sort of lethal damage it had inflicted in the Anfal campaign. Nevertheless, the south, particularly the marsh areas, was now a scene of sporadic military campaigns designed to limit the number of escapees and deserters, control contraband, and punish southerners who provided aid to the Shiʿi Islamist parties in Iran. To support its military campaigns, the regime began assigning the governorships of the southern provinces to military men, indicating the level of its concern about its own security in the south.[50]

The counterinsurgency campaign against Iraq's marsh population began soon after the suppression of the Intifada. It involved a two-pronged policy: territorial control and population dispersal. Ostensibly, the campaign took the form of an ambitious project to construct a Third River, dubbed the Saddam River, between the Tigris and Euphrates to drain the marshlands and resettle their populations. Plans for the project had started as early as the 1950s and continued throughout the 1970s. The Iran-Iraq war temporarily derailed the project, but highlighted the importance of transforming the marsh geography to control the movement of men and goods across the border with Iran.

In the aftermath of the uprising, the government began in earnest what it had started during the Iran-Iraq war. In April 1992, the Iraqi National Assembly approved the legal framework for the draining of the marshes. The body voted to approve a new housing program for the inhabitants of marsh areas that included their relocation to houses on the highway between Basra and al-Qurna. Their forced relocation was part of an attempt to turn them into "good citizens" and "civilize" them by

---

[50] Baran, *Vivre la Tyrannie*, p. 130. In the last six years of the regime, the governorships of Maysan, Babil, Muthanna, and Najaf were assigned to military men.

providing them with the amenities of modern life.[51] By 1994, four drainage canals, dubbed rivers, together with dams and small canals, deprived the marshes of the waters of the Tigris and the Euphrates and their tributaries, totally devastating the ecosystem that had sustained the marshes' more than two hundred thousand inhabitants.[52]

The campaign to drain the marshes involved cooperation between the Ba'thist, the military, and the security services. It took the better part of the 1990s to accomplish. Several military campaigns, search-and-seizure operations, mass arrests and disappearances, and economic blockades led to the mass exodus of the inhabitants or their resettlement. In carrying out its operations, the regime followed the template it had developed in the 1980s. Areas marked for operations in Dhi Qar, Muthanna, Wasit, Basra, and Maysan provinces were declared "prohibited areas" where trade was restricted or outlawed altogether.[53] Those detained while carrying unauthorized arms were imprisoned. The Southern Bureau played a central role in the operations, although it is not clear if it was as efficient as it had been earlier. In the summer of 1999, in a response to unrest in the cities of Basra and Nasiriyya in the wake of the execution of Ayatollah Muhammad Sadiq al-Sadr, the Southern Bureau coordinated with the leadership of the Third and Fourth Army Corps to conduct a military campaign against the marsh areas of Huwayza, which encompassed the provinces of Maysan, Dhi Qar, Wasit, and Basra. The operation took place within the areas declared "prohibited," involved the use of helicopter gunships and artillery, and included extensive search and seizure operations. Members of the Ba'th security committees of these provinces set up roadblocks, accompanied the military, and processed those taken prisoners. Present during the operation was the deputy director of the Southern Bureau and members of the Ba'th Central Committee. The military part of the operation was led by Lieutenant General Iyad al-Rawi, one of the principal architects of the Republican Guard's suppression of the Intifada.[54]

In addition to large military operations, the Southern Bureau's counterinsurgency work included pursuing deserters, absentees, escapees,

---

[51] Human Rights Watch, *The Iraqi Government's Assault on the Marsh Arabs*, Briefing paper, January 2003, http://www.hrw.org/backgrounder/mena/marsharabs1.htm accessed June 13, 2008, pp. 7–8.

[52] Ibid., pp. 5 and 11. The population of the marshes was reduced to twenty thousand people in 2003.

[53] Human Rights Watch, *Endless Torment*, pp. 8–13.

[54] BRCC 01–3521–0002–0344 to 0347. The operation led to the arrest of 2,659 people, 60 stolen vehicles, and 147 weapons.

and members of opposition parties. Although this had been part of its
function during the Iran-Iraq war, it now took on a different coloring.
Military mobilization was no longer needed: the government had introduced a law that allowed men unwilling to undergo military training to
pay a replacement fee.[55] The pursuit of deserters was to some degree an
attempt by local party cadres to raise funds, part of the corruption that
was rampant in the 1990s. More significant, the pursuit and apprehension of deserters became central to a larger campaign that sought to cur-
tail the movement of men, police their activities, and ensure that they did
not flee the country or join the opposition. Few of the deserters returned
to their units; fewer still could be rehabilitated. Rather, their apprehension or surrender was meant to keep track of them and raise funds for
local Ba'thist cadres. As punishment, their rations could be withheld and
they were excluded from public sector employment. Southern males were
thus targeted more than males elsewhere. Between January 1 and April
30, 1993, for example, the Southern Bureau reported that in the Dhi Qar,
Maysan, and Basra provinces, its cadres had recorded the surrender or
apprehension of some 25,968 deserters, absentees, escapees, "saboteurs,"
and infiltrators. That figure constituted 64 percent of the total number of
deserters in all fifteen provinces under central government control. Most
noticeable was the fact that where party cadres recorded 17,438 such
males in Basra province, there were only 287 in Ninewah, although their
populations were comparable.[56]

The government's counterinsurgency campaign was most successful in
destroying the marshland's ecosystem, but less so in ruling the southern
populations. Much of the southern part of the country, particularly the
provinces of Basra, Muthanna, Wasit, Maysan, and Dhi Qar, was only ten-
uously controlled. Both the Ba'th's General Secretariat and the Office of
the Presidency decentralized control in large part because of their limited
resources.[57] The populations of the south carried out campaigns against
government employees involved in draining marshes and building canals.

---

[55] *al-Qadisiyya*, August 26, 1994, p. 1. Revolutionary Command Council decree number
145, issued August 25, 1994. Those required to do military service were released after
they finished basic training (ninety days) if they paid half a million dinars, and those in
the reserve were released if they paid one million dinars. Another decree, number 116,
issued on the same day, prevented those who fled military service or those who did not
show up for service from contracting any transactions that sought to cultivate land for
agricultural or industrial purposes. They were also prohibited from buying or renting
through auction any of the state's resources.
[56] BRCC 02–3–6–0232 to 0424.
[57] Baran, *Vivre la Tyrannie*, pp. 113–48.

So routine were these acts of sabotage that the government felt compelled to designate those slain workers who had been sacrificed for the "*jihad* [holy war] of rebuilding" as martyrs.[58] The party's Southern Bureau reported on the proliferation of contraband in religious sermons by Shiʻi clerics from Lebanon and Iran, increased lawlessness, the ease with which the population crossed in and out of Iraq, and the continuous attempts by "saboteurs" to infiltrate from Iran.[59] Nevertheless, the campaign against the southern regions irreparably damaged the prospects of integrating the south into the central government's orbit, a process begun during the Iran-Iraq war but pursued with tragic results following the Intifada.

Between Charity and Mercy

In 1993, two years after the end of the First Gulf War, Saddam Hussain issued a decree that designated the Mother of All Battles as an ongoing series of confrontations "for justice and truth against untruth."[60] The Mother of All Battles included the confrontation with the coalition forces, the Intifada, the ongoing sanctions regime, and the continuing bombing campaigns. This view of the last twelve years of Baʻthist rule was not unrealistic. The loss of control over the three northern Kurdish provinces, where an active opposition funded by the United States was bent on dislodging the regime, meant its survival was constantly in jeopardy. At the same time, the government's control of the south was tenuous. Baghdad and the predominantly Sunni provinces of Anbar, Salah al-Din, and Diyali provided the basis of the regime's political power. These areas also contained the business elite, enriched through government reconstruction contracts and illicit trade. Saddam Hussain cultivated certain clan leaders, allowed their followers to carry light arms, and espoused the mantra of tribal values. Thus, for the first time since the establishment of the Republican regime in 1958, tribalism shaped elite alliances and became part of the political language of public culture. It was a politics invented by the regime to bolster its declining power.

The fallout from the Intifada and its handling by the regime did irreparable damage to the relations among sects. For four years after the uprising, the regime and the Baʻthists insisted on commemorating the "Page of Treachery and Betrayal" by reminding Iraqis, particularly in the south

---

[58] The phrase was officially espoused at the Tenth Regional Party Congress held in September 1991. *al-Qadisiyya*, September 14, 1991, 1.

[59] BRCC 01–3521–0002–0249 to 0250.

[60] BRCC 01–2214–0000–0187.

and in the holy Shi'ite cities of Najaf and Karbala, of the rebels' wanton depravity. In ceremony after ceremony, and in the various institutions of public culture, Iraqis were asked to commemorate the heroism of those who had remained loyal to the nation and to salute the regime's ability to forgive by rebuilding areas the rebels had destroyed. More corrosive was the distrust between Sunni and Shi'i communities. The tension was fueled by the regime and the party's increased watchfulness. Residents of the mixed quarters of Baghdad were encouraged to report rumors. Particularly during the early 1990s, when the memories of the Intifada remained fresh, rumors predicted the regime's diabolical intention against the Shi'i community, as well as the end of time.[61] One widely circulated rumor had Saddam Hussain, in a clear provocation of Shi'i sensibilities, granting those who chose to marry on the Shi'i day of mourning (the tenth day of Muharram) ten thousand dinars.[62] Rumors that highlighted the Sunni community's vulnerability were also rife. These included various plans hatched up by Iran to train Iraqi prisoners of war who had "converted" to infiltrate Baghdad's neighborhoods. Rumors also circulated about the cooperation and communication between residents of the predominantly Shi'i Kadhimiyya neighborhood of Baghdad and their relatives who had fled to Iran in the wake of the Intifada.[63] These rumors fueled sectarian tensions and were fed by the atmosphere of permanent war that existed in Iraq.

Sectarian tensions and tribalism do not alone explain the kind of political and governmental practices that governed Iraqis' daily lives during the embargo. To understand these, we need to view the transformation in the way the regime and the Ba'th Party attempted to solve the problems of diminished economic resources and circumscribed authority over the social and political life of Iraqis. The embargo created a host of new problems for the Iraqi government insofar as suffering was no longer contained to specific categories of people such as soldiers, but affected the entire population. The question of how to feed the population, pay salaries, maintain health and educational services, and rebuild the country's devastated infrastructure were of utmost importance. The pervasive lawlessness and crime in Iraqi cities, particularly Baghdad, was compounded

---

[61] BRCC 01–2465–0001–0674 and 0686 to 0691. Rumors circulated about the publication of an Arabic translation of Nostradamus that linked his predictions to the present and about papers circulated in Shi'i mosques that predicted the end of time; other rumors were reported by party cadres with a clearly sectarian slant.

[62] BRCC 01–3197–0001–0056.

[63] BRCC 01–3197–0001–0058 and 0127.

by the soldiers' demobilization and return. Poverty and unemployment were rampant, as was absenteeism from public posts. The lack of policing and the drastic weakening of the capacity of state institutions and the Ba'th Party to manage the population exacerbated these social problems. The regime's policies were improvised to deal with impending crises and implemented with inconsistency and incoherence. They were designed to project power and competency where both were lacking. The result for the Iraqi population most affected by such policies was confusion. Exhausted by war and the economic fallout of the sanctions, citizens struggled to understand and cope with a host of requirements, punishments, and political obligations essential for their survival.

For a regime bent on survival, the assertion of a modicum of control entailed restructuring the distribution of the state's dwindling economic resources and reworking the basis and projection of its political power. Undergirding the regime's policy of dealing with the embargo's economic fallout were two strategies. The first was transforming all decisions made to mitigate the embargo's impact into acts of charity, *makruma*, on the part of the leader. The second was creating a hierarchy among Iraqis of categories of people more deserving of this charity than others. The paternalism of the policy had its roots in the Iran-Iraq war, when Saddam Hussain instituted a system of rewards to soldiers and martyrs' families. He positioned himself as the father of the nation, dispensing *ikramat*, grants honoring the soldiers' heroism and their sacrifices in defense of the nation. They were not charitable grants but represented an enhancement of the rights of soldier-citizens. This practice was deployed differently during the embargo. It was now a charitable act by a leader generous enough to help his pauperized subjects and reward their loyalty and perseverance. It became a private act, enacted at will and doled out to old loyal Ba'thists, to technocrats who helped rebuild Iraq, and to tribes who had stood by the regime during the Intifada, Shi'i and Sunnis alike.[64] Grants were no longer only the privilege of soldiers and martyrs' families, but were extended to the entire Iraqi population, whose survival was dependent on the issuing of *ikramat* by Saddam Hussain and a host of intermediaries. The result has been aptly described as the "infantilization and extreme personalization" of politics.[65]

The strategy was fueled by economic and political realities. Ministries of state could no longer pay their employees salaries as they depended

---

[64] Baran, *Vivre la Tyrannie*, pp. 112–48.
[65] Ibid., p. 105.

for their funding on dwindling taxes on imports. Demobilized and retired soldiers had to fend for themselves, as the Ministry of Defense could not increase their pensions to keep up with hyperinflation. To continue functioning, ministries had to privatize their various services and to solicit "donations" from their staffs.[66] "Donations" were meant to bolster a new culture of charity that all Iraqis had to cultivate in face of the embargo. Sanctioned and openly embraced by the regime, charity gave cover to the privatization of social services that had been central to maintaining the social peace at home during the Iran-Iraq war. As early as October 1991, the president's wife founded the Committee of Solidarity and Perseverance to elicit donations to help the needy.[67] By 1992, the Chamber of Commerce of Baghdad was inveighed upon to create a fund supported by private businesses to help families. The Chamber of Commerce worked in coordination with the Baghdad municipality and bypassed the Ministry of Social Affairs.[68]

The privatization of key sectors of the Iraqi economy left a large section of the salaried population of Iraq vulnerable to malnutrition and black marketeering. This was particularly problematic in the distribution of basic foodstuffs essential for a population under siege. While the Ministry of Trade operated a rationing system starting in August 1990, it had provided essentials to both private suppliers and state-run cooperatives. That policy changed after the end of the First Gulf War. The shelves of government-run cooperatives and stores were left empty: most goods were now given to private retailers. By 1994, some eleven hundred sixty cooperatives that had serviced one hundred sixteen thousand citizens had closed because people had to shop at central markets.[69] Although the Ministry of Trade fixed prices on primary goods, it could do little to control price gauging. Nor could it do much about the corruption that ensued from such privatization. Ba'thist cadres and bureaucrats cooperated to ensure that goods were allocated to favored businesses.

While state institutions were left to struggle with funding, the Office of the Presidency increasingly took over the functions of state ministries, receiving returns from the illicit trade in oil and other goods and

---

[66] BRCC 01–2214–0000–0090 and 0091. A series of directives issued by the Council of Ministries asked that all ministries set a fund for donations toward defraying the cost of private transport, since ministries could no longer provide free public transport. Those who did not donate were to be fired.

[67] *al-Qadisiyya*, November 28, 1991, 5.

[68] *al-Qadisiyya*, June 11, 1994, 4.

[69] *al-Qadisiyya*, May 14, 1994, 4.

dispensing contracts to favored cronies to rebuild the country's infrastructure. Although little solid documentation exists on the economic basis of Saddam Hussain's power for this period, it seems fairly safe to conclude that much of the funding of state sectors became highly dependent on the largesse of the Office of the Presidency rather than on the established sources of revenue.[70] By 1994, when the economic situation was particularly dire and complaints about living conditions from employees of public sector enterprises, as well as soldiers, disabled veterans, and martyrs' families, flooded newspapers, Saddam Hussain made public the gradual process of the usurpation of public institutions' prerogatives that had begun in 1991. He announced that, in light of the "negativism and complaining" among the Iraqi population, and in order to ensure the "happiness" of the people, the leadership of the regime had decided to intervene directly in affairs usually handled by ministries and state directorates, "because small things become big in difficult circumstances."[71]

Hussain's interventions were politically motivated and intended to highlight his centrality to the population's survival, as well as to jettison scarce resources to bolster his regime. Thus, the rebuilding of Iraq's infrastructure, the construction of schools, the increase in public sector salaries to fight hyperinflation, and various other measures were framed as beneficent grants, not as policy decisions a modern state undertook to protect its citizenry during wartime. Equally important was the use of these grants to reward the loyalty of various sectors of the population during the First Gulf War and the Intifada. To allocate such rewards, the regime improvised a new hierarchy among its citizens of those more deserving of these grants than others. Perhaps the most striking example is the "medals mania" phenomenon. Tens of thousands of medals, attached to different ranks and entitlements, were granted with great fanfare to members of the party hierarchy who had remained loyal, clan and military leaders, soldiers, martyrs, and sectors of the population who rebuilt Iraq's infrastructure. Increases in salaries, land grants, and other entitlements depended on how many medals one accumulated.[72]

To bring order to this chaotic situation, Saddam Hussain encouraged the formation of an organization of the citizenry known as the "Friends

---

[70] Baran, *Vivre La Tyrannie*, pp. 87–112.

[71] *al-Qadisiyya*, June 9, 1994, 1.

[72] These medals ranged from the highest, the medal of Rafidayn, granted to party members after they had served a certain number of years, to medals of courage, to the insignia of martyrs, to medals commemorating the Mother of all Battles. Each came with some form of entitlement.

of Saddam." The category of citizens who comprised "Friends of Saddam"
consisted of individuals who had received three or more medals. While
the category of "Friends of Saddam" was created in 1983 to reward soldiers who had received three medals of courage, in the 1990s it became
a category that encompassed the entire "medal-receiving" population in
Iraq. It brought soldiers, clan leaders, martyrs, Ba'thists, and bureaucrats
together under a category of people who received periodic increases in
entitlements.[73] By 1998, the category of "Friends of Saddam" covered
nearly a fifth of the population. Its honorees were drawn equally from the
Shi'i and Sunni populations, although the percentage of "Friends" was
higher in the favored central provinces than in the south.[74]

Confused by the improvisational nature of this new system of appor-
tioning entitlements, Iraqi citizens continuously contested and negotiated
its meaning. These *ikramat* were, more often than not, without substance
and designed to project an ability to deal with the problems of state
disintegration. *Ikramat* grantees often could not cash in on the entitlements. There were no state mechanisms to implement them, causing mass
inter-ministerial confusion. When citizens were eligible for more than one
grant, neither they nor the various institutions that were supposed to help
them understood what these meant. In the words of one Iraqi, they often
meant very little. They presented an "insurance card" that a citizen could
deploy in moments of crisis.[75] Demobilized soldiers, martyrs' families,
prisoners of war, and the war disabled were among the most frustrated
with this new system of charity. The *makruma* that had previously honored their sacrifices for the nation was now being redefined. In February
1992, an editorial in *al-Qadisiyya* complained that misplaced charity
was unjust. Honorees were often undeserving. The purpose of bestowing an honor was to acknowledge an honorable social act in a special
way. The current practice of bestowing grants had erased the difference
between ordinary and exceptional Iraqis. Those who simply showed up
at work during bombing, those who engaged in rebuilding, and those
who worked in information bureaus (security and intelligence) were now
awarded grants where previously these were reserved for soldiers who

[73] *al-Qadisiyya*, February 5, 1994, 3. Dr. Salman Zaydan, head of the "Friends of Saddam"
association, attempted to give some moral significance to the meaning of friendship with
the leader by trying to borrow from *sufi* (Islamic mysticism) terminology of the relations
of the master to his student.
[74] Percentages culled from school registers of matriculating students in fifteen Iraqi provinces. See Appendix I.
[75] Interview with Tareq Ali, Damascus, Syria, March 13, 2009.

had exhibited courage at the war front. "This is what is dangerous about this system of *ikramat* [honors]" the writer concluded, "which is the policy of our wise leadership."[76]

If the language and politics of charity framed how the regime doled out resources to those deemed deserving, the politics of mercy shaped how it dealt with those who had "betrayed" it and those whom it perceived as a threat to the social and political order. The politics of mercy operated in two ways. First, the regime, the various security apparatuses that supported it, and the Ba'th leadership all assumed that a significant portion of the Iraqi citizens and their relatives were guilty of an expanding number of "infractions." Second, the regime instituted laws so draconian that they were difficult to implement systematically. They were designed to exact exemplary "justice," project power, and elicit mercy. This technique of governance was often touted as a security measure in colonial and authoritarian states and was practiced in Iraq during the Iran-Iraq war to "rehabilitate" political opponents and deserters. After the First Gulf War, the list of possible infractions was widened to include larger sections of the Iraqi population. Not only was guilt assigned based on political sympathies and desertion, it now covered the ill-defined concept of "attitude" toward the First Gulf War and the Intifada. The Ba'th Party and the security services developed a hierarchy of guilt to manage the proliferating number of "culprits" and to process the requests of those deemed redeemable and to forward them to the Office of the Presidency. Iraqis were classified according to the seriousness of the various infractions and allowed to "rehabilitate" themselves by asking for mercy, usually by writing to the president, informing on others, reporting on rumors, or simply admitting to their "guilt." If they did not, their food rations were threatened, their children banned from institutes of higher learning, their public sector positions terminated, or their freedom stripped by imprisonment. The efficacy of this governance did not lie in the punishment it exacted, which was sporadic at best. Rather it lay in the perpetual threat of punishment Iraqi citizens had to contend with as they tried to survive the embargo and the regime's predatory practices.

Take, for example, the regime's concept of measuring loyalty by "attitude." As early as 1992, citizens were given the Mother of All Battles insignia for their "attitude" during the battle and the uprising. "Attitude" clearly alluded to collaboration with the regime against the

---

[76] *al-Qadisiyya*, February 4, 1992, 8. It is not clear whether the author, a regular contributor to the newspaper in this period, was writing under the pseudonym of Hatif al-Thalj.

rebels.[77] By 1994, the Ba'th and the security service had made "attitude" into a category for the systemic assessment of male students' eligibility for admission into institutions of higher learning and technical and security training colleges. Gauging "attitude" was a problematic enterprise, negotiable and dependent on surveillance, information gathering, and connections. "Attitude" was elastic. It was not measurable by belonging to the Ba'th or an opposition party. It helped if a citizen or a family member had actively fought against the rebels in the Intifada or had reported on rebel activity. It also helped if one had a family member martyred during the First Gulf War or during the uprising. It was, however, no guarantee that one's "attitude" was "correct."[78] It had to be corroborated by the number of times a student or his family had attended the many celebrations and commemorations organized by the party around the Intifada and the First Gulf War. "Attitude" had much to do with local Ba'thist cadre reports from the neighborhood or the school. Thus, the practice of informing was a hallmark of the Ba'th mode of operations during the 1980s, but it became systematic in the 1990s and was used to assert control over the distribution of resources at the local level rather than for state security matters. It was partly a technique used by local cadres to elicit requests for their intercession by the "accused" citizens anxious to mitigate their situation either by asserting their innocence or by agreeing to inform on others. By the mid-1990s, informing had become so widespread that newspapers began to report on the difficulties of sorting through fabricated information and ensuring that what was reported was useful for the security of the regime.[79]

The usage and limitations of the politics of mercy was clearly manifested in the way the regime and the Ba'th Party dealt with one of the most intractable security problems that plagued them – how to control the movement of men, particularly returning prisoners of war, deserters from military service, and exiles. Their effectiveness and ability to pursue a systemic policy was limited. The pursuit of deserters took place in fits and starts in the first year after the war, during confrontations with the

---

[77] *al-Qadisiyya*, August 18, 1992, 2: 920 citizens given the insignia of Mother of All Battles for good attitude vis-à-vis the Mother of All Battles. These were from the clans in Ta'mim province.

[78] The 1994 school registers for example, added the category "attitude" toward the Mother of All Battles to the list of categories by which the Ba'th determined who was excluded from key educational institutions and academies.

[79] *al-Qadisiyya*, August 31, 1996, 7. The phenomenon was dubbed "artificial ruse conspiracy." People lied about infractions committed by others to settle scores, to extort money, or to settle personal issues that had to do with rent and access to resources.

United States and its allies, and in response to perceived threats from the Iraqi opposition in the Kurdish or Shi'i southern areas.

The regime devised several methods to deal with the problem of limited control over its population. One of the most common stripped deserters and exiles of their rights and then amnestied them. Once amnestied and repatriated, those who voluntarily surrendered were declared "repentant." However, rarely was the restoration of their rights automatic. They had to negotiate a dysfunctional bureaucracy and predatory intermediaries to regain their entitlements. Although amnesty was not a new policy devised by the regime to deal with desertion, its use in the regime's last decade was frequent and incoherent. The regime issued a general amnesty soon after the end of the war that allowed deserters, as well as Iraqis who had fled for political reasons in the wake of the Intifada, to return to Iraq. Security services and the Ba'th Party processed amnestied individuals and recorded their place of residence.[80] The information continued to be used throughout the 1990s to track down repeat deserters, punish their families, and exclude them from positions in public sector institutions, colleges, and academies.

The ration card was perhaps the most effective method of controlling the movement of men. The Ba'th Party became a linchpin in a policy that linked desertion with access to rations. Despite the involvement of its own cadres in profiteering activities, the government tasked the party with monitoring black marketeering by private retailers.[81] As they had done during the Iran-Iraq war, these cadres created information banks on the population affected by the embargo. They coordinated with the Ministry of Trade and local provisioning centers to develop forms that included information on the residence of each recipient of rations and the provisioning center to which he or she was attached. Rations became a means for controlling Iraqis' movements, as they could only receive their rations in the place of their registered residency.

The arrest and surrender of soldiers and men slated for military service after amnesties, particularly if they were poor and had no effective intermediary, did not guarantee the restoration of their rights to employment

---

[80] Starting in July and proceeding through December 1991, a series of Revolutionary Command Council decrees granted amnesty to those who had fled the country for political reasons as well as deserters and absentees. *al-Qadisiyya*, November 14 and December 13, 1991, 16.

[81] *al-Qadisiyya*, June 18, 1994, 1. Revolutionary Command Council decree number 70 gave Ba'th Party cadres and members of the Popular Councils the right to arrest and imprison for a year store owners who refused to sell food at government prices.

and other entitlements. In 1994, an order was issued to deprive deserters' families of their rations unless their sons surrendered or they delivered them in person to Ba'th Party offices. In one example, a mother from the poor neighborhood of Saddam City had been harassed by the neighborhood party cadres and deprived of her rations. She finally surrendered her son but found that her ration card was not restored.[82] Her situation was repeated on a wide scale. Men who had surrendered to their units found their families remained without ration cards months later.[83] Nor was the situation of deserters who had surrendered and been branded "repentant" much better. Their condition was dependent on the network of connections they could mobilize to restore their rights.[84]

Nowhere is the incoherence in the policy of dealing with deserters and "culprits" of all kinds more evident than in a series of draconian laws and regulations issued by the Revolutionary Command Council in 1994. Several converging factors made that year particularly threatening for the regime. The first was the realization by the regime and the Iraqi public that no relief would soon come from the dire economic situation created by the sanctions, given the UN's insistence that it needed to maintain control over the government's funds disbursement and purchasing. The Iraqi government refused to accept these conditions. To project an image of effectiveness in combating hyperinflation, it issued a series of draconian laws to fight the profiteers and "criminals." It issued a law that set the punishment of "culprits" as the amputation of their right hands.[85] To counter its inability to change the conditions of the embargo, the regime made threatening moves toward Kuwait, moving its forces closer to the border. The threat of military strikes by the United States and Britain turned the regime's attention to its military capabilities. It called on its reserves and created a paramilitary force, the *fida'yun*, led by Hussain's son.[86] However, despite all its efforts, the regime could not stop men from disappearing from their residences or choosing not to report to the military recruitment offices of their neighborhoods. To combat desertion, the Revolutionary Command Council issued a decree in

---

[82] BRCC 027-2-4-1012 and 1013.

[83] BRCC 027-2-4-0903 and 0984.

[84] BRCC 01-3465-0002-0102 and BRCC 01-3465-0002-0108 for the different outcomes of the cases of "repentants" from Ba'quba in Diyali province and from the village of al-Shatra in the Dhi Qar province.

[85] Amnesty International, *Iraq: State Cruelty: Branding, Amputation and Death Penalty*, 1996. http://www.amnestry.org/en/library/asset/MDE14/003/1996/en/ea126950-eb02–11dd-aad1-ed57e7e5470b/mde140031996een.pdf accessed September 19, 2011.

[86] Fida'iyun Saddam was organized in 1993–4 to defend the regime.

1994 that gave the Ba'th the authority to cut off the ear of an apprehended deserter. Another law outlawed medical treatment to repair the damaged ear.[87] These laws, however, were sporadically implemented and were soon shelved. In a particularly gruesome series of Ba'thist reports on the apprehension of deserters in 1994, a special heading was devoted to the number of apprehended deserters whose ears had been removed.[88] In both Basra and Baghdad, party cadres reported on the punishment inflicted on hundreds of deserters. The practice, however, seems not to have lasted beyond the initial months of issuing the decree. Not only did most doctors refuse to perform the operation, a large number of Ba'thist cadres could not condone it.

Contrast the extreme violence of these laws with the guidelines on how to rehabilitate deserters issued by the government during the same year. Arrested deserters were to be imprisoned in local police stations, then processed to different ministries to work for fifty dinars a day, a pittance during hyperinflationary times. To ensure that they did not absent themselves, a Ba'thist cadre was assigned to each deserter and paid another fifty dinars. Soon after this order was issued, it became clear that neither the ministries nor the Ba'thist cadres were able to accommodate it. Ministries did not have the financial resources or the manpower to oversee the work. As for Ba'thist cadres, few had the time to devote to their assigned tasks for such little remuneration. The order was eventually rescinded and apprehended deserters were ordered to report to their assigned units.[89] This oscillation between issuing of laws that required severe punishment and directives that could not be implemented reflected the regime's desperation to project its power and the incapacity of state institutions and the party to translate that power into practice.

Perhaps the best window into understanding the public projection of power is to grapple with the contradiction between the Ba'th Party's

---

[87] Revolutionary Command Council decree number 59, passed in July 1994, ordered the amputation of the right hand of offenders convicted of theft once, then the left foot if they were convicted twice. Another decree, number 117, prescribed that an "X" be branded on their forehead and made it punishable for doctors to remove the mark. Amnesty International, "Amputation and Branding, Detention of Health Professionals," October 20, 1994, http:www.amnesty.org/en/library/asset/MDE14/013/1994/en/da1766e6–614-c-4dd9-ba46–4b817a7cb2df/mde140131994.en.pdf accessed September 19, 2011. The punishment of those who had their ears or hands amputated was registered on their civil identity cards, their nationality documents, and their military identity card. The stamp could be erased only if the culprit performed a heroic act in the presence of a credible witness.

[88] BRCC 027–2–4–1069.

[89] BRCC 023–3–6–0846 to 0850 and 0011.

diminished resources and ideological bankruptcy and its ability to recruit and promote members and mobilize the Iraqi population for the innumerable celebrations and commemorations decreed by the regime. The Ba'th Party survived the Intifada, but it was greatly weakened. Many of its cadres had participated, and numerous party offices had been ransacked. The embargo wreaked havoc on the party's finances. If the numerous directives issued by the General Secretariat to party offices calling on the party cadres to conserve paper in its record-keeping are any indication, the party was having a hard time finding the paper so essential for its information banks.[90] Nor could it keep up with the numerous calls to print posters of the leader or pictures to celebrate various occasions. The financing of these continued to be a problem.[91] More important, perhaps, was the inability to pay salaries. The purging and retirement of many older members had temporarily alleviated the party's financial situation, but its capacity to run its offices through regular disbursement was limited.[92] Like a large number of other state enterprises, the Ba'th was privatized. It no longer had a monopoly over managing Iraqis' social lives. Nor was it as crucial to protecting the regime's security. Its cadres had to compete with myriad other entrepreneurs, security and military figures, religious and tribal leaders, businessmen, and intellectuals, all clamoring for attention from the Office of the Presidency. To maintain its operations, the party's General Secretariat unofficially allowed its cadres, much like the ministries of state, to "elicit" donations, offer its services for a fee to intervene on the part of the Iraqi population and solicit funds for its security committees. The General Secretariat incentivized its cadres to attract and promote as many new members as possible, making promotion and benefits contingent on new member enrollment. This was particularly the case in 1994 and 1998, years that witnessed a drive to strengthen the party in the face of increased threats from the United States, the UN, and the Iraqi opposition.

During 1998, the Ba'th Party leadership undertook a campaign to increase its members and promote those within the party even if they had

---

[90] The General Secretariat issued several directives urging local offices to conserve paper and to conduct its business by phone.

[91] By 1993, a special committee within the Ministry of Culture and Information was formed to oversee the pictures of Saddam Hussain and coordinate expenses. BRCC 023–5–4–0000. The committee faced especially acute problems in finding funds to post "before" and "after" pictures of buildings fixed after the destruction of the war and the uprising. BRCC 01–3373–0000–0007 to 0011.

[92] BRCC 01–2855–0002–0000. The file is the purging of the Ba'th cadres in the aftermath of the Intifada.

not served the requisite years that made them eligible for promotion. The reasons for this policy were varied. Perhaps the most important was the need to create a leadership cadre from the new generation of Iraqis who were born in the 1970s, had no memory of Iraq without Saddam Hussain, and did not have any grounding in Ba'th ideology. The regime itself had encouraged this move in large part because of the increasing problems with the lawlessness that its own policies of devolving security and other powers to favored clans had created. Neighborhood party cadres were encouraged to target schools and promised promotion within the Ba'th and security responsibilities within their neighborhoods. Recruitment was now parceled out to individuals within subdivisions. Each individual was rewarded according to how many new recruits he or she was able to bring in.[93] Thus, if the school registers of matriculating male students for the year 1998–9 are any indication, more than 90 percent of students were Ba'thists.[94] Even more significant is the remarkable increase in general party membership. It more than doubled between 1986 and 2002.[95] Yet the numbers are deceiving. Even if we are to accept the statistics presented by Ba'th party cadres as reality, membership in the party was but one of many designated categories the regime used to measure Iraqis' political affiliations and their "attitudes." The push to reinvigorate the party created the illusion for its cadres that their fortunes might be turning if they proved capable of expanding their reach. It also offered an opportunity for a younger generation of Iraqis to find a place for themselves should they prove sufficiently entrepreneurial.

Despite its diminishing resources, the Ba'th Party remained the main arm of the regime in creating public festivals that brought out the masses in a public show of support for its decisions and the frequent celebrations and commemorations the Iraqi population had to attend. These were meant as spectacles to assert, as Lisa Wedeen has shown for Yemen, that the regime was "acting like a state" despite the weak capacity of its institutions and of the Ba'th Party.[96] The national calendar of Iraq was crammed with all kinds of celebrations – commemorations of battles of both wars, milestones set by the regime for surviving yet another year of

---

[93] Baran, *Vivre la Tyrannie*, pp. 27–36, and interview with Abu Muhammad, Amman, Jordan, August 7, 2007.
[94] See Appendix I.
[95] Sassoon, *Saddam Hussein's Ba'th Party*, p. 52. The numbers increased from 1,637,444 in 1986 to 3,971,762 in 2002.
[96] Wedeen, "Seeing Like a Citizen, Acting Like a State," *Comparative Studies in Society and History*, p. 681.

sanctions, and a host of other fictions of national endurance and heroism – for which Iraqis had to show public support. This "eventfulness" was an essential part of the perpetual attempts of the regime to assert its presence. Early in 1998, when negotiations over the return of weapons inspectors were at an impasse and talk of military action against Iraq was once again floated by the United States, the regime turned to the Ba'th to organize military exercises by the masses to defend Iraq. In April, the Ba'th Party organized a "Day of Dignity and Chivalry" as a culmination of the months of military exercises by "volunteers," who, despite eight years of sanctions, had not lost their "abilities ... to rise and defend their country ... [Iraqis] are a people that will not be dishonored."[97] To encourage participation, five extra grades were added to the grade point average of students who came out for the festivities.[98] A special identity card was issued to participants. Those who elected not to participate were excluded from applying to colleges and academies, their "attitude" deemed incorrect.[99] Surveys of matriculating male students for that year showed close to 100 percent participation rate.

Conclusion

Four years after the massive mobilization for the "Day of Dignity and Chivalry," the regime proposed the creation of another militia, the Army of Jerusalem. Its declared purpose was to march into Jerusalem to help the Palestinians in their second uprising. That this was a spurious claim and one that elicited a great number of jokes among Iraqis was beside the point. It was, according to one commentator, a "pantomime" army, designed to create the illusion, for the regime itself as well as for the Iraqi population, of effectiveness and action.[100] Yet Iraqis "volunteered" and continued to participate in these massive events. Coercion, threat of punishment, the creation of a culture in which citizens were made "culpable" of an infraction if they did not participate, may explain why people complied with calls for participation in these rituals. No less significant were the ways in which the arbitrariness of power and the improvisational nature of governance had become firmly tied to routine spectacles, meant to make the presence of Saddam Hussain's rule and of the Ba'th Party

---

[97] *al-Jumhuriyya*, April 19, 3. The description was that of the editor in chief of the newspaper.
[98] *al-Jumhuriyya*, March 23, 1.
[99] BRCC 01–2496–0003–0001 and 0003.
[100] Baran, *Vivre la Tyrannie*, p. 30.

real to the Iraqi public. To a citizenry with diminished economic, social, and intellectual opportunities, these spectacles provided the background din to their daily lives. They were endured as everything else in embargoed Iraq. For Ba'thists who ran these spectacles and helped manage the new politics, they provided the illusion of stability. Spectacles of mobilization, despite their ideological emptiness, explain the durability of the regime and its brittleness.

Abu Muhammad, a Ba'thist commissar in the Iraqi army during the Iran-Iraq war and the First Gulf War, provides a window into the effectiveness and limits of the politics of the last decade of Ba'thist rule.[101] Born to a lower-middle-class family of A'dhamiyya merchants in 1971, Abu Muhammad was one of twelve children. He had volunteered quite young to become a low-level commissar in the Republican Guard in 1987, a year after his older brother had deserted the army, causing his Ba'thist family embarrassment and harassment by the neighborhood party cadres. Abu Muhammad was demobilized after the end of the Iran-Iraq war, and let his membership in the Ba'th Party lapse. Mobilized again during the First Gulf War, he was stationed in Nugra in Kuwait, but soon found himself back in Basra. He was by then a full working member within the party with loyalty to the person of Saddam Hussain rather than to Ba'thist ideology. Saddam, for Abu Muhammad, was a charismatic, firm, and strong father figure whose claims for regional leadership were deserved. Abu Muhammad was demobilized from his unit at the end of the First Gulf War, but stopped going to party meetings even though he had attained the relatively high level of working member of a subdivision. The economic sanctions had forced him to devote his energies to private business and he had little time for the party. In 1998, after several years of struggling to make a living, his fortunes began to turn. The regime had decided to reactivate the role of the Ba'th Party in the wake of the buildup to Operation Desert Fox. Ba'thist cadres were enjoined to become more active and recruit new members. Abu Muhammad stepped up to the challenge and became the leading recruiter in his neighborhood. He was also an active member of the party's security committee. He opened a café that he turned into the headquarters for all festivities and for marches organized by the Ba'th. Two years later, he felt confident enough to approach one of the directors of the leading privately owned contracting companies in Iraq and asked him to secure a position for him in the Ministry of Housing as a security officer tasked with overseeing

---

[101] Interview with Abu Muhammad, Amman, Jordan, August 7, 2007.

supplies in a major building project funded by the government. By his own account, his world in A'dhamiyya was stable and he was at the center of it.

In 2002, he and other employees were volunteered into the Army of Jerusalem. It was in his capacity as a Ba'thist commissar that he was stationed in the al-Rashidiyya area to protect Republican Guard supplies when the bombing of military supplies and installments started in March 2003. He had fought in the Iran-Iraq and First Gulf wars as a Ba'thist commissar and thought the world he helped shape would last indefinitely. He could not imagine that Ba'thist Iraq would not survive this latest war with the United States. He had seen his role as a fighter in the last days of Ba'thist rule as a heroic defense of the nation and had no inkling that the armed forces would not put up a significant resistance. His commanding officer had simply worn his civilian clothes and abandoned him and his comrades in their position. When Abu Muhammad asked him why he had done this, the man simply told him "it is over" and advised him to go home.

6

War's Citizens, War's Families

Ammar Hasan once estimated that there must be twenty-one levels of citizens' rights in Iraq:

There are entitlements and privileges that distinguish one citizen from the other. I consider myself, for example, a citizen of the fifteenth degree.... No one of my family was martyred in the war, no one had medals of courage, I don't have any relatives who were prisoners of war, I do not have any party rank, my father is an independent not a Ba'thist, neither my family nor I belong to the party. At the same time, I have no one in my family against the regime, no one among my family who is outside the country working with the opposition. According to this logic I am grade fifteen ... Because if my daughter applies to college and had a perfect grade average [sic] and the person who competes with her has a father who has a high party rank, or has a medal of courage or has a connection, or is among the Friend of the President, or ... or ... or.... All these privileges, I have nothing of these.[1]

Ammar's bitter comment captures three features of Iraqi citizens' rights during wartime: the proliferation of categories that determined access or denial of citizens to entitlements, the importance of martyrdom and soldiering in bestowing privileges, and the primacy of family in the assignation of rights.

At the onset of the Iran-Iraq war, Iraq's political leadership found that it had to rework the legal and administrative infrastructure of the system of privileges and exclusion that had underpinned citizens' rights in the Ba'thist state. Starting in October 1980, to garner support for the war, the Revolutionary Command Council (RCC) enacted a series of laws

---

[1] Interview with Ammar Hasan, Damascus, Syria, August 16, 2007.

161

intended to reshape the rights of soldiers and martyrs by elevating both
to favored citizens' status and granting them privileges formerly reserved
to Ba'th Party members. To enforce its version of national security and
to counter desertion, the Council reworked the nationality law to deny
citizens of "Iranian affiliation" their national rights, and changed military law to deprive deserters and their families of their civil and social
rights. These laws marked the beginning of an ambitious effort by the
state to regulate its citizens' claims of belonging to a nation at war. The
efforts were often piecemeal because laws and resolutions were devised
to deal with the short-term exigencies of the war effort and in response
to citizens' demands for entitlements. No long-term policy was developed to deal with the far-reaching social impact of such regulations. To
complicate matters, during the last twelve years of Ba'thist rule (1991–
2003), the Iraqi regime created a multitude of categories of inclusion and
exclusion that further upended Iraqis' rights as citizens to claim routine
entitlements that had existed during the early 1970s. Iraqi citizens' rights
became increasingly differentiated and dependent on a set of specific
"contributions" to the nation or the regime.

The systematic use of family and kin to bestow privileges and punish
opponents became part of Ba'thist state policy in the 1970s. Families
of those deemed enemies of "the nation and revolution" lost full rights
of citizenship. By contrast, families of loyal and old-time Ba'thists were
granted privileged access to employment and promotion within key government institutions. The Iran-Iraq war brought changes to this policy.
Not only were rewards previously reserved for Ba'thists extended to martyrs' families, but punishments once levied against families of political
opponents were now extended to families of deserters and absentees. In
a country that had lost some six hundred thirty thousand martyrs and
had an annual desertion rate in the tens of thousands, the policy of using
families as instruments of reward and punishment had a multiplier effect
and transformed the rights of millions of citizens.[2]

No attempt to understand Ba'thist methods of rule can overlook the
critical role of the family. Nor can we fully comprehend the claims made
by Iraqis to their rights or their exclusion from such rights without coming to grips with the ways in which the state regulated families to ensure
support, loyalty, and obedience.

---

[2] For the use of family to punish opponents in Stalinist Soviet Union, see Golfo Alexopolous, "Stalin and the politics of kinship: Practices of collective punishment, 1920s-1930s," *Comparative Studies in Society and History*, vol. 50 1(2008), 91–117.

Defining Martyrdom

The legal underpinnings of Iraqi citizens' rights under the Ba'thist regime were spelled out in the Interim Constitution of 1970. Iraqis, defined as belonging to two ethnic groups, Kurds and Arabs, were equal citizens of a socialist Arab state the primary goals of which were the "planning, directing and steering of the national economy" and the protection of the nation's territorial integrity. The state was the caretaker of national resources, so it could "make available, the means of enjoying the achievements of modernization, by the popular masses and to generalize the progressive accomplishments of contemporary civilization on all citizens."[3] As a state focused on development, the regime's primary goal was to foster "social solidarity" by ensuring that citizens had equal rights to free education, health care, and full employment. These rights remained the mainstay of the Ba'thist government's policies and central to its claims to legitimacy until the middle of the 1970s. However, these rights became increasingly circumscribed by a series of exclusions that denied to non-Ba'thists as well as to those who had belonged to outlawed parties access to vital government institutions and agencies. By 1979, the Iraqi government's definition of social and civil rights had become bound to one's political affiliation and was based on the concept of "comprehensiveness" (*shumuliyya*). To have full citizen's rights in the Ba'thist state, one had to belong to the party because its ideology and practice fused party, state, and nation into one.[4] Political organizations opposed to the Ba'th, whose existence had been legal under the 1970 Interim Constitution, were now declared treasonous, and their followers and their families were excluded from select rights accruing to other Iraqi citizens. After the suppression of the Kurdish rebellion and the dissolution of the alliance with the Iraqi Communist Party, a new category of citizenship was devised to deal with those who belonged to these parties but had left them because they were outlawed. They had returned to the "national fold," although their and their families' full social and civic rights were still curtailed. In the absence of any alternative legal political organization, the options available to Iraqis were to remain "independent" by not joining the party or

---

[3] The 1970 Interim Constitution of Iraq remained functional until 2005. For text, see http://www.mpil.de/shared/data/pdf/constitution_of_iraq_1970-_engl.pdf accessed February 26, 2012.

[4] Hasan al-'Ubaidi, *Dirasat Qanuniyya fi Qiyadat al-Hizb li al-Dawla wa al-Mujtama'* (A Legal Study of the Leadership of the Party/State and Society) (Baghdad: Dar Wasit, 1982).

to become Ba'thists. As "independents," they retained the majority of
their social rights, but were excluded from select institutions of higher
education and denied employment or promotion in the military, security, and police apparatus.

At the outset of the Iran-Iraq war, a series of resolutions and decrees
issued by the RCC further redefined the rights of citizenship laid out in
the 1970 Interim Constitution. A new system of entitlements was created
to reward those who had contributed to the war, notwithstanding their
party affiliation. At the same time, increasingly draconian rules governed
the disenfranchisement of categories of people deemed detrimental to
the war effort, in particular those of "Iranian affiliation."[5] Such drastic
reworking of the legal basis of Iraqi citizens' rights had to do with the
monopolization of legislation on such issues by the RCC at the expense
of civil and military courts as well as ministries. The process had started
a year before the beginning of the Iran-Iraq war. When Saddam Hussain
took power in July 1979 and became chairman of the RCC, he initiated
a series of laws and resolutions that undermined the autonomy of many
state institutions, including the ministries of Justice, Labor and Social
Affairs, Youth, Higher Education, Finance, and Defense and Interior.[6]
The RCC now had oversight over much of the nation's decision making
on development, finance, and law. Most significant for our purposes was
the Council's ability to circumvent and reshape laws governing military
entitlements, which had been the cornerstone of the system of promotion
and retirement for the armed forces and which were managed by the
Ministry of Defense. Thus, mobilizing and rewarding soldiers, managing

---

[5] Abd al-Husayn Sha'ban, *Man Huwa al-'Iraqi? Ishkaliyat al-Jinsiyya wa al-la-Jinsiyya
fi al-Qanunayn al-'Iraqi wa al-Duwali*, (Who is Iraqi? The Problem of Nationality and
Non-nationality in Iraqi and International Laws) (Beirut: Dar al-Kunuz al-Dhahabiyya,
2002). Between 1924 and 1968, there were two major laws on nationality and citizenship in Iraq with few amendments. The resolutions issued by the RCC outside direct
amendments to the nationality law were always justified as being part of national security legislation.

[6] The reorganization of ministries, institutions, and professional and popular organizations
began in earnest in 1980 and continued throughout the 1980s. The legal fiction maintained by the RCC to justify this intervention in various state institutions was Article 43
of the Interim Constitution of 1970, paragraph (a). The reorganization of the Ministry
of Justice was done under Amendments 6 and 7 to the Law of the Ministry of Justice
of April 30, 1980. See *Official Gazette*, December 31, 1980 (*al-Waqa'i' al-'Iraqiya*), no
53, p. 18. The Ministry of Youth was reorganized in 1981, *Official Gazette*, February
10, 1982, no 6, pp. 6–8. The General Federation of Writers dissolved the two writers'
federations that had existed and put the new Federation under a reorganized and more
pliant Ministry of Culture and Information under Law 70, issued in April 1980, *Official
Gazette*, no. 1983, pp. 2–11.

martyrs' affairs, and punishing absentees and deserters became some of the Council's primary legislative functions.[7]

The underlying logic of much of the legislation was that Qadisiyat Saddam was the first war of national security and, as such, was unprecedented in Iraqi history. From the outset, the process of expanding older entitlements required redefining categories of citizens' rights. Determining the official boundaries of martyrdom, for example, soon proved more challenging than the government had initially envisioned. Was the fallen soldier a martyr of the nation or the party, or did his death in Qadisiyat Saddam grant him a different status as a citizen? Two organizations dealt with martyrs' rights in 1980: the Ministry of Defense and the Ba'th Party. Each had its own definition of martyrdom. For the Ministry of Defense, the martyr was an enlisted soldier who had died in the line of fire. His rights and those of his survivors were governed by laws and regulations issued in 1975 that covered retirement, martyrdom, and disability under the rubric of "Law of Service and Retirement in the Military."[8] Compensation to the fallen soldier's family included his retirement salary according to his grade, medical care, the right to shop at armed forces stores, the right to use armed forces clubs, and other entitlements accruing to officers and enlisted men.

For the Ba'th Party, a martyr was an individual – civilian or military – who had died in the service of the party and in the cause of the Arab nation as defined by the Ba'th. A directive issued by the party's General Secretariat in January 1979 spelled out the benefits accruing to a martyr and his family. The martyr's rank in the Ba'th Party hierarchy was posthumously elevated, so that if he had had the rank of an advocate, he was promoted to a member after his death. The party took upon itself the responsibility to protect the martyr's family much as the father had done. The martyr's children were inducted into the party and given the rank of advocate. With that came a host of benefits, including an accelerated track up the party ladder and the prospects of joining government and state institutions reserved for Ba'thists. Party officials were expected to visit the martyrs' families and give them gifts on national and religious occasions.[9]

---

[7] In the first year of the war alone, the RCC issued eleven resolutions dealing with entitlements of fallen soldiers. Many involved the state in the legal issues of inheritance to the relatives of the deceased. "Social cohesion and the battle of Qadisiyya," *al-Jumhuriyya*, May 28, 1981, 3.

[8] *al-Jumhuriyya*, October 30, 1980, 7.

[9] NIDS/serial 322164.

Soon after the Iran-Iraq war began in 1980, the government issued resolutions that amended military laws and reshaped Ba'th policies covering entitlements to soldiers and martyrs. These eventually became classified as the rights of soldiers and martyrs of Qadisiyat Saddam, to be distinguished from rights accruing to soldiers who had fought in other wars or individuals who had been martyred in defense of the nation and the party in other ways. The resolutions were enacted to deal with two problems. The first had to do with the government's need to create a reward system that would motivate conscripts to keep fighting and put them on a par with enlisted men who had volunteered to join the armed forces, attended military schools, and whose entitlements were covered by military laws. The second problem went to the heart of the definition of the Ba'thist state at war. Were soldiers who had died defending the nation to be considered martyrs of the Ba'thist "revolution" which had now melded the party, state, and nation?

To deal with the first problem, the RCC issued a resolution amending the "Law of Service and Retirement" that governed compensation for enlisted men. Martyred or injured conscripts were entitled to the same rights as enlisted men in the armed forces if they had fallen in the war with Iran.[10] The resolution also allowed the president of Iraq to override laws governing compensation and promotion within the military, granting him the prerogative to issue compensation and medals. The president could also expand the benefits to the martyr's family beyond those required by military laws of promotion and retirement. For example, the martyr was promoted one grade above his rank as an enlisted man or pay grade if he was a government employee at the time of his service and death. His heirs received a lump sum amounting to eighteen months of salary and full retirement benefits. The children and grandchildren of martyrs were exempt from the general requirements set by the ministries of Education, Interior, and Defense, particularly governing grades, should they decide to enter military and police academies. A martyr's children were also given special consideration when entering universities and priority in public sector jobs. To facilitate their affairs, members of martyrs' families were given a special identifying insignia.[11]

In the 1980s, especially during the first five years of the Iran-Iraq war, the RCC issued copious resolutions governing compensations for

---

[10] The resolution alluded to categories of people as those employed in the public and socialist sectors.

[11] *al-Jumhuriyya*, October 30, 1980, 7.

martyrs' families that included increases in salary, land, residence, and other entitlements. Largely in response to claims by families of men who fought in the war and were drawn from the security forces and the party militia and who did not fall under the purview of the Ministry of Defense, the Council further expanded the category of martyrs to include members of the Popular Army as well as members of the security and police apparatus.[12] As the number of dead mounted, citizens' petitions, processed through local Ba'th Party offices, clamored for the designation of martyr for all who had died as the result of the war, even if the manner of their death did not strictly fall within the Ministry of Defense's definition of "death under fire."[13]

In the early months of the Iran-Iraq war, the RCC issued a resolution posthumously inducting all non-Ba'thist martyrs into the Ba'th Party and promoting enlisted and conscripted party members within the party. The decision had an ideological underpinning. Since the nation, armed forces, and party were synonymous, to die serving one meant to die serving all. Within this definition of martyrdom, it was difficult to assert that martyrs who did not belong to the party had no rights. To die for the nation in Qadisiyat Saddam was to die for the party as well. Beyond the ideological meaning ascribed to martyrdom in Ba'thist Iraq, induction into the party meant more entitlements for enlisted and conscripted soldiers alike. Martyrs' membership certificates were published in the *al-Jumhuriyya* and *al-Thawra* dailies. The entitlements that had accrued only to party members before the war were now extended to martyrs' families, even if they had not been party members or had served at a low level in the party hierarchy. In addition, since all martyrs were now party members, it was incumbent on party cadres to become custodians of martyrs' families. By the end of the war, the definition of the rights of martyrs as citizens had gone beyond those determined by military laws governing retirement and benefits within the Ministry of Defense and well beyond the ceremonial and paternalistic definition of the Ba'th Party martyrs. With the emergence of a citizen army and the increasing number of casualties, martyrdom was now elevated to an exalted category of citizen, accompanied

---

[12] RCC Resolution 712, issued June 1, 1982, granted rights of martyrs to fighters in the Popular Army. BRCC 01-2993-0001-0673.

[13] BRCC 01-2459-0002-0448 and 0449. By 1988, the definition of martyrs included but was not confined to death by friendly fire and death due to the explosion of military ordnance. In the aftermath of the Anfal campaign, soldiers in both the Popular Army and regular armed forces were declared martyrs if they had died fighting "saboteurs" or if they had been subjected to chemical weapons.

by a widely expanded number of rights and bolstered by a cultural and social apparatus that privileged claims of martyrdom.

From the beginning, however, martyrs' entitlements were confusing and negotiable. To claim benefits (to land, cars, educational privileges, etc.) martyrs' families had to deal with multiple institutions with overlapping jurisdictions, which was confusing. Families often found that they could petition the government to have a late relative categorized as martyr, even if the way he died was not within the military's legal definition. Increasingly as the war progressed, the rights of martyrs became particularistic. Entitlements were granted according to military and party rank and to the number of medals. Entitlements were also subject to periodic modifications by the state. These modifications happened with remarkable regularity during the many national celebrations, when the leader and the party rewarded a certain category of martyrs with new entitlements. Families of martyrs within the party, for example, wrote to the General Secretariat seeking a further promotion of their dead relative in order to garner specific entitlements disbursed by the leader or the party on national occasions.[14]

The families' experiences while interacting with the bureaucracy differed depending on the rank of their soldier-martyr. Families of dead officers and enlisted soldiers navigated the relatively organized bureaucracy of the Ministry of Defense. They could appeal to the Committee for the Protection of Soldiers of Qadisiyat Saddam, a veterans' organization and intergovernmental agency devoted to the problems of enlisted men within the armed forces.

The families of martyred conscripts, however, particularly those drawn from poorer sectors of Iraqi society, often found that they had to resort to local branches of the Ba'th Party to help them interpret the various resolutions that continued to redefine the meaning of martyrdom and families' rights. Even when the conscript's death was supposed to have entitled him to land, an apartment, or privileges for children, the majority of such families received the initial sum given on the soldier's death and his meager retirement benefits.[15] If the dead soldier was a

---

[14] BRCC 01–3252–0002–0004. This is a ledger dated 1998 that lists petitions from family members of martyrs requesting that their martyred relatives be granted a higher rank within the party.

[15] BRCC 035–3–4–0076 and 0077. In 1984, for example, the families of two martyrs from Basra, border guards in the Zurbatiya area in 1980, wrote to the head of the Southern Bureau. They had only been given the martyrs' retirement salaries and a residence. They were not given any other grants as other martyrs of Qadisiyat Saddam had been.

self-employed petty trader or farmer, his family was often left penniless. In such cases, privileges accruing to children as well as possession of the insignia of martyrdom assured them special consideration from the party and the leader on national holidays. Such consideration could sometimes include monetary compensation and land, but it was more often confined to ceremonial gifts. While important in allowing relatives to make claims on the state and the party, such gifting remained unpredictable and was rarely construed as a rightful entitlement by its recipients.

So acute was the problem of managing the multiple claims by martyrs' families that, in 1989, the Ba'th was tasked by the Office of the Presidency with issuing recommendations on how to streamline the process. The resultant recommendation was to create an intergovernmental agency, similar to that created to deal with the war injured, and attach it to the Office of the Presidency. Among the agency's proposed functions was coordination among the various state agencies that determined and dispensed the entitlements of martyrs.[16] Its recommendations were never acted upon, as the First Gulf War ushered in a new set of problems that further complicated matters.

The First Gulf War and the ensuing Intifada compelled a reexamination of the official definition of martyrdom. Bombardment of civilian targets and the killing of a number of Ba'th Party cadres by the rebels erased the clear distinction between civilian and combatant deaths. At the same time, the rebels challenged the sanctioned definition of martyrs of Qadisiyat Saddam soon after they took control. In Basra, for example, rebels in control of the city's hospital issued certificates of martyrdom to those killed by government forces during the uprising.[17] The rebel actions were informed by an alternate definition of martyrdom endorsed by Iraqi opposition parties who fought with Iranians against their countrymen during the Iran-Iraq war. Iraqi Islamist opposition parties in Iran as well as Kurdish parties had from the war's outset declared that those of their men who had died fighting the Iraqi army were martyrs fighting an unjust Ba'thist war. The uprising, according to this view, was an extension of the fight against the Ba'thist regime. The rebels' claim was soon countered by the Ba'th Party, which now asserted that those of its civilian members killed by the rebels should be accorded the same rights as soldiers who had died in Qadisiyat Saddam. They had died in the line of fire

---

[16] BRCC 01-2124-0000-0212 to 0220.
[17] BRCC 01-3455-0002-0102.

defending the nation against its enemies, who were "agents" of a foreign government.[18]

By September 1991, the RCC had begun to set up mechanisms to assess who would be considered a martyr in its latest war. It determined that the Mother of All Battles (the First Gulf War), had started on August 2, 1990, the date of the Iraqi invasion of Kuwait, and that it was ongoing. Those conscripted or enlisted soldiers killed during the invasion and the ensuing forty-two-day war, as well as those from the security, intelligence apparatus, and Popular Army were considered martyrs. They were accorded the same rights as martyrs of Qadisiyat Saddam. To determine martyrdom eligibility during the uprising, however, a special committee under the direction of the Ministry of Interior was established. The committee was tasked with distinguishing legitimate martyrs (those who died fighting on the government's side) from fraudulent ones.[19]

The RCC extended the martyrs' rights that accrued to combatants during the Iran-Iraq war to those of the First Gulf War as well. The designation of the Mother of All Battles as an ongoing war, however, created the means by which various constituencies in Iraq could claim the rights of martyrs. The Ba'th Party was among the first to insist that those of its members slain by the rebels be considered martyrs of the Mother of All Battles. In the first months after the uprising, it proceeded to create application forms for members who wanted to file claims to martyrs' entitlements on behalf of a slain relative. This helped ensure that the flood of claims from party members who had lost family during the war and the uprising were legitimate. The General Secretariat's approval of the certificates of martyrdom allowed a family to receive the land and other entitlements assigned to it by Saddam Hussain.[20] Other party members challenged this narrow definition. If the Mother of All Battles was an ongoing war, one party member from Mosul wrote in 1994, Iraq was in the third phase of that battle, having withstood the coalition's attacks and the "page of treachery and betrayal." This third phase was characterized by:

smuggling and economic destruction, by the avariciousness of merchants, and the devastation of the psyche by the enemies. As the situation escalates to actual battles and as the smuggler and saboteur obtain all kinds of weapons to resist our squads [of the party's security committees] and some injuries and deaths occur,

[18] BRCC 01–2124–0000–0212 to 0220.
[19] BRCC 01–2993–0001–0669 to 0671.
[20] BRCC 01–2993–0001–0548 to 0705.

we suggest that those martyred in the confrontation be considered martyrs of the Mother of All Battles ... and be awarded the same privileges.[21]

To deal with the proliferating claims, the regime established levels of martyrdom and made entitlements dependent on one's position in a hierarchy of victimhood. On December 24, 1993, an RCC resolution declared all the families of martyred soldiers of Qadisiyat Saddam and the Mother of All Battles "Friends of Saddam."[22] They now received the periodic salary raises and entitlements granted by Hussain on many national occasions. Those families whose martyrs had received badges of courage before their deaths were accorded more privileges than those who had merely died serving the nation. In 1999, the heads of families who had given three martyrs or more to Qadisiyat Saddam and the Mother of All Battles were granted the Rafidayn Civilian Badge, one of the highest honors in the country. With that badge came additional privileges.[23] This increased differentiation of categories aroused great confusion among martyrs' families. Not only were they now required to obtain further identifications to claim their entitlements, but they also had to go through a bureaucratic wrangle to do so. Complaints by citizens led the Ministry of Defense and other organizations dealing with martyrs' families to designate special days just to process the entitlements of "Friends of Saddam."

The line between martyred combatant and civilian victim continued to erode throughout the 1990s. The erosion was partly encouraged by a government cognizant of the changed rules of engagement that came with the First Gulf War and the sanctions regime when civilian populations became the primary victims. It was equally fueled by the rising clamor of a population with rapidly diminishing resources. Death and victimhood became a means of negotiating a measure of security and survival in an otherwise precarious economic environment. A woman who had lost twelve family members when U.S. warplanes bombed her family home in Basra asked that she receive the same entitlements as the families of al-'Amiriyya shelter, which was hit by the United States in February 1991. The wife of a policeman who had died fighting Shi'i Islamist parties in the south in 1978, well before any war, asked that he be declared a martyr.[24] Whether their requests were taken into consideration is difficult

---

[21] BRCC 01–2993–0001–0131.
[22] *al-Qadisiyya*, December 30, 1993, 1.
[23] BRCC 01–2857–0001–0044.
[24] BRCC 01–3465–0002–0056 to 0057.

to say, but they highlight the extent to which claims to martyrdom had become entrenched in the vocabulary of citizenship.

Regulating Families

Ba'thist ideology, like other nationalist ideologies, regarded the patriarchal family as the primary productive unit of the society it sought to create.[25] Saddam Hussain often invoked the metaphor of the nation as a family with himself as its patriarch. He drew on his own family and extended kin to man key positions within the party and the security services, leading Iraqis to describe the party as the "family party." The deployment of personal, kin, and tribal networks outside and within the party was highly informal, unstable, and given to factional conflict. This kind of politics has alternatively been described as patrimonial or "neo-tribal," an Iraqi iteration of similar forms of authoritarian rule in one-party states.[26] The Ba'thist state, however, also engaged in regulating families to create obedient and modern citizens in a more formal and institutionalized manner. The nuclear family, according to Article 11 of the 1970 Interim Constitution, provided "the nucleus of the Society. The State secures its protection and support, and ensures maternal and child care."[27] Thus, the family constituted the foundation of modern citizenship, and the state's role was to protect mother and child legally and socially. The Ba'thist state's developmental and modernizing social policies targeted the family by issuing legislation that provided the legal underpinnings for women's autonomy in matters of marriage and divorce and weakened the extended family's role in the same domain.[28]

State policies and Ba'thist practices, however, did not conceive of family as merely a social reform and modernizing project. The family was also at the heart of its political project. Beginning in the 1970s, on applications to join the Ba'th Party, inductees had to list their extended

---

[25] Noga Efrati, *Women In Iraq: Past Meets Present* (New York: Columbia University Press, 2012).

[26] Amatzia Baram, "Neo-tribalism in Iraq," *International Journal of Middle East Studies*, 29 (1997), 1–31; and Faleh Abdul Jabar, "Shaykhs and ideologues: Detribalization and retribalization in Iraq, 1968–1998," *Middle East Report*, 215 (2000), 28–31.

[27] http://www.mpil.de/shared/data/pdf/constitution_of_iraq_1970-_engl.pdf.

[28] Amal Rassam, "Revolution within the revolution? Women and the state in Iraq," in Tim Niblock (ed.), *Iraq: The Contemporary State* (New York: St. Martin's Press, 1982), pp. 88–99; Suad Joseph, "Elite strategies for state-building: women, family, religion and state building in Iraq and Lebanon," in Deniz Kendiyoti (ed.), *Women, Islam and the State* (Philadelphia: Temple University Press, 1991), pp. 176–200.

families' history of political activism, their criminal records if any, and their place of origin.[29] By the early 1980s, the process of categorizing Iraqi individual citizens as members of extended families had expanded to cover the majority of the population. At several levels of the party hierarchy, from organizations operating in high schools and universities, to committees set up at the level of neighborhood and townships, a systematic process of forming "information banks" on Iraqi citizens placed every individual within kinship networks in order to dispense punishment and entitlements. Access to state resources was determined by one's family's political affiliation and rank within the Ba'th party hierarchy. Denial of rights was predicated on whether any member of one's family had been considered an enemy of the "nation and revolution." The whole apparatus was bolstered by the RCC. It passed decrees and amended laws that set the boundaries of rights within the family, particularly on issues governing women, martyrs, deserters, and others considered enemies of the Ba'thist state. Ba'thist institutional practices ensured that various government agencies approved and denied entitlements within a prescribed hierarchy of inclusions and exclusions. Precise and particular definitions of what constituted family and clear demarcation of "culpability" were part of the systematic and institutionalized process of granting or denying rights to citizens.

Two constructions of family undergirded much of the RCC legislation and Ba'thist practice in its dealing with martyrs and deserters: the first was of a patriarchal nuclear family household headed by a male that formed the basis of modern citizenship; the second was that of extended family, which encompassed first- and second-degree relatives.[30] The government deployed these definitions of family to grant entitlements and deny rights during the Iran-Iraq war. To recognize a martyr, it allocated rights and rewards to his nuclear patriarchal family household; to punish an enemy of the state or a deserter, it levied various sanctions against his extended family or kin. Thus, when it came to family, Ba'thist legal and institutional practice was often contradictory. On one hand, the government sought to strengthen the nuclear family at the expense of kin and clan; on the other, it created a set of regulations that tied an individual citizen's rights to those of his kin, thereby augmenting the regulatory

---

[29] Sassoon, *Saddam Hussein's Ba'th Party*, pp. 34–70.
[30] In dealing with the Kurdish population, the government used a third definition of family. Kurdish men were located within kin networks of the first and second degree and within their clan and tribal kin. See Chapter 4 for how the government used family and clan networks to punish Kurds during the Anfal campaign.

power of kin and entrenching clan loyalties. As an ideal citizen, one was part of a nuclear patriarchal family that served to build a modern state. As a dissident citizen, one was part of an extended kin network.

During the early years of the Iran-Iraq war, RCC legislation and regulations attempted to retain this neat division strengthening the nuclear family and women's rights within it when rewarding martyrs' widows and using extended kin to punish opponents as well as deserters. The large number of war casualties, however, severely strained patriarchal family structures, as more women became the heads of households. Compounding matters was the rising tide of desertion and absenteeism the government was unable to control. To deal with both problems, the RCC issued numerous resolutions and regulations that reshaped citizen rights. In so doing, it acquired unprecedented legal power over such civil matters as marriage, divorce, inheritance, and a myriad of other private rights. In particular, the state singled out the regulation of women's rights to cope with the crisis afflicting the patriarchal family structure. While some of its early policies sought to enhance the rights of widows, these fell to the wayside in the face of social pressures from extended kin and security concerns. When dealing with families of deserters, the state sought to use extended kin networks to punish and control desertion and broke up nuclear families by disenfranchising spouses and children of deserters.

In May 1989, the Ba'th Party General Secretariat sent letters to its various bureaus and popular organizations asking them to address the delinquency and criminality that had become rampant among martyrs' children.[31] The series of reports that ensued attributed the problem to the fact that so many patriarchal families were stressed by the death of their male heads. In particular, widows who became heads of households faced enormous difficulties, notably challenges to their rights to their husband's entitlements from in-laws, siblings, and other wives. Whether these entitlements included land, apartments, a car, or just the martyr's retirement salary, in-laws and siblings often forced the widow to live under drastically reduced economic circumstances. Even if she were able to retain a substantial portion of these entitlements, she found herself preyed upon by dishonest building contractors intent on profiting off her construction on land received from the state or victimized by interfering male family members who wanted to usurp her resources.

Complicating matters, the reports continued, were the continual attempts of wives and other family members to understand and expand

[31] BRCC 01–2124–0000–0274.

the definition of martyrdom and to navigate the complicated bureaucracy necessary to obtain their entitlements.[32] The government was aware of these problems and, through several laws and regulations, it encouraged Iraqi men to marry martyrs' widows to protect these families. Many of these unions, often entered into for economic convenience, were fraught with difficulty. Particularly in rural areas, social tradition forced a widow to marry her martyred husband's brother; these marriages allowed the new heads of household to claim the children's patrimony and mistreat them, creating economic and psychological stress. Delinquency and criminality rates among children rose as a result.[33]

The General Secretariat analyses, based largely on home visits, were remarkably accurate and insightful. They were also implicitly critical of the role of the state's social policy. From the beginning of the war, the state had targeted martyrs' families as a means to regulate the social and human costs of the war. It had not, however, anticipated the continuous need to issue resolutions governing private life, particularly those pertaining to women's rights to their late husbands' entitlements. During the first few years of the war, RCC resolutions allowed a martyr's wife sole access to the martyr's entitlements, granting her land, residence, and other rewards.[34] From the beginning, however, the government ran into myriad problems with respect to matters of inheritance. Was a childless widow the sole heir to her slain husband's benefits? Or must she share them with his parents and siblings as prescribed by Islamic law, which normally governed inheritance in Iraq? The RCC had to issue a resolution specifically addressing that question that stipulated that the wife should inherit most of the martyr's benefits rather than share them.[35] Another problem arose over the financial responsibility for martyrs' minor children, which was supposed to devolve to the new male heads of household, either the martyrs' fathers or eldest male siblings. In this matter, the state appears to have left it up to the new patriarchs and the widows to negotiate

---

[32] Shirin Saeidi, "Creating the Islamic Republic of Iran: wives and daughters of martyrs, and acts of citizenship," *Citizenship Studies*, 14 (2010), 113–26. Saeidi provides insight into the ways that martyrs' widows and daughters navigated and reshaped their citizenship within Iranian society.

[33] BRCC 01–2124–0000–0012 to 0020.

[34] RCC resolution 4550, issued in October 1980, allowed interest-free real estate loans to the wife of the martyr or to his father if he was single, to build on land obtained through the state. Resolution 1750, issued in 1981, granted an apartment or house to the martyr's widow or his parents. Resolution 585 granted equal rights to all the martyrs' widows.

[35] The widow could sell the apartment or the piece of land and keep the proceeds to herself. *al-Jumhuriyya*, May 28, 1981, 3 and *al-Qadisiyya*, December 1, 1991, 3.

the management of the minors' inheritance, which tended to place the women at a disadvantage due to traditional patriarchal hierarchy.[36]

The clamor from martyred soldiers' families played a central role in limiting widows' rights. Parents and siblings challenged widows' rights to their husbands' benefits. They took their cases to local party offices, the state Islamic courts, and relevant ministries. In response, the RCC had to issue rulings on inheritance minutiae that brought the state into the vortex of intimate family relations. In 1981, for example, the family of a martyr who had not consummated his marriage before he was sent to the front claimed that his widow had no right to a sedan or the money granted to her after her husband's death. An RCC decree was issued granting the entitlement to his parents.[37] Although several RCC decrees reaffirmed the primary right of the widow to inherit, pressure from kin influenced government decisions to encourage men to marry widows and compensate the men "protecting" the widows, which gradually undermined the widows' autonomy and eroded women's rights to their martyred husbands' benefits. In 1989, for example, the state issued a new grant of land in Basra to families of martyrs. This grant excluded widows who had remarried, because they had come under the "protection" of a new head of household and thus needed no further compensation. Furthermore, in a clear attempt to undercut the autonomy of female heads of household in managing their children's inheritance, the state granted martyrs' children who were minors the right to inherit their fathers' benefits, thus circumventing widows' role as financial guardians.[38]

By the end of the Iran-Iraq war, the state retreated from its policy of legislating in support of the nuclear family and widows' rights within it. The Ba'th Party reports cited earlier had blamed the delinquency and criminality of martyrs' children on the patriarchal order that allowed kin and uncaring second husbands to undermine the stability of the nuclear family. It had, however, called for a governmental agency to prevent the abuses of extended kin, but no such agency was created under the austerity of the embargo. Therefore, just as it had privatized most of the social services, the regime devolved the regulation of nuclear families to kin, part of the re-tribalization of Iraqi society in the 1990s. In December 1991, the government issued a resolution granting men interest-free loans

---

[36] This is the language used by a 1984 amendment to RCC decree Number 736 granting all wives and children of the martyr equal entitlements. Contested inheritance matters should be settled between patriarch and the widow. NIDS/serial 329084.

[37] *al-Jumhuriyya*, August 12, 1981, 6.

[38] BRCC 01-2126-0001-0628.

to marry widows even if such marriages necessitated taking on a second wife. An editorial by a theologian in support for this call observed that Iraqi men were merely following the example of the Prophet, who had encouraged his followers to marry the widows of martyred Muslims to preserve the community.[39]

The regulation of the patriarchal nuclear family was at the heart of the system of entitlements set up by the Ba'thist state. However, in its efforts to punish those it regarded as its enemies, the government sought to break up the nuclear family household to punish the individual "culprit" and extended kin. The regulations against kin functioned in two ways. The first was exclusionary. The person executed or accused of belonging to an outlawed political party was considered a criminal with no rights, and his extended kin were banned from employment in key institutions, particularly those concerned with security, military affairs, and propaganda. The regulations also gave the "culprit's" family members an opportunity to petition the government for amnesty should they prove that their kin had no influence on them. To do so, family members could report on their relatives, join the party, or perform any act deemed redemptive by the security apparatus and the Ba'th. The state's definition of "family" in this case included both the nuclear and the extended family. For those who could not exempt themselves from punishment, the severity of punishment depended on how closely family members were related to the accused. First-degree relatives were punished more severely than second-degree relatives. Only when the accused had been executed was the crime viewed seriously enough to penalize second-degree relatives.[40] State security agencies as well as the Ba'th Party expended much effort to determine the types of exclusions relatives of varying degrees were to endure for different crimes.

During the Iran-Iraq war, the policy of punishing relatives of political dissenters was extended to deserters' families. Parents, wives, and children were held hostage as a means to control the movement of soldiers. As early as 1982, the Ministry of Defense issued a directive calling for the arrest of first-degree family members of deserters who fled to Iran to escape military service. These included the wife, children, and parents of deserters, whose imprisonment was liable to induce the deserter to return to service.[41] If the deserter joined the insurgents, then punishment extended

[39] *al-Qadisiyya*, December 28, 1991, 6.
[40] BRCC 003–1–1–0289 to 0291.
[41] NIDS/serial 717546.

to second-degree kin as well. The same applied to kin whose male relatives had been executed for desertion. In these cases, first- and second-degree relatives were excluded from key educational institutions and employment in government agencies. They could not bring civil suits against the deserter's execution squads.[42] How consistently this policy was followed is difficult to gauge, but it remained a powerful incentive for soldiers to remain at the front. The pressure exerted on the family by party organizations and by the various institutions of the state was inestimable. In one case, the party arrested the seventy-eight-year-old mother of a deserter, whose brother wrote a telling letter to a high-ranking party member. The author complained that his family was still being harassed by party cadres, despite the fact that his family had no knowledge of his brother's whereabouts, to no avail – the mother was held hostage until her son surrendered.[43]

From the outset of the Iran-Iraq war and until the fall of the regime in 2003, the erosion of the social and civil rights of families of deserters extended and reshaped those policies that the Ba'thist state had created to punish political dissent. However, the 1980s marked the first time that the RCC created legislation to break up nuclear family units to punish deserters, a policy it had earlier used to punish enemies of the state it branded as of "Iranian affiliation."[44] RCC resolution 1529, issued on December 31, 1985, decreed that the wives of the deserters absent from their units for more than six months or who had fled to Iran must ask for a separation. The civil courts were to issue a legal separation without either party's consent. The separation was suspended if the husband rejoined his unit, but became a divorce if he deserted again.[45] Thus, marriage became part of a national security and counterinsurgency policy even though it had originally been contracted according to Islamic legal precepts and sanctioned by the civil courts.

Conclusion

The transformation of Iraqi citizenship during wartime is evident in the series of surveys conducted by the Ba'th Party of matriculating male

---

[42] BRCC 01–2126–0001–0015 to 0023. An RCC resolution issued in July 1982 decreed that deserters who did not surrender within thirty days were subject to execution. Although families as well as captured deserters could bring their case to an investigative committee, the committee was tasked to take into consideration the fact that the deserter had resisted arrest and that the squads were forced to execute him.

[43] BRCC 029–3–7–0492 to 0495.

[44] Sha'ban, *Man Huwa al-'Iraqi?* p. 229.

[45] NIDS/serial 321751.

students over the course of the last twenty years of Ba'thist rule. These surveys highlight the differentiated and contextual nature of the rights of Iraqi citizens. To access their entitlements, students and their families were classified under one or more of a number of categories that had to do with performance of acts of loyalty to the state and the regime. Thus, Iraqi males were surveyed, located within a grid of family, locality, and political affiliation, and assessed as to their eligibility for admission into institutions of higher learning reserved for Ba'thists, military, police, and security academies. Based on these surveys, the Iraqi government and the party determined whom to include or exclude from full privileges of citizenship.

The surveys of 1987–8, the first year these surveys are available for most Iraqi provinces, list the name of the student, his political affiliation (Ba'thist or Independent), his level within the Ba'th Party hierarchy, his and his family's reputation, his ethnicity, his address, the name of the chief of his neighborhood (*mukhtar*), his place of birth, and his father and grandfather's place of birth. Under a separate section devoted to comments, the surveys detailed the reasons for excluding certain students from academies. The family's politics played a crucial role. If the student had a first- or second-degree family member who had belonged to out-lawed opposition parties or who had been executed for belonging to one, he was automatically excluded. And while the contribution to the war effort by family members was mentioned, it was not listed as a separate category that gave students automatic rights. Belonging to the Ba'th was the crucial prerequisite that determined inclusion; opposing the Ba'thist state marked one and one's family for exclusion.

By the late 1990s, citizen's rights were characterized by increasing differentiation within a larger number of categories. The 1998–9 surveys added five more categories to those listed in 1987–8 surveys. All, save for one, were introduced for the first time in that year. Separate categories were devoted to the student's family's attitude and his or his family's participation in the Intifada, whether members of his family were "Friends of Saddam," and whether family members had been martyred in the Iran-Iraq war or the First Gulf War. Other categories listed membership in the paramilitary force of Fida'iyun Saddam created in 1994 and participation in the "Day of Chivalry and Dignity." The rights to which a given citizen was entitled were determined by his or her location in one or more of these categories. If, on one hand, a student had a martyr in the family and attended the "Day of Chivalry and Dignity," he stood a better chance of getting into his desired college. If, on the other hand, the same

TABLE 6.1. *Classifications used in school registers*

Categories in 1987–8 Registers	Categories in 1998–9 Registers
Name	Name
Political Affiliation	Political Affiliation
Party Rank	Party Rank
Reputation of Student and his Family	Reputation of Student and His Family
Address	Address
Name of Neighborhood Headman (*mukhtar*)	Name of Neighborhood Headman (*mukhtar*)
Ethnicity	Ethnicity
Place and Date of Birth	Place and Date of Birth
Place of Father's Birth	Place of Father's Birth
Place of Grandfather's Birth	Place of Grandfather's Birth
Comments	Student and his Family's Attitude to 1991 Uprising
	Number of Martyrs in the Iran-Iraq and First Gulf wars in Student's Family
	Family Members who are "Friends of Saddam"
	Fida'iyun Saddam
	Participation in Day of Chivalry and Dignity
	Comments

student had a family member who had died in a war and another family member who had participated in the Intifada, then he had to petition the government for admission to a college (Table 1).

The hierarchical and differentiated nature of Iraqi citizens' rights introduced during the war years left a profound impact on Iraqis' practices of citizenship. Rather than associate citizenship with a stable set of legal rights defined by equal status, they came to view it as a relational enterprise in which every individual was connected to his family and to the state in a complex web of privileges and exclusions. As a result, Iraqi citizens found that they had to continuously lay claim to their privileges or negotiate exclusions.

7

Memory for the Future

Like all states fighting national wars that require mass mobilization, the Iraqi government needed to generate consent among its citizenry to ensure their acquiescence to the costs of conflict with Iran. To that end, state cultural institutions and the Ba'th Party created a public iconography and language to portray the experience of war as national and transformative. Two cultural idioms dominated the efforts to shape the narrative of the Iran-Iraq war. The first was bombastic, authoritarian, militant, and panegyric, particularly of Saddam Hussain. This idiom was assiduously reinforced in all public media outlets and in the visual arts. At its center was Saddam Hussain, who was portrayed as leading a new generation of men and women in a war that would give birth to a militant Iraq that would spearhead Arab and anti-imperialist struggles. He stood for all aspects of the nation – its ancient past, its contribution to Arab-Islamic civilization, and its "revolutionary" present. Like a good revolutionary, he embodied all Iraqi classes and ethnicities. He was a peasant and tribal leader, an educator to his middle classes, and an intellectual and military planner. Above all, he was the embodiment of the ideal soldier who merged all these attributes in his person.

The extent to which this project to link the war and its conduct to the person of Saddam Hussain carried resonance with the population is difficult to gauge. As Eric Davis has concluded in his study of public culture during this period, the personalization of the war undermined the narrative of an Iraqi state as the caretaker and protector of a diverse nation in favor of an exclusivist narrative of Iraqi national history focused on Saddam Hussain and the Ba'th.[1]

---

[1] Davis, *Memories of State*, pp. 176–99.

The second cultural idiom of the narrative of the war, the subject of this chapter, was biographical. It focused on the existential and transformative impact of what state cultural institutions and the mass media called the "war experience" (*tajrubat al-harb*). The experience of war was not linked to the personality cult of Saddam Hussain nor with a necessarily Ba'thist interpretation of the war. Rather, as articulated by Iraqi media and literature, it was associated with the formulation of an Iraqi private self shaped by new existential realities created by the war. The building blocks of the war experience were based on remembrance of the individual's experience of heroism, violence, and death. The soldier's experience became the moniker of the new Iraqi self: his service and death attested to the merging of the individual with the nation. The government sought to create a "memory for tomorrow," one that underscored sacrifice and the experience of war as formative of the current and future generations of Iraqis.[2] Thus, the cultural institutions of the Ba'thist state defined the war experience in generational and gendered terms. This biographical idiom marked the generation of men and women who came of age under the 1968 Ba'thist revolution and set them apart from an earlier generation whose sensibility had been formed in the melee of the leftist and contentious politics of 1960s and 1970s Iraq.[3] The experience of war, according to the official narrative, forged a unity among the mass of Iraqis who had benefited from the progressive modernization projects of the Ba'thist revolution. War engagement was the crucible of new memories and bonds forged by the shared collective experience of battle.

The war experience was also a gendered one. At its heart was the male soldier, whose manliness and honor exemplified the new Iraqi subject.[4] The soldier was at the center of an extensive literature on the war experience produced under the auspices of the Ministry of Culture and Information and geared primarily to young adult males. Posters rendered the soldier's masculinity as the embodiment of an Iraqi male. Television and radio programs exulted his prowess, as did ubiquitous popular songs and poetry. The Iraqi soldier was an amalgam of an idealized version of a

[2] Warid Badr Salem, Hamza Mustafa, and Muhammad al-Hayyawi eds., *Dhakirat al-Ghad, Shahadat, Ru'a wa Tajarib* (*Memory for Tomorrow, Testimonies, Visions and Experiences*) (Baghdad: Dar al-Shu'un al-Thaqafiyya al-'Amma, 1989).

[3] For a preliminary sociological study of the war generation, see Faleh Abdul Jabar, "Iraq's war generation," in Lawrence G. Potter and Gary G. Sick (eds.), *Iran, Iraq and the Legacies of War* (New York: Palgrave Macmillan, 2004), pp. 121–40.

[4] Achim Rohde, "Opportunities for masculinity and love: Cultural production in Ba'thist Iraq during the 1980s," in Lahouchine Ouzgane (ed.), *Islamic Masculinities* (London: Zed Press, 2006), pp. 148–201.

modern, militant, and military archetype drawn from European and Third World iconography and literature, and a tribal archetype whose notions of loyalty, love, honor, and courage emerged from Iraqi folklore.[5]

The new masculinity embraced by the government marked a shift from the ideal Iraqi male as worker, peasant, party militant, and committed intellectual to a mixture of the former combination of traits with a tribal archetype. The reification of a tribal masculinity was particularly evident in the popular song and poetry of the war. It was assiduously cultivated by Saddam Hussain, who saw the panegyric and defamatory traditions of tribal poetry and song as sources for the glorification of militarism and the diminution of threat. The government's cultivation of cultural forms that exulted in tribal masculinity was as much directed to its rural population as it was to its middle-class urban soldiers, who were supposed to draw lessons from their simple tribal brethren. Although – as objects of the soldier's love, symbols of land, and militant fighters in the Popular Army – women also played a crucial role in shaping the war narrative, its essence as propagated by the state emanated from the soldier's battle experience.

Central to the government's efforts to render the individual soldier's experience one that exemplified a generation's collective memory was the act of witnessing – albeit witnessing that was homogenized and highly controlled.[6] Journalists and literary figures wrote vignettes, short stories, and novels; photographers and filmmakers shot a purported narrative of the soldier's experience even as they manipulated the product to fit the guidelines of the Directorate of Political Guidance. Although the majority did not have battle experience, almost all spent time at the front with soldiers. They called their time "*mu'ayasha*" or "cohabiting," and they took their limited and controlled visits to the front as authentic reflections of the war experience. They were both journalists and writers; they created the documents of the war experience and transformed these documents into literary narratives. In her general study of the relationship of mass media to the war story, Miriam Cooke has observed that in its construction of a narrative of the encounter with violence, "the media have deliberately blurred the line between the representation of actual events and the choreography of historical images in the service of propaganda."[7]

---

[5] Davis, *Memories of State*, pp. 170–6.

[6] On the relationship of witnessing to memory, see Jay Winter and Emmanuel Sivan eds., *War and Remembrance in the Twentieth Century* (Cambridge: Cambridge University Press, 1999), pp. 6–39.

[7] Miriam Cooke, *Women and the War Story* (Berkeley: University of California Press, 1997), p. 75.

As they appeared in the Iraqi press, the stories of people at war sentimentalized and trivialized what was essentially a violent traumatic experience. They introduced a standard limited vocabulary to speak about what was in reality a complex and diverse experience. They blurred the distinction between fact and fiction, biography and autobiography, and described fighting in a stylized fashion that did not remotely describe the reality. They elided the army's role in the suppression of the Kurdish insurgency, and they excluded any mention of the role of death squads, Ba'thist commissars, or hierarchical distinctions on the battlefront. Thus, even biographical accounts written to create the illusion of truthfulness failed to convey the horrors of battle. Only in less widely read literary accounts, particularly in short stories that were part of the sanctioned war literature during the 1980s, did a more complex and subtly critical narrative of the war experience emerge.

The first part of this chapter expounds on the elements of the war experience sanctioned by the state by focusing on two of its pillars: photojournalism, which created an iconography of a martial and modern masculinity as it did of landscapes of war; and war literature, which professed to give voice to a generation of Iraqi men shaped by the war experience. It is important, however, not to think of the war experience narrative as a solely manufactured and state-controlled cultural project. The repertoire of words and images the media and literary culture deployed to construct the war experience built on soldiers' accounts and distorted and simplified them, but nevertheless provided the language and iconography that soldiers employed in their own remembrances of the war.

The second part of this chapter explores how soldiers' actual remembrances converge and challenge the official narrative. I draw on interviews with nineteen soldiers and one war correspondent. Most interviewees were born between 1955 and 1967. All were beneficiaries of the educational and economic opportunities created by the Ba'thist state after 1968. They represent what the state viewed as the generation of the revolution. While few defined themselves in these terms, most viewed their experience at the front as one that shaped their generation's view. For several, anxieties about death and masculinity belied the state's heroic and militarized war narrative. Most noticeable was the language they used to describe their battle experience and the landscapes of war. They drew on the vocabulary and images widely disseminated in the mass media and the literature of the war, but disaggregated the narrative, often confusing time and space and in most cases portraying a dystopic landscape of mayhem and destruction.

The Iconography of the War Experience

From its earliest days, the Iran-Iraq war was a mass media event. It was the first war in the Arab world that produced, despite vigilant censorship, a professional crop of print, photography, and television journalists embedded with the armed forces.[8] As in the Soviet Union during World War II, journalism was not supposed to be objective, but was to conform to the party line, form part of the state's propaganda machine, and help mobilize the population for war.[9] For its part, the state tackled the enormous task of shaping the culture of war as if it was another battlefront. Saddam Hussain was reported to have said that the Ministry of Culture and Information constituted the eighth army corps. The policy of the state was designed to co-opt older intellectuals who were not fully committed to the Ba'thist war narrative and hesitant about becoming part of its machinery of cultural production. Its ability to do so was bolstered by its sponsorship of a younger generation of ambitious and relatively inexperienced young would-be intellectuals and professionals eager to be part of the expanding bureaucracy of cultural organizations. The Ministry's various departments and directorates, together with the Ba'th Party's Directorate of Political Guidance, oversaw a massive effort to create consent among the public at large, and, more important, among the urban Iraqi educated middle class and the lower middle class, beneficiaries of its economic and social policies, who were now asked to contribute their lives to the war. They constituted the main audience for the mass media outlets and the literary culture that purportedly depicted the war experience.[10]

Working with various professional unions, particularly those of the writers, photographers, actors, and filmmakers, the Ministry and the party helped create the cultural artifacts that defined the war experience. Journalists covering the front, whether reporting for civilian or military newspapers, were steered by the Directorate of Political Guidance personnel stationed in the rear lines of military brigades. The party censored journalists' reports on the progress at the front, cleared the nightly battle

---

[8] *Alif Ba'*, no. 627, October 1, 1980, pp. 48–50.

[9] Louise McReynolds, "Dateline Stalingrad, newspaper correspondents on the front," in Richard Stites (ed.), *Culture and Entertainment in Wartime Russia* (Bloomington: Indiana University Press, 1995), pp. 28–43.

[10] Davis, *Memories of State*, pp. 148–204. Davis's work remains one of the most incisive on the role of intellectuals in supporting the Ba'thist state's version of history. He also highlights the importance of this culture to the growing ranks of middle-class and lower-middle-class urbanites.

footage broadcast on Iraqi television sets every evening, and directed their coverage of human interest stories.[11] War reporting, developed in its early stages in a piecemeal fashion, played a crucial part in this undertaking.[12] On television and in print, war reporting stressed the soldiers' martial and masculine prowess and recorded a sanctioned sanitized version of their testimonies and those of their families. It introduced a new militarized vocabulary into public discourse. The party and the Directorate of Internal Information (*da'irat al-i'lam al-dakhili*) within the Ministry of Culture and Information heavily promoted photography, poster art, and cartoons that collectively depicted the ideal Iraqi citizen and demonized the enemy.[13]

War photographers, in particular, created the visual iconography of the war experience. They saw themselves as part of the war story, cohabiting with soldiers on the front lines, providing "testimony to the truth," risking their lives and sometimes dying in their efforts to "document" battle realities.[14] From the onset, however, photographers considered their work part of the national mobilization effort. They attempted to bridge the gap between the truth their images purported to convey about the war and the images' ideological content by insisting that propagandistic images were stylized testimonials to the heroism of soldiers and, by extension, of the Iraqi people. It was, according to war photographer Jasim al-Zubaydi, important to choose images that would remain in viewers' memories.[15] Photography became the basis of poster art, partly derivative of Soviet, Palestinian, and Algerian models that portrayed mustached soldiers in a variety of clichéd heroic stances – standing on tanks or near armored vehicles, sporting victory signs, smiling from trenches, carrying their weapons. Soldiers' stylized images were plastered in public venues and created a homogenized national image of the ideal soldier-citizen.[16] The sheer repetitiveness of imagery and of the stories they purported to tell undermined their credibility as truthful testaments. Their function was, above all, to leave an abstracted memory – a distant snippet – of the war at the front.

---

[11] Interview with Waddah Hasan, Amman, Jordan, June 23, 2007. Hasan was a radio reporter and worked for the Directorate of Political Guidance at the front.

[12] Interview with Haytham Ali, Amman, Jordan, August 8, 2007. Ali was the war correspondent for *al-Thawra*.

[13] *al-Jumhuriyya*, October 3, 1980, 3.

[14] *Alif Ba'*, "al-futughraph wa malamih fan al-ma'raka" ("The photograph and features of the art of battle"), no. 777, August 17, 1983, pp. 56–7.

[15] Ibid.

[16] *Alif Ba'*, "al-ma'na al-jadid li al-mulasaq al-siyasi," ("The new meaning of the political poster"), no. 630, October 22, 1980, p. 45; *al-Jumhuriyya*, October 3, 1980, 8.

Images created by photojournalists filled the daily pages of the newspapers as testimonials to the "continuous" victories of the Iraqi armed
forces. They hid the reality of Iraqi retreats; they stood in place of military analysis of developments at the front; they rarely portrayed the death
or injury of Iraqi soldiers. As photojournalist for the daily *al-Jumhuriyya*,
Rahim Hasan helped shape the iconography of soldiering during the Iran-
Iraq war. Born in Basra to a poor family in 1949, he grew up in Baghdad
and began honing his skill as a photographer in the 1970s. The conflict
with Iran provided him with the opportunity to turn himself into a war
photographer par excellence. One of his photographs was turned into
the very first war poster. Five others followed, all of which contributed to
creating a heroic image of the soldier. He exhibited his work at home and
abroad, and acquired a reputation among his peers as a fearless photojournalist. As he said in 1987, he believed that his work at the front:

lay in photographing the event so it remains a document to future generations. I
transport the image that agrees with the public proclamations of the leadership
when it declares the military developments to the citizens of the nation, the Arab
nation and the world.... I was always happy despite all the difficulties [of covering the front] because I realized my important role in informing my compatriots
of developments at the front so that they can feel they are close to their sons and
brothers.... The front for me is the honor of my mother's milk, it is the bread of
the glorious Iraqi women, and it is the bridge to our radiant future.[17]

In 1987, a selection of his published photographs was compiled and
introduced by Najman Yasin in a book entitled *Man and War*. Yasin
presented his compilation of the photographs as witness (*shahada*) to
the soldier's heroism, "who had allowed us to surpass flaccidity, lassi-
tude and defeatism and stand at the doors of a sunny future," and to
the intrepidness and courage of Rahim Hasan, who was, according to
Yasin, one of the few photojournalists who ventured onto the front lines
of battle in the southern sector.[18] Published in the wake of the fall of the
Faw Peninsula to the Iranians, the book's images were meant to provide
testimony in the two meanings of the Arabic word *shahada* (which also
means martyrdom): as a photographic witness of the heroism of soldiers
and as a reminder that their martyrdom, their act of witnessing for their
country, would ultimately lead to victory. To highlight the importance of
the southern front, particularly after Iraq's retreat, all the photographs

---

[17] Najman Yasin, *al-Insan wa al-Harb, Qadisiyyat Saddam if 'A 'mal Rahim Hasan* (Man and
War, Qadisiyat Saddam in the Works of Rahim Hasan) (Baghdad: al-Dar al-Wataniyya li
al-Tiba'a wa al-Nashr, 1987), p. 16.
[18] Ibid., p. 2.

chosen for the book were drawn from Hasan's time as an embedded journalist there. Hasan's photographs, according to Yasin, told the story of
men and landscapes transformed by the experience of war. Whereas the
focus of Hasan's work before the war had been men and women in the
alleyways, coffeehouses, and popular markets of the city and the countryside, his camera was now directed at men's daily lives as fighters. While
their lives were hard and violent – for war is "not a picnic" – they were
experiencing the fullest meaning of their humanity as they protected the
nation's soil. They "fight and celebrate," for war has become "habitual
and man is the son of habit. They are the sons of war."[19] War was an
adventure – a paean to soldiering and the ultimate test of the masculinity
of men removed from the accoutrements of civilian life.

   War transformed landscapes as it did men. Of all the landscapes on
the Iraqi front, the southern marshes (*al-Ahwar*) carried the greatest
significance in Iraqi public culture. The inhabitants of the marshlands,
the marsh Arabs, furnished the basis of the earliest and most sophisticated folkloric studies. The ecology of the marshes, its long reeds, the
houses built from these reeds, its distinctive boats, its water, and its fowl
appeared in songs, poetry, and literature as an authentic feature of a specifically Iraqi national landscape that linked its present to its ancient past.
This bucolic national imagining of the marshlands stood in stark contrast to the Iraqi government's policies toward their populations as it did
to the rampant destruction of these marshlands that began during the
Iran-Iraq war. Soldiers and journalists who sought to convey this experience to audiences at home had to contend with the romanticized view of
the marshlands and their meaning to Iraqi national culture. The marsh
was transformed, according to Yasin's reading of Rahim Hasan's images,
from the romantic and poetic symbol it had been before the war to the
"insurgent mountain and barbed wires," to "a grave and a fence and a
presence filled with heroism." As they inhabited and fought in the space
of the marshlands, soldiers established a communion with the habitat of
the marshes rarely achieved in the distant imagining of poets.[20]

   The story of war told in the collection of Rahim Hasan's photographs
unfolds in the southern marshlands. The images in the book are grouped
into three sections: the first, "War is Their Playground," presents soldiering as men's adventure; the second, "Defenders of Life," is meant to portray everyday life at the front and the camaraderie created by soldiering;

[19] Ibid., p. 5.
[20] Ibid.

the third, "Humiliated and Humbled," depicts Iranian prisoners of war. The narrative arc of the first section of war as adventure highlights the movement of men against landscapes of war. Soldiers are photographed in groups or as individuals: disembarking from inflatable boats in the marsh waters; climbing up barren hills divided by barbed wire; walking down dusty roads surrounded by reeds and decapitated palm trees; sitting in trenches and fox holes; looking into the horizon where plumes of smoke signify the bombardment of enemy lines; hoisting the Iraqi flag in conquered Iranian territory; and sitting in boats against the bucolic background of the marshlands.

The marshlands and the surrounding areas appear tamed by the modern machinery of war and the soldiers who use it. In one image, a helmeted soldier sits atop a tank obscured by the smoke of battle and surrounded by the corpses of Iranian soldiers. In the right corner of the picture, the side of a tank appears suspended over two Iranian soldiers' corpses. Only the head of one of these soldiers appears in the corner of the picture, creating the impression that it is pinned under the tank's wheels. In another iconic picture, an Iraqi soldier is firmly holding onto his rifle in one arm and raising the other arm in a call to combat. In the background, an armored vehicle shoots missiles at the enemy (see Figure 7.1). Another image juxtaposes the helmeted heads of soldiers peering from the trench with their guns directed toward an enemy with the movement of a tank and sand plumes marking its path, in a parallel line to the trench that stretches across the seemingly endless horizon of desert. These and other images in the first section of the book introduce the readers at home to the landscape in which the adventure of soldiering takes place. As an action hero, the soldier is no longer defined by his social and class origins but rather by the moment of battle. He is neither peasant nor marsh dweller; neither citified educated man nor clan leader; but rather a proud Iraqi fighter.

The images also convey another story – one only implicit in the choice of landscape and subjects – a story of the destruction of landscape and the dangers inherent in the adventure of soldiering and of death. In five sequential images, shot with clear allusions to images of American soldiers walking through the jungles of Vietnam, Iraqi soldiers are photographed walking as a group down an unpaved road in the southern marshlands. They are surrounded by tall reeds and palm trees, many of which have lost their fronds to Iranian bombardment. The first shot is taken from the back with soldiers marching forward on both sides of the road, walking into a horizon of palm tree trunks that resemble black spirals in a war

FIGURE 7.1. Rahim Hasan photo: Soldier on attack, Najman Yasin, *al-Insan wa al-Harb, Qadisiyat Saddam fi 'A'mal Rahim Hasan.*

film. The second, still shot from the back at a distance, has them stop and look into the reeds in expectation of enemy fire. The third is shot at closer range, focusing on four soldiers pointing their guns at Iranian soldiers hiding in the vegetation. The fourth is of two soldiers shooting at close range. The fifth is of Iraqi soldiers moving toward the photographer but past Iranian soldiers' corpses, partially undressed, lying on the marsh's edge (see Figure 7.2). Inured to death, they march forward.

The landscape is quintessentially Iraqi, the images universal. War is for men who have to acclimate to death and destruction. Battle takes place in remote, uninhabited places where one's death often goes unreported, unregistered, and unmourned. Few of the bucolic images of the marshes survive in this war – fewer still are the images of people outside the band of brothers marching toward their next inevitable encounter with death. While the images portray the enemy's death, often reducing him to an anonymous, dehumanized, partially clothed body, the implication in these images is that death is omnipresent in the Iraqi soldier's life. One got used to it and moved on. War concentrates action as it brutalizes men. Iraqi state propaganda sought to project this brutalization as part of the

FIGURE 7.2. Rahim Hasan photo: Soldiers marching in al-Ahwar, Najman Yasin, *al-Insan wa al-Harb, Qadisiyat Saddam fi 'A'mal Rahim Hasan.*

creation of new men, but the images chosen for Hasan's portrayal of war as adventure do not always reflect the state's sanctioned version.

The second section of the collection features the persistence of the ordinary in extraordinary circumstances. Camaraderie between men sidesteps divisions that might have existed in civilian life; the mundane lends humanity to what is essentially a violent and dangerous experience. The opening image of this section is of two Iraqi soldiers sitting on empty wooden boxes, perhaps of ammunition, playing a game of chess. In the background, a soldier, mounted on an armored personnel carrier, scrutinizes the surroundings, ever on alert. Other images portray soldiers at rest: a soldier cooking eggs over an open fire, a jar of Iraqi ghee on one side and a carton of eggs on the other; a soldier sitting in the trench reading a tiny Quran, his gun standing against the trench wall, his magazine in his helmet on the floor; an officer, in partial profile, in his tent feeding a bird a drop of tea; a group of soldiers in the trench reading newspapers; a soldier shaving; another having his hair cut by a comrade in view of a stack of empty ammunition boxes resembling wooden coffins; and another praying in the open air as his comrades sit surrounded by sandbags manning an antiaircraft gun.

FIGURE 7.3. Rahim Hasan photo: Iraqi soldier aiming his weapon, *al-Jumhuriyya*, October 2, 1980.

According to this narrative, life at the front, despite its harshness, brought its own measure of joy born of the friendships forged with soldiers from diverse backgrounds. Rarely do these images highlight the military hierarchies that existed on the front line, or the division between those who remained at the rear and those out on the front lines. Photographs of soldiers walking and smiling into the camera, raising the obligatory victory sign, and performing mundane tasks with members of their units created a narrative of an ideal experience and an ideal soldier in communion with comrades compatible with him. Individual images of soldiers posed them in heroic stances, carrying their guns with ease and confidence. The gun was part of their body, whether it was slung over the shoulder like a hoe or aimed threateningly at an enemy. Two of Hasan's images became iconic: one features a soldier wearing goggles and pointing the wide mouth of his gun at the viewer (this photo was published in *al-Jumhuriyya* in 1980); (Figure 7.3) and the other shows a soldier posing, smiling at the camera underneath four long cannons that provide a sort of canopy over his head (Figure 7.4). In the first, the soldier is portrayed as an action hero, his modern machinery slung comfortably on his shoulder and directed against

FIGURE 7.4. Rahim Hasan photo: Soldier smiling with missiles in the background, Najman Yasin, *al-Insan wa al-Harb, Qadisiyat Saddam if 'A'mal Rahim Hasan.*

the enemy. The image targets the viewer and projects the aggressive masculinity of the new male as well as his invincibility. The other image is less threatening. The smiling soldier is wearing the accoutrements of modern warfare – a helmet, binoculars, a transmitter – and stands in the shadow of guns. But the assertion of masculinity is less threatening and is meant to highlight the efficiency of the war machine as well as the humanity and accessibility of the people who operate it. Variations of these images were reproduced as posters and in newspapers. All highlighted the symbiotic relation between man and machine, the modernity of war and its disciplined, efficient, and ordered nature.

The masculinity, modernity, and heroism of the Iraqi soldier stood in marked contrast to the subjugation, humiliation, and emasculation of the Iranian soldier shown in the third section of Hasan's collection. The first image is of a young Iranian soldier, perhaps in his teens, unarmed and bareheaded, his injured leg exposed, being hoisted by two fully armed and helmeted Iraqi soldiers. The inexperienced youth of the Iranian and his injury contrast vividly with the assured competence, masculinity, and invincibility of the Iraqis. The Iraqi soldier, the image seems to say, is both strong and humane as he protectively helps the injured vulnerable youth who had been duped into fighting by the

FIGURE 7.5. Rahim Hasan photo: Iranian prisoner of war, Najman Yasin, *al-Insan wa al-Harb, Qadisiyat Saddam fi 'A'mal Rahim Hasan.*

manipulative and exploitative Ayatollahs. This portrayal of the Iranian reappears in an image of an Iranian boy, barely in his mid-teens, with a full head of hair, gazing blankly at the ground, flanked by two Iraqi soldiers. The profile of the mustachioed Iraqi soldier, placed in the foreground, frames the upper left-hand corner of the image, while the background of the right-hand corner is dominated by another Iraqi soldier, his chiseled face under the ubiquitous helmet looking haughtily at the young boy (Figure 7.5).

The contrast reinforced one of the popular narratives propagated by the media – that Khomeini readily sent young men in human waves to die fighting the Iraqis. Clearly, however, not all Iranian prisoners of war were teenagers. Hasan's images of imprisoned Iranian men depict them as young, humiliated, and subjugated. They are rarely photographed standing. A number of images show Iranian prisoners, their heads shaved, sitting hunched over their knees behind barbed wires; others show them lying on the ground, sometimes partially clothed, in various positions. Iraqi soldiers mill around them unconcerned.

War photography like Hasan's provided the visual language of the war experience for the Iraqi public. The essence of that experience lay in the landscape of the front and in soldiering. Its narrative arc was the orderly movement of invincible and archetypal men and modern machinery across a landscape of barbed wire, trenches, and burned vegetation. Men became soldiers when they donned their helmets, wore their khakis and their boots, and embraced their guns. Soldiers became men in the heat of the battle as they mounted their tanks, trudged through marshlands, and killed their enemies. The story the images purport to tell is the story of soldiers' experience of battle everywhere. It is, as Miriam Cooke has demonstrated in her work on the building blocks of the war story, a narrative that omits as much as it reveals.[21] In the Iraqi case, the narrative homogenizes the soldiers' experience, leaving out the distinctive features of the individual life story. War, according to these images, is an orderly exercise of well-planned slaughter – it leads to the degradation and death of the enemy only. Moreover, war is quintessentially a story about men, not women; it takes place in trenches and on empty terrain that the soldier and the machines he mans tame, master, and inhabit.

The Language of the War Experience

In February 1989, a group of Iraqi and Arab writers and literary critics gathered in Baghdad for a conference devoted to the examination of a genre of literature, the "literature of war" (*adab al-harb*) that had dominated literary production during the Iran-Iraq war. The proceedings of the conference were published in a book entitled *The Memory of Tomorrow: Testimonies, Visions and Experiences* and edited by three Iraqi writers who emerged as authors of war novels and short stories during the Iran-Iraq war. In their introduction, these editors state that they hoped to assess the aesthetic merits of a literature that had been, by their own admission, part of the state's mobilizing efforts and hence of uneven quality. War literature, according to the editors, was the literature of the battlefield, produced in rapid abundance: some ninety-five short story collections and seventy-five novels penned by eighty-seven authors over just eight years.[22] This literature, based in some cases on firsthand experience and testimonies and bolstered by authors' cohabitation with

---

[21] Cooke, *Women and the War Story*, pp. 16–43.
[22] Al-Salem, Mustafa, and Hayyawi eds., *Thakirat al-Ghad*, pp. 5–7 and pp. 377–400 for list of authors, short story collections, and novels. For a trenchant critique of this literature, see Salam Abboud, *Thaqafat al-'Unf fi al-'Iraq* (*The Culture of Violence in Iraq*) (Köln: Dar al-Jamal, 2002).

soldiers at the front, provided ostensibly authentic documentation of the war experience. Now that the war was over, the editors opined, the task of literary critics and of writers was to take these testimonies, which comprised the collective memory of the war experience, and determine their literary worth for future generations.

At the outset of the war, in the fall of 1980, the leadership within the Ministry of Culture and Information decided to sponsor a literature focused exclusively on the battle of Qadisiyat Saddam. In hindsight, the decision to do so appears remarkable given that there was no indication then that the war would last eight years. Nor was there a precedent in Iraq or in the Arab world of a literature of war at the center of which was the troops' battle experience. The Ministry of Culture and Information sponsored and published the war literature through its cultural division, the Directorate of General Cultural Affairs. It measured the support for the war as well as literature and poetry produced under the Ba'th by the willingness of intellectuals and writers to publicly endorse or participate in the production of a genre of literature focused on soldiering.[23] From the outset, however, the genre of war literature generated controversy among writers and literary critics who questioned whether a literature about the war experience could be produced in the heat of battle and without much distance and reflection. To what extent could a literature for mobilization be truthful or have any aesthetic value?[24]

The debates on the war literature were not confined to the relatively insular circles of writers and intellectuals within the Union of Iraqi Writers or in the pages of cultural journals. Rather, the cultural pages of the *al-Jumhuriyya* and *al-Thawra* dailies together with the popular weekly magazine *Alif Ba'* were filled with commentary and interviews with intellectuals, poets, and writers who were asked about the relationship of writing a "committed" literature geared to mobilization and the "authenticity" of the literary product as a work of art. Among the most commonly posed questions was whether writers and artists whose work was produced after the 1968 Ba'thist "revolution" had surpassed their intellectual forebears among the 1950s and 1960s generation of writers.

---

[23] *Alif Ba'*, "al-nahda al-thaqafiyya hiya nahdat al-hayat," ("The cultural renaissance is the rebirth of life") no. 776, August 10, 1983, pp. 44–5. The title is of a speech given by the Minister of Culture and Information, Lutayif Nasif Jasim, at the third annual awards for the literature of war.

[24] *Alif Ba'*, "al-'isalah wa al-fann fi qissat al-harb" ("Authenticity and art in the war story") and "al-adab al-haqiqi wa khida' al-qari'" ("Truthful literature and the deception of the reader"), no.777, August 24, 1983, pp. 44–5.

The question was as much about the support the Ba'thist state sought from mostly leftist intellectuals as it was about aesthetics and culture.[25]

Established writers and literary critics – such as Jabra Ibrahim Jabra, novelist and artist, and Muhsin al-Musawi, literary critic and secretary general of the General Federation of Arab Writers and head of the Directorate of General Cultural Affairs that published the war literature – expressed their ambivalence toward this literature and the politics behind it indirectly, through literary critique. For Jabra, the new generation's work lacked the maturity and depth of the work of the earlier generation in large part because it was prolific and apt not to adhere to aesthetic convention.[26] Even as head of the cultural organization that published the short stories and novels on the war experience, al-Musawi remained hesitant about endorsing them.[27] In 1983, he and Jabra Ibrahim Jabra, Fuad al-Takarli, and Musa al-Kreidi, leading writers and cultural critics whose intellectual formation owed little to Ba'thist education, were tasked by the Directorate of General Cultural Affairs with undertaking a study of the literary merits of the hundreds of short stories and novels published under its auspices or in the press and literary magazines. In particular, they examined the short stories published in nine volumes entitled *Qadisiyat Saddam: Stories Under the Flame of Fire.*[28] Clearly, the Directorate was hoping to lend legitimacy to the new literature by asking Iraq's skeptical intellectuals and cultural critics to endorse it. When it eventually appeared, the endorsement, though lukewarm, was critical for legitimizing the literature and, by extension, the state's attempt to create a cultural product that had soldiering at its heart.

In 1986, al-Musawi judged that enough time had elapsed since the emergence of the genre to assess its literary merits and its distinctive contributions. It was time as well to speak to the fraught question of the truthfulness and authenticity of a literature geared toward mobilization to portray the reality of the war experience. In his book on the topic, al-Musawi conceded that the war literature marked a departure in form

---

[25] For the most recent analysis of these debates as they touched on poetry, see Leslie Tramontini, "The struggle for representation: The internal Iraqi dispute over cultural production in Baathist Iraq," in Stephen Milich, Friederike Pannewick, and Leslie Tramontini (eds.), *Conflicting Narratives, War, Trauma and Memory in Iraqi Culture* (Wiesbaden: Reichert Verlag Wiesbaden, 2012), pp. 25–48.

[26] *al-Jumhuriyya*, August 30, 1980, 5.

[27] *Alif Ba*,' no. 781, September 14, 1983, pp. 44–7.

[28] Muhsin al-Musawi, *Al-Mar'i wa al-Mutakhayal, Adab al-Harb al-Qisasi fi al-'Iraq* (The Visible and the Imagined, The Narrative Literature of War in Iraq) (Baghdad: Dar al-Shu'un al-Thaqafiyya al-'Ama, 1986), pp. 3–9.

and content from earlier Iraqi literature. It was produced by a generation
of writers with a different sensibility than the generation of the 1960s.
The new literature signaled the emergence of a new voice and vision and
was in many respects more democratic because its main characters were
ordinary people, rather than educated, middle-class intellectuals, facing
extraordinary situations. The narrative of the new literature was based on
reporting the concrete, whereas the earlier literature had focused on the
abstract. The themes that had dominated the older generation's literary
writings, such as struggles between tradition and modernity or between
the protagonist's interior life and his or her external circumstances, were
no longer relevant in the new literature. Nor did the coffeehouse, the bar,
or the city street, the main landscapes in which the characters played
out their internal alienation in the earlier literature, resonate with the
new realities of wartime. The new literature replaced the bucolic landscapes with those of the front; writers portrayed the trench, rather than
the urban coffeehouse, as a place of alienation. In addition, in marked
contrast to the poeticism of the older generation of writers, the new generation wrote with an economy of language that was close to reportage,
an archive of the experience of war rather than a reflection on it.[29]

The hero of the war literature was the soldier. His experience brought
together the battle and home fronts, the city and the countryside, the
family and society at large. His story erased differences within Iraqi society and helped lay the foundations for a "culture of war." According to
al-Musawi, the soldier's experience – not the literary critic's opinion –
was the arbiter of good literature. Unlike the U.S. war in Vietnam, which
had no consensus within the American intellectual community, or Nazi
Germany, which saw a clear decline in cultural production as a result of
the acquiescence of intellectuals to state propaganda, Iraqi intellectuals
supported the war, were allowed space for critical thinking and discussion, and helped create new literary forms.[30]

al-Musawi hedged his endorsement of the war literature. Rather than
dismiss the literature of the previous generation of leftist writers, he
insisted that the new literature had different aesthetics and protagonists
than that of the earlier generation's, an aesthetic in keeping with the war.
He avoided passing judgment on the truthfulness and literary value of
this literature by stating that the soldier's experience was the ultimate
arbiter of quality. Finally, his claim that Iraqi writers and intellectuals

[29] Ibid., pp. 11–38.
[30] Ibid., pp. 53–76.

supported the war was not, at least in the early years of the war, that far from the truth.[31] There was also some truth to his statement that the state allowed for a critical examination of the war experience, provided this examination did not become outright opposition to the war effort or to the regime. Particularly after the third year of the Iran-Iraq war, when Iraq was in retreat and actively seeking a ceasefire agreement, the state awarded a number of literary prizes to stories that highlighted the human costs of the war and its destructiveness.

What was the content of this new literature? To what extent did it express criticism of the Iran-Iraq war and the version of the war experience propagated by the mass media? In the first two years of the war, the literature that purported to convey the war experience was derivative and adhered closely to the more propagandistic aspects disseminated in the mass media. Writers derived their templates from the novels and journalistic accounts written by Western and Soviet authors about the two world wars. Hemingway's *A Farewell to Arms*, Remarque's *All Quiet on the Western Front*, Gheorghiu's *The Twenty Fifth Hour*, Smirnov's *Heroes of Brest Fortress*, and Siminov's war diaries as correspondent for the Red Star, *From Black to Barents Sea*, were translated into Arabic and widely read. Iraqi writers also drew on films depicting World War II.[32] Although the government sent a number of young, ambitious, would-be writers as well as older established ones on visits to the front to cohabit with soldiers, few had firsthand experience of battle; fewer still could access the soldiers' interior lives.

The novels and short stories produced about the war experience in the first two years of the Iran-Iraq war had three recurring themes. War was a journey of discovery and adventure for youthful men of the generation of the "revolution;" it allowed them to discover Iraq's geography and bond with Iraq's diverse population; war was also a story of sacrifice in defense of the nation and the achievements of the "revolution." Most of the stories were set on the front or in Iranian territory. When Iraqi villages appeared in soldiers' remembrances, they furnished a bucolic contrast to the front. Soldiers who came from cities remembered their encounters with loved ones, their lives at the university, or their pampered existence before they were transformed by their military experience. As in Europe, the narrative of the war experience cultivated the myth of the common man: it

---

[31] Davis, *Memories of State*, pp. 150–66 and 193–9. Poet Buland al-Haydari expressed his support of the war and called for the production of a committed literature and art. *al-Jumhuriyya*, February 18, 1981, 3.

[32] *al-Jumhuriyya*, May 20, 1981, 5; and *al-Qadisiyya* May 8, 1994, 6.

brought peasants, tribesmen, and citified middle-class men together in the trench.[33] All were portrayed as sentimentalized types whose engagement with violence provided a means of transcendence. In a trope familiar in European war literature, martyrs returned from the dead to visit their families, request that they not be mourned, and reassure grieving loved ones that their deaths had been for a worthy cause.[34]

Perhaps the most representative novel of this early period was Adel Abd al-Jabar's *Mountain of Fire, Mountain of Snow*, winner of the 1982 Ministry of Culture and Information's competition for best novel on the war.[35] al-Jabar was a novelist, screenwriter, and playwright from the 1960s generation who was among the first recruited into writing about the war. He visited the front lines in the fall of 1980 and wrote several short stories before he produced his novel.[36] The novel was widely read by a generation of young adults and was conceived as an adventure story. It follows four soldiers charged with infiltrating Iranian territory and traversing difficult mountainous terrain in the battle of Dezful in the dead of winter. They accomplish their mission, but are ambushed by the enemy as they attempt to return to their unit. The story revolves around their relationships and their interactions with their captors, who are Iranian Kurds. The protagonists of the novel represent four Iraqi archetypes. Khalid is a university-educated Baghdadi in his early twenties who represents the generation of the revolution; Asim is a tribesman from Anbar province; Fattah is a peasant from the southern city of Amara; and Aziz is a slightly older Baghdadi who represents a transitional generation of Iraqis who, although not formed by the revolution, are grateful for its achievements.

The novel is told from the perspective of these soldiers, moving from one to the other. Khalid is a sensitive Baghdadi, educated in European languages, who has ambitions of becoming a writer. His literary abilities are the product of his education under the Ba'th and his first essay was written in school on the occasion of the anniversary of the Ba'thist revolution. He represents a generation of modern Iraqis who intermingle with

[33] Mosse, *Fallen Soldiers*, pp. 15–50.

[34] Jay Winter, *Sites of Memory, Sites of Mourning: The Great War in European Cultural History* (Cambridge: Cambridge University Press, 1998), pp. 15–28; Paul Fussell, *The Great War and Modern Memory* (New York: Oxford University Press, 2000), pp. 3–35.

[35] Adel Abd al-Jabar, *Jabal al-Nar, Jabal al-Thalj* (*Mountain of Fire, Mountain of Snow*) (Baghdad: Dar al-Rashid li al-Nashr, 1982).

[36] *al-Jumhuriyya*, October 18, 1980, 5–6. Abd al-Jabar and a number of other writers were taken to "liberated" Muhammarah to spend time with soldiers.

young women, frequent coffeehouses and drink at bars.[37] He is, however, plagued by ennui, and his battle experience allows him to transcend his sense of alienation. His first engagement with the enemy is a life-changing experience:

> He transcended himself for the first time – everything in him, his feelings, his consciousness and his bodily strength was directed towards one goal on the other side, directed against the enemy, and how to eliminate him and protect oneself. As for firmness of hand, his hand became part of the rifle – iron connected to iron – he remembers this with clarity – and all seemed quiet to him during the battle.[38]

Khalid is made acutely aware of his shortcomings as a fighter at the front. He befriends Asim, even though he thinks of him as a simple and childlike Bedouin prone to reminiscing about his fifteen-year-old village love, Abla. Khalid soon gains respect for his comrade when he sees him in battle single-handedly downing an enemy plane with his rocket-propelled grenade. The tribesman becomes the essence of everything courageous and honorable in the Iraqi character, and he has a few things to teach young men like Khalid about manhood. Much of the interaction among the different protagonists revolves around a gradual process of discovery that, despite their divergent backgrounds, they share a common humanity and a commitment to defend their homeland and the revolution. No tensions exist between soldiers at the front, and their commanding officers represent models of leadership and discipline. When Asim dies, Khalid remembers him with sadness as he walks along the Tigris, reflecting that his death was a small price to pay for preserving the nation.

Abd al-Jabar's novel was meant to portray war as an adventure on the front that taught citified and educated men how to become strong and helped integrate them into the Iraqi nation. The love interests of Khalid and Asim provide part of the adventure, humanizing them and reminding them that their defense of the nation was also the defense of women. Most striking in the novel, however, was the manner in which Abd al-Jabar introduces a military vocabulary to educate his readership about the realities of the front. The hierarchy of military units and rank, the mechanics of planting landmines, the ubiquitous East German transport truck IFA, the terms of military ordnance – all became part of the language of young adults who sought to relive the war experience as a rite of initiation into manhood.

---

[37] Abd al-Jabar, *Jabal al-Nar*, p. 239. This is the assessment of Aziz, who comments on the modernity brought on by the revolution and the importance of defending it.
[38] Ibid., p. 63.

This clichéd and ideological narrative of the war experience began to be challenged, after the third year of the Iran-Iraq war, by a crop of young writers, many of them now more familiar with the realities of battle and its human costs through their interviews of soldiers or their visits to the front. The change is evident in the short stories that appeared after 1983 and won prizes in *Qadisiyat Saddam, Stories under the Flame of Fire*.[39] Some of the prize-winning short story writers convey a sense of resigned exhaustion. Soldiers are no longer seeking adventure, anxious to cut short their furloughs to return to their units, or marching with great bravado to their deaths. Soldiers are, as often as not, portrayed as loners who perform their duty with resignation rather than enthusiasm. Their characters are now more complex, with rich interior lives, less like the action-adventure archetypes of the earlier literature. Death is not always portrayed as meaningful or heroic. War leads to injury and imprisonment – the stories of prisoners of war and handicapped veterans appear in the collections. Anxieties about masculinity and love also appear as some of the soldiers reflect on whether their loved ones will continue to wait for them or abandon them. The stories in the last three volumes of the collection do not always eschew the nationalistic language. Many continue to use Ba'thist and highly ideological language, but others speak of a war experience that had gradually eroded the heroic narrative of soldiering. The vocabulary is no longer militaristic, concerned with creating the illusion of truthfulness by reenacting a literal representation of the front. The landscapes are dystopic, populated by portents of doom and ghosts of the past. The clear division between the battle and home front is now erased as the war reaches the cities, particularly the southern city of Basra, threatening the security of home.

In Muhsin al-Khafaji's story, "The fifth day in the valley of the sun," which earned the first prize in 1983, six soldiers and their officer set out on a reconnaissance mission in no-man's-land.[40] They accomplish their mission, but get lost on their way back to their unit. Part of the responsibility for their predicament lies with their officer, who is unable to read the maps of the terrain correctly. They trudge aimlessly in the scorching July sun and soon run out of provisions. By the time they reach their unit five days later, three of the six soldiers had variously expected to be taken

39 Salim Abd al-Qadir al-Samarra'i ed., *Qadisiyat Saddam: Qisas Tahta Lahib al-Nar* (*Qadisiyat Saddam, Stories under the Flame of Fire*) (Baghdad: Dar al-Rashid, 1981).
40 Muhsin al-Khafaji, "al-Yawm al-khamis fi wadi al-shams" ("The fifth day in the valley of the sun") in *Qadisiyat Saddam: Qisas Tahta Lahib al-Nar* (Baghdad: Dar al-Shu'un al-Thaqafiyya wa al-Nashr, 1983), vol. 6, pp. 9–27.

prisoner by the Iranians, fallen in exhaustion, and been threatened with abandonment by their officer. Back safely in his unit, one soldier wonders about the meaning of his martyrdom had he died of hunger or thirst in an unfamiliar and hostile landscape under the leadership of an inept and uncaring officer.

al-Khafaji's story has little to do with sketching heroic national archetypes or glorifying death. Similarly, the third-prize short story winner in the collection in 1983, Muhammad Abd al-Majid's " The gazelle runs towards the East," focuses on the prisoner of war and reflects on the despair and meaningless of death in the prison camps.[41] The story begins with a scene of Iraqi soldiers forced to dig the grave of one of their comrades killed by an Iranian soldier. They huddle in a prison cell listening to the screams of their fellow prisoners, who are being tortured. They are determined to resist, even though some are overwhelmed with fear and despair. Before his captors march him to his execution, the protagonist reflects that:

No one writes the history of the oppressed present and the precarious moment, surrounded by barbed wires and by bullets and by the curses of constant siege, and by the delusion that does not bring forth except a long and stubborn silence.[42]

Jasim Helou's short story, entitled "The Lotus tree," which won the first prize in 1985, upends the division between the home and battlefront and situates the battle in the streets of Basra, whose civilians are now victims of the war.[43] The story alternates between the battle and the city, where the protagonist's family lives in a house fronted by a lotus tree. The voice of the narrator moves between the first and third person, providing a contrast between his memory of his family and his engagement in battle. The protagonist's family is martyred by Iranian shelling while its members are tending the garden and hanging the laundry. Two of the lotus tree's branches are destroyed. The protagonist fights at the front to avenge his wife's death and to restore the lost branches of his tree in the hope of bringing back the nightingales that used to perch on it. The juxtaposition of the destroyed bucolic domestic landscape with the visceral description of the landscape of the front highlights the breakdown of the

[41] Muhammad Abd al-Majid, "al-Ghazal al-rakid nahwa al-sharq" ("The gazelle that runs towards the East"), in *Qadisiyat Saddam, Qisas Tahta Lahib al-Nar* (Baghdad: Da'irat al-Shu'un al-Thaqafiyya wa al-Nashr, 1984), vol. 6, pp. 57–69.
[42] Ibid., p. 65.
[43] Jasim Helou, "al-Sadra" ("The Lotus tree"), in *Qadisiyat Saddam: Qisas Tahta Lahib al-Nar* (Baghdad: Da'irat al-Shu'un al-Thaqafiyya wa al-Nashr, 1985), vol. 8, pp. 9–27.

line between civilian and military life. The protagonist returns to Basra in search of his dead wife. He finds that:

Summer has rushed with speed this time spreading its hated heat over the streets of the city.... It is the thirty-fourth summer of my life.... It appears to me more lonely than other summers.... The alleyways are mute and the cars rarely run in the streets. Quiet surrounds closed houses.... Two or three children play and scream on the pavement carpeted with hot sand.... A tall man with a rifle emerges from behind the houses and soon goes to right and disappears.... All is surrounded by silence.... I have to walk between the high walls of sandbags and to turn with it along the pavement of the road.... These walls were not as high during my last furlough.[44]

This small selection of prize-winning short stories is a far cry from Abd al-Jabar's narrative of the war story. Its protagonists do not represent archetypes; they say little about the "revolution" or defense of national territory. They do not portray war as an efficient and orderly march of men and machines toward a clear goal. Their protagonists' engagement with death and destruction is transformative, but their narratives lay bare the myth that war is an adventure or that it forges a militant masculinity. The voices are infused with a sense of resignation and despair, and their encounters with their comrades are often fraught.

The government tolerated the implicitly critical stance of this literature in large part because it was not widely read beyond literary circles. It never explicitly challenged the conduct of war and it was not picked up in mass media outlets, which continued to glorify the war experience in film, photography, and print. The war literature, however, was critical to the government's efforts to create a literary culture and vocabulary centered on soldiering, and to do so by co-opting older intellectuals and recruiting a cadre of younger authors who established themselves by writing about the war experience.

Remembrance and the War Experience

The government's attempt to render the war experience as transformative of the "revolution" generation was directed at an expanding middle- and lower-middle-class educated, largely urban population. The generation's sensibility as articulated in outlets of public culture was above all modern, defined by a set of signs that distinguished it from an earlier generation. This generation's members were characterized by social mobility as

[44] Ibid., p. 22.

distinct from the generations of their fathers and grandfathers who were uneducated and relatively poor. They were, as the war literature called them, the "children of schools" (*awlad al-madaris*), beneficiaries of the expansion in institutions of higher education as well as the state's investment in entertainment and sports venues.[45] They were also products of the new values governing male and female relationships. They studied beside women in universities, had romantic relationships, frequented bars and literary venues, read voraciously, and attended the theater and cinema. According to the government, these accoutrements of modernity were central to this Iraqi generation's sensibility and should in part motivate it to fight against the Iranian brand of Islamic government. They were, to put it in American terms, defending a way of life.

The government's attempt to define a generational sensibility of men who came of age under the Ba'th as modern as well as socially and culturally expansive resonated with middle- and lower-middle-class urban conscripts, particularly those drafted after graduating from college. Although only a few clearly associated this modernity with the Ba'thist "revolution," almost all insisted that, in addition to defending Iraq in a conflict imposed by the Iranian regime, they did not wish to live in a society governed by religious strictures on social public behavior. In hindsight, many expressed doubts about the necessity and conduct of the war, but few questioned the need to defend Iraq against what they called an "imposed war." Among conscripts, those who entered the war in their late teens or early twenties saw their lives as overshadowed and frequently truncated by a long conflict that produced few tangible results. Enlisted men, that is to say those who joined military colleges voluntarily, rarely expressed themselves in explicitly generational terms. They did view their encounter with violence as a transformative life experience; it allowed them to perform their duty as patriotic soldiers. It also helped transform the Iraqi armed forces, according to many of them, into a high-performance, powerful, modern military machine.

Waddah Hasan was in his final year at the Academy of Fine Arts when he and dozens of other young short story writers were recruited by the Directorate of Political Guidance to spend a few weeks at the front cohabiting with soldiers. He had come to the attention of the Directorate after he had published, in the early months of the war, short stories about soldiers at the front in the party newspaper, *al-Thawra*. He was sent to the southern sector, spent about a month with soldiers in the Third

---

[45] The phrase was used in Abd al-Jabar's novel, *Jabal al-Nar, Jabal al-Thalj*, pp. 77–82.

Army Corps stationed outside Basra, and produced a number of short stories, which he published in various dailies. He viewed his visit as one of recording information about life at the front and rendering it into an accessible literary form. The first stories he produced were a mixture of reportage, adventure, and propaganda. They were, by his admission, derivative and clichéd. One of his stories, a recreation of a battle in a building in Khorramshahr (Muhammarah) was drawn, as he told me, from watching the 1949 Soviet film *The Battle of Stalingrad*. He was conscripted into the armed forces soon after graduating from college, and spent the first three years in Baghdad writing radio programs for the Directorate of Political Guidance before being posted to the East Tigris Command in the south. There he continued his work as a reporter for military newspapers and for the radio, only to fall afoul of one of his commanding officers and be posted to the north for combat duty. His narrative of his experience provides a bridge between the claims made by the war literature and the mass media to document soldiers' memories of their actual war experience.[46]

Unlike the majority of the soldiers I interviewed, Waddah told his story in formal literary Arabic (*fusha*) rather than in the Iraqi colloquial dialect. He was forever the journalist and short story writer seeking to narrate his war experience within the boundaries of the larger story using vocabulary he and others like him had popularized. Waddah had a remarkable memory for dates, battles, and names. He recalled for my benefit the exact size of trenches, the models of equipment and arms, and the minutiae of life on the front, from the kind of utensils used to feed soldiers to the kind of radio programs broadcast and theater productions watched in the rear lines. He was, however, more reticent about his actual battlefield experience after he was posted to the Rawanduz area in the north, and opted to render his experience in the training camp in a short literary piece that he gave me after our interviews. It is difficult to judge whether his decision was driven by his need to maintain control over his narrative or by his unwillingness to talk about his experience, more than twenty years later, in the more direct and emotive colloquial and outside the confines of ordered literary forms disseminated by the media and the literature of war.

Despite hewing closely in literary form to the sanctioned narrative of the war experience, Waddah's recollections point to the complex manner by which the language and imagery propagated by the mass media and literary culture shaped the soldiers' remembrances even as the latter

[46] Interviews with Waddah Hasan, Amman, Jordan, June 21, 23, 28, 2007.

challenged its content. Waddah's remembrance of the war was often at odds with the heroic descriptions that he himself helped create and disseminate among soldiers and to the larger public.

Waddah Hasan represents the generation of young Iraqi men to whom the government sought to appeal. He was born in 1956 to a family of illiterate peasants who migrated to Kirkuk in 1959. A product of the public educational system set up well before the Baʻth came to power, his intellectual life was formed by the pluralistic cultural milieu of the city of Kirkuk that brought together Kurds, Turcomans, and Arabs. Trilingual, he spent the 1970s frequenting cafés in the city, socializing with like-minded literary friends, and acting in local productions of plays performed in public theaters in the city. By his own reckoning, he was a secular, well-read, tolerant, and artistic intellectual committed to defending the modernity of his way of life. In his early twenties, while still in the Academy of Fine Arts as a theater student, he, like a number of ambitious would-be intellectuals, began writing in the cultural pages of daily newspapers. Although not a militant Baʻthist, he saw his contribution to the culture of war as a short story writer and journalist as necessary for the defense of the nation and of the secular modernity of Iraq. Until his posting to the front lines in the last years of his service, Waddah enjoyed a relatively privileged position. He worked for the Directorate of Political Guidance, first in Baghdad and at the rear lines, meeting a large number of artists and intellectuals mobilized for the war effort. They formed, in his remembrance, a nucleus of a community of comrades that shaped his war experience as a journey of intellectual and social discovery. When he was posted to the front lines, however, his attitude changed:

We [he and his friend] had a difficult life in this battalion for a month [of intense training].... Our suffering was great because we were older than the new conscripts, and sensitive intellectuals who love life and we had a great number of artistic and cultural projects. I had met the Minister of Culture and Information Lutayif Nasif Jasim and asked for his help to cancel my posting.... But he angrily told me, "If you don't go to the front and others do not go to the front on the excuse that they are writers and intellectuals, who will fight the enemy?" ... We are a tragic generation.... For the state we were the generation of heroes and sacrifice and liberation.... We did not have the courage to write about this [the tragic experience] in our journals and articles and our literary output.[47]

A strong sense of grievance about their call to the front pervaded the remembrances of college-educated men who felt a deep sense of alienation

---

[47] Interview with Waddah Hasan, Amman, Jordan, June 23, 2007.

about the violence of battle as they did about the forced proximity to men from different social and regional backgrounds. Tareq Ali, a Baghdadi from a family of professionals, some of whom leaned left politically, was only sixteen at the onset of the war with Iran. He was immersed in the youth culture of middle-class Baghdad, listening to Western pop and rock and roll, consuming pop culture magazines, reading Western literature in translation, and, by the time he was in college, dating a young woman. His self-identification as a modern young Baghdadi was bound with certain practices and mannerisms, many inspired by Western youth culture, that had as much to do with outward signs such as grooming and socializing as it did with the defiance of the social and cultural conventions of his parents and their peers. His identity, as he saw it, had little to do with the Ba'thist "revolution" and much to do with the leftist-inspired and pluralistic cosmopolitan literary culture of Baghdad of the 1960s and 1970s. Unlike Waddah, he had little ambition to join the cultural Ba'thist apparatus. He trained as a radar operator and was posted, in 1984, to the front, where he performed well enough to earn a medal of courage. At the front:

> I avoided those who were older than me, in fact I used to hate dealing with them or forming friendships with them. My friends were all my age or they were college graduates like me. You notice that in the training camps, people congregated according to age, or around other identities like ethnic, religious or regional. I had my own group, who were interested in reading, writing and other refined pursuits.[48]

For a number of soldiers of this generation, both conscripts and enlisted men, the war years were a wasted part of their lives. Of the nineteen soldiers I interviewed, more than half remembered missed opportunities to escape outside the country as some of their friends had done or acknowledged having serious thoughts about deserting. A few were continuously late for reporting back to their units; others did not desert out of fear or a sense of resignation to their situation. For Tareq Ali, the country that had allowed him to live the ordinary life of a young, sometimes rebellious, modern man had become a burden when he became a soldier, "I am entangled in a nation," he said, unable to flee it except through the creation of an alternative world derived from Western books and music.[49] Abu Faruk, a Ba'thist and an officer from the city of Ana who lost his leg while planting landmines in no-man's-land, spoke regrettably

---

[48] Interview with Tareq Ali, Amman, Jordan, July 17, 2007.
[49] Ibid.

of the lost opportunity to emigrate to Detroit just before the Iran-Iraq war.[50] Haytham Abbas, the son of a dockworker in the city of Basra with communist sympathies, viewed the war as a farce. The Iraqi mass media insisted on claiming victory even as his city was being bombed, evacuated, and overrun by military vehicles bringing the dead and injured from the front:

I used to feel that this war was a personal loss for me, because I used to dream that after I am twenty ... a person when he reaches twenty there is something beautiful in life. This thing [beauty] I did not see, this is the first and most important loss in my life.... The war was a personal loss, it was not a [war of] defense and I do not know what.... Then this loss became a farce because we saw the work of death as many of our friends died.... Ha! ... we used to see people coming [while] holding the keys to heaven and riding on motorcycles and wearing shrouds ... Something absurd.[51]

Nostalgia and mourning for a lost youth infused many of the remembrances of conscripts and enlisted men. The war experience had transformed them as a generation, but not in the ways originally anticipated by state propaganda. Despite the state's repeated attempts to equate the defense of the nation with the defense of a modern way of life to its urban middle- and lower-middle-class conscripts, the soldiers' remembrances point to cynicism about the state's claims of the liberating promise of modernity. In particular, the death and destruction brought on by the modern technology of war, the ability of the state to manipulate modern media to lie about the war, and the chaos of battle belied the sanctioned story of a progressive modern Iraqi self that finds transcendence of social difference and existential apathy in the violence of war. Even lower-ranking members of the enlisted officer corps who expressed great pride in the achievements and modernity of the Iraqi military machine described, with trepidation and terror, the destructive power of these machines. In recalling his experience in the battles to regain the Faw Peninsula after 1986, Abu Faruk, who was an officer in a unit to plant and remove landmines, remembers that he was manning a powerful armored shovel used to remove soil and build sand barriers between Iranian and Iraqi lines:

In the hell that was Faw, they used to get extraordinary equipment, they did not get a regular shovel. I went on the armored shovel to accompany its driver.... I was shaking with fear while talking to the corporal.... The world was upside down, I mean, there were tanks shelling and mortars shelling and [the Iranians]

[50] Interview with Abu Faruk, Damascus, Syria, March 20, 2009.
[51] Interview with Haytham Abbas, Amman, Jordan, July 5, 2007.

were hitting us.... The colonel spoke to me quickly and said, "Lets retreat....
Take the armored shovel and retreat." ... I had to take it on the only paved road
which was very dangerous because it was continuously being shelled and it (the
shovel) was heavy, weighing more than thirty-five tons.... I was in the shovel
here, and the Iranian forces were here and the Iraqi forces on the other side....
There is a line of mortar cannon on both sides.... I see looking in front of me ...
the first one was hit and burned, the second was hit and burned ... and then they
burned all the mortar cannons.... The Iranians were not easy.... This sight is
overwhelming.... I did not know what to think.... For sure terror, not fear ... this
terror is normal ... the shaking and terror I went through, I cannot forget.[52]

For Abu Faruk, as for other soldiers, the experience of battle at the
front lines upended his understanding of modern warfare as organized
death. It was, above all, the experience of living on the front lines, rather
than the rear lines, that defined their memories. It was on the front lines
that social and regional distinctions among Iraqi men were least visible, and it was at the front where Ba'thist commissars made only occa-
sional appearances and officers showed their mettle. This was part of the
mythology of the war experience propagated by the state and it was pivotal in the stories soldiers told about their experiences. Most striking was
their vivid portrayal of the landscapes of the Iraqi warfront, particularly
in the feared southern front.[53] Soldiers eschewed the bucolic or romanticized vision of the front, but often alluded to moments of communion
with the landscape before and during the chaos of battle. They often
described these moments in cinematic terms, alluding to the film-like
quality of their experience. Nor did soldiers' remembrances convey the
triumphalism of the mass media in its celebration of the militarization of
Iraqi landscapes. Soldiers confused battle dates, did not remember when
they fought at what front, and rarely spoke of their battles in terms of
victories. Many, however, grounded their remembrance in a specific place
on the front. They located their experience not in time, or in the name of
a battle, but on a battlefront: East Basra, al-Ahwar, Faw, Majnoon, Nahr
Jasim. The war heightened the awareness of many men to the power of
nature and its fragility.

My interviewees' encounters with the landscape of the front was transformative. Few had traveled outside their cities before the war. Fewer still
had gone to the border areas of Iraq. Their posting to the front was their

---

[52] Interview with Abu Faruk, Damascus, Syria, March 20, 2009.
[53] The centrality of frontline landscapes to the construction of a narrative of war was
    not unique to Iraq during wartime. George Mosse, among others, has observed that
    the destruction brought on by the First World War was masked by what he called an
    "appropriation" and idealization of nature in the arts. Mosse, *Fallen Soldiers*, pp. 107–25.

introduction to the geography of their country as it was to the architecture of the front with its division into front and rear lines, its concrete shelters, its trenches and foxholes, and its military barriers. Some, like Mazin Hadithi, began their description of their experience at the front with the story of their initial encounter of their division's or unit's officer in the rear lines and their movement from the relative safety of the rear lines to the front. The sight of the trench on the East Basra front overwhelmed Mazin:

We left Basra ... we left the city, a desert road, and every now and then there are stations of soldiers, but you don't see them, its just their heads sticking out of the ground, nothing is over the ground, everything is under the ground.... I was taken to the headquarters of my unit, it was such a headquarter, it is as if it was a grave, it is a world different than this world, a world under the ground, you walk so underground, there is an administrator, a cook, an officer and military police, all of this underground.... I was supposed to fight, eat and sleep in a little hole.... I decided that when I get my furlough, I am going to Baghdad and never coming back.[54]

Soldiers learned to live life in the trenches and developed a certain rhythm: relatively calm and monotonous days punctuated by hellish nights of bombardment. Morning meant counting the dead and injured and taking stock of equipment losses. For most who fought on the southern front, however, descriptions of battles in the marsh regions of southern Iraq were infused with both terror and fascination with the harshness of the landscape and its threat to their survival; others were interwoven with a romanticized notion of the marshes. In his description of a 1987 battle in the Amara marshes, Ammar Hasan reflects this fear and fascination with the marshes. He had been taken with a number of soldiers by boat to the marsh and left on a sandy part of the marsh that had been drained to make way for tanks. During the battle, half buried in the sand, he slept:

In this situation I slept ... with the tanks behind my head shooting [at the enemy] and spewing sand in our direction.... I do not know how long I slept.... I woke with the first break of light, I mean the light had become the color of indigo.... I woke up with the smell of gunpowder, the smoke and the steam of the water forming clouds. Like that, when I stuck my head out [of the foxhole] I saw an enchanting scene, as if I remembered a scene from films.... It meant that there will be calm but afterwards there will be shelling.... It meant that we will get in boats to cleanse the marshes ... but the state I woke in![55]

---

54 Interview with Mazin Hadithi, Damascus, Syria, March 1, 2009.
55 Interview with Ammar Hasan, Damascus, Syria, August 16, 2007.

The government deployed a definition of heroic masculinity that drew on the tropes of militant Ba'thist nationalism and what it viewed as traditional tribal values marked by personal loyalty, instinctive courage, and authentic and unmediated attachment to a militarized way of life. Soldiers' remembrances sometimes drew on the latter version of masculinity, but also often belied this stereotypical archetype. Conscripts drawn from second-generation middle and lower-middle classes who hailed from major cities like Baghdad and Basra rarely alluded to tribal notions of courage and honor in their descriptions of their battle experience. Their remembrances, however, attest to the brutalization of their sensibilities as exhibited by their gradual hardening toward death; their intimate familiarity with the vocabulary of military hierarchy; and their description of battle. Insofar as they articulated the transformation in their sense of themselves as men, they often framed it in terms of brutalization, anxiety (*qalaq*), and weariness (*ta'ab*), terms that are a far cry from the certitude of the militant masculinity embraced in the mass media and in heroic tribal narratives.

Abu Ali's story attests to the power of tribal tropes of manhood for some soldiers. Born in Karbala in 1955, Abu Ali was a Ba'thist college graduate who was teaching English to middle-school children in his city when he volunteered to join the Popular Army less than three months after the war began. He had been watching the aggressive moves of the Iranian government since late August 1980, and as a Ba'thist, had frequented his neighborhood party offices to partake in city security checks. After hearing of the fall of Khorramshahr, he volunteered to join the Popular Army. He and thousands of other local volunteers were briefly trained in Basra and deployed to Khorramshahr as guards. Less than two months into his service, he lost a leg and part of an arm when an Iranian missile fell nearby. When I asked him why he volunteered and was eager to forego more extensive training, he said that he came from a tribal culture in the mid-Euphrates where hunting with rifles was an integral part of their lives. He viewed fighting in battle as a natural extension of this experience. Abu Ali eventually secured, through connections to the Presidential Palace, a meeting with Saddam Hussain to request medical treatment for his injuries in Europe. His description of this meeting speaks to the power of the kind of masculinity that drew on the Iraqi traditions of tribal leadership. When Abu Ali, in a wheelchair, was ushered into the presence of Saddam Hussain, the latter embraced him and at some point wept as he heard of how the injury happened. Hussain then personally pushed the veteran's wheelchair to his administrative office and ordered his staff to ensure that Abu Ali, accompanied by his wife, be sent to Europe for treatment.[56]

The cultivation of the image of manliness based on generosity, emotiveness, and personalized bonds defined for Abu Ali and many Iraqis who fought at the front the boundaries of an "inherently" Iraqi masculinity that drew in part on tribal leadership traditions. Three of the seasoned soldiers I interviewed, two of them enlisted lower-ranking officers, alluded to Saddam Hussain as a manly leader who was severe with his enemies but generous with his subjects.[57] As one soldier who spent twelve years in Iranian prison camps and was frequently punished for his refusal to "convert" told me, Saddam Hussain was a "*zalmy*," a tough guy.[58] For Sabir Farah, a soldier in the Republican Guard, the Iraqi man "is authentic and has zeal and honor ... when his rights are taken away by force ... he defends them with all his emotions ... our people [soldiers in the Republican Guard] all threw themselves at death, it is usual, they were not afraid."[59]

In their remembrances of their battle experiences, conscripts and enlisted soldiers often invoked Sabir's idealized vision of soldiering as the incubator of manly honor and fearlessness to describe some of their fallen comrades. However, in their descriptions of their own encounters with death and killing, their narratives are far more ambiguous. They point to a conflicted notion of honor where the courage and fearlessness of some coexisted with the ubiquitous presence of death squads, corruption, and complicity in the conduct of war and counterinsurgency. At the same time, the majority of my interviewees spoke of their war experience as brutalizing, beginning with the first shocking encounter with the landscape of the front and with death and killing, and proceeding to a gradual deadening of emotion, a process commonly encountered among soldiers fighting wars anywhere. Those who fought on the southern marshes and the Faw Peninsula drew on a repertoire of similar images to talk about their experience: the body parts of soldiers floating in marshes and the salty water of the Faw; their ability to eat and function in the midst of this carnage; and the gradual erosion of their commitment to their comrades as they struggled to survive Iranian assaults and life on the front lines.

[56] Interview with Abu Ali, Damascus, Syria, March 22, 2009.
[57] Interviews with Hanna Khoshaba, Amman, Jordan, July 19, 2007; Issa Youhanna, Amman, Jordan, July 23, 2007; and Abu Muhammad, Amman, Jordan, August 7, 2007.
[58] Interview with Abu Mukhlis, Amman, Jordan, August 7, 2007.
[59] Interview with Sabir Farah, Amman, Jordan, July 21, 2007.

Mazin Hadithi was one of less than a handful of soldiers I interviewed who was willing to talk about his initial experience of killing an Iranian soldier. His narrative framed this first act of killing as a turning point in a process of brutalization of his sensibility as a man, a process he resisted by bribing his superiors for longer furloughs and failing to return on time, a choice that often landed him in prison. He spent the first six months of his time in the trench in complete terror, trying to avoid firing direct shots into enemy lines. It was only after an attack by Iranian forces and his unit's subsequent chaotic withdrawal that he threw a hand grenade toward an Iranian soldier who was pursuing him and his commanding officer. In his words:

I hit him with hand grenade, as if you are hitting with a stone or something ... it exploded.... When we returned [after the battle] to look for who was martyred and who was injured.... I went to the Iranian that I had hit with the hand grenade.... He was dead, he had a light red beard.... I mean he looked like a Dutchman ... he had a pocket that had a zipper.... I opened the zipper like that ...there were identity cards or something in his pocket ... I opened his wallet, it had a photograph of a woman with two children, the woman did not mean anything to me but his children, they also had red hair like his beard. The world exploded for me and I started crying as I held onto the photograph ... my commanding officer came and I told him, "Look. The poor guy had a family." He said, "Why? Don't you have a family? Don't we also have families? Those people who were killed did not have families?" I threw the wallet back at him [the Iranian soldier] and we left.... This "Battle of the Great Day" [the official title for the battle] was a cursed day for me because I had killed and I had not done so before now.[60]

By the time he had been transferred to the Faw front, Mazin had become a hardened soldier. To paraphrase his colorful language, he had lost his initial terror through the camaraderie he developed with other soldiers over the stench of death, rockets, and the detritus of other men. He, like other soldiers, told of the absolute quiet and terror that gripped him and his comrades before they undertook an attack, and, in Mazin's case, the need to sing dirty limericks and songs to help prepare for the confrontation to come. It was an assertion of aggressive masculinity and of camaraderie belied by Mazin's description of the most scarring battle he fought in the salty waters of the Mamlaha region of Faw. He came closest to dying in Faw, and he found that he had to cross the line that had hitherto set the limits of his endurance; one did not abandon

---

[60] Interview with Mazin Hadithi, Damascus, Syria, March 1, 2009.

comrades, one helped pick up the dead, and one rescued the injured. These formed his understanding of his duties as a man and his continued survival. His experience in Faw upended this understanding and distilled for him, at least in the way he told me his story, the essence of his war experience.

I swear by God, the attack in Mamlaha ... the shouting, the screaming of wounded the screaming of people, I thought it would reach Kuwait.... So strong was the screaming on the front ... and the injured, he who had lost his hand and the other had his abdomen open, what are they supposed to do.... On that day ... I have told this story to my friend ... I had seen death but had never seen the dismemberment of legs, feet, heads.... I mean I lost my control.... I spit on God.... I started talking to God.... If God is present why does he accept this.... This happened in Mamlaha.... I had partaken in Majnoon and Nahr Jasim [earlier deadly battles in difficult terrain] ... This only happened in Mamlaha.[61]

At the battle's end, Mazin had to escape an area covered by an Iranian sniper. While he managed to find his way to the rear lines, he refused en route to help an injured soldier because he could not carry him, and he had to persuade his own army's execution squad that he was not fleeing his front line unit. He was prepared to shoot at them if they were not convinced. Meeting them after he had barely survived a battle in which he had lost his commanding officer and numerous comrades, they represented the enemy within. As he put it, they always had "clean boots." They did not conform to the code of honor and manhood that supposedly governed soldiering in defense of the nation.

Fighting at the front lines gradually inured men to their comrades' deaths. It also exposed them to their own state's violence against its people and made them complicit in it, although they insisted in interviews that they had no choice. Less than a month after the hostilities ended, Ammar Hasan, a graduate of the Academy of Fine Arts, joined his unit in what he was told was a military training maneuver in the southern marshes. He was to take photographs and videotape of the operation. Initially excited by the adventure of shooting live footage from a military helicopter, he soon realized that the operation was not innocuous but rather an assault on civilian marsh populations suspected of harboring Islamist party members. His commanding officer seized his video and photographs of the victims and directed him to remain silent about what he had seen. Speaking about his experience two decades later, Ammar

[61] Ibid.

placed it in the narrative of the atrocities of wartime Iraq that he and others could not fathom or publicize at the time.[62]

Hanna Khoshaba, however, was fully aware of the orders issued against Kurdish villagers in the Anfal campaign. His division was stationed in Dyana in the Kurdish north when their orders came to move into the village of Malgan in the Rawanduz area of Arbil province. His order was to eradicate the village. He drove the car of the commander of his division and:

reached the village and found it totally empty. Its people had fled a few hours earlier and left their animals and their properties. We found a bread kiln still hot. It seems that they had heard of the attack and they fled. The Kurds had intelligence and they knew that those areas that had rebel presence were going to be attacked ... the rest of the division walked for about five hours and then met with Kurdish resistance which they annihilated.[63]

When I asked Hanna what he thought when he received his orders to eradicate the village, his response was:

It is not important what I think. These are military orders, who can disobey them? He will be executed for sure, because of this I am with myself and against my enemy. We were told that these were rebels against the government and army. The army annihilated most of these rebels. After a short while, in February 1989 I was demobilized from the army even though *Anfal* was still going on. I went to my family in Baghdad to rest.[64]

For most soldiers, the core of their war experience lay in the gradual militarization of their sensibility: their familiarity with military ordnance and hierarchy; their internalization of the routines at the front; their acceptance and cynicism about corruption and politicization of relations; and their hardening toward death. These were the elements that marked them as men who fought in the Iran-Iraq war. Soldiering was indeed transformative, but rarely in the ways the officially sanctioned version of war claimed.

Conclusion

The First Gulf War put an end to the state-sponsored mythology built around soldiering and the war experience. The military's performance in the war, the widespread looting undertaken by soldiers, the deadly

[62] Interview with Ammar Hasan, Damascus, Syria, August 16, 2007.
[63] Interview with Hanna Khoshaba, Amman, Jordan, July 19, 2007.
[64] Ibid.

and chaotic withdrawal of the armed forces, and the role they played in the uprising and its suppression – all made it difficult for the government to continue promoting the soldiers' experience as the essence of Iraqi selfhood. Instead, the defining features of the new war experience in the wake of the First Gulf War and during the embargo were survival, steadfastness, and victimhood. Mass media outlets portrayed women and children as the heroes of the realities of a new kind of war. They defined masculinity using increasingly tribal and rural rather than militant and modern tropes.

Photographers were now asked to document the destruction wrought by the coalition forces' bombing of Iraq, as they were to document the new struggle (*jihad*) of rebuilding in the aftermath of the First Gulf War and the Intifada. The Ministry of Culture and Information could no longer afford to sponsor any literature on the war experience. Abd al-Sattar Nasir, a prolific writer of the war literature genre, attributed the paucity of short story writers in the 1990s to the lack of funds.[65] Others wrote that the war literature was propagandistic and called for a more reflective and truthful literature on the war experience.[66] It was only among the Iraqi diaspora, however, that the first non-state-sponsored literature on the war experience began to emerge at the end of the 1990s. Insofar as any writing on the Iran-Iraq war experience emerged in the Iraqi press and in literature, the hero of that experience was no longer the soldier, but the prisoner of war who had endured torture and had returned to Iraq. He, like his fellow Iraqis under the embargo, had remained steadfast in the face of insurmountable odds.[67]

Nevertheless, the state's attempts to elevate and manipulate the experience of war with Iran into a narrative of militant masculinity and the birth of a new sensibility for a Ba'thist generation of Iraqis has left a profound imprint on the cultural politics of Iraq and on the politics of memory that continue to play themselves out in the present. It has created generational fissures between Iraqis whose formative years were in the 1960s and those who grew up under the Ba'th and have no memory of life without war. It has split the intellectual communities of Iraq between those who fled the country rather than work within Ba'thist cultural

---

[65] *al-Qadisiyya*, September 2, 1991, 6.

[66] *al-Qadisiyya*, January 17, 1994, 6; *al-Qadisiyya*, August 28, 1995, 6; and *al-Jumhuriyya*, March 25, 1997, 7.

[67] Abd al-Mu'min Hammadi, *Lughat al-Siyat* (*The Language of Whips*) (Baghdad: Dar al-Huriyya, 1999).

institutions and those who remained and wrote in support of the war.[68] Last, but not least, the Ba'thist state's attempts to monopolize the narrative of the war experience, has meant, in the current climate in Iraq, that the experience of those who fought and survived the war continues to be intertwined with the politics and the conduct of that war.

---

[68] For some of these divisions see Abboud, *Thaqafat al-'Unf fi al-'Iraq*; Fadhil al-Azzawi, *al-Ruh al-Hayya, Jil al-Sitinat fi al-Iraq* (*The Living Spirit, The Sixties Generation in Iraq*) (Damascus: Dar al-Mada, 1997); Fatima Mohsen, "Debating Iraqi culture: Intellectuals between the inside and the outside," in Milich, Pannewick, and Tramontini, *Conflicting Narratives*, pp. 5–23; and for a satirical novel on the conflict see Ali Bader, *Baba Sartre* (*Papa Sartre*), 2nd edition (Beirut: al-Mu'assasa al-'Arabiyya li al-Dirasat wa al-Nashr, 2006).

8

Commemorating the Dead

On February 16, 1981, the mayor of Baghdad, Samir Abd al-Wahab al-Shaykhli, made public the government's intention to build a $40 million monument commemorating the dead of the Iran-Iraq war.[1] Conceived by artist Isma'il Fattah al-Turk and drafted by a team of architects from the Baghdad School of Architecture, the monument consisted "of a circular platform, 190 meter in diameter, floating over an underground museum and carrying a 40-meter high split dome." Set in the middle of an artificial lake, the monument stood apart from the city's high rises and bustle, and was meant to create a space for reflection on the meaning of death.[2] The Martyr's Monument signaled the intention of the state to offer a distinct place to those martyred in the war with Iran. It distinguished them from martyrs for the nation among the armed forces and from the Ba'th Party who had come before them. The Martyr's Monument, officially titled the *Monument of the Martyrs of Qadisiyat Saddam*, commemorated the death of citizen soldiers in the first national war in which mass death became the norm. The government's goals were to nationalize that death, create rituals that commemorated the fallen, render their deaths acceptable to their families, and do so while controlling the meaning of that loss.

In the first years of the war, cultural institutions in cooperation with the Ba'th Party undertook a systematic effort to sanctify the deaths of soldiers by developing rituals that gave meaning to their deaths within the narrow confines of a secularized reading of martyrdom in Islam and a Ba'thist interpretation of Iraqi Arab nationalism. These efforts were

---

[1] *al-Jumhuriyya*, February 16, 1981, 7.
[2] Kanan Makiya, *The Monument: Art and Vulgarity in Saddam Hussein's Iraq* (New York: I.B. Tauris, 2004), p. 23.

centralized and authoritarian. They did not allow for any development of community-based rituals of mourning or the formation of independent organizations of martyrs' families. Their purpose was to depersonalize and routinize death. Above all, they were designed to foster and project unity of Iraq's diverse population and bolster national support for the war by highlighting the martyrs' families' contributions and the leadership's generosity. The routine and ritualized practices created a modicum of consensus among the majority of Iraqis on the meaning of death for the nation: soldiers died to protect Iraqi soil from Iranian aggression, even if such death did not have, for their families or many in the nation, the same meaning ascribed to it by Ba'thist ideology.

The consensus on the commemoration and meaning of martyrdom was shattered in the aftermath of the First Gulf War. A debate ensued within the Ba'th Party and the regime leadership on how to commemorate the Mother of All Battles. Not only was the heroic version of martyrdom for the nation shattered, it had become clear to most Iraqis that the nation itself was a precarious community that could disintegrate into chaos and violence. Faced with the breakup of the heroic national narrative on the meaning of death, the political leadership sought to highlight a narrative of victimization. The choice of al-'Amiriyya shelter, bombed by the United States on February 13, 1991, as the site of commemoration of the First Gulf War dead, was driven by two factors. The popular and often spontaneous grief over the bombing of the shelter demonstrated by the Iraqi population gave the Iraqi regime impetus to channel popular sentiment toward a national symbol that could unite Iraqis and divert their attention from the regime's disastrous politics and the divisiveness of the Intifada. Equally important, al-'Amiriyya shelter allowed the political leadership to speak the language of humanitarianism, linking the deaths that ensued from the First Gulf War to the human costs of the embargo. According to the new narrative of memorialization, the Iraqi nation was united by its victimization. Its citizens were defined by their steadfastness (*sumud*), a term used by the government to describe the essence of Iraqi national traits as well as a new generation of Iraqis who had grown up under the UN sanctions. Despite the government's manipulation of the rituals and meaning of al-'Amiriyya shelter as a site of commemoration, however, it provided Iraqis with an emotional narrative that used the vocabulary of humanitarianism and suffering to protest the embargo.[3]

---

[3] Lara Deeb has drawn attention to the dual power of memorials and museums to speak a counter-hegemonic language within a transnational setting and to impose a hegemonic

The Invention of the Cult of Martyrs

On January 16, 1982, a Revolutionary Command Council directive designated December 1 as Martyr's Day. The choice of the date was significant. It marked the day, six weeks earlier, of the execution of Iraqi prisoners of war by the Iranian Revolutionary Guard at Bostan in Iran. It was chosen to underscore the contravention by the Iranian government, in the words of the directive, of "international, moral and religious laws and injunctions."[4] It constructed martyrdom for the nation around the twin poles of heroism and victimhood, and provided the government with the opportunity to remind Iraqis of the "immorality, hypocrisy and inhumanity" of the Iranian Islamic regime. It collapsed the times and places of the deaths of individual fallen soldiers into one symbolic day of mass commemoration. In the words of Saddam Hussain, "The Day of the Martyr is a blessed day and it is one of our immortal days.... It is an immortal day because it is the day of martyrs who defended principles, honor and the nation so that they deserved that honor by the people.... A day of remembrance.... And a day of memory.... For remembrance because it is the day of the martyrs, and for memory so that we do not forget the betrayal of the Persians and their hatred and their lowliness when they executed Iraqi prisoners of war while their hands were tied."[5]

Saddam Hussain's distinction between collective historical memory on one hand and remembrance and its attendant public rituals of mourning on the other demarcated the two components of the policy to create and shape a cult of martyrdom around Qadisiyat Saddam. It was important, above all, to situate martyrdom in the war within the narrative of sacrifice for the Iraqi nation while highlighting the distinctive nature of martyrdom in the Iran-Iraq war. To ascribe meaning to the deaths of fallen soldiers, the organizations of public culture (particularly those run by the Ministry of Culture and Information), drew on three related nationalist discourses. The first was thoroughly secular and derived from the rhetoric of anticolonial struggles. The martyrs of the war against Iran were the children of martyrs who had fought British colonial subjugation, first

---

narrative within a national setting in her discussion of memorials and museums built by Hizbullah. Lara Deeb, "Exhibiting the 'Just-Lived-Past': Hizbullah's nationalist narratives in the transnational political context," *Comparative Studies of Society and History*, vol. 50, 2(2008), 369–99.

[4] NIDS/serial 695815.

[5] Quoted by Abd al-Jabbar Mahmud al-Samarra'i, "hawla mafhum al-istishhad," ("On the meaning of martyrdom"), *Afaq 'Arabiyya*, 4 (January 1984), 8.

during the 1920 revolution, and again during the 1941 British occupation of Iraq. They carried the torch of the anti-imperialist and anti-Zionist
Arab revolutionary governments who had failed to restore Palestinian
rights. Muhsin al-Musawi, editor of the respected cultural journal *Afaq
'Arabiyya (Arab Horizons)*, articulated this view clearly in the opening
editorial of a special issue on martyrdom in 1984. Martyrdom was an
essential component of citizenship, he argued, because it was a building
block of the nation. Within Iraq, martyrdom should be understood as part
of the price Iraqis had to pay for the march of progressive forces engaged
in the fight against Zionism and imperialism. Iraqis' heroism and martyrdom countered the defeat of the progressive Arab forces after 1967. Iraqi
martyrs were assuming the mantle of all Arabs in their fight against the
Islamic Republic of Iran. They were as much fallen soldiers of the nation
as they were fallen revolutionaries for the defeated "progressive" forces
in the Arab world.[6]

The other nationalist discourse on martyrdom drew on a Ba'thist
reading of Iraqi history. The Iraqi Ba'th Party saw itself as the sole representative and protector of Arab nationalism within Iraq, and designated
all those who had died fighting for its sanctioned version of Arab nationalism as its own martyrs. Thus, Arab nationalists who died in 1941 for
their support of the Gaylani coup against the pro-British government,
those who had been killed for their role in the failed 1959 coup against
Abdul Karim Qasim, and Ba'thists killed in defense of the first Ba'thist
takeover of the state in 1963 – all were considered martyrs of the Arab
revolution. Except for those who died in 1941, the martyrs of the Ba'th
had died fighting nationalist Iraqi governments.[7] Ba'thist ideology, however, viewed their deaths through the lens of a national struggle between
true Arab Iraqis and Iraqis who were agents of foreign ideologies and
foreign interests. Parallel to the pantheon of martyrs for the nation in its
fight against external enemies were Iraqis who were martyred fighting
internal enemies, enemies whose loyalty to the nation was suspect. Any
Iraqis who did not die for the Arab Ba'thist version of Iraqi history were
excluded from the narrative of sacrifice for the nation because they were
putatively outside that nation. The war with Iran was a war to preserve
the Arab greatness of Iraq against the sectarian and divisive intentions
of an outside enemy, just as the struggle against Iraqi enemies of the

[6] Muhsin al-Musawi, "hawla mafhum al-istishhad" ("On the meaning of martyrdom"),
Afaq 'Arabiyya, 4 (January 1984), 4–7.
[7] BRCC 01–2065–0001–0012 to 0014. In 1984, a proposal to expand the museum of the
Ba'th Party highlighted these events as crucial in the struggle of the Iraqi Arab Ba'th.

Ba'th preserved the unity of the nation against the sectarianism of internal opponents to that unity.

In constructing the cult of martyrdom of Qadisiyat Saddam, the government had to address the fact that the war with Iran pitted it against an Islamic revolutionary government that tapped into the rhetoric and rituals of martyrdom inherent in an emotional Shi'i historical narrative of death and redemption. The Iranian government linked the seventh-century martyrdom of Imam Hussain on the plains of Karbala with its "holy defense" against Iraq. In the former, Imam Hussain was martyred while fighting against the establishment of an unjust Islamic political order; in the latter, Iranians were dying in defense of a just Islamic order. Elaborate rituals of mobilization and mourning accompanied by a visual iconography that situated martyrdom for the nation in the context of Shi'i suffering provided powerful means of creating consensus on the human costs of the war.[8] The Iraqi government eschewed the appeal of Shi'i rituals and enlisted the support of prominent Shi'i clerics to place martyrdom for the nation within a sanctioned Islamic context. Shaykh Ali Kashif al-Ghita', one of the foremost Shi'i clerics of Najaf, explained that martyrdom in Islam was an act of witnessing for the truth of one's cause. Martyrs acquired the sanctity of those who died in a holy war and were accorded a special place in the afterlife.[9] Kashif al-Ghita' was careful not to employ the ethnic and racial language that pitted Arab against Persian in a historical struggle stretching from the birth of Islam to the present. Martyrdom was sanctioned in the war against Iran because it was a war of defense against an enemy that was behaving toward another Muslim neighbor as the crusaders had behaved against the Muslims. His version of martyrdom was at some variance with that deployed in official commemorative activities and in the press. Martyrdom in Qadisiyat Saddam, according to the more propagandistic constructions, yoked the religious reading of martyrdom to a secular and ethnic reading of history.

The concept of martyrdom, according an article in the daily *al-Jumhuriyya*, was based on a belief in the preservation of honor, dignity, and sovereignty. This belief has been passed down through generations of Iraqis from the earliest Islamic conquests that united people in defense of the Islamic nation (*umma*). The mother of all martyrs was Khansa', who lost four sons in the seventh-century battle of al-Qadisiyya

---

[8] Monachehr Dorraj, "Symbolic and utilitarian value of a tradition: Martyrdom in the Iranian political culture," *Review of Politics*, vol. 59, 3(1997), 489–521.

[9] *Alif Ba'*, no. 844, November 28, 1984, p. 11.

against the Persian Empire. Her equanimity about her loss was a result of her belief that her sons were guaranteed a place in heaven as a reward for their sacrifice.[10] The figure of Khansa' as the historical mother of the modern martyrs of Qadisiyat Saddam was frequently invoked by Saddam Hussain in his well-publicized visits to the families of martyrs.[11]

The folding of history into a national memory in the service of the cult of martyrs was revisited in a pseudo-academic article written by Abdul al-Jabbar Mahmud al-Samarra'i, a Ba'thist commissar. Samarra'i traced the history of martyrdom in Iraq from ancient times until the advent of the Ba'th. Six pages long and peppered with footnotes, the article sought to find an uninterrupted and homogenous history in the development of martyrdom from pagan times to the present. Happiness in the after-life in ancient Mesopotamia, according to Samarra'i, was contingent on a man's sacrifices for his "society and nation." The notion of sacrifice for the greater good also informed the ideas of the afterlife among pre-Islamic Arabs, as is clear from their sacrifice in the pre-Islamic battle of Dhi Qar waged by Arabs against Persians. Arab Islamic society built on this tradition. Arab Muslim soldiers carried with them a liberationist ideology that helped them build an Arab Islamic empire. It was the advent of the Persian element (*shu'ubiya*) that brought the heroic period to an end. The rupture with this Arab revolutionary past was now resurrected by the martyrdom of Iraqi soldiers in the second Battle of Qadisiyya.[12]

This fusion of pre-Islamic, Islamic, and modern history was not very effective. Few Iraqis accepted the link between the first Qadisiyya and the Iran-Iraq war. This narrative did, however, succeed in setting the boundaries of the enactment of the narratives of martyrdom during the rituals of remembrance of the dead. Martyrdom was sanctified because it defined a specific nationalist message that set Arabs against "Persians" in a struggle that linked the current war to historical Persian designs on Iraq. This struggle was made all the more palpable after 1982 by Iran's refusal to accept a ceasefire. Martyrdom in the Iran-Iraq war unified Iraqis across the religious, sectarian, and ethnic divide; their personal histories submerged in an epic fight against historic enemies. The rituals of commemoration were notable for their elisions of differences among the Iraqi dead. Although much was made in the first of the year of the unity of Kurds and Arabs in fighting Iran, there was no official acknowledgment of the

[10] *al-Jumhuriyya*, January 19, 1981, 5.
[11] *al-Jumhuriyya*, February 19, 1981, 1.
[12] al-Samarra'i, "Hawl mafhum," pp. 8–15.

martyrdom of Kurds within the National Defense Battalions or Iraqis of "Iranian affiliation," who were excluded from full citizenship despite their death in the nation's defense. Little effort was made to connect the martyrdom of the nation to the martyrdom of Imam Hussain because the government viewed rituals of commemoration associated with his death as foreign to Iraq's Arab Shi'a. Any attempt to incorporate them into the mourning rituals associated with fallen soldiers could reinforce the sectarian allegiances of the Shi'a at the expense of their allegiances to the nation. While official commemorations incorporated aspects of religious rituals, these were highly circumscribed and closely controlled. They were meant to reify death, associating it with abstract symbols and highly ritualized practices of public remembrance. The state did not create special cemeteries for the dead of the Iran-Iraq war that could serve as spaces of collective mourning. Nor did it allow community or local organizations in various areas of Iraq to erect memorials for the dead.[13] Any such memorials were government funded and controlled by the Ba'th Party.

Commemorating the Heroes of Qadisiyat Saddam

The Martyr's Monument (Figure 8.1) and the rituals built around Martyr's Day were at the heart of the state's project to sanctify the deaths of soldiers. The design of the monument blends Islamic and nationalist motifs, linking death for the nation to martyrdom in Islam. The split dome of the monument is covered in blue tile, referencing the tiling of Shi'i mosque domes in Iraq, allowing for the souls of the dead to rise to heaven. A sculpted Iraqi flag "ascends from the underground level of the monument, passes through the symbolic martyr's grave [which bears the Quranic verse] on the ground level and flutters upward a few feet to the center of the two halves of the dome."[14] The monumentality of the structure is tempered by its successful abstraction of the domes of a mosque inviting people to reflection and prayer for the martyrs' souls. Nothing in the structure of the monument specifically references the Ba'thist interpretation of the war with Iran. Its relevance to Iraqis comes

---

[13] Jay Winter, *Sites of Memory. Sites of Mourning* (Cambridge: Cambridge University Press, 1998); and Jay Winter and Emmanuel Sivan (eds.), *War and Remembrance in the Twentieth Century* (Cambridge: Cambridge University Press, 1999). Winter argues that the development of nongovernmental "communities of mourning" played a crucial role in normalizing death in Europe.

[14] Sinan Antoon, "Monumental disrespect," *Middle East Report*, 228 (2003), 28–30. The Qura'nic verse is "Deem not those who were killed for God deceased, but alive with their Lord."

FIGURE 8.1. Iraqi children visit Martyr's Monument, February 1998 (Eric Marti/
AP photo).

in its power to unite diverse communities and classes in Iraq in mourning. It stands as a testament to the reification and nationalization of mass
death during the Iran-Iraq war.

When the Revolutionary Command Council designated December 1
the official day to commemorate the martyrs of Qadisiyat Saddam, the
Martyr's Monument had not yet been completed. Discussions were under
way between the Office of the Presidency, the mayor of Baghdad, and
various members of the Council's leadership on the organization of the
museums of the monuments of the Unknown Soldier and the Martyr's
Monument.[15] In January 1982, Saddam Hussain convened a conference to "study the philosophical, cultural and civilizational philosophy"
that should inform the museums. Deputy Prime Minister Tariq Aziz was
tasked with writing recommendations for the museums of both monuments. His recommendations for the Martyr's Monument were notable
for their narrow Ba'thist and hierarchical vision. He proposed that the

[15] For a historical overview of national celebrations in Iraq, see Elie Podeh, "Iraq: Changing
regimes, changing celebrations," in *The Politics of National Celebrations in the Middle
East* (New York: Cambridge University Press, 2011), pp. 108–67 and Amatzia Baram,
Achim Rohde, and Ronen Zeidel, "Between the Unknown Soldier monument and
the Cemetry," in Milich, Pannewick, and Tramontini (eds.), *Conflicting Narratives*,
pp.109–24.

monument be given the name *The Monument of the Martyrs of Qadisiyat Saddam*. He further recommended, clearly with no foreknowledge as to the length and human cost of the war, that the names of martyrs and their ranks be carved on the marble columns of the project. Pictures of martyrs who had shown exceptional courage should be exhibited in the museum. A special tablet should list the names of martyred soldiers and officers who had been awarded medals of courage. A library for documentation, research, and information on Qadisiyat Saddam, together with paintings and pictures of battle, would commemorate the battle for future generations. Finally, a permanent collection of the spoils of battle should be installed in a special courtyard within the space of the monument. Of all these recommendations, Saddam Hussain only approved the creation of a library, suspending judgment on the rest for a later time.[16]

In March 1983, Samir Abd al-Wahab al-Shaykhli, the mayor of Baghdad, submitted his recommendations for the museum and monument grounds to the Office of the Presidency. He accepted Aziz's recommendation for the naming of the monument as well as his plan for an exhibit of the spoils of war. He recommended that the soil for the gardens of the monument be brought from the battlefronts. Against this literalism in representation, however, al-Shaykhli's suggestions for the commemoration and burial of the dead sought abstraction. Rather than the hierarchical organization of martyrs proposed by Aziz, al-Shaykhli recommended that a 450 m wall be erected around the museum to make the "names of the martyrs eternal" and to highlight the "historical struggle between Arabs and Persians." The museum should be devoted to honoring martyrs and link their martyrdom to the first battle between the Arab Muslims against Persians and the current Qadisiyya. In place of an archive of the battle itself as Aziz had suggested, the mayor proposed founding a library devoted to the "meaning of the monument." Al-Shaykhli recommended against proposals to place a cenotaph of a martyr within the museum and a cemetery on the site for military leaders. When a proposal was put forth, it is not clear by whom, that a cemetery devoted to the martyrs of the Iran-Iraq war be founded, al-Shaykhli sidelined it by insisting that the city plan could not accommodate the space needed for such a cemetery.[17]

When Saddam Hussain inaugurated the monument's ground to great fanfare in July 1983, most of al-Shaykhli's recommendations had been

---

[16] BRCC 038–5–23–0029 to 0033.
[17] BRCC 038–5–23–0037.

put in place. The museum told Iraqi citizens why their sons and husbands had died in the war. In the words of Yousef al-Sa'igh, a prominent
Ba'thist poet and intellectual, the monument and its environs formed
a sacred valley in which the eternal meaning of the martyrs' sacrifice
became real to the citizens of Iraq.[18] The martyrs had died heroically to
protect the nation from "Persian" aggression. Within the museum, a list
of the historical battles between Arabs and Persians traced them to the
pre-Islamic battle of Dhi Qar all the way to the battle of Bostan in 1980.
The wall itself was erected, but the names of the martyrs of the war were
only carved after 1991. The wall's visual impact reminded viewers of the
equalizing and homogenizing effect of death for the nation. The representation of death as a list of names individualized the loss as it highlighted
the equalizing nature of war. National mourning for the dead took place
on official occasions according to prescribed rules. Personal mourning
and the burial of the dead remained a family and community undertaking.
In marked contrast to Iran, where national cemeteries for the war dead
created a potent link between the rituals of mourning by martyrs' families and the national justification for their martyrdom, Iraqi martyrs were
buried in community cemeteries along with their co-religionists who had
not been martyred. When the bodies of the dead soldiers were brought to
a neighborhood, the families held days of mourning prescribed by traditional practice, put up a black banner outside their home, and were often
visited by the Ba'thist cadres within their neighborhood.

Over the following two years, the national political leadership and the
Ba'th Party set the parameters for the rituals of national remembrance of
the dead. Their goals were threefold: to garner support of the families of
martyrs by reminding them of the state's largesse; to remind citizens
of the sacrifice of the families of martyrs and engender support for the
war effort; and to ensure that commemorations remained strictly controlled affairs that did not foment unrest. On its first official celebration
of Martyr's Day in 1983, the government chose to commemorate fallen
soldiers by organizing a festival. To die for the nation was to allow it to
be reborn. The organizers took the metaphor of death for rebirth literally.
Young women wearing white wedding dresses, together with members
of the youth organization dressed in white trousers and shirts, came to
the monument to perform songs and plays.[19] The cover of the popular

---

[18] Yousef al-Sa'igh, "Ta'amulat fi nasb al-shahid," ("Reflections on Martyr's Monument"),
Alif Ba', no. 776, August 10, 1983, p. 39.
[19] *Alif Ba'*, no. 793, December 7, 1983, pp. 5–6.

magazine *Alif Ba'* showed a white flower being watered by blood sprouting from the cracked soil of Iraq. Flower wreaths reminiscent of wedding décor were laid at the base of the flag that represented the martyrs' rising souls.[20]

By 1985, in the face of the retreat of Iraqi forces and the rising death toll, the commemorations of Martyr's Day were no longer festivals but rather more somber and ritualized activities. Every November, the Office of the Presidency issued directives to all ministries, popular organizations, and the General Secretariat of the Ba'th outlining the official commemorative activities and the slogans that should be emblazoned on public venues and repeated in schools. Dawn prayers in mosques and churches were said over martyrs' souls. At eight o'clock in the morning a five-minute period of silence was observed in all public spaces only to be filled by the sounds of the Muslim call for prayer and the ringing of church bells. Government institutions, industries in the socialist sector, and every school and university devoted the first hour of their working day to speeches, poetry, and reminders of the martyrs' sacrifices. In schools, martyrs' children were recognized, as were martyrs' family members who worked in public sector institutions. Speeches and poetry reminded attendees of the treacherous, evil Iranians who had executed defenseless Iraqi prisoners of war. Party youth belonging to the Vanguard organization, together with representatives of all popular and government organizations, visited the Martyr's Monument to pray and to lay floral arrangements.[21] Iraqis were required to wear a special pin, called the Martyr's pin (Figure 8.2), which portrayed the soul of the martyr as a red rose ascending between the two domes of the Martyr's Monument.[22]

Plays and music reenacted stories of sacrifice by fallen soldiers. The press published homogenized (perhaps fictionalized) testimonies of martyrs' families expressing great pride in the sacrifice of their sons, fathers, and husbands and giving fealty to the leader.[23] Their photographs and those of fallen soldiers graced newspapers' pages and attested to the diversity of Iraq's population. Mothers and wives dressed in traditional

---

[20] *Alif Ba'*, no 792, November 30, 1983. The magazine cover read, " The blood of martyrs nourishes the flower of victory."

[21] BRCC 01–2792–0003–0559 to 0588.

[22] *Alif Ba'*, no. 949, December 3, 1986 was a whole issue devoted to the commemoration of martyrs. Saddam Hussain was photographed presenting martyrs' children with medallions and pinning the martyr's pin on their lapels.

[23] See as an example *al-Jumhuriyya*, October 29, 1980, 10, for an interview with a woman in Thawra city and *Alif Ba'*, no. 792, November 30, 1983, pp. 34–6.

FIGURE 8.2. Martyr's pin, private collection.

black cloak or modern Western-style clothes and posed seated in more traditional homes or in homes with all modern amenities – proud of the sacrifices of their men. These personal narratives and photographs intended as testimonies helped depersonalize bereavement through their use of repetition of sanctioned tropes. They presented archetypal martyrs and archetypal families. Television and radio programs covered all commemorative activities, highlighting the victimization of Iraqi prisoners of war at the hand of the "Persians" and the latter's continued intransigence despite offers of a ceasefire agreement. This message was relayed to a national as well as to an international audience through commemorations of Martyr's Day in Iraqi embassies abroad. Foreign powers were to be reminded of the violations of human rights the Iranian government had perpetrated and its refusal to agree to peace despite international pressure.[24]

The activities of public remembrance were meant to integrate martyrdom into a national narrative of struggle and to highlight the collective investment of Iraqis in the defense of the nation. Martyrs, after all, were the most honorable of the citizens of the nation, a slogan that accompanied every remembrance activity and was emblazoned on much

[24] BRCC 01–2792–0003–0636 to 0645.

ثارة الشهيد
تـضيء بـيـوت المنتصرين

FIGURE 8.3. Martyr's medallion, adapted from cover of *Alif Ba'*, December 12, 1984. The Martyrs' Medallion illuminates the homes of the victorious.

of the official state correspondence. The activities were also meant to homogenize and control mourning by rendering it through a series of iconic images and rituals that belied the enormity and familial nature of the loss. Martyr's Day, however, provided the government with a venue to remind martyrs' families of their entitlements. Every Martyr's Day, Saddam Hussain and the local Ba'th Party leadership dispensed more entitlements on chosen martyrs' families. Children, mothers, and widows of martyrs were awarded special medallions meant to commemorate their loved ones' deaths and single out their families for special recognition. On the medallion (Figure 8.3) were two inscriptions: Saddam Hussain's declaration, "Martyrs are more honorable than all," and the Quranic verse, "Deem not those who were killed for God deceased, but alive with their Lord." Alongside these were carved an Iraqi flag, an olive branch, a gun, and a soldier's helmet, a reiteration of the government's message that martyrs had fought a war while continuously suing for an elusive peace denied them by the Iranians.[25]

By 1989, when the Iraqi government had, according to its own war narrative, emerged triumphant, commemoration rituals had become routine. Ba'th Party cadres managed these rituals at the level of district and neighborhood. In Baghdad, for example, visits to martyrs' families by party cadres and members of popular organizations included the distribution of the martyrs' medallions to families who had not received them and a reiteration of the Iranian regime's crimes. The Federation of Student and Youth's local branches organized posters, poetry readings, and speeches at various high schools. They staged a singing performance by martyrs' children and planned a soccer tournament named after a martyr. Some neighborhood party cadres singled out families who had lost more than one martyr by hanging an Iraqi flag on their door. Others organized a small neighborhood march. In some cases, they themselves took the families of the martyrs to visit the Martyr's Monument.[26]

The state- and party-sponsored commemoration of martyrs allowed for little space for affected families and communities to challenge the official narrative of martyrdom. No semi-official intergovernmental agency for martyrs' families was allowed to exist. All aspects of remembrance were prescribed, and public questioning of the state-assigned meaning of martyrdom was not possible. Burials and rituals built around family condolences, however, were organized independently of the state. It is here that some challenge to the officially sanctioned meaning of martyrdom might have been possible. As a result, these occasions were closely monitored by the state. Individual acts of defiance were quickly reported by the security apparatus or Ba'th Party cadres. In one reported instance, a mother had torn the Iraqi flag that draped her son's coffin, decrying the Ba'th and its war. She was quickly reported and party cadres visited her home.[27]

Despite the highly controlled nature of the rituals surrounding remembering the dead of the Iran-Iraq war, it is difficult to dismiss their efficacy in creating a measure of consensus about the meaning of death. They served to cement a narrative of sacrifice for a nation fighting a defensive war against an implacable enemy. They created a cult of martyrdom

---

[25] *Alif Ba'*, no. 846, December 12, 1984.
[26] BRCC 01–2792–0003–0445 to 0471.
[27] BRCC 01–2062–0001–0023 to 0026.

centered on a system of privileges assigned to the families of martyrs and bolstered by rituals of remembrance that nationalized the deaths of citizens drawn from Iraq's diverse population. The sanctioned slogans for the Martyr's Day commemorations in 1989 were remarkably triumphant and militant. Two such slogans exalted martyrdom as the wedding of heroes and promised that every Iraqi was "a perpetual project of martyrdom."[28] The slogans effectively hid the underbelly of the Iran-Iraq war, erasing the cost in lives as well as the government's campaign of counterinsurgency against its own population and its violence against deserters. By the end of the war with Iran, Iraq had developed a standardized, highly ideological cult of the dead supported by closely planned rituals of commemoration and by the public media. Had Iraqis been afforded the time to examine with some distance the costs of the war with Iran, the government's official meaning of rituals of remembrance might have been challenged, as they have been in Iran and Israel, for example, by returning soldiers or a by younger generation within Iraq.[29] The invasion of Kuwait, the ensuing war, and the uprising, however, violently shattered the heroic meaning of death for the nation.

Commemorating the Victims of the Mother of All Battles

On March 12, 1994, the Office of the Presidency issued a circular addressed to the General Secretariat of the Ba'th and the Office of the Minister of Culture and Information. It designated February 13, the date of the bombing of the al-'Amiriyya shelter, as the official day for commemorating the martyrs of the Mother of All Battles. It tasked the Secretariat and the Ministry with developing ceremonies and rituals for the occasion.[30] The decision on the date and site of commemorating the martyrs of the First Gulf War came after three and a half years of deliberations among the political leadership of the party and the regime. Much of the discussion centered on the meaning of martyrdom for the nation. It was clear to many within the regime and the party that the heroic narrative of martyrdom would no longer stand in the face of the poor performance of the military and the popular uprising. Instead, most who presented proposals for the commemoration of the Mother of All Battles highlighted the

---

[28] BRCC 01–2792–0003–0535.
[29] For Israel see, Meira Weiss, "Bereavement, commemoration and collective identity in contemporary Israeli society," *Anthropological Quarterly*, vol. 70, 2(1997), 91–101; for Iran see Varzi, *Warring Souls*.
[30] BRCC 01–2993–0001–0141.

victimhood of martyrs. The shift from martyr as glorified hero to martyr as victim was informed by the regime's need to speak the language of human rights and humanitarianism with the international community. It was fueled, as well, by the necessity of creating a narrative of martyrdom that could erase the memory of the crushing defeat and the divisive uprising. Disagreements within the party leadership and the regime were over determining who was most worthy of the honor of the martyr for the nation. Was the martyr the soldier strafed by enemy planes as he was retreating? Was he a Ba'thist cadre or security officer who had died at the hands of the rebels? Or was he or she a civilian victim who had died as the result of airstrikes by an imperialist power?

The project of commemorating the war dead and the uprising began taking shape during and in the immediate aftermath of the war. On February 17, four days after the bombardment of the al-'Amiriyya shelter, the Office of the Presidency issued a directive to the Ministry of the Interior, the General Secretariat, and the Ministry of Culture and Information asking them to photograph the destroyed shelter and to document the loss of life – 408 women, children, and elderly – for a special publication on the atrocity. Early in 1992, the Ministry of Culture and Information began fielding proposals for the site as a space for the commemoration of the war dead.[31] If the proposal to portray the al-'Amiriyya shelter as the symbol of inhumanity and hypocrisy of imperial aggression was politically safe, proposals to render soldiers the martyrs-victims of the war were more problematic.

In September 1991, a few months after the suppression of the uprising, a member of the Ba'th intelligence office proposed to the General Secretariat that a day of mourning be dedicated to the remembrance of Iraqi soldiers strafed by U.S. warplanes earlier that year, on February 26. The United States had perpetrated a crime against "human conscience" and its actions stood in clear contradiction to America's declared aims of protecting human rights. A day of mourning for the soldier-victims could be an effective way of alerting the world to the human costs of the war. Saddam Hussain asked the Ba'th and the political leadership of the country to consider the proposal together with a suggestion to erect a special monument for the soldiers of the Mother of All Battles. Both matters were taken up by the Revolutionary Command Council in December, only to be shelved. The Council's leadership felt that that any attempt to designate a day of mourning around the victimization of Iraqi soldiers

---

[31] BRCC 028–1–4–0007 to 0073.

had to draw attention to the treachery of the United States and the ability of the Iraqi soldier to withstand the U.S. military machine with much less advanced military capabilities. Furthermore, the choice of February 26 might have internal repercussions, as it would raise questions about the ineffectiveness of the Iraqi political and military leadership. Thus, the suggestion was rejected. Another suggestion to build a monument for the martyrs of the First Gulf War was also not adopted, in large part because it might highlight Iraq's defeat. The representation of soldier as victim was too politically fraught to become iconic of martyrdom in the First Gulf War.[32]

Even more burdened with political meaning was the question of martyrdom during the Intifada. The violence of the uprising destroyed the myth of national cohesion and any consensus on the meaning of martyrdom. Three competing narratives of martyrdom emerged. For Kurdish rebels, those killed by the regime during the suppression of the uprising joined the pantheon of martyrs of the Anfal and Halabja campaigns and stood as testament to the suffering of the Kurdish nation.[33] For Shi'i rebels, those killed by the regime became martyrs of an uprising against a tyrannical power and were part of the mythology of the historical oppression of the Shi'a in Iraq. Throughout the 1990s, in the three provinces of Iraqi Kurdistan as well as within the large Shi'i diaspora that fled to the south, the Intifada became the basis of a powerful narrative of victimization.[34] In Iraq itself, the first three years after the uprising saw a serious attempt by the Ba'th Party and the regime to commemorate the uprising in a manner that would resurrect public awareness of the violence and mayhem wrought by the rebels. Interviews and testimonies of Iraqi citizens and Ba'th Party members stressed the rebel's destructiveness, their criminal behavior, and the government's heroic efforts to restore order and rebuild.[35] At the same time, however, it was equally important for the regime to ensure that the enormity of the political implications of the uprising be forgotten. As much as possible, the public narrative after 1994, when the regime had secured itself in power and punished rebels, had to affirm that the Intifada was a brief interlude, an aberration. This, in part, might explain its reluctance to act on the suggestion of a party

[32] BRCC 01–2993–0001–0202 to 0208.
[33] Sheri Laizer, *Martyrs, Traitors and Patriots: Kurdistan after the Gulf War* (London: Zed Books, 1996).
[34] Haddad, *Sectarianism in Iraq*, pp. 117–41.
[35] See as an example *al-Qadisiyya*, May 3, 1991, 3 and *al-Qadisiyya*, November 23, 1991, 8.

leader in Basra to build a monument listing the names of party members martyred in the "The Page of Treachery and Betrayal" in every province that had risen against the regime.[36]

Just as the Martyr's Monument was an attempt to stress the unity of the Iraqi nation through the martyrdom of its soldiers, remembrance on the anniversary of the bombing of the al-ʿAmiriyya shelter was a reminder of the victimization of Iraqi civilians and of the humanitarian toll of the war and sanctions. The bombing of the shelter generated international outrage and condemnation by human rights organizations worldwide.[37] Representatives from the press, international agencies, and peace organizations visited the shelter hours after its destruction. It was with the international community in mind that the government decided in the first days after the bombing to keep the shelter as close to its initial state of devastation as possible and to collect firsthand victims' testimonies and photographs. Situated in the crowded middle-class district of al-ʿAmiriyya, a western suburb of Baghdad, Public Shelter number 25 had been built in 1984 to protect civilians from Iranian shelling during the Iran-Iraq war. A Finnish company had built a two-level structure to withstand nuclear bombs, its roof reinforced by layers of meshed steel used to support bridges and highways. The first floor was meant as a public area for socializing, while the lower underground floor housed showers, kitchen, a medical clinic, and storage areas. When two "smart bombs" hit the shelter a little after four o'clock on the morning of February 13, occupants on the upper floor were incinerated. On the lower floor, the water tank overheated and burst, severely burning those who had taken shelter there.

The impact of the bombing of the shelter on Baghdad's population, which had endured nearly four weeks of heavy bombardment by the coalition forces was immense. In 2004, Riverbend, the Baghdad blogger, remembered:

After the 13th of February, it [al-ʿAmiriyya district] became the area everyone avoided. For weeks and weeks the whole area stank of charred flesh and the air was thick with grey ash. The beige stucco houses were suddenly covered with black pieces of cloth scrolled with the names of dead ones. "Ali Jabbar mourns the loss of his wife, daughter, and two sons....," "Muna Rahim mourns the loss of her mother, sisters, brothers and son." ... Within days, the streets were shut with

[36] BRCC 01–2993–0001–0301.
[37] Human Rights Watch, "Needless deaths in the Gulf War: Civilian casualties during the air campaign and violations of the laws of war," http://www.hrw.org/reports/1991/gulfwar/index.htm accessed February 12, 2012.

the black cloth of tents set up by grief stricken families to receive mourners from all over Iraq who came to weep and ease some of the shock and horror.[38]

Within a few weeks, Baghdadis began independently organizing public rituals of mourning for those who had died in the bombing. These were often arranged by artists and community leaders without much direction from the government. Naseer Shamma, a musician and preeminent lute player, was then a talented twenty-eight-year-old composer. He witnessed the bombing of the shelter and the ensuing rescue operation. He viewed the bombing and its victims as an emblem of the "collapse of the new world order and all ethical values that control human destiny." He approached the director of the National Museum of Iraq and suggested that they organize a memorial service for the victims a few days after the end of the war on the museum's premises. The commemorative concert, entitled "Coming from the Past – Going to the Future," was held in the Sumerian Hall. Flanked by two Sumerian winged bulls and sitting in front of the statue of Nabu, the god of wisdom, Shamma reminded his audience that the present was not the friend of Iraqis. They had to start reconfiguring their future by drawing inspiration from their rich cultural heritage.[39] The piece he composed for the occasion, "It Happened in al-'Amiriyya" begins softly, reenacting a mood of playfulness of children and the movement of people attempting to live ordinary lives during wartime. The tune then rises to a crescendo of dissonant notes, recreating the sound effects of the bombing, the voices of people calling for help, and the wail of sirens. It ends with the theme of rebirth and a rearrangement of the Iraqi national anthem.

Shamma's piece marked a stark contrast to the music of mobilization and militant nationalism played on television and radio stations during the commemoration of the dead of the Iran-Iraq war. It linked private and community mourning to national suffering and rebirth. It captured the popular mood of mourning and defiance at the coalition's bombing of Iraq's infrastructure, as well as the loss of civilian lives to smart bombs. Shamma, like a number of artists and intellectuals in the first years after the end of hostilities, invoked the memory of Iraq's cultural past as an antidote to the destruction of the present, and insisted that it provide the basis of regeneration. International activists, Iraqi citizens, and the Ba'thist regime embraced his explicit critique of the new international

---

[38] Riverbend, *Baghdad Burning: Girl Blog from Iraq* (New York: The Feminist Press at CUNY, 2005), p. 209.
[39] http://www.youtube.com/watch?v=V7a_K6kQ8po. Accessed February 20, 2012.

order dominated by the United States. "It Happened in al-'Amiriyya" inspired some thirty additional artistic works in theater, visual arts, documentaries, and dance within Iraq. Shamma, who ran afoul of the regime and left Iraq in 1993, played it in international venues, particularly at events organized by opponents of the embargo.[40]

The Iraqi government built on this popular and international sentiment and recast the themes of community mourning and national suffering to convey its own political message. The shelter became a memorial and a mausoleum rather than a monument. The ideal martyr of the new memorial was not the heroic soldier but rather the defenseless woman and child – a stark contrast to the militancy and agency of the soldier. Unlike the Martyr's Monument's abstractions of the meaning of death, the al-'Amiriyya shelter left on exhibit the remains of the victims' bodies and the detritus of their lives.[41] It provided a venue for an on-site reenactment of those deaths by survivors. By the second anniversary of the bombing, the shelter had been turned into a public mausoleum. Located in a nondescript area, its very ordinariness served to highlight the precariousness of life and the injustice of the war against Iraq. Visitors, both Iraqi and foreign, were ushered into a building with an open gaping hole in the roof where the bombs had hit, which exposed the meshed reinforced steel. The blackened walls of the shelter were preserved, as were the ashes of those incinerated by the bombs. In the early years, visitors often commented on the stench of burnt bodies and the persistence of a haze of smoke within the shelter. The dried blood of victims provided visceral testament to their violent deaths. On the first level, the outline of a woman holding her child as she burned remained seared onto the wall, while the lower floor's ceiling had the imprints of palms of men and women trying to escape.[42]

The literalism of the memorial was designed, by the Baghdad municipality, in consultation with the Office of the Presidency and the Ministry of Culture and Information, to elicit visitors' grief, mourning, and anger. By displaying the photographs of the dead – a child with his mother, a young woman with her college graduation cap and gown, a whole family looking into the camera – and contrasting them with their remains now reduced to ashes or seared on the shelter's walls, the organizers created

---

[40] http://www.naseershamma.com/; http://www.alarabiya.net/programs/2010/06/17/111561. html; and http://www.alarabiya.net/programs/2010/06/24/112176.html, all accessed February 20, 2012.

[41] For comparisons with Palestine and Lebanon, see Khalili, *Heroes and Martyrs of Palestine*, Deeb, "Exhibiting the 'Just-Lived-Past'," and Volk, *Memorials and Martyrs*, pp. 115–23.

[42] *al-Jumhuriyya*, February 14, 1993, 2 and 7, *al-Jumhuriyya*, February 13, 1995, 3.

FIGURE 8.4. Child lighting a candle at the al-'Amiriyya shelter, February 1998 (Eric Marti/AP photo).

a powerful before and after effect. Photographs of the shelter before the bombing were exhibited alongside photographs of its condition in the bombing's immediate aftermath. The victims' charred bodies, stacked out on the street while civil defense squads struggled to find survivors inside, were also displayed. The vibrancy of the young in the photographs allowed visitors to mourn their loss and provoked rage at the perpetrators. Flowers left by the victims' families reminded visitors on any day that the memorial was also a mausoleum, a mass grave to the First Gulf War dead (Figure 8.4).

In the first three official commemorations of the anniversary of the bombing of the al-'Amiriyya shelter, the organizers attempted to strike a balance between the community's need to mourn the dead and the regime's manipulation of the symbol of al-'Amiriyya for its political ends. In 1993, the Ministry of Culture and Information asked artist Muhsin al-Azzawi to organize the ceremonies. The purpose of the commemoration of the martyrs was to remember:

but we have to remake memory into a remembrance that can inspire the spirit of struggle, hope and optimism that life goes on and is uninterrupted ... through this internal power we will learn by an understanding that employs the tragic sense but at the same time [points to] – the pile of the martyrs in this place [to] become a symbol of goodness and hope.[43]

---

[43] *al-Jumhuriyya*, February 7, 1993, 3.

The honoring of the martyrs of al-'Amiriyya, according to al-Azzawi, allowed for grieving but also reminded Iraqis of the need to remain steadfast.

Most exhibits and performances took place in the courtyard of the shelter. Sound and light elements, according to al-Azzawi, were meant to recreate the sense of loss for the thousands expected to visit the shelter on the anniversary of its bombing. The National Symphony Orchestra chose two classical selections to play, and the orchestra of the College of Fine Arts played four pieces: two dirges and two anthems to the dead. Students in the School of Music and Ballet performed an operetta about the value and meaning of martyrdom written by poet Nizar Jawad. Readings from the Quran and a prayer by church leaders were also included in the ceremonies.

If the commemorative performances within the shelter centered on mourning the dead, the Ba'th Party organizations' activities focused on disseminating the government's political message. Booklets in both Arabic and English were printed and circulated. These pointed to the contravention of humanitarian law and the embargo's continued impact on civilian populations. In neighborhood schools and among different popular organizations, party cadres reminded audiences of the victimization of the Iraqi civilian population under the embargo and their steadfastness in face of their suffering. They organized marches to protest the embargo and solicited essays from schoolchildren on the meaning of martyrdom.[44] Interviews with survivors, family members of the dead, and civil defense workers appeared in the press on every anniversary of the bombing. The interviewees relived their experience and warned against forgetting.

A potent rhetoric of suffering and victimization accompanied by set images informed a great deal of the remembrance: the unexpectedness of the bombing, the contrast between the celebrations of the Muslim Feast the day before the bombing and the hell of being trapped in the shelter, the listing of family members killed en masse, the charred bodies retrieved from the shelter, the innocence of the victims caught unprepared. Umm Ghayda', a women who had lost eight family members to the bombing, served as a poignant volunteer guide. Riverbend, reflecting the emotional impact of Umm Ghayda's testimony, recalls:

Her face was stern, yet gentle – like that of a school principal or ... like that of a mother of eight children. She shook hands with us and took us around to see the shelter. This is where we were. This where the missiles came in.... This is where

---

[44] *al-Qadisiyya*, February 13, 1994, 6, *al-Qadisiyya*, February 13, 1995, 7.

FIGURE 8.5. Umm Ghayda' at the al-'Amiriyya shelter, September 1996 (John Moore/AP photo).

the water rose up to.... This is where the people stuck to the wall.... Her voice was strong and solid in Arabic. We didn't know what to answer.... She pointed to the vague ghosts of bodies stuck to the concrete on the walls and ground and the worst one to look at was that of a mother, holding a child to her breast, like she was trying to protect and save it. "That should have been me ... " the woman said (Figure 8.5).[45]

The rituals and performances at the al-'Amiriyya mausoleum and memorial continued until the regime fell in 2003. By 1995, however, when February 13 became the official date for the commemoration of the martyrs of the Mother of All Battles, the victims of the al-'Amiriyya shelter were no longer the sole focus of national remembrance. All those martyred in the First Gulf War were to be honored. On June 11, 1995, the Office of the Presidency issued a directive on the official commemorative activities. Many of the activities planned by the Ministry of Culture and Information and Ba'th Party organizations replicated the activities of the December 1 Martyr's Day with some notable differences. In addition to the requisite official visits to the Martyr's Monument, party cadres organized a candlelight vigil on the night of February 12/13 at the al-'Amiriyya shelter. Care was given to the remembrance of martyred children in the

[45] Riverbend, *Baghdad Burning*, pp. 211–12.

FIGURE 8.6. Stamp commemorating the martyrs of Umm al-Ma'arik, private collection. In memory of the martyrs of the Mother of All Battles. Note that the Arabic term used for the attack is "crime" whereas the English term is "disastrous."

shelter, linking their fates to those of children of embargoed Iraq.[46] A book devoted to the First Gulf War martyrs was printed in English and distributed to foreign visitors as well as to Iraqi embassies abroad. It included the pictures of victims of the coalition forces' bombardment at al-'Amiriyya, the Falluja market, and the residential quarter of Ma'qal in Basra.[47] Special stamps (Figure 8.6) were issued highlighting the victimization of children and the mourning of mothers against a background of the devastated shelter itself.

The political leadership had chosen February 13 as day of national mourning for the First Gulf War martyrs in the hope of forging a modicum of national consensus on the meaning of martyrdom under the embargo. It attempted to induce amnesia about its responsibility in the First Gulf War and the suppression of the uprising. In choosing to subordinate the remembrance of fallen soldiers to that of civilian victims, the leadership sought to erase its abandonment of the military and its humiliating surrender or withdrawal. In publically excluding the commemoration of

[46] BRCC 01–2993–0001–0105 to 0110.
[47] BRCC 01–2993–0001–0160 to 0183.

Ba'thist martyrs, the leadership omitted its own contribution to the violence of the uprising. The First Gulf War and the Intifada, however, had created deep fissures within Iraqi society and had destroyed the power of national commemorations to unite Iraqi citizens. While the al-'Amiriyya shelter commemorations reminded Baghdad's civilian population of their victimization by coalition forces and by the embargo, they did not have the same resonance in the south, which had experienced the Intifada. Among Ba'thists in these provinces, commemorative activities on February 13 were devoted to the remembrance of Ba'thists martyred by the rebels, while the military office of the Ba'th continued to call for erecting memorials to the martyred soldiers of the war.[48] Among all, however, the narrative of victimization had become central to the definition of martyrdom.

Conclusion

Writing on the cult of fallen soldiers in Western Europe in the first half of the twentieth century, historian George Mosse found that the proliferation of commemorations, monuments, and memorials represented "tangible symbols" of the development of the idea of death as sacrifice for the nation.[49] As in Europe, an Iraqi national cult of martyrdom sanctified mass death as the only means to preserve the nation during the Iran-Iraq war. Unlike Western Europe, however, where rituals of remembrance were, as often as not, locally planned affairs without the government's direction, remembrance of martyrs in Ba'thist Iraq remained a state-sponsored and highly centralized affair. The unwillingness of the Iraqi government to allow any form of commemorative activities by independent, community-based organizations can partly be attributed to its authoritarian practice as a one-party state. The Iraqi government and the Ba'th Party, however, were equally concerned with the politics of meaning in their control of all aspects of commemoration. The heroic meaning of death, the Ba'thist interpretation of sacrifice for the nation, and the centrality of Saddam Hussein to all rituals of public remembrance allowed little room for other types of collective mourning rituals. This centralized and ideological nature of rituals associated with the cult of martyrs during the Iran-Iraq war has meant that those who fought and died in the war have had an ambiguous place in the Iraqi national

---

[48] Ibid.
[49] Mosse, *Fallen Soldiers*, p. 34.

narrative of sacrifice in post-Ba'thist Iraq. Did they die for a national or a Ba'thist war? Do they deserve to be mourned as national heroes or as pitied victims of an unnecessary war?

The First Gulf War eroded the heroic meaning of martyrdom for the nation. Soldiers and civilians became victims of aerial bombardment in a war in which the rules of engagement were radically different than those that had governed the Iran-Iraq war. In addition, the divisiveness and violence of the Intifada, particularly the use of the army to suppress the population, shattered Iraqis' view of the army as a national organization. The narrative of the fallen soldier as the heroic defender of the nation was discarded in favor of that of the civilian victim. The Iraqi government cultivated this narrative, but it built on the sentiment of a population that had experienced death and privation after the First Gulf War. Iraqis, despite deep fissures created by the Intifada and its suppression, were united in their victimization and steadfastness in face of the U.S. aggression and the UN-imposed embargo. They were victims of the designs of a much more powerful enemy and an unjust international system. The themes of unequal power and the absence of justice gave popular sanction within Iraq to the government's attempts to shape the rituals of mourning around the al-'Amiriyya shelter. However, despite the government's attempts to create a national narrative of oppression around the coalition's conduct of war and the UN embargo, it was unable to impose a monopoly over the meaning of martyrdom. Inside and outside Iraq, a powerful challenge to its narrative came from parties and groups who constructed an alternative meaning of victimization, particularly around the Intifada, the Anfal, and Halabja. During much of the 1990s and until the regime's fall, they employed the language of human rights and humanitarianism to appeal to the international community and to call for the prosecution of the regime for crimes against humanity. The U.S. invasion and occupation of Iraq has brought these political groups to power and has allowed them to assert their own narratives of martyrdom.

9

Postscript

The legacies of the Iran-Iraq and the First Gulf wars continue to shape current Iraqi politics. They are a perpetually present past. They infuse the politics of the governing elite, and they manifest themselves in the pervasive political language of victimization that shapes the way Iraqis stake their claims as citizens. The 2003 U.S.-led invasion and occupation of Iraq brought to power Shi'i Islamist opposition and Kurdish nationalist parties that had drawn support from Iran during the Iran-Iraq war and from the United States during and after the First Gulf War. They were party as well as victim to the divisive politics and conduct of these wars. They came to power intent on creating the legal and bureaucratic mechanisms that would allow for the restoration of justice to the victims of the Ba'thist regime's violence, but they willfully neglected to acknowledge the deaths of Iraqi soldiers and compensate their families. The legacies of the Iran-Iraq and the First Gulf wars are distilled, for the current political elite in Iraq, into the regime's genocidal politics toward the Kurds and its violent suppression of the Intifada. As a result, as of this writing, neither the Baghdad nor the Arbil government has attempted to develop a war narrative in a manner that could forge a pluralistic, non-authoritarian, national consensus on the legacies of Iraqis' encounter with violence during the last twenty-three years of Ba'thist rule.

For the Kurdish Regional Government, the legacy of the Iran-Iraq war is the ethnic cleansing of the Kurds and the complicity of the Iraqi military and the Ba'th in the genocidal policy of the regime. The High Iraqi Tribunal, established with U.S. support after 2003, tried the architects of Anfal for crimes against humanity. Anfal and Halabja have become central to the development of a Kurdish exclusivist national identity and crucial to claims of citizenship in Iraqi Kurdistan. For the Shi'i Islamist parties that dominate the political terrain and government of Iraq, the Iran-Iraq war was a Ba'thist rather than a national war and their complicity in the war's conduct is rarely addressed. Public discourse on the costs of the First Gulf War and the embargo has been jettisoned in favor of mythologizing the Intifada as a Shi'i uprising against Ba'thist rule. Fifteen of the Ba'th regime's henchmen who led the suppression of the uprising were brought to trial before the High Iraqi Tribunal in 2007 on the charge of crimes against humanity. Intifada victims' families have become a powerful constituency clamoring for privileges and access.[1] The Intifada continues to be an authoritative marker of Shi'i identity, setting Shi'is apart from their Sunni compatriots. It provides Shi'i politics with a narrative of victimization deployed by different constituencies to ensure that former Ba'thists, often equated with Sunnis, are excluded from access to state resources and political power. In the current climate of sectarian politics in Iraq, Sunni politicians and a substantial portion of the Sunni population are loathe to acknowledge the suffering endured by their Shi'i compatriots under the Ba'th.[2]

In the past five years, however, Iraqis have begun to grapple with the legacies of the Iran-Iraq and the First Gulf wars outside the narrow confines set by the ruling elites. Two issues have dominated the public discourse on the wars: how to define martyrdom and how to deal with the memory of the wars. On January 8, 2006, the Presidential Council in Iraq issued Law No. 3, governing the formation of a Martyrs' Foundation independent of any government ministry and funded by the Office of the Prime Minister. The Foundation's mandate was to determine who was a martyr, provide martyrs' families with entitlements, and ensure that they receive priority in government positions and educational institutions. The Foundation's overall mission was to "glorify martyrdom by inculcating the values of sacrifice in society through political, social and cultural activities." It was charged with creating branches in all provinces of Iraq outside Iraqi Kurdistan, where the Kurdish Regional Government created a separate ministry dealing with Kurdish martyrs' affairs. The

---

[1] A political association of families of victims of the Intifada ran in the 2005 election in various provinces in the south. www.almustaqbal.com.lb/storiesprintpreview. aspx?storyid=109263 accessed June 24, 2008. Representatives from the association for Karbala and Najaf pushed the government to allocate special privileges for families of victims of the Intifada. http://www.parliament.iq/Iraqi_Council_of_Representatives. php?name=articles_ajsdyawqwqdjasdba46s7a98das6dasda7das4da6sd8asdsawewqeqw 465e4qweq4wq6e4qw8eqwe4qw6eqwe4sadkj&file=print&sid=1755.

[2] Haddad, *Sectarianism in Iraq*, pp. 143–210.

martyr, according to the new national law, was every Iraqi citizen who had lost his or her life for opposing the Ba'thist regime or for being supportive of those who had opposed it.[3] A few months after issuing the law establishing the Martyrs' Foundation, the government passed the Law of Mass Graves. It designated the Ministry of Human Rights as the sole body responsible for the excavation and exhumation of these graves.[4] The Ministry determined the manner and time of the victims' deaths and passed the information onto the local offices of the Martyrs' Foundation, which then determined compensation.

The passage of the laws marked the government's attempt to regulate the process of assigning victims' privileges. They came in the wake of the clamor of victims' families demanding that their losses be acknowledged and compensated. In particular, Shi'i constituencies in the south, who had lost family members during the Intifada, exerted great pressure on the government to recognize their sacrifice.[5] The laws, however, were meant to exclude a number of Iraqis. Among them were those killed during the U.S.-led invasion and occupation of Iraq and the ensuing chaos. These included civilians and members of the security forces. Their families claimed that their loved ones had been martyred and demanded compensation.[6] The government initially tried to respond, but soon became overwhelmed with the proliferation of claims. The law also excluded all those declared martyrs of the Iran-Iraq and the First Gulf wars. Soldiers who had fought in those wars, according to one statement by an Iraqi politician allied to a Shi'i Islamist party, were not martyrs but were merely dead men who had fought in an illegal Ba'thist war.[7] The government conceived the law on martyrdom and mass graves in part to limit and regulate the multiplicity of claims to martyrdom by Iraqis who had endured and continue to endure all manners of violence.

The passage of Law No. 3 and its implementation, however, were questioned from the outset. The law was challenged by the families of fallen soldiers and missing in action, as well as by the families of victims of the

[3] www.iraq-lg-law.org/ar/content/2006 accessed February 20, 2012.

[4] www.almadapaper.com/paper.php?source=akbar&mlf=interp accessed June 4, 2008.

[5] http://www.parliament.iq/Iraqi_Council_of_Representatives.php?name=articles_ajsdyaw qwqdjasdba46s7a98das6dasda7das4da6sd8asdsawewqeqw465e4qweq4wq6e4qw8eqw e4qw6eqwe4sadkj&file=print&sid=1755 accessed June 10, 2008.

[6] *al-Mada*, August 6, 2006. www.almadapaper.com/sub/08–737/p.07.htm#2 accessed June 6, 2008. *al-Mada*, October 8, 2006, www.almadapaper.com/sub/10–787/p.10.htm#1 accessed June 4, 2008.

[7] *Azzaman*, December 14, 2008.www.Azzaman.com/qpdfarchive/2008/12/12–13/P15.pdf accessed January 15, 2012.

post-invasion violence. The narrow definition of martyrdom espoused
by the Baghdad government was criticized as sectarian and divisive. It
offered no narrative of Iraqi sacrifice for the nation. Iraqis with secular, nonsectarian political leanings, as well as those sympathetic to Sunni
opposition parties, objected to the exclusion of the Iran-Iraq war martyrs.[8]
Even among constituencies in the Shi'i south, where many benefited from
the law, the press often voiced criticism of the government's definition
of martyrdom and the politicization of its implementation. There was,
according to a 2009 article in the Basra newspaper *al-Mannarah*, popular
anger at the classification of martyrs into hierarchies and the political
nature of the assignment of privileges. There is, according to the article,
a descending hierarchy of privileges that is highly dependent on political
connections rather than clearly defined legal rights. Martyrs were now
classified into five or six hierarchical categories. For example, those connected to the ruling Shi'i Islamist political parties that dominate the government in Baghdad, and who had died within Iranian territories fighting
with the Badr Brigade, were martyrs of the first order; those who died in
Iraqi prisons under the Ba'th are of the second order. As for those southerners who had died or had been imprisoned during the Iran-Iraq or the
First Gulf wars, they are excluded from all privileges.[9]

The popular challenges to the government's narrow definition of martyrdom are as much about claims to redress and privileges of citizenship
as they are about the legacies of the Iran-Iraq and the First Gulf wars.
More than thirty years later, a contentious but relatively open debate is
taking place about the long-term impact of the Iran-Iraq war. The debate
is unfolding in the context of post-invasion politics and the efforts by
the Iraqi and Iranian governments, coordinated through the International
Red Cross Committee, to account for prisoners of war and missing in
action and to repatriate Iraqi soldiers who died on Iranian soil.[10] Three

---

[8] Ibid., and *Azzaman*, December 16, 2008. www.Azzaman.com/qpdfarchive/2008/12/16–12/
P13.pdf accessed January 13, 2012.

[9] *al-Mannarah*, March 13, 2009. www.almannarah.com/NewDetails.aspx?NewsID=9254&
CatID=6 accessed February 14, 2012. In one particularly egregious case, a former Iraqi
prisoner of war joined the Badr Brigade during the Iran-Iraq war and died in Iran. His
family receives privileges from three sources: the Iraqi government, which pays his retirement benefits, the Badr Brigade, and the Martyrs' Foundation attached to the Prime
Minister's office.

[10] The repatriation of the remains of Iraqi soldiers was overseen by the Ministry of Human
Rights and coordinated by the International Red Cross Committee. As of 2008, there had
been twenty-two exchanges of remains of dead soldiers between Iraq and Iran. *Azzaman*,
December 1, 2008. www.Azzaman.com/qpdfarchive/2008/12/01–12//P2.pdf accessed
January 10, 2012. See also *al-Mada*, November 19, 2009. www.almadapaper.net/news.

competing narratives of the war inform most of these debates. The first, espoused by the Kurdish Regional Government and the Shiʻi Islamist parties that presently dominate Iraq's politics, is that the war was a Baʻthist project rather than one of national defense. Insofar as these wars are remembered, it is in the context of Baʻthist repression of the Shiʻa and Kurds. All other war narratives are excised in the name of a de-Baʻthification policy. The second trend, expressed by Iraqis across the sectarian divide, is an Iraqi nationalist one that sees the war as a legitimate war of defense. Iraqis who adopt this narrative of the war point to Iran's continued influence on Iraqi politics and the intransigence of its allies in Iraq who refuse to publically deny Iran's insistence that Iraq instigated the war and that it has legitimate claims to reparations from Iraq.[11] The third trend, espoused mostly by secular intellectuals and human rights activists, can perhaps be described as postnationalist. Its proponents argue for a national reckoning with the human and social costs of the war, blaming the Baʻthist regime for its instigation and conduct, but rejecting the politicized nature of the dominant sectarian and the anti-Iranian Iraqi nationalist narrative of the war.[12]

The controversial legacies of the wars under the Baʻth are evident in the erosion of national consensus on the meaning and practices of commemorating the dead. The most hallowed martyr in the Iraqi official narrative is the victim of the mass grave. Between 2006 and 2007, the Kurdish Regional Government and the central government in Baghdad determined that there were between 250 and 350 mass graves of victims of Baʻthist violence. The exhumation of these graves became central to the evidence presented in the post-2003 trials of the Anfal campaign and the

php?action=view&id=9408&spell=0&highlight=%CD%D1%5C8+%C7%CE%E1%ED%CC accessed January 26, 2012.

[11] *Azzaman*, December 25, 2008. www.Azzaman.com/qpdfarchive/2008/12/02/02–12/pdf accessed January 10, 2012. *al-Mada*, December 21, 2009. www.almadapaper.net/news.php?action=view&id=7330&spell=0&spell=0&highlight=%CD%D1%C8+%C7%E1%DA%D1%C7%DE%ED%C9+%C7%E1%C7%ED%D1%C7%E4%ED%C9 accessed February 1, 2012.

[12] *al-Mada*, September 29, 2009. www.almadapaper.net/news.php?action=view&id=489&spell=0&highlight=%CD%D1%C8+%C7%E1%DA5D1%C7%DE%ED%C9+%C7%E1%C7%ED%D1%C7%E4%ED%C9 accessed January 27, 2012. *al-Mada*, June 1, 2010. www.almadapaper.net/news.php?action=view&id=19416&spell=0&highlight=%CD%D1%C8+%C7%E1%DA%D1%C7%DE%ED%C9+%C7%E1%C7%ED%D1%C7%E4%ED%C9 accessed February 4, 2012. See also *al-Mada*'s long article on the thirtieth anniversary of the Iran-Iraq war, September 24, 2010. www.almadapaper.net/news.php?action&id=27170&spell=0&highlight=%CD%D1%%C8+%C7%E1%DA%C7%DE%ED%C9+%C7%E1%C7%ED%D1%C7%E4%ED%C9 accessed February 4, 2012.

Intifada. The decision, in 2007, by the Baghdad government to organize national commemorative activities around the Shi'i and Kurdish victims of mass graves was an attempt, in part, to remind Iraqis of the regime's crimes in the hope of forging a national reconciliation. But the tone of the ceremonies was often accusatory, holding Iraqis who were not victims of mass violence collectively responsible for their silence. The government declared May 16, the day of the discovery of the first two mass graves in the provinces of Babil and Karbala, as the official national date for the commemoration of martyrs. It chose the date, according to the deputy minister of human rights who presided over the Baghdad ceremony, to remind Iraqi citizens as well as the international community and Arab nations that they had stood silent and sometimes denied the Ba'thist regime's atrocities. In Karbala, a special cemetery for the victims of mass graves was planned with a stone monument at its entrance. A women's organization in the city arranged an exhibit of pictures and martyrs' possessions near the tombs of Imams Hussain and Abbas. The clothes of victims of mass graves, their pictures, and their identity cards were also exhibited. In other southern cities, ceremonies of remembrance were organized by local civil society organizations or local members of national political parties working with personnel of the Ministry of Human Rights. Mass graves were, according to one such representative, the real monuments of the Ba'thist regime.[13]

May 16, however, was one of many days of commemoration. The Kurdish Regional Government built memorials and organized ceremonies commemorating the victims of Anfal and Halabja.[14] Soon these were followed by a day of remembrance of the dead among Fayli Kurds.[15] The martyrs of the Kurdish Intifada are commemorated on March 5, the anniversary of the beginning of the uprising in the Kurdish north.[16] Local organizations of martyrs' families in southern provinces arrange their own commemorations of the martyrs of the Intifada.[17] The Iraqi

[13] *al-Mada*, May 16, 2007. www.almadapaper.com/paper.php?source=akbar&mlf=interp accessed June 4, 2008

[14] *al-Mada*, February 18, 2010. www.almadapaper.net/news.php?action=view&id=1184&spell=o&highlight=%C7%D4%E5%CF%C7%C1 accessed December 5, 2011.

[15] *al-Mada*, April 9, 2011. www.almadapaper.net/news.php?action=view&id=38433&spell=o&higlight=%ED%E6%E3+%C7%E1%%D4%E5%ED%CF accessed December 15, 2011.

[16] *al-Mada*, March 5, 2008. www.almadapaper.com/paper.php?source=akbar&mlf=interp accessed June 3, 2008.

[17] *al-Mada*, March 25, 2007. www.almadapaper.com/paper.php?source=akbar&mlf=interp accessed June 4, 2008.

Communist Party commemorates its dead on the "Day of the Communist Martyr," and special days of commemoration are organized in provinces to highlight each province's contribution to the "culture of witnessing and martyrdom."[18]

Iraq's calendar is replete with days of remembrance of the dead. None, however, include any commemoration of the death of the hundreds of thousands of fallen soldiers and thousands of civilian victims who fall outside the currently sanctioned definition of martyrdom. The Martyr's Monument, occupied by U.S. troops in the first months of occupation, fell into disrepair. Today, official ceremonies no longer take place there. The al-'Amiriyya shelter was ransacked in the aftermath of the 2003 invasion and is currently occupied by the units of the Iraqi army.[19] The neglect of the Ba'th-established monuments and memorials is a result of the current government's systematic policy to de-Ba'thify the "visual landscape" of Iraq. In 2005, Prime Minister Nuri al-Maliki created a Committee to Remove the Remains of the Ba'th Party and Consider Building New Monuments and Murals.[20] Its mandate was to erase or rededicate edifices built under the Ba'th. A statue commemorating prisoners of war was destroyed, as was a memorial to schoolchildren who had died under Iranian bombardment.[21] Only the Victory Arch, built by the Ba'thist regime in 1989 as a monumental and triumphal declaration of victory in the Iran-Iraq war, is being rededicated to preserve the memory of all the lives lost as a result of Ba'thist policies.[22] Ironically, of all the monuments and memorials of remembrance, it has the least meaning and legitimacy among Iraqis who lived through the last two decades of Ba'thist rule.

The thirtieth anniversary of the Iran-Iraq war and the withdrawal of U.S. troops resurrected once again a debate in the Iraqi press on the de-Ba'thification of Baghdad's landscape. Those who support preserving

---

[18] *al-Mada*, February 13, 2011. www.almadapaper.net/news.php?action=view&id=35143& spell=0&highlight=%ED%E6%E3+%C7%E1%D4%E5%ED%CF accessed December 15, 2011. The quote is from the secretary general of the Union of Prisoners of Dhi Qar province, himself a son of a martyr. *al-Mada*, April 20, 2006. www.almadapaper.com/sub/04-648/p23.htim#2 accessed June 6, 2008.

[19] *al-Mada*, February 6, 2011. www.almadapaper.net/news.php?action=view&id=34663 &spell=0&highlight=%E3%E1%CC%C3+%C7%E1%DA%C7%E3%D1%ED%C9 accessed December 13, 2011.

[20] Sinan Antoon, "Bending history," *Middle East Report*, 257 (2010), 29–31.

[21] *al-Mada*, February 10, 2010. www.almadapaper.net?news.php?action=view&id=11180 &spell=0&highlight=%C7%E1%D4%E5%CF%C7%C1 accessed December 3, 2011.

[22] Its survival owes much to pressure exerted by Kanan Makiya, the founder of the U.S.-based Iraq Memory Foundation and a supporter of the U.S. invasion, and to the U.S. Embassy.

the monuments insist on their importance for Iraq's national heritage and point to the politicized decisions of the al-Maliki government and its supporters. Others argue that monuments and memorials are central to the construction of an Iraqi collective memory that seeks reconciliation rather than retribution. A strong and powerful constituency, however continues to seek to eradicate these monuments.[23] The Martyr's Monument has survived the vicissitudes of the government's policy in large part because its aesthetics eschews any reference to the Ba'th. Since 2009, it has been undergoing a process of renovation and beautification, even as the names inscribed on its wall do not figure in the sanctioned Iraqi national narrative.[24] Despite the neglect of the al-'Amiriyya shelter, its memory has been resurrected in a number of articles that recreate the tragic loss and highlight the atrocity committed by U.S. smart bombs.[25] Last, but not least, the explosion in electronic media has created spaces for public but often divisive discourse on the Iran-Iraq and the First Gulf wars. On Ba'thist and Sunni Islamist websites, images, songs, and poetry from the Iran-Iraq war are tributes to the Ba'th and attacks on the current Iraqi government as a stooge of Iran and the United States. Images of mass graves and of Intifada violence are reproduced on Shi'i websites to highlight Ba'th atrocities against the Shi'a of Iraq.

Clearly, the legacies of Iraq's wars under the Ba'th continue to work themselves into the politics of post-Ba'thist Iraq. A language of victimization and mourning pervades public discourse and shapes the claims that Iraqis make to their rights as citizens. The practices of the Baghdad and, to a lesser extent, the Arbil governments, reproduce, in ways that merit deeper examination, the authoritarian practices of the Ba'th. This is particularly evident in the privileging of certain martyrdom narratives at the expense of others, in the amnesia that characterizes readings of certain aspects of the Iran-Iraq and the First Gulf wars, and in the paternalism that informs the doling out of the entitlements of citizenship. Yet, while there are continuities between Ba'thist and post-Ba'thist Iraq, the breaks are equally important to highlight. The central government no

[23] *al-Mada*, October 2, 2010. www.almadapaper.net/news&id=11180&spell=0&higlight= %C7%E1D4%E5%CF%C7%C1 accessed December 3, 2011.

[24] *al-Mada*, October 13, 2009. www.almadapaper.net/news.php?action=view&id=1774& spell=0&highlight=%E4%D5%C8+%C7%E1%D4%E5%ED%CF accessed December 5, 2011 and *al-Mada*, July 29, 2010, www.almadapaper.net/news.php?action=view&id =23459&spell=0&highlight=%E4%D5%C8+%C7%E1%D4%E5%ED%CF accessed December 5, 2011.

[25] *al-Mannarah*, February 13, 2009. www.almannarah.com/NewsDetails.aspx?NewsID= 8503&CatID=5 accessed February 9, 2012.

longer monopolizes public discourse, and its hold over the country's various regions continues to be contested by local civil society and political organizations that do not subscribe to the new government-sanctioned narratives of the legacies of the wars under the Ba'th. Insofar as Iraqi citizens insist on reworking the history and memory of these wars through challenging the government's prerogatives in doling out entitlements and its decisions on memorializing the dead, they continue to forge a new narrative of these wars that opens the door for reconciliation across the social, sectarian, and ethnic divides.

Any such prospects, however, are hampered by the legacy of the U.S.-led occupation and the continuous violence it has engendered. Scholars and practitioners, who write and work on transitional justice and post-conflict reconciliation, assume that reconciliation is possible only when violence has become part of the recent past. However, in Iraq, memories of regime violence and the violence of Iraq's wars continue to be reworked in the context of sectarian and often violent polarization, ethnic tensions, and massive displacement of populations. Three generations of Iraqis have now inherited and construct conflicting narratives of their experiences of the devastation of their lives and their landscapes of belonging. A pervasive sense of lives postponed and of fatalism about the nature of Iraq's history informs a great deal of the remembrances of the generation of Iraqi men I interviewed for this book. Perhaps it is fitting to conclude by quoting one of them. Born in 1967, Najm Faris and three of his brothers were conscripted into the army to fight in the Iran-Iraq war. A stage artist and illustrator, he expressed, as he was sitting in a small gallery in Amman, what he believed was his generation's narrative of Iraqi history. "Iraq," according to Najm:

has not had a respite except for a few years since the 1920 revolution [against the British] ... Wars that have no meaning, wars that are useless envelop us.... This is the tragedy of Iraq in the latest war.... The army did not fight because it was deprived, tormented, crushed and hungry.... How can an army like that fight a Great Power? Does it fight for love of party and revolution? Can a man driving a 1960s model Volkswagen compete with a man driving the latest Mercedes model? ... Why should Iraqi art express anything but grief? Look at these paintings no matter how beautiful they are they carry a tone of sorrow.... Our life, we Iraqis, is built on sorrow.... Take for example the song of the singer Ilham al-Madfa'i ... He sings that "joy comes infrequently to our midst," ... My generation has endured a great deal."[26]

---

[26] Interview with Najm Faris, Amman, Jordan, July 17, 2007.

APPENDIX I

Distribution in Percentage of Ba'th Party Members,
"Friends of Saddam," and Martyrs in Fifteen
Iraqi Provinces, 1998–1999

Province / Register Number	Select Districts	Party Rank: Supporter	Party Rank: Advocate	Party Rank: Advanced Advocate	Party Rank: Member	Friends of Saddam	Martyrs
1. Anbar		42.1	31.1	8.5	2.6	20.7	5.3
H 63-10	Ramadi	43.6	36.9	5.4	0.1	8.7	2.7
63-11	Haditha	41.4	33.7	8.2	4.6	31.5	11.5
2. Babil		69.1	17.1	13.2	0.5	14.9	7.7
H 60-13	Hilla	63.7	14.1	3.6	0.2	10.8	4.1
60-15	al-Hashimiyya	73.3	22.9	2.9		14.4	3.7
3. Baghdad		37	10.7	3.9	0.3	14.7	4.6
H 59-04	A'dhamiyya	39.9	14.9	8.7	0.3	15.8	9.5
59-20	Karkh	36.6	15.2	4.9	0.2	9.2	7.1
60-01	Kadhimiyya	29.6	7.7	1.5	0.1	14.1	4.5
to 60-10	Madinat Saddam	55.9	6.7	1.9	0.2	12.5	5.7
4. Basra		40.9	42.3	16.6	0.8	12.2	5.4
H 61-23	Basra City	50	36.3	11.7	0.3	12.4	6.8
	al-Madinah	10.5	78	7.2	0.3	10.8	9.6
61-24	Abu Khasib	44.1	38.2	15.2	1.7	8.7	2.3
61-25	Zubayr	58.1	37.9	1.8	1	12.6	2.1
5. Dhi Qar		32.7	53.6	10.5	2.68	20.9	7.7
H 61-13	Nasiriyya	14.2	72.6	0.7	1.8	15.5	6.3
61-14	Suq al-Shuyukh	46.2	38.3	12	2.9	19.8	7.1
	Al-Chibayish	22.6	44.4	28	4.8	32.8	11.5

	1	2	3	4	5	6
6. Diyali H 62–04 62–05	59.1	27.6	9.1	1.1	22	7.3
Miqdadiyya	64.32	24.3	9.5	0.7	29.9	9.1
Khalis	52.5	29.9	11.4	1.4	21.7	7.8
Khaniqin	72.9	22	3.1	0.4	18.3	4.4
7. Karbala H 60–22	74.5	16.8	5.2	1.2	13.9	6.8
Karbala City	73.1	16.8	6.5	1	12.7	5.2
al-Hindiyya	78.1	16.9	3.1	1.7	16.5	7.4
8. Maysan H 60–37	76.8	14.3	2.7	1.1	11.3	5.3
Amara	74.3	10.1	3.1	1.3	9.3	4.3
Qal'at Saleh	68.3	29.3			27	9.1
al-Majar al-Kabir	85.5	13.3			11.1	4
9. Muthanna H 61–18	57.5	27.8	10.9	2.7	13.9	10.5
Samawa	54.3	31.9	10.7	1.6	15.7	11.2
al-Rumaytha	63.4	20.4	11.8	4.8	11.5	7
al-Khidr	52.9	23.5	7.3	5.8	7.3	20.5
10. Najaf H 60–28	58.5	9.1	2.8	0.6	9.6	3.7
Najaf City	41.7	6.9	2.6	0.5	6.5	1.9
al-Manathira	24.5	6.5	0.9		7.1	3.9
Kufa	92	6.2	1.1		13.9	7.3
11. Ninewah H 62–26 62–27	43.9	16.7	4	1.7	23.9	5.2
Mosul	38	13.8	3	1.7	25.9	5.7
Sinjar	39.1	35.7	11	3	25.8	6
Tel Affar	70.4	18.6	5.4	3.6	24.9	5.7
Tel Kayf	49.3	22.8	10.5	3.6	24.2	4.5

(continued)

257

Province Register Number	Select Districts	Party Rank: Supporter	Party Rank: Advocate	Party Rank: Advanced Advocate	Party Rank: Member	Friends of Saddam	Martyrs
12. Qadisiyya H 61-06		71.6	20.6	5.4	0.4	14	5
	Diwaniyya	76.5	15.7	2.9	0.2	16.8	4.5
	Hamza	42.8	28	12.2	0.2	10.8	5.7
13. Salah al-Din H 62-14		35.8	35.9	16.6	1.7	28	5.1
62-15	Takrit	9	39.8	17.5	3	29.1	4.4
	Bayji	34.3	27.1	34.6		37.4	8.4
	Balad	38.4	36	15.3	2.1	22.3	5.2
14. Ta'mim H 63-05		39	21	4.8	2.6	21.4	7.4
63-06	Kirkuk	33.9	17.4	3.9	2.1	21.9	6.1
	al-Huwayia	35.7	45.5	9	3.8	19.8	8
15. Wasit H 60-34		63.2	28.2	6.8	1.2	15.8	7.5
60-35	Kut	77.7	20.7	3.7	0.7	19.3	8.7
	Suwayra	52.7	37.3	4.5	1.2	12.5	4.8
	Nu'maniyya	75.3	18.9	3.6	1.5	11.4	4.5

Percentages are derived from matriculating students in sixth secondary (1998–9). Registers do not survey all schools. I have chosen to list select districts within provinces.

Percentage of Ba'th Party Membership among Matriculating Students (Sixth Secondary) in Ten Iraqi Provinces, 1987–1988

Province Register Number	Supporter	Advocate	Advanced Advocate
1. Anbar H 31–92 23–84	53.4	28.8	7.7
2. Babil H 54–11	53.1	26.2	8.3
3. Baghdad H 02–04 to 02–09	32.2	11.5	2.9
4. Basra H 42–32 40–36	75.1	14.3	1
5. Diyali H 59–33 H 23–33	60.8	17.8	1.7
6. Karbala H 22–32	70.8	26.5	1.3
7. Najaf H 20–49	88	6.6	1.1
8. Ninewah H 27–34 33–45	62.3	16.8	2.9
9. Ta'mim H46–02	52.8	24.3	7
10. Wasit H42–49	60.4	32.8	4.9

APPENDIX III

Report Issued by Ali Hasan al-Majid, Head of the Northern Bureau of the Ba'th Party to the General Secretariat, August 1987

"In order to give a full picture of the results that have been achieved from the operation of the eradication of prohibited villages, we present the following census: A census table of achieved results of the operation of the resettlement of villages (*tajamu'al-qura*) distributed among provinces from 25/4/87 to 15/7/87"*

Province	Number of Expelled Families	Number of Eradicated Villages	Number of Martyrs**	Number of Surrendered Saboteurs	Number of Surrendered Deserters	Number of Surrendered Absentees
Ninewah	626	157		12	193	95
Ta'mim	2,923	183	29	1	220	22
Sulaimaniyya	11,413	296	12	13	159	671
Dohuk	4,835	378	51	425	6,022	6,250
Arbil	6,464	338	55	124	4,660	3,937
Salah al-Din		26	20		58	
Diyali	135	63	13	8	25	
Total	26,399	1,441	190	663	11,337	11,077

Source: Table reproduced from BRCC 01-2140-0003-0064.
Notes:
 * April 25, 1987 to July 15, 1987.
** Martyrs are those among army, security, and Ba'th party apparatus killed in operation.
Courtesy of the Iraq Memory Foundation.

Sources and Bibliography

Primary Sources

I. Hoover Institution/Iraq Memory Foundation Archives
Box Files:
Ba'th Regional Command Council (BRCC)
School Registers:
School registers for years 1987–8 and 1998–9 are all those compiled by the party and with the designation of (H) for *Hizb* (party) preceding each number. Numbers of registers used are listed in appendixes I and II.
School registers for the year 1991 are drawn from the surveys of the General Directorate of Security (*Amn*) and that of the Ba'th Party (*Hizb*). The number of the registers with correct designation can be found in notes to Chapter 5.
North Iraq Data Set (NIDS)
II. Iraqi newspapers and magazines:
al-Jumhuriyya
al-Thawra
al-Qadisiyya
Alif Ba'
Afaq 'Arabiyya
Electronic newspapers
al-Mada
Azzaman
al-Mannarah
III. Iraqi Gazette

Interviews

1. Sabir Farah. Amman, Jordan, July 21, 22, 23, 2007.
2. Waddah Hasan. Amman, Jordan, June 21, 23, 28, 2007.

3. Haytham Ali. Amman, Jordan, August 8, 2007.
4. Abu Faruk. Damascus, Syria, March 20, 2009.
5. Haytham Abbas. Amman, Jordan, July 5, 2007.
6. Ammar Hasan. Damascus, Syria, August 16, 2007.
7. Tareq Ali. Amman, Jordan, July 14, 2007, Damascus, Syria, March 13, 2009.
8. Hamza Jubayli. Damascus, Syria, April 28, 2009.
9. Najm Faris. Amman, Jordan, July 18, 2007.
10. Su'ud Muhammad. Amman, Jordan, July 18, 2007.
11. Mazin Hadithi. Damascus, Syria, March 1, 2009.
12. Hanna Khoshaba. Amman, Jordan, July 19, 2007.
13. Husayn Ahmad. Amman, Jordan, June 23, 2007.
14. Isa Youhanna. Amman, Jordan, June 23, 2007.
15. Hazim Najm. Amman, Jordan, July 15, 2007.
16. Sabri Asad. Amman, Jordan, July 4, 2007.
17. Abu Muhammad. Amman, Jordan, August 7, 2007.
18. Abu Ali. Damascus, Syria, March 22, 2009.
19. Abu Ayham. Damascus, Syria, April 8, 2009.
20. Abu Mukhlis. Amman, Jordan, August 7, 2007.
21. Bulus Isa. Amman, Jordan, July 19, 2007.
22. Abu Safa'. Amman, Jordan, July 24, 2007.

Bibliography

Abboud, Salam, *Thaqafat al-'Unf fi al-'Iraq* (*The Culture of Violence in Iraq*), Köln: Dar al-Jamal, 2002.

Abd al-Jabar, Adel, *Jabal al-Nar, Jabal al-Thalj* (*Mountain of Fire, Mountain of Snow*), Baghdad: Dar al-Rashid li al-Nashr, 1982.

Abd al-Majid, Muhammad, "al-Ghazal al-rakid nahwa al-sharq" ("The gazelle that runs towards the East"), in *Qadisiyat Saddam: Qisas Tahta Lahib al-Nar* (*Qadisiyat Saddam: Stories Under the Flames of Fire*), vol. 6, Baghdad: Da'irat al-Shu'un al-Thaqafiyya wa al-Nashr, 1984, pp. 57–69.

Abdul Jabar, Faleh, "Iraq's War Generation," in Lawrence G. Potter and Gary G. Sick, eds., *Iran, Iraq and the Legacies of War*, New York: Palgrave Macmillan, 2004, pp. 121–40.

  "Shaykhs and ideologues: Detribalization and retribalization in Iraq, 1968–1998," *Middle East Report*, 215 (2000), 28–31.

Abrahamian, Ervand, *Tortured Confessions, Prison and Public Recantation in Modern Iran*, Berkeley: University of California Press, 1999.

Abu al-Fawz, *Tadharis al-Ayam fi Dafatir Naseer* (*The Traces of Days in the Journals of an Advocate*), Damascus: Dar al-Thaqafa wa al-Nashr, 2002.

Abufarha, Nasser, *The Making of the Human Bomb: The Ethnography of Palestinian Resistance*, Durham: Duke University Press, 2009.

Alexopolous, Golfo, "Stalin and the politics of kinship: Practices of collective punishment, 1920s-1930s," *Comparative Studies in Society and History*, vol. 50, 1(2008), 91–117.

al-Ali, Nadje, *Iraqi Women: Untold Stories from 1948 to the Present*, London: Zed Press, 2007.

al-Alusi, Manal Yunus Abd al-Raziq, *al-Mar'a wa al-Tatawur al-Siyasi fi al-Watan al-'Arabi* (*Women and Political Development in the Arab Nation*) Baghdad: Ministry of Culture and Information, 1989.

al-Azzawi, Fadhil, *al-Ruh al-Hayya, Jil al-Sitinat fi al-'Iraq* (*The Living Spirit, The Sixties Generation in Iraq*) Damascus: al-Mada Press, 1997.

al-Khafaji, Isam, "The parasitic base of the Ba'thist regime," in Committee Against Repression and for Democratic Rights in Iraq (CADRI), *Saddam's Iraq, Revolution or Reaction*, London: Zed Press, 1986, pp. 73–88.

"War as a vehicle for the rise and demise of a state-controlled society: The case of Ba'thist Iraq," in Steven Heydemann, ed., *War, Institutions and Social Change in the Middle East*, Berkeley: University of California Press, 2000, pp. 258–91.

al-Khafaji, Muhsin, "al-Yawm al-khamis fi wadi al-shams"("The fifth day in the valley of the sun"), in *Qadisiyat Saddam: Qisas Tahta Lahib al-Nar* (*Qadisiyat Saddam: Stories under the Flames of Fire*), vol. 5, Baghdad: Dar al-Shu'un al-Thaqafiyya wa al-Nashr, 1983, pp. 9–27.

al-Majid, M., *Intifadat al-Sha'b al-'Iraqi* (*The Uprising of the Iraqi People*) Beirut: Dar al-Wifaq, 1991.

al-Marashi, Ibrahim, "Iraq's security and intelligence network: A guide and analysis," *Middle East Review of International Affairs*, vol. 7, 2(2003), 1–13.

al-Marashi, Ibrahim and Sammy Salama, *Iraq's Armed Forces: An Analytical History*, London: Routledge, 2008.

al-Musawi, Muhsin, *al-Mar'i wa al-Mutakhayal, Adab al-Harb al-Qisasi fi al-'Iraq* (*The Visible and the Imagined, the Narrative Literature of War in Iraq*) Baghdad: Dar al-Shu'un al-Thaqafiyya li al-Nashr, 1986.

Reading Iraq, Culture and Power in Conflict, London: I.B. Tauris, 2006.

al-Samarra'i, Abd al-Qadir, ed., *Qadisiyat Saddam: Qisas Tahta Lahib al-Nar* (*Qadisiyat Saddam: Stories under the Flame of Fire*), vol. 1, Baghdad: Dar al-Rashid, 1981.

al-'Ubaidi, Hasan, *Dirasat Qanuniyya fi Qiyadat al-Hizb li al-Dawla wa al-Mujtama'* (*A Legal Study of the Leadership of the Party/State and Society*) Baghdad and London: Dar Wasit al-Markaz al-Dusturi li Hizb al-Ba'th al-'Arabi al-Ishtiraki, 1982.

al-Zaydi, Staff Colonel Ahmad, *al-Bina' al-Ma'nawi li al-Quwwat al-Musalaha al-'Iraqiyya*, (*The Structure of Morale of the Iraqi Armed Forces*) Beirut: Dar al-Rawda, 1990.

Antoon, Sinan, "Monumental disrespect," *Middle East Report*, no. 228 (2003), 28–30.

"Bending history," *Middle East Report*, no. 257 (2010), 29–31.

Arab Ba'th Socialist Party, *Revolutionary Iraq, 1968–1973, The Political Report Adopted by the Eighth Regional Congress of the Arab Ba'th Socialist Party*, Baghdad: np 1974.

Arab Ba'th Socialist Party-Iraq, *al-Taqrir al-Markazi li al-Mu'tamar al-Qutri al-Tasi'*, June, 1982 (*The Central Report of the Ninth Regional Congress, June 1982*), Baghdad: np, 1983.

Arendt, Hannah, *On Violence*, USA: Harvest, 1970.

Bader, Ali, *Baba Sartre (Papa Sartre)* Beirut: al-Mu'assasa al-'Arabiyya li al-Dirasat wa al-Nashr, 2006.

Baram, Amatzia, *Culture, History and Ideology in the Formation of Ba'thist Iraq, 1968–89*, New York: St. Martin's Press, 1991.

"Neo-tribalism in Iraq: Saddam Hussein's tribal policies 1991–1996," *International Journal of Middle East Studies*, vol. **29**, no.1 (1997), 1–31.

Baram, Amatzia, Rohde, Achim and Zeidel, Ronen, "Between the Unknown Soldier monument and the Cemetry: Commemorating the Fallen Soldiers in Iraq, 1958–2010," in *Conflicting Narratives, War, Trauma and Memory in Iraqi culture*, Milich Stephan, Friederike Pannewick, and Leslie Tramontini, eds., Wiesbaden: Reichert Verlag Wiesbaden, 2012.

Baran, David, *Vivre la Tyrannie et lui Survivre, L'Irak en Transition (Living Tyranny and Surviving It: Iraq in Transition)* Paris: Mille et Une Nuits, 2004.

Barber, John and Harrison, Mark, *The Soviet Home Front*, London: Longman, 1991.

Bayart, Jean François, Ellis, Stephen and Hilou, Béatrice, *The Criminalization of the State in Africa*, trans. Stephen Ellis, Bloomington: Indiana University Press, 1999.

Bengio, Ofra, "Iraq," *Middle East Contemporary Survey*, vol. **6** (1981–1982), 582–3.

"Iraq," *Middle East Contemporary Survey*, vol. **10** (1986), 364–69.

"Iraq," *Middle East Contemporary Survey*, vol. **13** (1987), 376–95.

"Iraq," *Middle East Contemporary Survey*, vol. **14** (1990), 386–412.

Saddam's Words, Political Discourse in Iraq, New York: Oxford University Press, 1998.

Brown, Ian, *Khomeini's Forgotten Sons, The Story of Iran's Boy Soldiers*, London: Gray Seal, 1990.

Brown, Wendy, *Regulating Aversion, Tolerance in the Age of Identity and Empire*, Princeton: Princeton University Press, 2006.

Butler, Judith, *Precarious Life: The Powers of Mourning and Violence*, New York: Verso, 2006.

Caswell, Michelle, "Thank you very much, now give them back: Cultural property and the fight over the Iraqi Baath records," *American Archivist*, vol. **74** (2011), 211–40.

Chatterjee, Partha, *The Politics of the Governed, Reflections on Popular Politics in Most of the World*, New York: Columbia University Press, 2004.

Chelkowski, Peter and Dabashi, Hamid, *Staging the Revolution: The Art of Persuasion in the Islamic Republic of Iran*, London: Booth-Clibborn Editions, 2000.

Chubin, Shahram and Tripp, Charles, *Iran and Iraq at War*, Boulder: Westview Press, 1988.

Corboz, Elvire, "Uneasy Humanitarianism, The ICRC and the prisoners-of-war during the Iran-Iraq conflict," unpublished MA thesis, Oxford University (2005).

Cooke, Miriam, *Women and the War Story*, Berkeley: University of California Press, 1977.

Davis, Eric, *Memories of State, Politics, History and Collective Identity in Modern Iraq*, Berkeley: University of California Press, 2005.

de Bellaigne, Christopher, *In the Rose Garden of the Martyrs: A Memoir of Iran*, New York: HarperCollins, 2005.

Deeb, Lara, "Exhibiting the 'Just Lived Past': Hizbullah's nationalist narratives in the transnational political context," *Comparative Studies of Society and History*, vol. 50, 2(2008), 369–99.

Dorraj, Monachehr, "Symbolic and utilitarian value of tradition: Martyrdom in Iranian political culture," *Review of Politics*, vol. 59, 3(1997), 489–521.

Efrati, Noga, "Productive or reproductive? The roles of Women during the Iran-Iraq war," *Middle Eastern Studies*, vol. 35, 2(1999), 27–44.

Women in Iraq: Past Meets Present, New York: Columbia University Press, 2012.

Fanon, Franz *The Wretched of the Earth*, trans. C. Farrington, New York: Grove Weidenfeld, 1991.

Farhi, Farideh, "The antinomies of Iran's war generation," in *Iran, Iraq and the Legacies of the War*, Lawrence Potter and Gary Sick, eds., New York: Palgrave Macmillan, 2004, pp. 101–20.

Federation of Arab Journalists, *No to War, Yes to Peace: Stop the Gulf War, Save Iraqi POWs*, Baghdad: Federation of Arab Journalists, 1986.

Foucault, Michel, "Governmentality," in *The Foucault Effect: Studies in Governmentality*, Graham Burchell, Colin Gordon and Peter Miller eds., Chicago: University of Chicago Press, 1991, pp. 87–104.

The Birth of Biopolitics, Michel Senellart ed., New York: Palgrave Macmillan, 2008.

Security, Territory and Population, Michel Senellant ed., New York: Palgrave Macmillan, 2009.

Franzén, Johan, *Red Star over Iraq: Iraqi Communism before Saddam*, London: Hurst and Company, 2011.

Freedman, Lawrence and Karsh, Ephraim, *The Gulf Conflict, 1990–1991*, Princeton: Princeton University Press, 1995.

Fussell, Paul, *The Great War and Modern Memory*, New York: Oxford University Press, 2000.

Galli, Carlo, *Political Spaces and Global War*, Elisabeth Fay, trans., Minneapolis: Univesity of Minnesota Press, 2010.

Gordon, Joy, *Invisible War, The United States and The Iraq Sanctions*, Cambridge: Harvard University Press, 2010.

Gordon, Neve, *Israel's Occupation*, Berkeley: University of California Press, 2009.

Graham-Brown, Sarah, *Sanctioning Saddam: The Politics of Intervention in Iraq*, London: I. B. Tauris, 1999.

Haddad, Fanar, *Sectarianism in Iraq: Antagonistic Visions of Unity*, United Kingdom: C. Hurst & Co., 2011.

Hamadani, Lieutenant General Ra'id Majid, *Qabla 'an Yughadiruna al-Tarikh* (*Before History Leaves Us Behind*) Beirut: Arab Scientific Publishers, 2007.

Hashim, Ahmad, "Saddam Husayn and civil-military relations in Iraq: The quest for legitimacy and power," *Middle East Journal*, vol. 57, 1 (2003), 9–41.

Haugbolle, Sune, *War and Memory in Lebanon*, Cambridge: Cambridge University Press, 2010.

Heydemann, Steven ed., *War, Institutions, and Social Change in the Middle East*, Berkeley: University of California Press, 2000.

Hiltermann, Joost, *A Poisonous Affair, America, Iraq, and the Gassing of Halabja*, Cambridge: Cambridge University Press, 2007.

   Bureaucracy of Repression, The Iraq Government in Its Own Words, New York: Human Rights Watch, 1994.

Hiro, Dilip, *Desert Storm to Desert Shield, The Second Gulf War*, New York: Routledge, 1992.

   The Longest War, The Iran-Iraq Military Conflict, New York: Routledge, 1991.

Isin, Engin, "Theorizing acts of citizenship," in *Acts of Citizenship*, Engin, I. and Nielsen G. M. eds., London: Zed Press, pp. 15–43.

Islamic Action Organization, *al-Intifada al-Sha'biyyah fi al-'Iraq: al-Asbab wa al-Nata'ij was Mustaqbaluha bi Nadhar Ayatollah al-Sayyid Muhammad Taqi al-Din al-Mudarissi (The Popular Uprising of Iraq: Its Causes, Consequences and Its Future in the View of Ayatollah al-Sayyid Muhammad al-Mudarissi)* Beirut: Islamic Action Organization, 1991.

Jabar, Faleh A. *The Shi'ite Movement in Iraq*, London: Saqi Press, 2003.

The Joint Working Committee of the Iraqi Opposition Forces, *Watha'iq al-Mu'tamar al-'Am li Qiwa al-Mu'arada al-'Iraqiyya (The Documents of the General Congress of Iraqi Opposition Forces)* Beirut: np, 1991.

Joseph, Suad, "Elite Strategies for state-building: Women, family, religion, and state-building in Iraq and Lebanon," in *Women, Islam and the State*, Deniz Kendiyoti, ed., Philadelphia: Temple University Press, 1991, pp. 176–200.

Khalili, Laleh, *Heroes and Martyrs of Palestine: The Politics of National Commemoration*, Cambridge: Cambridge University Press, 2009.

Kimmerling, Baruch, *The Invention and Decline of Israeliness: State, Society and the Military*, Berkeley: University of California Press, 2005.

Klein, Kerwin Lee, "On the emergence of memory in historical discourse," *Representations*, vol. 69 (2000), 127–50.

Kligman, Gail, *The Politics of Duplicity, Controlling Reproduction in Ceausescu's Romania*, Berkeley: University of California Press, 1998.

Laizer, Sheri, *Martyrs, Traitors and Patriots: Kurdistan after the Gulf War*, London: Zed Books, 1996.

Makiya, Kanan, *Cruelty and Silence: War, Tyranny, Uprising and the Arab World*, New York: W.W. Norton, 1993.

   The Monument: Art and Vulgarity in Saddam Hussein's Iraq, New York: I.B. Tauris, 2004.

   Republic of Fear, The Politics of Modern Iraq, Berkeley: University of California Press, 1998.

Maroun, Ibrahim, *L'économie Pétrolière pour L'économie de Guerre Permenante, Ètude Socio-Èconomique des Problèmes du Dévelopment en Irak*, Beirut: Lebanon University Press, 1986.

Marr, Phebe, *The Modern History of Iraq*, Boulder: Westview Press, 2003.

McReynolds, Louise, "Dateline Stalingrad, newspaper correspondents on the front," in *Culture and Entertainment in Wartime Russia*, Stites, Richard ed., Bloomington: Indiana University Press, 1995, pp. 28–43.

Mbembe, Achille, "Necropolitics," trans. Libby Meintjes, *Public Culture*, vol. 15, 1(2003), 11–40.

On the Post-Colony, Berkeley: University of California Press, 2001.

"The banality of power and the aesthetics of vulgarity in the post-colony," *Public Culture*, vol. 4, 2 (1992), 1–30.

Milozc, Czelslow, *The Captive Mind*, London: Penguin Books, 2001.

Mitchell, Timothy, "Society, Economy and the State Effect," in George Steinmetz, ed., *State/Culture: State Formation After the Cultural Turn*, Ithaca: Cornell University Press, 1999, pp. 76–97.

Mohsen, Fatima, "Debating Iraqi culture: Intellectuals between the inside and the outside," in *Conflicting Narratives, War, Trauma and Memory in Iraqi culture*, Milich, Stephan, Friederike Pannewick and Leslie Tramontini, eds., Wiesbaden: Reichert Verlag Wiesbaden, 2012.

Montgomery, Bruce, "Immortality in the secret police files: The Iraq Memory Foundation and the Baath Party archive," *International Journal of Cultural Property*, 18(2011), 309–36.

Mosse, George L. *Fallen Soldiers, Reshaping the Memory of the World Wars*, New York: Oxford University Press, 1990.

Omar, Suha, "Women: Honor, Shame, and Dictatorship," in *Iraq Since the Gulf War: Prospects for Democracy*, Hazelton, Fran, ed., London: Zed Books, 1994.

Parasaliti, Andrew and Antoon, Sinan, "Friends in need, foes to heed: The Iraqi military in politics," *Middle East Policy*, vol. 7, 4(2000), 130–41.

Perelli, Carina, "Youth, politics, and dictatorship in Uruguay," in *Fear at the Edge: State Terror and Resistance in Latin America*, Corradi, Juan E., Fagen, Patricia Weiss, and Garretón, Manuel Antonio, eds., Berkeley: University of California Press, 1992, pp. 212–35.

Podeh, Elie, *The Politics of National Celebrations in the Middle East*, New York: Cambridge University Press, 2011.

Ram, Haggay, *Myth and Mobilization in Revolutionary Iran: The Use of the Friday Congregational Sermon*, Lanham: American University Press, 1994.

Ramadan, Taha Yasin, *Qadisiyat Saddam wa al-Jaysh al-Sha'bi (Qadisiyat Saddam and the Popular Army)*, Baghdad: The General Leadership of the Popular Army, 1988.

Rassam, Amal, "Revolution within the Revolution? Women and the state in Iraq," in *Iraq: The Contemporary State*, Niblock, Tim ed., New York: St. Martin's Press, 1982, pp. 88–99.

Riverbend, *Baghdad Burning: Girl Blog from Iraq*, New York: The Feminist Press at CUNY, 2005.

Rohde, Achim, *Facing Dictatorship: State-Society Relations in Ba'thist Iraq*, London: Routledge, 2010.

"Opportunities for masculinity and love: Cultural production in Ba'thist Iraq during the 1980s," in *Islamic Masculinities*, Ouzgane, Lahouchine ed., London: Zed Press, 2006, pp. 148–201.

Rosenhek, Zeev, Maman, Daniel, and Ben-Ari, Eyal, "The study of war and the military in Israel: An empirical investigation and reflective critique," *International Journal of Middle East Studies*, vol. 35 (2003), 461–84.

Saeidi, Shirin, "Creating the Islamic Republic of Iran: Wives and daughters of martyrs, and acts of citizenship," *Citizenship Studies*, vol. 14 (2010), 113–26.

Salem, Warid, Hamza, Mustafa, and Hayyawi, Muhammad eds., *Dhakirat al-Ghad, Shahadat, Ru'a wa Tajarub (Memory of Tomorrow, Testimonies, Visions and Experiences)* Baghdad: Dar al-Shu'un al-Thaqfiyya al-'Ama,1989.

Sassoon, Joseph, *Saddam Hussein's Ba'th Party: Inside an Authoritarian Regime*, New York: Cambridge University Press, 2012.

Sayer, Derek, "Everyday forms of state formation: Dissident remarks on hegemony," in *Everyday Forms of State Formation; Revolution and the Negotiation of Rule in Modern Mexico*, Joseph, Gilbert and Nugent, Daniel eds., Durham: Duke University Press, 1994, pp. 367–78.

Sayigh, Yezid, "War as leveler, war as midwife: Palestinian political institutions, nationalism, and society since 1948," in *War, Institutions and Social Change, in the Middle East*, Heydemann, Steven ed., Berkeley: University of California Press, 2000, pp. 200–39.

Sha'ban, 'Abd al-Husayn, *Man Huwa al-'Iraqi? Ishkaliyat al-Jinsiyya fi al-Qanun al-'Iraqi wa al-Duwali (Who is Iraqi? The Problem of Nationality and non-Nationality in Iraqi and International Laws)*, Beirut: Dar al-Kunuz al-Dhahabiyya, 2002.

Smolansky, Oles M. and Smolansky, Bettie, *The USSR and Iraq, the Soviet Quest for Influence*, Durham: Duke University Press, 1991.

Sluglett, Peter and Sluglett, Marion-Farouk, *Iraq Since 1958: From Revolution to Dictatorship*, revised edition, London: I.B. Tauris, 2001.

Thompson, Elizabeth, *Colonial Citizens*, New York: Columbia University Press, 2000.

Tilly, Charles, *Coercion, Capital and European States, AD 900–1990*, Cambridge: Basil Blackwell, 1990.

Tilly, Charles, ed., *The Formation of National States in Western Europe*, Princeton: Princeton University Press, 1975.

Tramontini, Leslie, "The struggle for representation: The internal Iraqi dispute over cultural representation in Baathist Iraq," in *Conflicting Narratives, War, Trauma and Memory in Iraqi culture*, Milich, Stephan, Friederick Pannewick, and Leslie Tramontini, eds. Wiesbaden: Reichert Verlag Wiesbaden, 2012.

Tripp, Charles, *A History of Iraq*, second edition, Cambridge: Cambridge University Press, 2002.

Van Bruinessen, Martin, *Agha, Shaikh and State: The Social History and Political Structures of Kurdistan*, London: Zed Books, 1992.

Varzi, Roxane, *Warring Souls: Youth, Media and Martyrdom in Post-Revolutionary Iran*, Durham: Duke University Press, 2006.

Volk, Lucia, *Memorials and Martyrs in Modern Lebanon*, Bloomington: Indiana University Press, 2010.

Walker, Barbara, "(Still) searching for a Soviet Society: Personalized political ties and economic ties in recent Soviet historiography," vol. 43, 3(2001) *Comparative Studies of Society and History*, 631–42.

Wedeen, Lisa, *Ambiguities of Domination: Politics, Rhetoric and Symbols in Contemporary Syria,* Chicago: University of Chicago Press, 1999.

"Seeing like a Citizen, Acting like a State: Exemplary Events in Unified Yemen," *Comparative Studies in Society and History,* vol. 45, 4 (2003), 680–713.

Weiss, Meira, "Bereavement, commemoration and collective identity in contemporary Israeli society," *Anthropological Quarterly,* vol. 70, 2(1997), 91–101.

Weizman, Eyal, *Hollow Land: Israel's Architecture of Occupation,* New York: Verso Press, 2007.

Winter, Jay, *Sites of Memory, Sites of Mourning,* Cambridge: Cambridge University Press, 1998.

Winter, Jay and Sivan Emmanuel, *War and Remembrance in the Twentieth Century,* Cambridge: Cambridge University Press, 1999.

Yasin, Najman, *al-Insan wa al-Harb, Qadisiyat Saddam fi 'A'mal Rahim Hasan (Man and War: Qadisiyat Saddam in the Works of Rahim Hasan),* Baghdad: al-Dar al-Wataniyya li al-Tiba'a wa al-Nashr, 1987.

Youssef, Saadi, *Without an Alphabet, Without a Face,* Khaled Mattawa trans., Saint Paul: Graywolf Press, 2002.

Yurchak, Alexei, "Soviet hegemony of form: Everything was forever, until it was no more," *Comparative Studies in Society and History,* vol. 45, 3 (2003), 480–510.

Zizek, Slavoj, *Violence* (New York: Picador, 2008).

Electronic Resources

al-Salhi, Najib. "al-Zilzal (The Earthquake)."*Iraq 4 All News* 1998. Accessed April 28, 2008. http://www.Iraq4all.dk/Zlzal/Zm.htm.

"Amputation and Branding, Detention of Health Professionals." *Amnesty International.* Accessed September 19, 2011. http://www.amnesty.org/en/library/asset/MDE14/013/1994/en/da1766e6–614c-4dd9-ba46–4-b817a7cb2df/mde140131994.en.pdf.

"The Central Report of the Ninth Regional Congress of the Ba'th Party, June 1982." *Al-Moharer.* Accessed June 18, 2008. http://www.al-moharer.net/iraqi_files/ninth_regional_congress82.htm.

Eakin, Hugh, "Iraqi Files in US: Plunder or Rescue." *New York Times.* Accessed July 9, 2009. http://www.nytimes.com/2008/07–01/books/01hoov.html.

"Endless Torment: The 1991 Uprising in Iraq and its Aftermath" *Human Rights Watch.* Accessed June 12, 2008. http:// www.hrw.org/file://G:\Iraq926. htm.

"Genocide in Iraq: The Anfal Campaign Against the Kurds" *Human Rights Watch.* Accessed October 27, 2010. http://www.hrw.org/legacy/reports/1993/iraqanfal/.

Hiltermann, Joost, "Case Study: The 1988 Anfal Campaign in Iraqi Kurdistan" *Online Encyclopedia of Mass Violence* 2008. Accessed April 6, 2011. http://www.massviolence.org/The-1988-Anfal-Campaign-in-Iraqi-Kurdistan?artpage=9–11.

Interim Iraqi Constitution, 1970. Accessed February 26, 2012. http://www.mpil.
de/shared/data/pdf/constitution_of_ira1970_eng.pdf.

"Iraq: State Cruelty: Branding, Amputation and Death Penalty." *Amnesty
International.* Accessed September 19, 2011. http://www.amnesty.org/en/
library/asset/MDE14/003/1996/en/ea126950-eb02–11dd-aad1-
ed57e7e7e5470b/mde140031996een.pdf.

"The Iraqi Government's Assault on the Marsh Arabs." *Human Rights Watch.*
Accessed June 13, 2008. http://www.hrw.org/backgrounder/mean/marshar-
abs1.htm.

"Needless deaths in the Gulf War: Civilian casualties during the air campaign and
violations of the laws of war." *Human Rights Watch* Web. Accessed February
12, 2012. http://www.hrw.org/reports/1991/gulfwar/index.htm.

Salem-Pickartz, Josi (prep.) "Iraq Watching Brief: Child Protection" *UNICEF.*
Accessed February 24, 2012. http://www.google.com/url?sa=t&rct=j&q
=&esrc=s&source=web&cd=6&ved=0CF8QFjAF&url=http%3A%2F%
2Firaq.undg.org%2Fuploads%2Fdoc%2FWatching%2520BriefChild%
2520Protection%252028.08.03.doc&ei=2TlIT73cH6P20gGF18mLDg
&usg=AFQjCNHXlpQie7zV2HjvgILCloh4tPA_dQ&sig2=sBMUkIWJ-
2UYwTFa1snFzA.

Sen, Biswat, "Iraq Watching Brief: Overview Report, July 2003." Accessed April
23, 2011. http://www.icrc.org/eng/resources/documents/misc/5x5drb.htm.

Shamma, Naseer, "It happened in Amiriya." Accessed February 20, 2012. http://
www.youtube.com/watch?v=V7a_K6kQ8po.

Shamma, Naseer, webpage. Accessed February 20, 2012. http://www.naseers-
hamma.com.

Shamma, Naseer, Interview with Naseer Shamma. Accessed February 20, 2012.
http://www.alarabiya.net/programs/2010/06/17/111561.html.

Index

absentee soldiers, 101–3
  See also deserters
Africa, normalization of war in, 3
Afwaj al-Khafifa (Light Cavalry), 100
al-'Amiriyya shelter, 220, 233, 234,
  236–43, 251, 252
al-Azzawi, Mushin, 239–40
al-Bakr, Ahmad Hasan
  becomes president of Iraq, 20
  pushed aside by Hussain, 27–8
Algiers Agreement, 26–8, 38
al-Hakim, Muhammad Baqir, 106
al-Hakim, Muhsin, 24, 25
al-Huda, Bint, 28
Alif Ba' (newspaper), 196
Alif Ba', 228–9
al-Jawihiri, Muhammad Mahdi, 127
al-Jumhuriyya (newspaper), 55, 78, 167,
  187, 192, 196, 223–4
al-Khafaji, Isam, 6
al-Khafaji, Muhsin, 202–3
al-Kho'i, Abu Qasim, 24, 28
al-Kreidi, Musa, 197
al-Majid, Ali Hasan, 32, 38, 111, 117–19,
  128, 135, 260
al-Majid, Muhammad Abd, 203
al-Maliki, Nuri, 251
al-Musawi, Muhsin, 197–9, 222
al-Musawi, Sajida, 78
al-Rawi, Iyad, 126
al-Sabah, Jaber, 35–6
al-Sadr, Muhammad Baqir, 24, 28
al-Sadr, Muhammad Sadiq, 143
al-Sa'igh, Yousef, 228

al-Samarra'i, Abdul al-Jabbar Mahmud,
  224
al-Sharqi, Amal, 78
al-Shaykhli, Samir Abd al-Wahab, 219, 227
al-Takarli, Fuad, 197
al-Thawra (newspaper), 167, 196, 205
al-Turk, Isma'il Fattah, 219
al-Zubaydi, Muhammad Hamza, 61,
  115–16, 117
amnesty decrees, 73, 75, 99
Anfal campaign, 33, 41, 118, 119–21, 216,
  235, 245–6
"apostates," 109–10
Arab nationalism, 10, 20, 24
Arbil government, 245, 252
Arendt, Hannah, 54
armed forces
  cultural differences among, 96
  expansion of, 86
  manipulation of furloughs of, 98
  morale of, 86, 89
  National Defense Battalions in Kurdish
    north, 95, 100–2
  party affiliation and recruitment, 85–6
  Popular Army (*see* Popular Army)
  promotions, 31, 84, 85–6, 95, 166
  reservists, 95
  shortage of soldiers, 94–5
  social mobility of, 97
  See also conscripts; Directorate of
    Political Guidance; prisoners of war
Army of Jerusalem, 158, 160
'*Ashura* commemoration, 23–4, 25–6, 63–5
Assyrians, 120

and journalists, 185
language of, 184, 195–204
and photojournalists, 186–8
and remembrance, 184, 204–16
and romanticizing of marshlands,
   188–91
Wedeen, Lisa, 157
women
   participation in Shi'i rituals, 64

participation in Shi'i rituals, Ba'thist
   view on, 65
See also families; martyr families

Yasin, Najman, 187–94
Younus, Manal, 80

Zionism, 10, 37, 59–60, 222
Zizek, Slavoj, 8–9